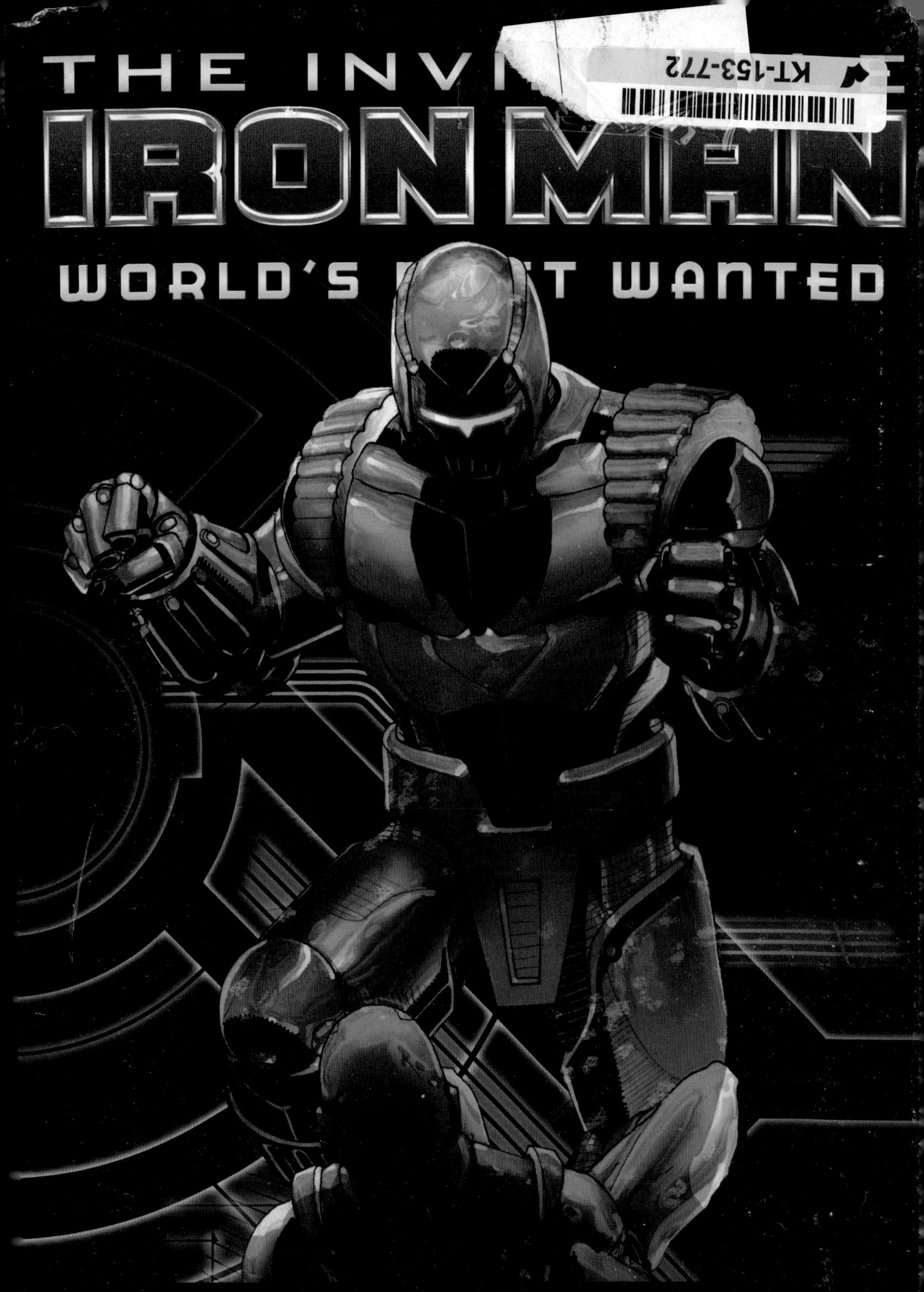

THE INVINCIBLE IRON MAN
WORLD'S MOST WANTED

INVINCIBLE IRON MAN VOL. 3: WORLD'S MOST WANTED BOOK 2. Contains material originally published in magazine form as INVINCIBLE IRON MAN #14-19. First printing 2009. Hardcover ISBN# 978-0-7851-3935-5. Softcover ISBN# 978-0-7851-3685-9. Published by MARVEL PUBLISHING, INC., a subsidiary of MARVEL ENTERTAINMENT, INC. OFFICE OF PUBLICATION: 417 5th Avenue, New York, NY 10016. Copyright © 2009 and 2010 Marvel Characters, Inc. All rights reserved. Hardcover: $19.99 per copy in the U.S. (GST #R127032852). Softcover: $14.99 per copy in the U.S. (GST #R127032852). Canadian Agreement #40668537. All characters featured in this issue and the distinctive names and likenesses thereof, and all related indicia are trademarks of Marvel Characters, Inc. No similarity between any of the names, characters, persons, and/or institutions in this magazine with those of any living or dead person or institution is intended, and any such similarity which may exist is purely coincidental. **Printed in the U.S.A.** ALAN FINE, EVP - Office Of The Chief Executive Marvel Entertainment, Inc. & CMO Marvel Characters B.V.; DAN BUCKLEY, Chief Executive Officer and Publisher - Print, Animation & Digital Media; JIM SOKOLOWSKI, Chief Operating Officer; DAVID GABRIEL, SVP of Publishing Sales & Circulation; DAVID BOGART, SVP of Business Affairs & Talent Management; MICHAEL PASCIULLO, VP Merchandising & Communications; JIM O'KEEFE, VP of Operations & Logistics; DAN CARR, Executive Director of Publishing Technology; JUSTIN F. GABRIE, Director of Publishing & Editorial Operations; SUSAN CRESPI, Editorial Operations Manager; ALEX MORALES, Publishing Operations Manager; STAN LEE, Chairman Emeritus. For information regarding advertising in Marvel Comics or on Marvel.com, please contact Mitch Dane, Advertising Director, at mdane@marvel.com. For Marvel subscription inquiries, please call 800-217-9158. **Manufactured between 11/16/09 and 12/23/09 (hardcover), and 11/16/09 and 4/21/10 (softcover), by R.R. DONNELLEY, INC., SALEM, VA, USA.**

10 9 8 7 6 5 4 3 2 1

THE INVINCIBLE IRON MAN

WORLD'S MOST WANTED

WRITER: **MATT FRACTION**
ARTIST: **SALVADOR LARROCA**
COLORS: **FRANK D'ARMATA**
LETTERS: **VC'S JOE CARAMAGNA**
ASSISTANT EDITOR: **ALEJANDRO ARBONA**
EDITORS: **WARREN SIMONS & RALPH MACCHIO**
SPECIAL THANKS TO SANA AMANAT & YANA CHAPKIS

COLLECTION EDITOR: **JENNIFER GRÜNWALD**
ASSISTANT EDITORS: **ALEX STARBUCK & JOHN DENNING**
EDITOR, SPECIAL PROJECTS: **MARK D. BEAZLEY**
SENIOR EDITOR, SPECIAL PROJECTS: **JEFF YOUNGQUIST**
SENIOR VICE PRESIDENT OF SALES: **DAVID GABRIEL**
BOOK DESIGNER: **RODOLFO MURAGUCHI**

EDITOR IN CHIEF: **JOE QUESADA**
PUBLISHER: **DAN BUCKLEY**
EXECUTIVE PRODUCER: **ALAN FINE**

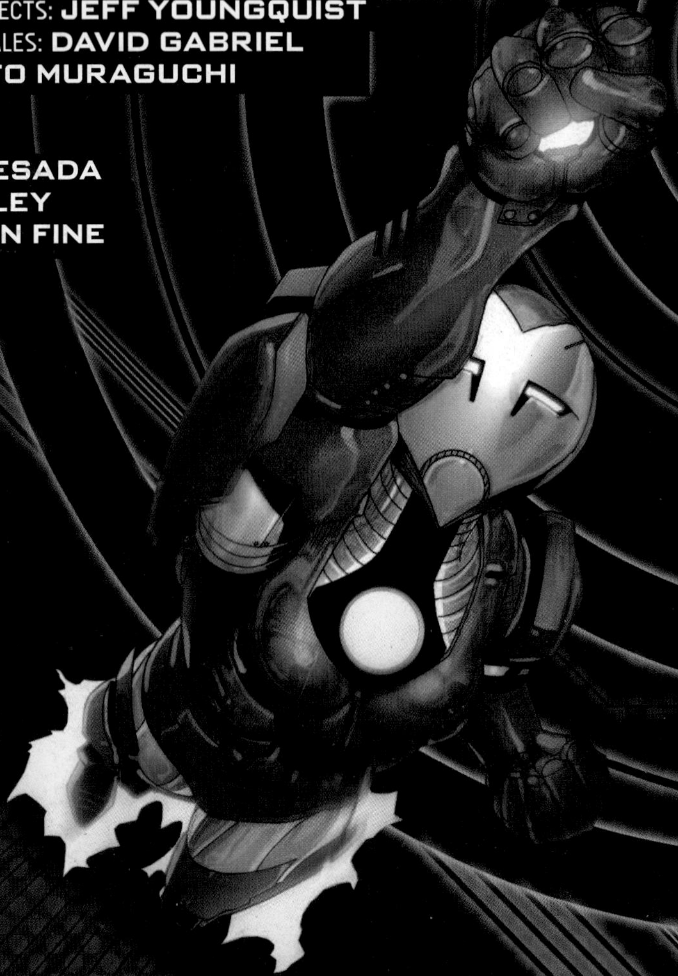

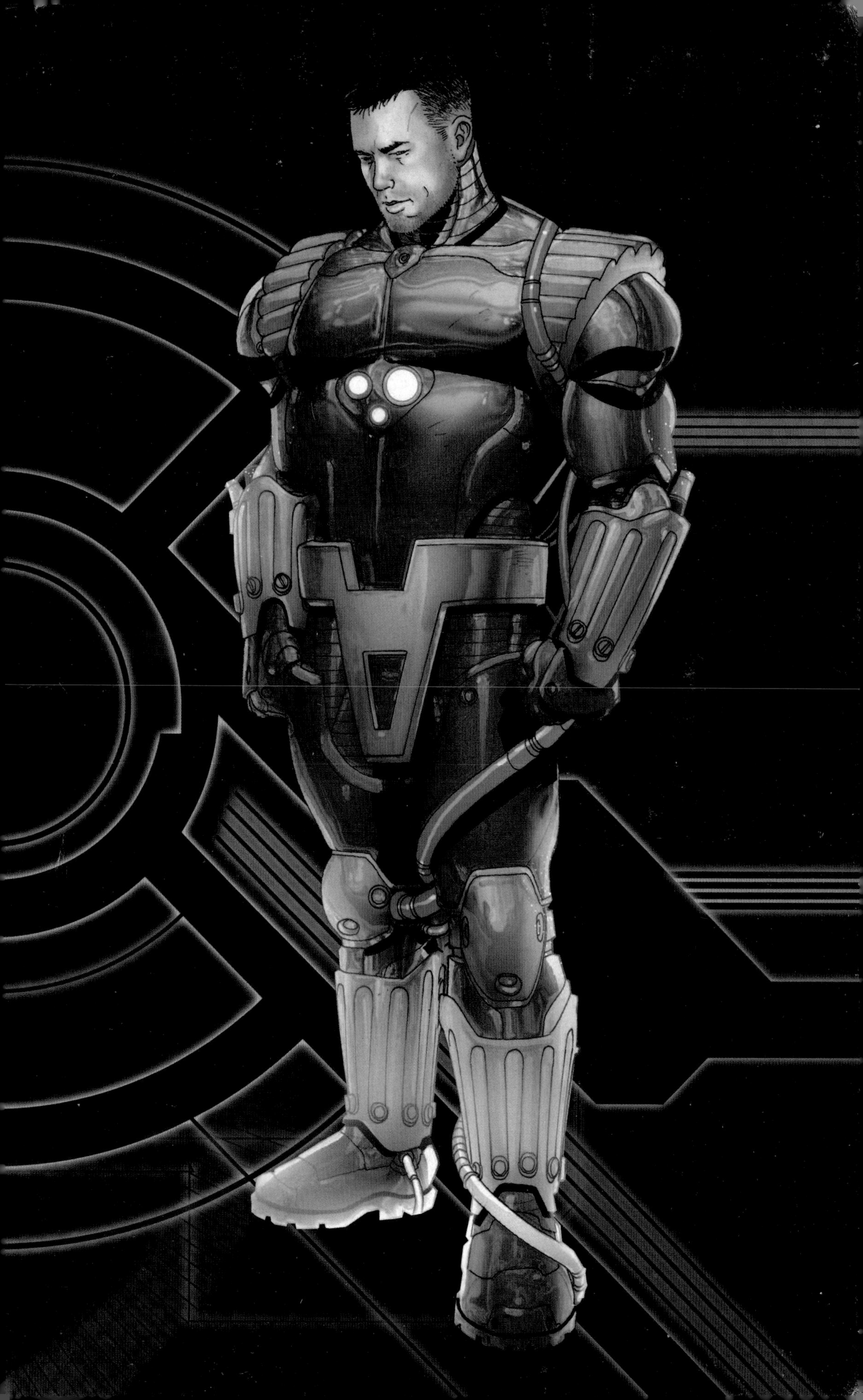

PREVIOUSLY:

In the wake of the disastrous Skrull invasion, Tony Stark was stripped of his roles as leader of the Avengers and director of S.H.I.E.L.D. Now Tony's on the run, and Norman Osborn — leader of the corrupt government agency known as H.A.M.M.E.R. — is after him. Tony's got the secret identity of every super hero in his head, and Osborn will stop at nothing to get that information.

As Osborn's web tightens, Tony frantically makes his way across the globe to each of his hidden armories, using extraordinarily powerful technology to delete the database that is his mind. The process, however, has dramatically diminished Tony's intelligence...which makes evading Osborn's lackeys increasingly difficult. Osborn now dispatches Tony's former flame — the super villain Madame Masque — to bring him in...

Meanwhile, Maria Hill has completed the first step in her mission for Tony, retrieving very sensitive data for her former boss. However, she encountered the brutal Controller, and the villain might have severely damaged her. Now she continues her mission to find Captain America...but is she well?

And Pepper — equipped with her very own Stark-tech suit for aid and rescue — has gotten Osborn's attention. After several acts of heroism, Pepper was detained by Osborn and strong-armed into turning over Stark. She refused...but Osborn's put her on notice. He'll have her arrested or shot down if she flies again...

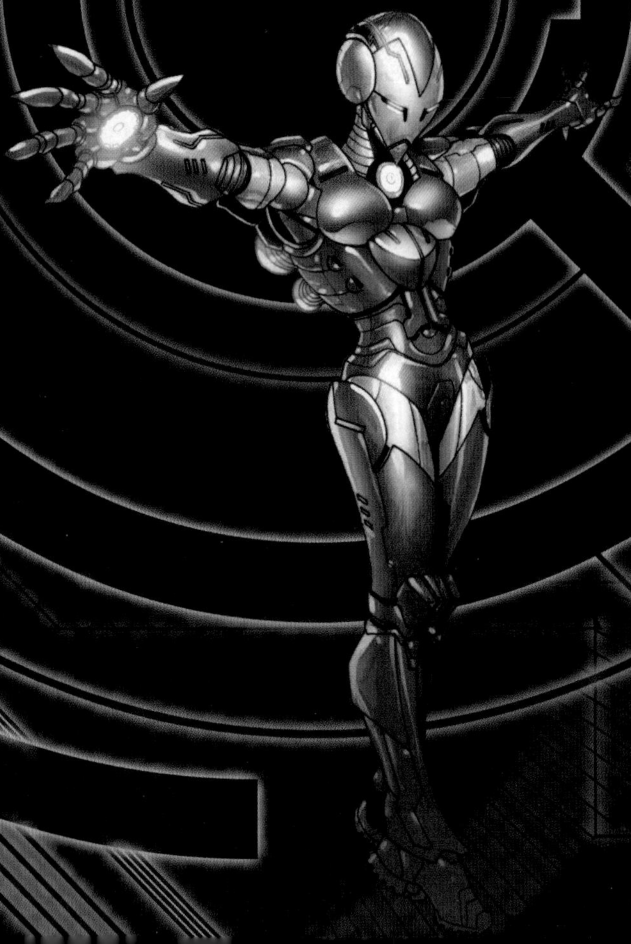

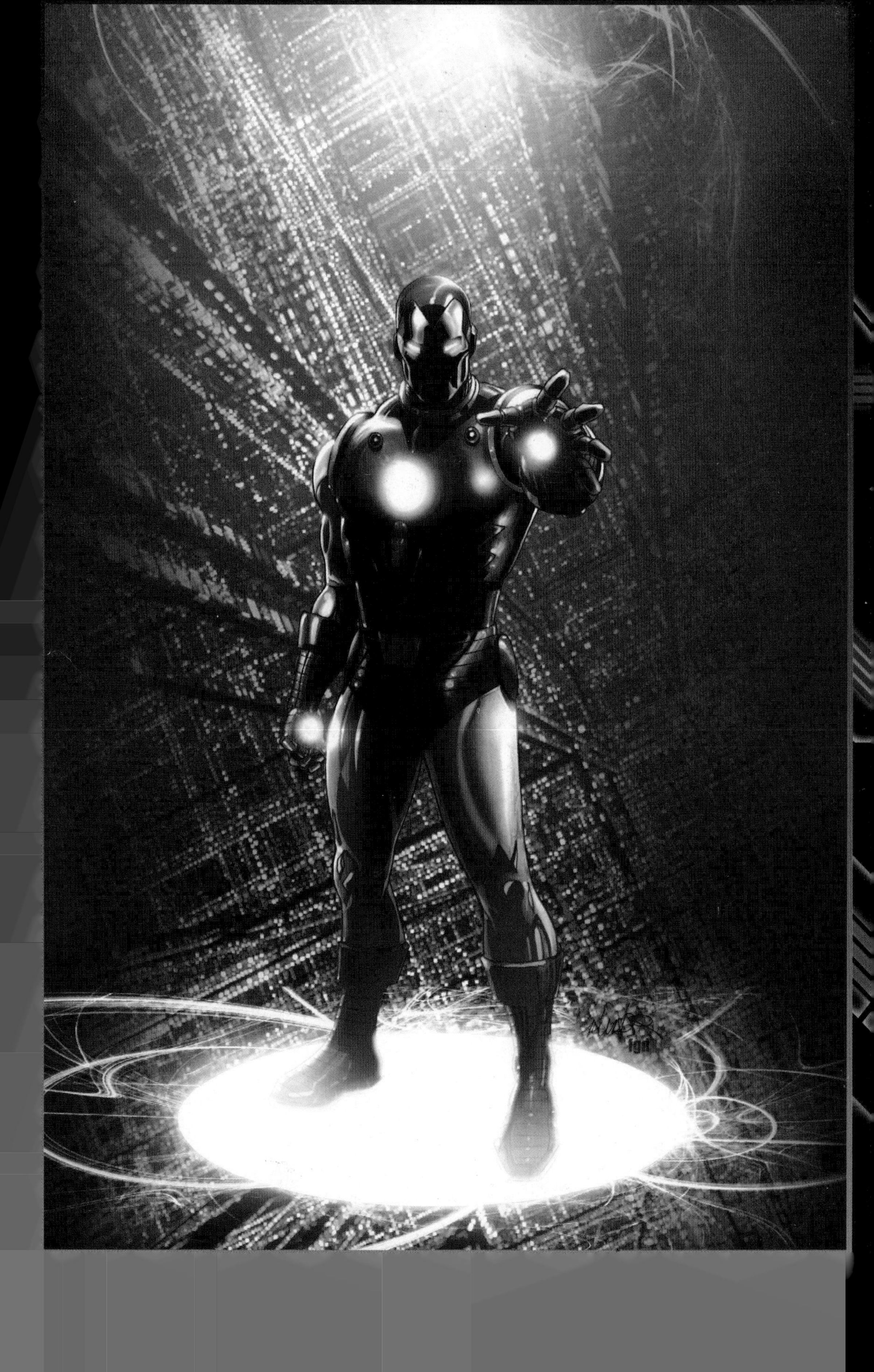

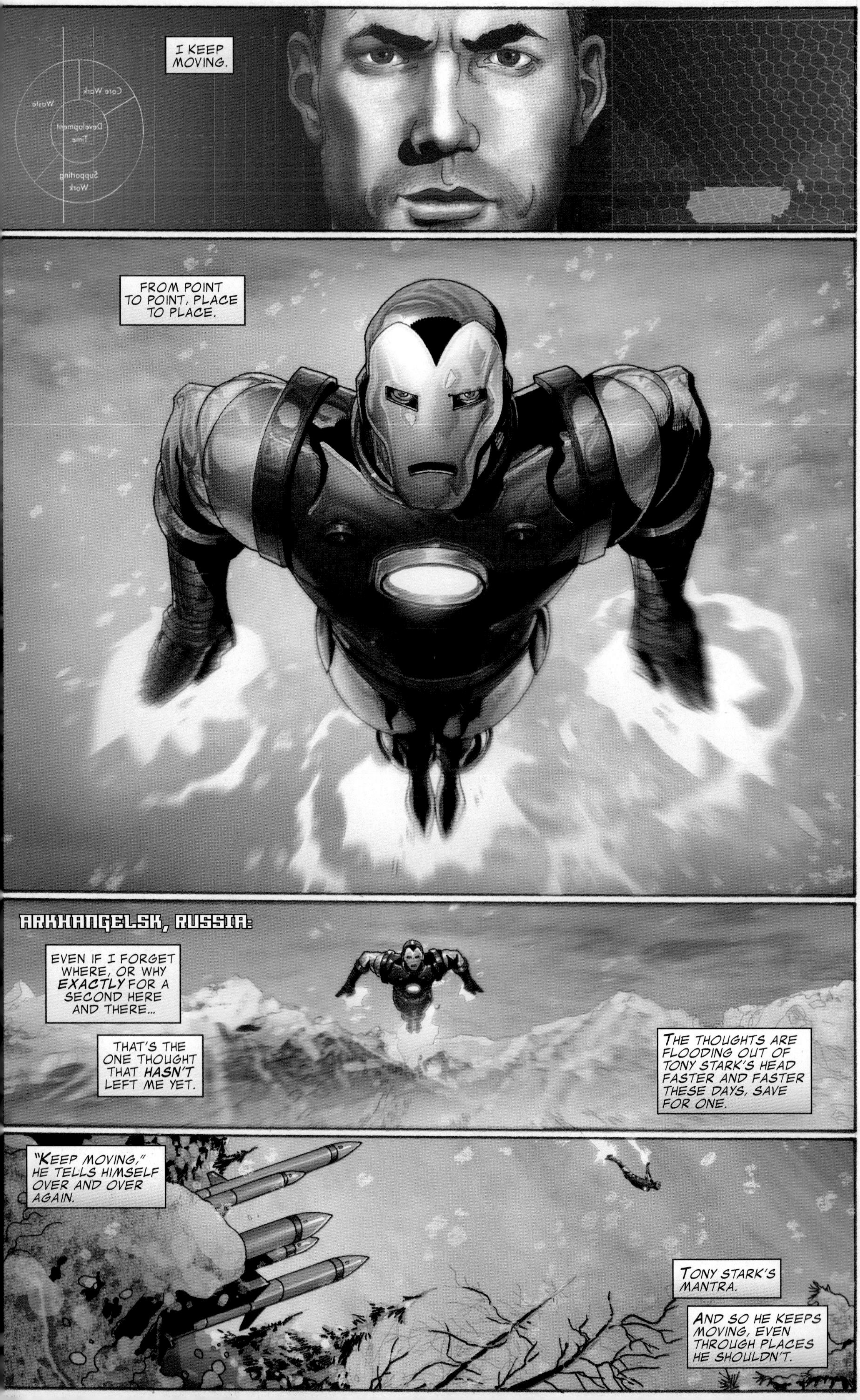

I KEEP MOVING.
FROM POINT TO POINT, PLACE TO PLACE.
ARKHANGELSK, RUSSIA:
EVEN IF I FORGET WHERE, OR WHY EXACTLY FOR A SECOND HERE AND THERE...
THAT'S THE ONE THOUGHT THAT HASN'T LEFT ME YET.
THE THOUGHTS ARE FLOODING OUT OF TONY STARK'S HEAD FASTER AND FASTER THESE DAYS, SAVE FOR ONE.
"KEEP MOVING," HE TELLS HIMSELF OVER AND OVER AGAIN.
TONY STARK'S MANTRA.
AND SO HE KEEPS MOVING, EVEN THROUGH PLACES HE SHOULDN'T.

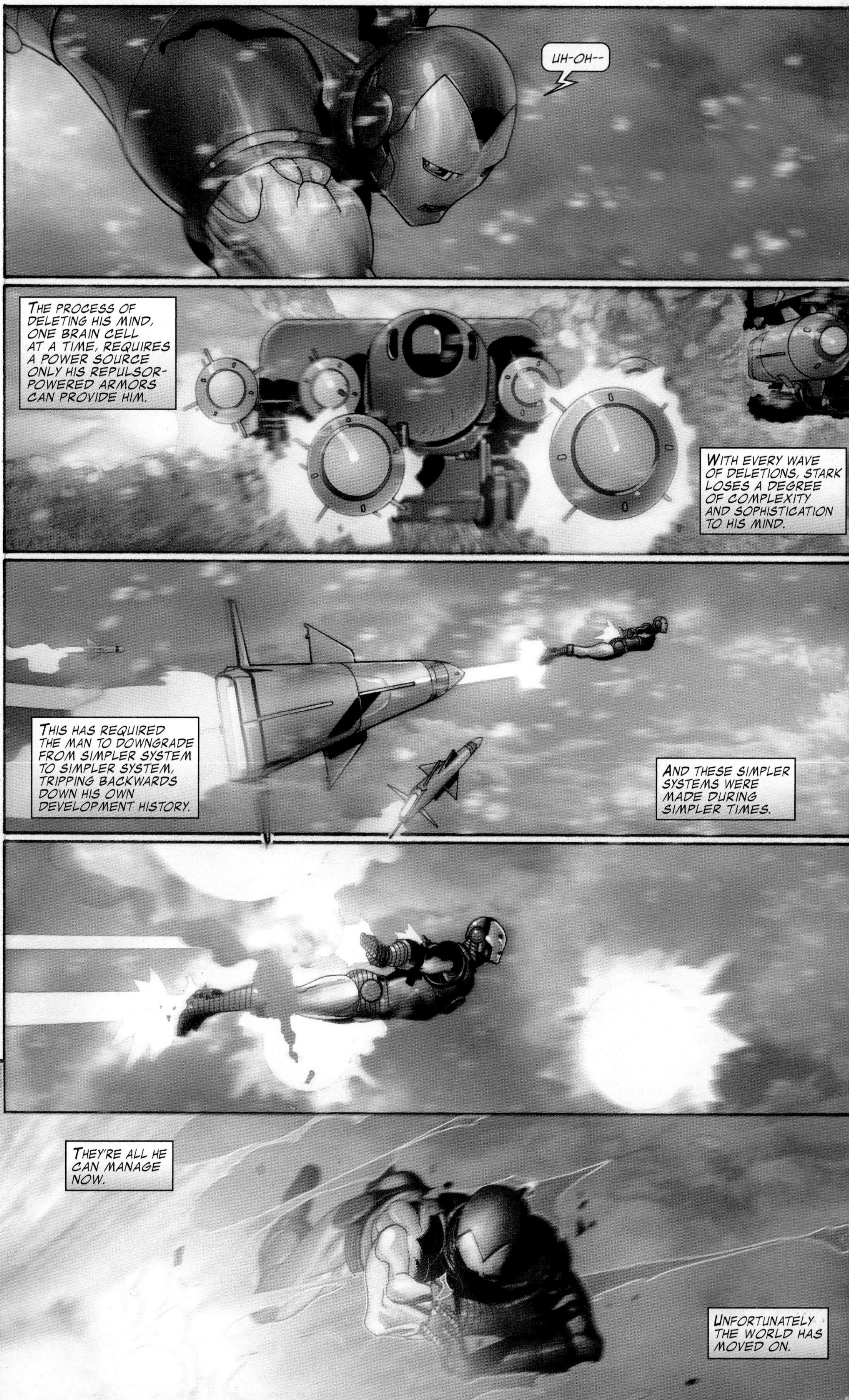
UH-OH--
THE PROCESS OF DELETING HIS MIND, ONE BRAIN CELL AT A TIME, REQUIRES A POWER SOURCE ONLY HIS REPULSOR-POWERED ARMORS CAN PROVIDE HIM.
WITH EVERY WAVE OF DELETIONS, STARK LOSES A DEGREE OF COMPLEXITY AND SOPHISTICATION TO HIS MIND.
THIS HAS REQUIRED THE MAN TO DOWNGRADE FROM SIMPLER SYSTEM TO SIMPLER SYSTEM, TRIPPING BACKWARDS DOWN HIS OWN DEVELOPMENT HISTORY.
AND THESE SIMPLER SYSTEMS WERE MADE DURING SIMPLER TIMES.
THEY'RE ALL HE CAN MANAGE NOW.
UNFORTUNATELY THE WORLD HAS MOVED ON.

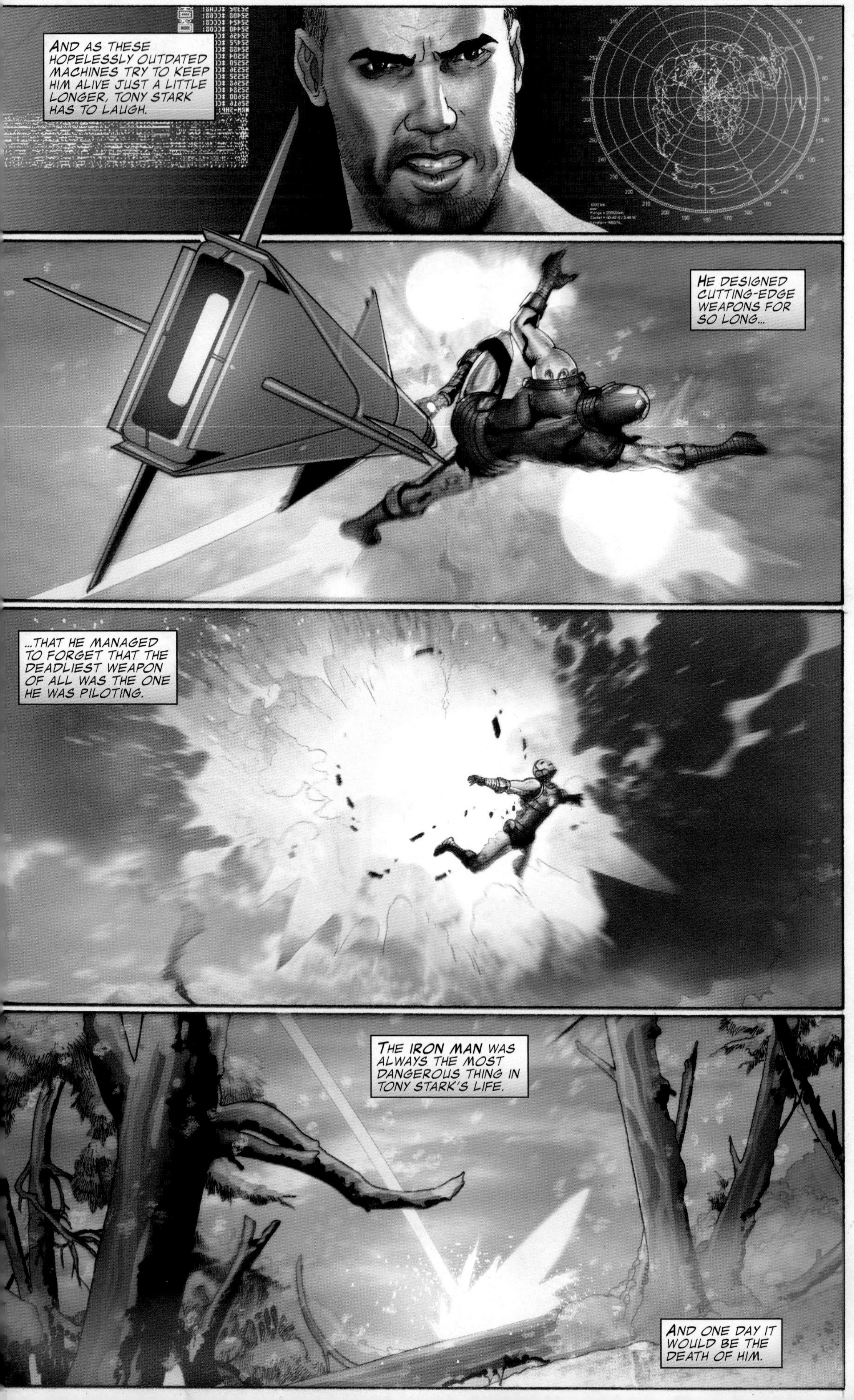
AND AS THESE HOPELESSLY OUTDATED MACHINES TRY TO KEEP HIM ALIVE JUST A LITTLE LONGER, TONY STARK HAS TO LAUGH.
HE DESIGNED CUTTING-EDGE WEAPONS FOR SO LONG...
...THAT HE MANAGED TO FORGET THAT THE DEADLIEST WEAPON OF ALL WAS THE ONE HE WAS PILOTING.
THE IRON MAN WAS ALWAYS THE MOST DANGEROUS THING IN TONY STARK'S LIFE.
AND ONE DAY IT WOULD BE THE DEATH OF HIM.

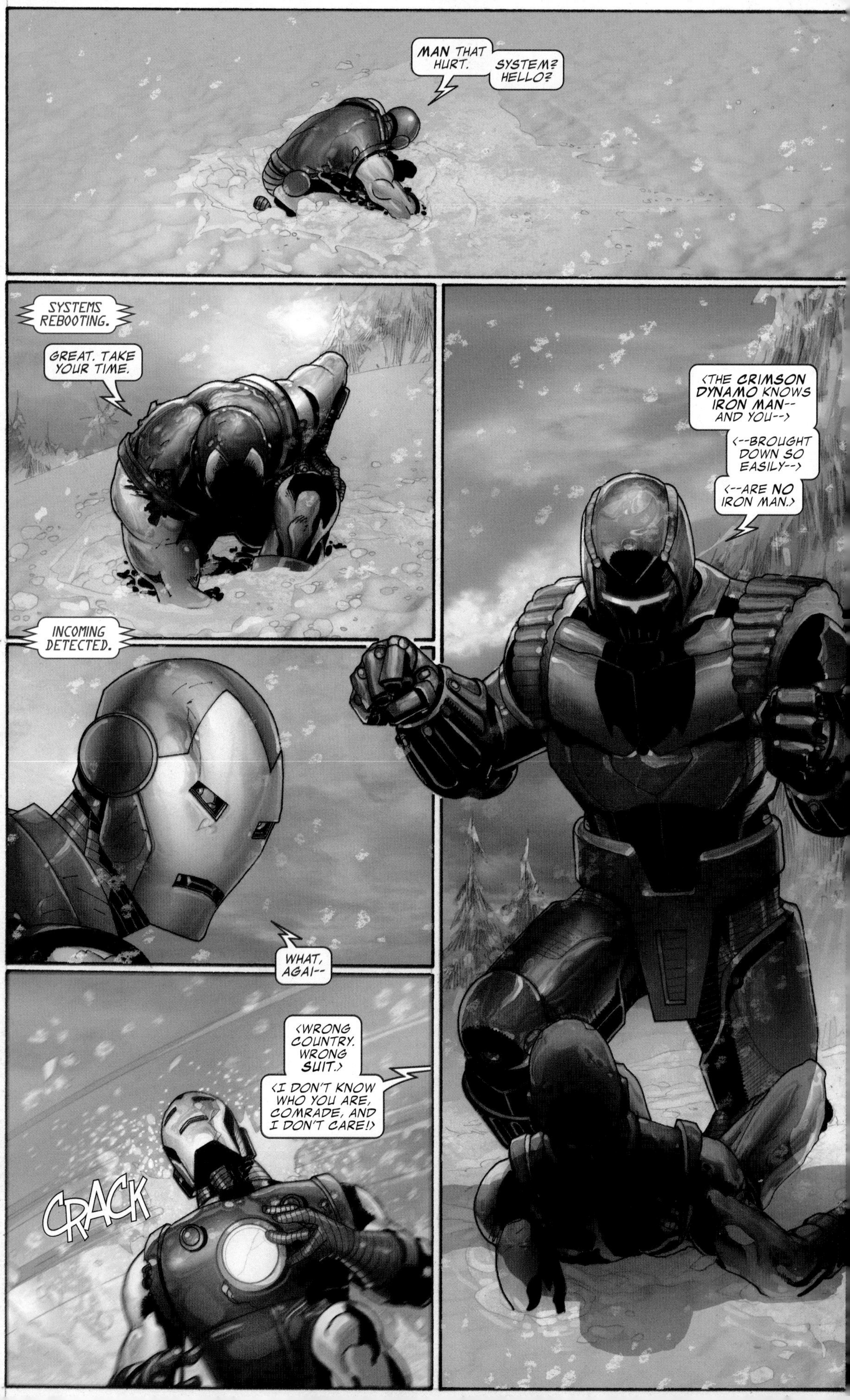
MAN THAT HURT.
SYSTEM? HELLO?
SYSTEMS REBOOTING.
GREAT. TAKE YOUR TIME.
INCOMING DETECTED.
WHAT, AGAI--
<THE CRIMSON DYNAMO KNOWS IRON MAN-- AND YOU-->
<--BROUGHT DOWN SO EASILY-->
<--ARE NO IRON MAN.>
<WRONG COUNTRY. WRONG SUIT.>
<I DON'T KNOW WHO YOU ARE, COMRADE, AND I DON'T CARE!>
CRACK

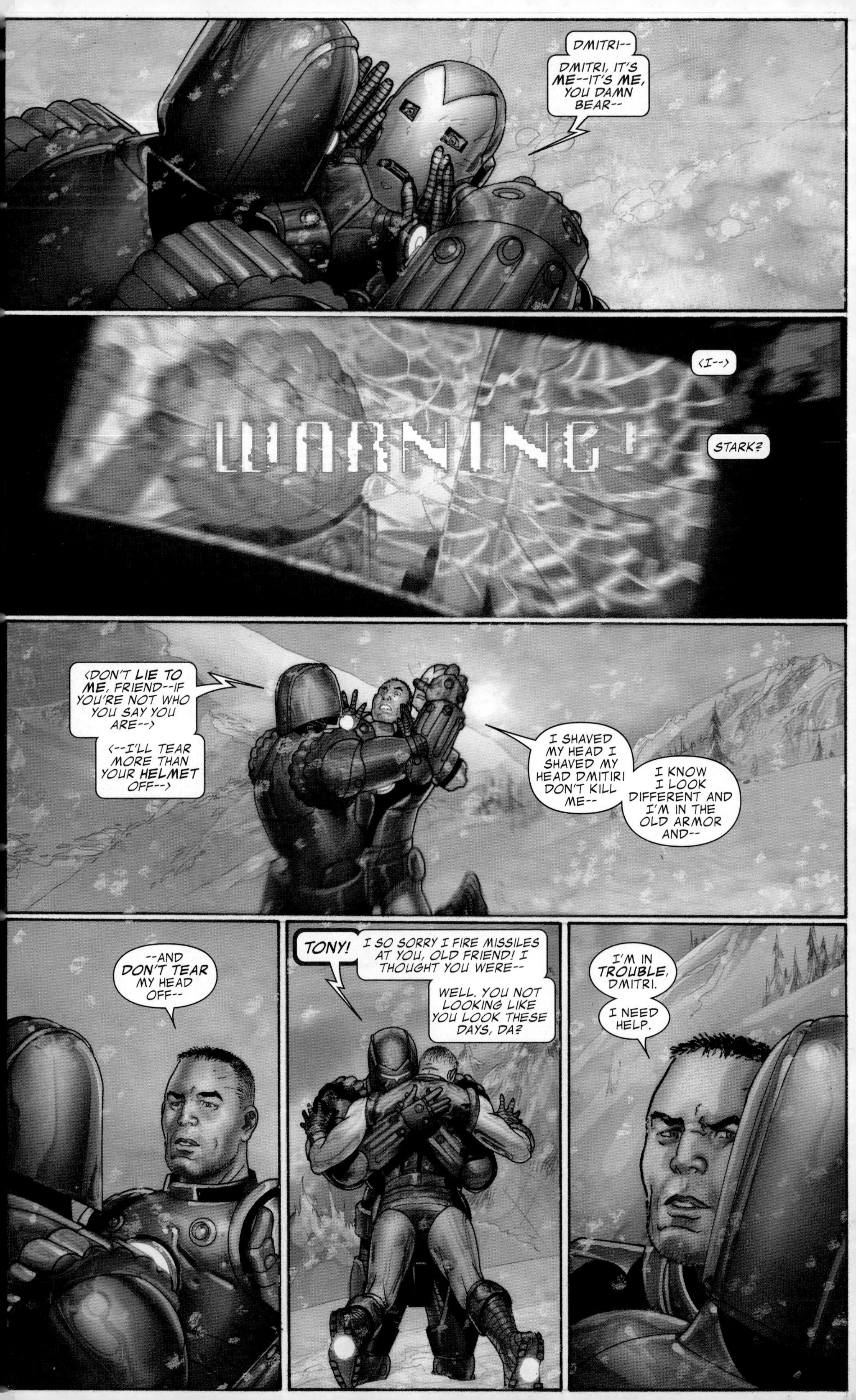
DMITRI--
DMITRI, IT'S ME--IT'S ME, YOU DAMN BEAR--
<I-->
WARNING!
STARK?
<DON'T LIE TO ME, FRIEND--IF YOU'RE NOT WHO YOU SAY YOU ARE-->
<--I'LL TEAR MORE THAN YOUR HELMET OFF-->
I SHAVED MY HEAD I SHAVED MY HEAD DMITIRI DON'T KILL ME--
I KNOW I LOOK DIFFERENT AND I'M IN THE OLD ARMOR AND--
--AND DON'T TEAR MY HEAD OFF--
TONY!
I SO SORRY I FIRE MISSILES AT YOU, OLD FRIEND! I THOUGHT YOU WERE--
WELL. YOU NOT LOOKING LIKE YOU LOOK THESE DAYS, DA?
I'M IN TROUBLE, DMITRI.
I NEED HELP.

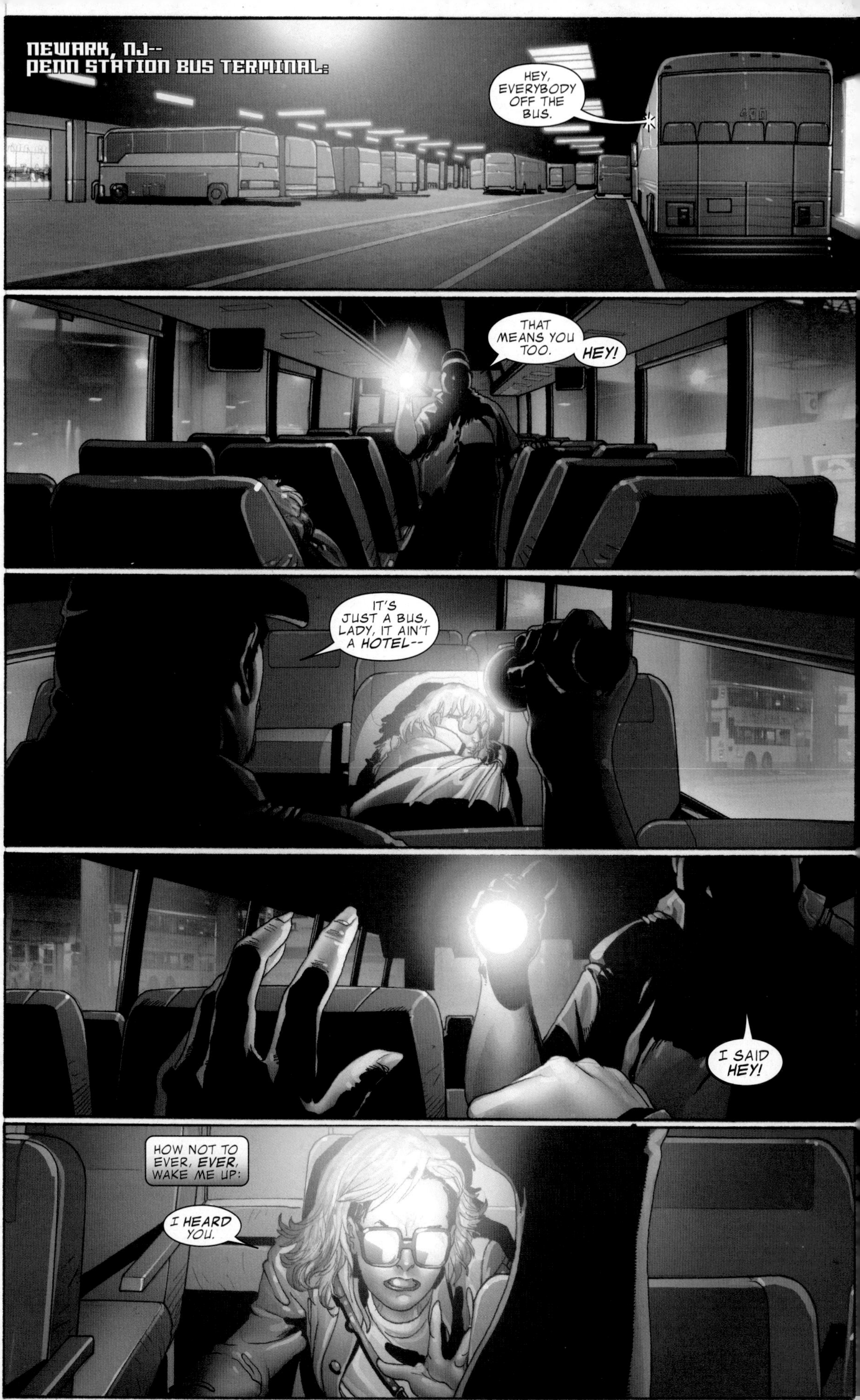
NEWARK, NJ--
PENN STATION BUS TERMINAL:
HEY, EVERYBODY OFF THE BUS.
THAT MEANS YOU TOO.
HEY!
IT'S JUST A BUS, LADY, IT AIN'T A HOTEL--
I SAID HEY!
HOW NOT TO EVER, EVER, WAKE ME UP:
I HEARD YOU.

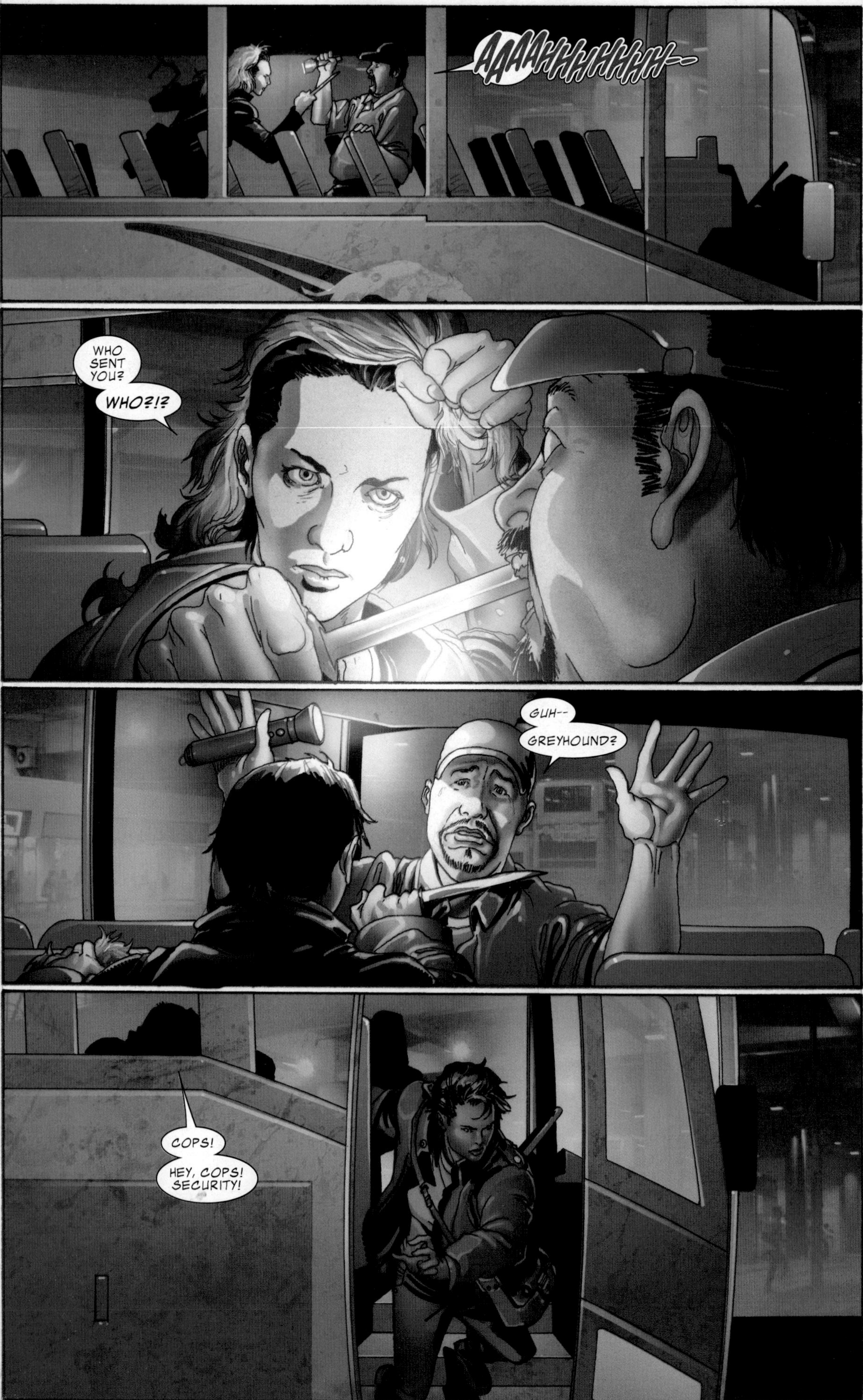
AAAAHHHHHHHHH--
WHO SENT YOU?
WHO?!?
GUH-- GREYHOUND?
COPS!
HEY, COPS! SECURITY!

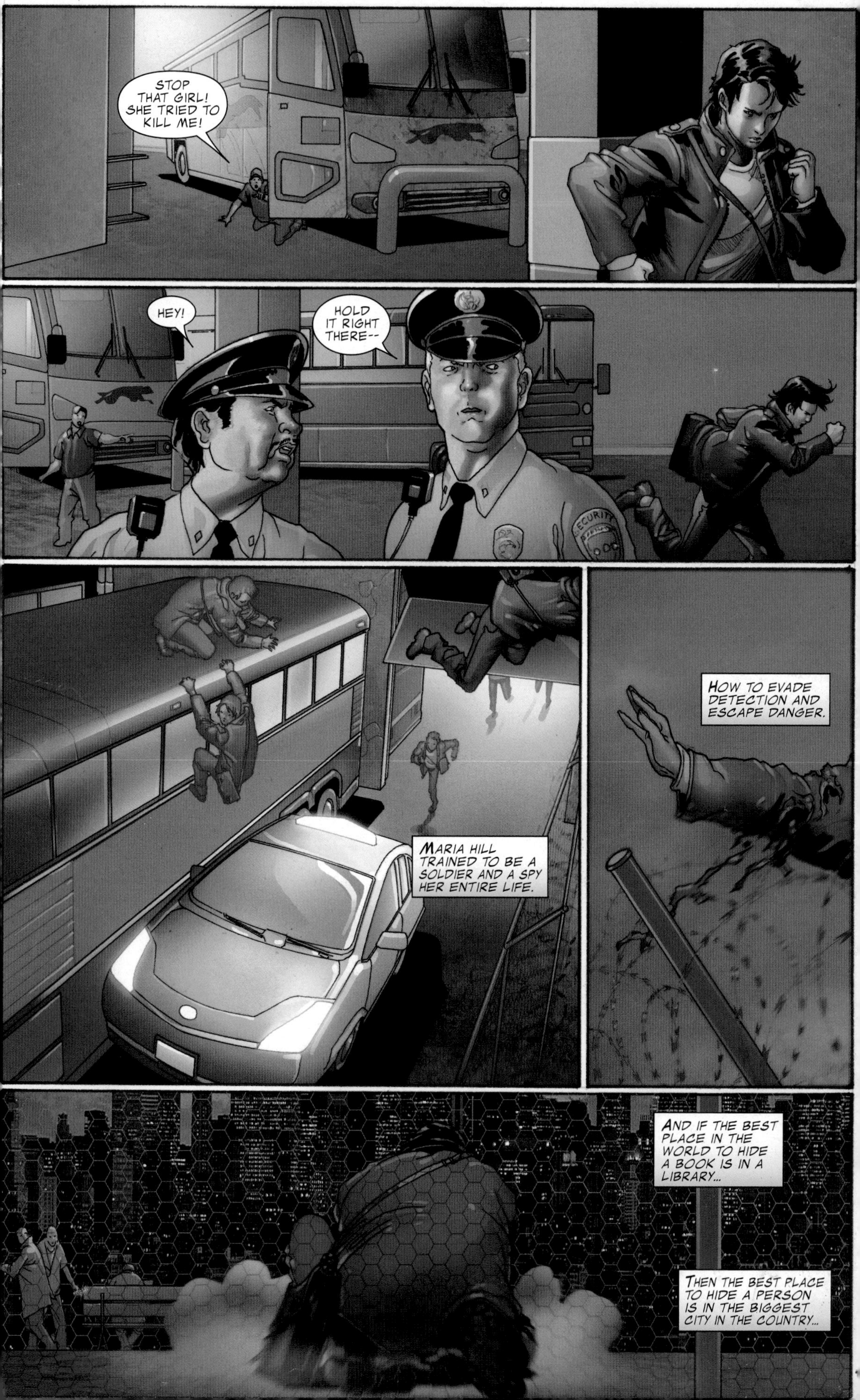
STOP THAT GIRL! SHE TRIED TO KILL ME!
HEY!
HOLD IT RIGHT THERE--
HOW TO EVADE DETECTION AND ESCAPE DANGER.
MARIA HILL TRAINED TO BE A SOLDIER AND A SPY HER ENTIRE LIFE.
AND IF THE BEST PLACE IN THE WORLD TO HIDE A BOOK IS IN A LIBRARY...
THEN THE BEST PLACE TO HIDE A PERSON IS IN THE BIGGEST CITY IN THE COUNTRY...

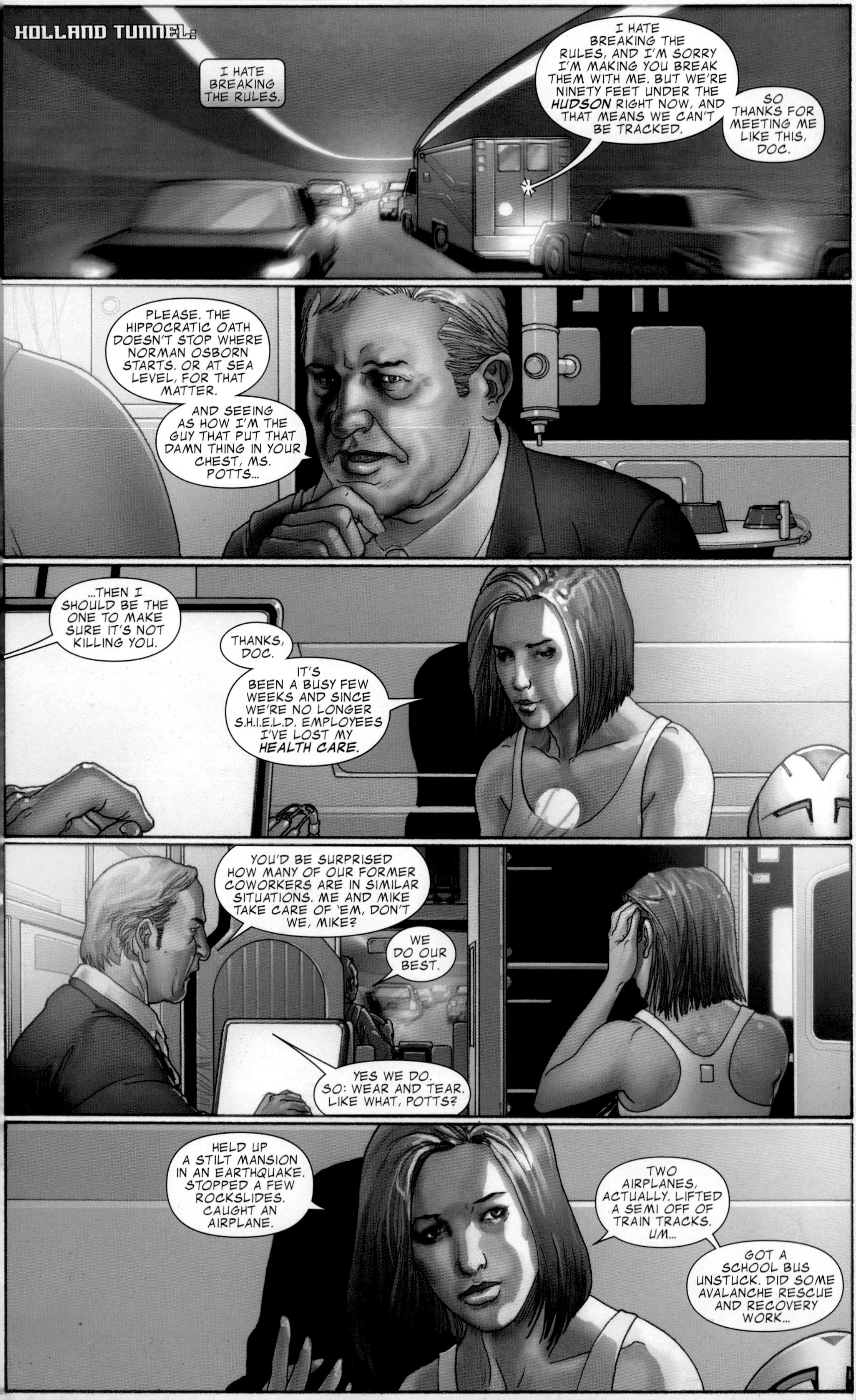
HOLLAND TUNNEL:
I HATE BREAKING THE RULES.
I HATE BREAKING THE RULES, AND I'M SORRY I'M MAKING YOU BREAK THEM WITH ME. BUT WE'RE NINETY FEET UNDER THE HUDSON RIGHT NOW, AND THAT MEANS WE CAN'T BE TRACKED.
SO THANKS FOR MEETING ME LIKE THIS, DOC.
PLEASE. THE HIPPOCRATIC OATH DOESN'T STOP WHERE NORMAN OSBORN STARTS. OR AT SEA LEVEL, FOR THAT MATTER.
AND SEEING AS HOW I'M THE GUY THAT PUT THAT DAMN THING IN YOUR CHEST, MS. POTTS...
...THEN I SHOULD BE THE ONE TO MAKE SURE IT'S NOT KILLING YOU.
THANKS, DOC.
IT'S BEEN A BUSY FEW WEEKS AND SINCE WE'RE NO LONGER S.H.I.E.L.D. EMPLOYEES I'VE LOST MY HEALTH CARE.
YOU'D BE SURPRISED HOW MANY OF OUR FORMER COWORKERS ARE IN SIMILAR SITUATIONS. ME AND MIKE TAKE CARE OF 'EM, DON'T WE, MIKE?
WE DO OUR BEST.
YES WE DO. SO: WEAR AND TEAR. LIKE WHAT, POTTS?
HELD UP A STILT MANSION IN AN EARTHQUAKE. STOPPED A FEW ROCKSLIDES. CAUGHT AN AIRPLANE.
TWO AIRPLANES, ACTUALLY. LIFTED A SEMI OFF OF TRAIN TRACKS. UM...
GOT A SCHOOL BUS UNSTUCK. DID SOME AVALANCHE RESCUE AND RECOVERY WORK...

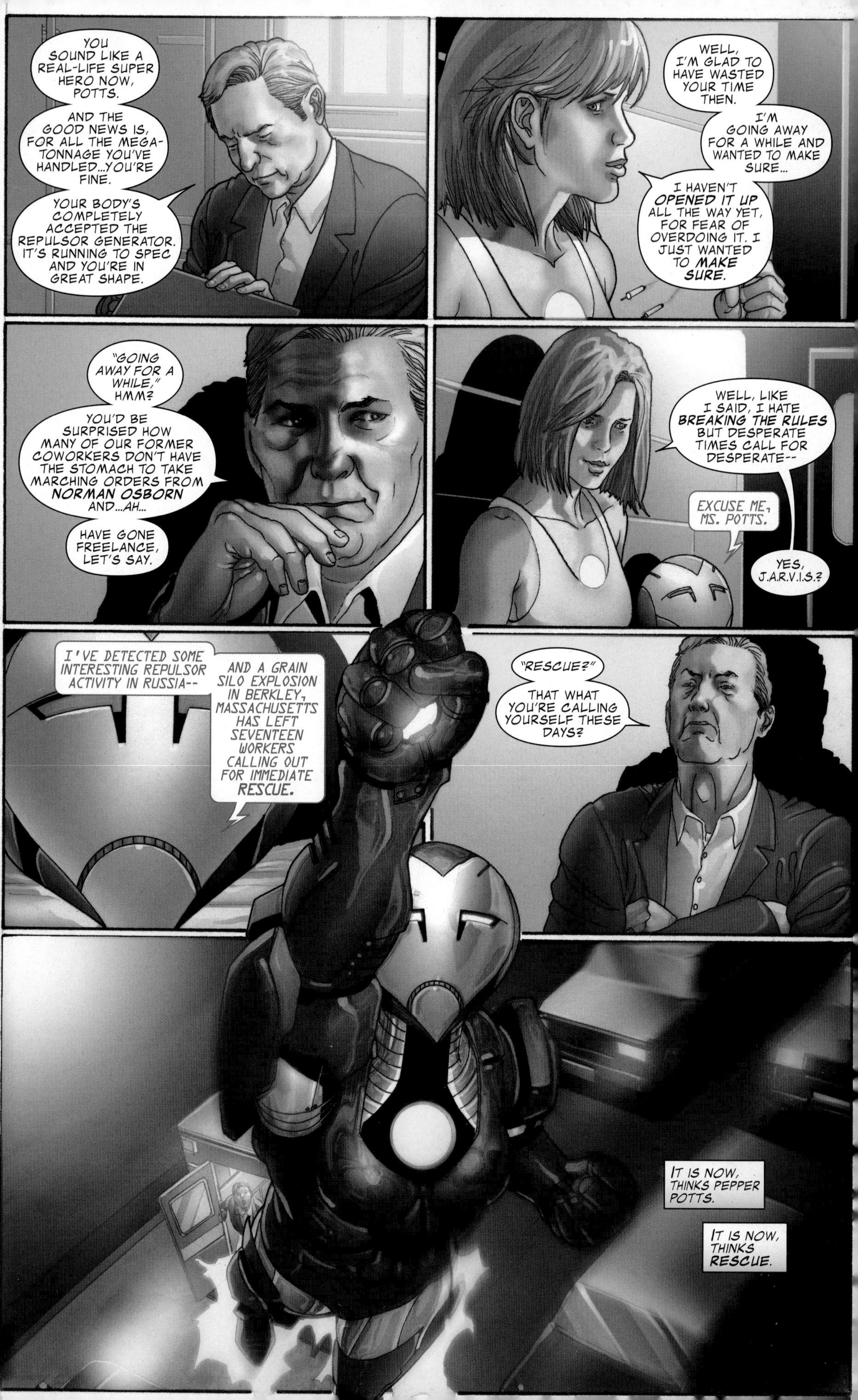
YOU SOUND LIKE A REAL-LIFE SUPER HERO NOW, POTTS.
AND THE GOOD NEWS IS, FOR ALL THE MEGA-TONNAGE YOU'VE HANDLED...YOU'RE FINE.
YOUR BODY'S COMPLETELY ACCEPTED THE REPULSOR GENERATOR. IT'S RUNNING TO SPEC AND YOU'RE IN GREAT SHAPE.
WELL, I'M GLAD TO HAVE WASTED YOUR TIME THEN.
I'M GOING AWAY FOR A WHILE AND WANTED TO MAKE SURE...
I HAVEN'T OPENED IT UP ALL THE WAY YET, FOR FEAR OF OVERDOING IT. I JUST WANTED TO MAKE SURE.
"GOING AWAY FOR A WHILE," HMM?
YOU'D BE SURPRISED HOW MANY OF OUR FORMER COWORKERS DON'T HAVE THE STOMACH TO TAKE MARCHING ORDERS FROM NORMAN OSBORN AND...AH...
HAVE GONE FREELANCE, LET'S SAY.
WELL, LIKE I SAID, I HATE BREAKING THE RULES BUT DESPERATE TIMES CALL FOR DESPERATE--
EXCUSE ME, MS. POTTS.
YES, J.A.R.V.I.S.?
I'VE DETECTED SOME INTERESTING REPULSOR ACTIVITY IN RUSSIA--
AND A GRAIN SILO EXPLOSION IN BERKLEY, MASSACHUSETTS HAS LEFT SEVENTEEN WORKERS CALLING OUT FOR IMMEDIATE RESCUE.
"RESCUE?"
THAT WHAT YOU'RE CALLING YOURSELF THESE DAYS?
IT IS NOW, THINKS PEPPER POTTS.
IT IS NOW, THINKS RESCUE.

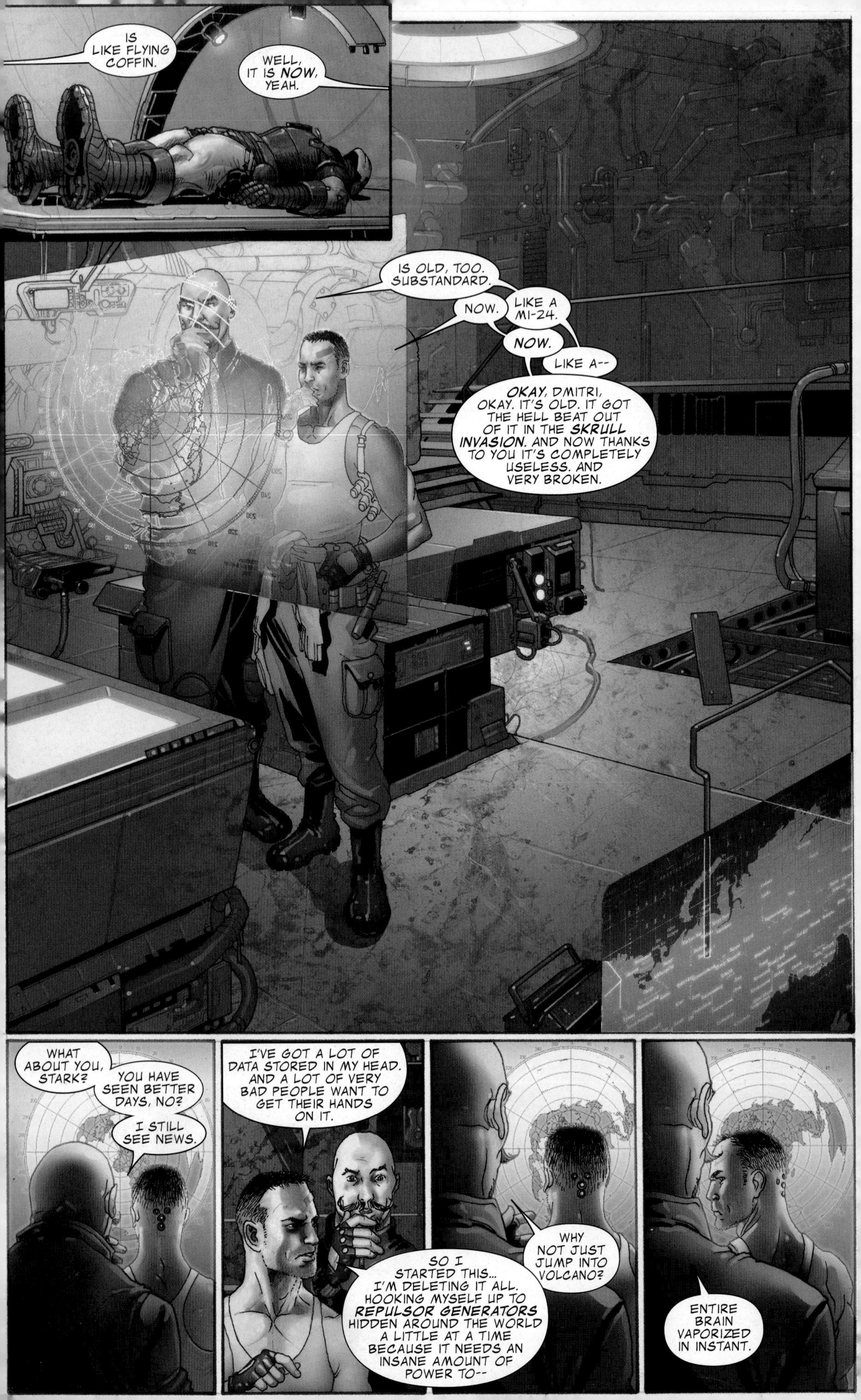
IS LIKE FLYING COFFIN.
WELL, IT IS NOW, YEAH.
IS OLD, TOO. SUBSTANDARD.
LIKE A MI-24.
NOW.
NOW.
LIKE A--
OKAY, DMITRI, OKAY. IT'S OLD. IT GOT THE HELL BEAT OUT OF IT IN THE SKRULL INVASION. AND NOW THANKS TO YOU IT'S COMPLETELY USELESS. AND VERY BROKEN.
WHAT ABOUT YOU, STARK?
YOU HAVE SEEN BETTER DAYS, NO?
I STILL SEE NEWS.
I'VE GOT A LOT OF DATA STORED IN MY HEAD. AND A LOT OF VERY BAD PEOPLE WANT TO GET THEIR HANDS ON IT.
SO I STARTED THIS... I'M DELETING IT ALL. HOOKING MYSELF UP TO REPULSOR GENERATORS HIDDEN AROUND THE WORLD A LITTLE AT A TIME BECAUSE IT NEEDS AN INSANE AMOUNT OF POWER TO--
WHY NOT JUST JUMP INTO VOLCANO?
ENTIRE BRAIN VAPORIZED IN INSTANT.

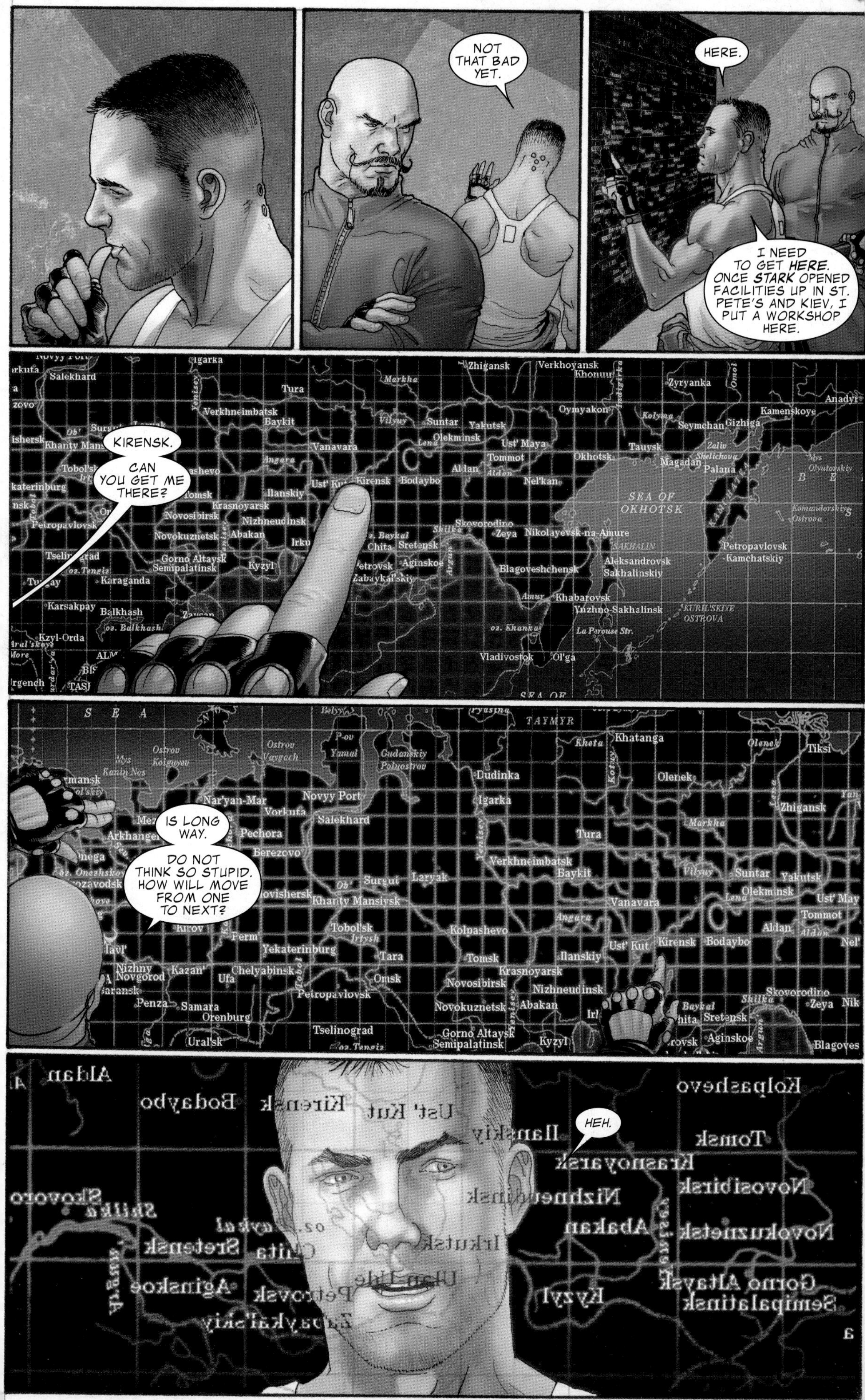
NOT THAT BAD YET.
HERE.
I NEED TO GET HERE. ONCE STARK OPENED FACILITIES UP IN ST. PETE'S AND KIEV, I PUT A WORKSHOP HERE.
KIRENSK.
CAN YOU GET ME THERE?
IS LONG WAY.
DO NOT THINK SO STUPID. HOW WILL MOVE FROM ONE TO NEXT?
HEH.

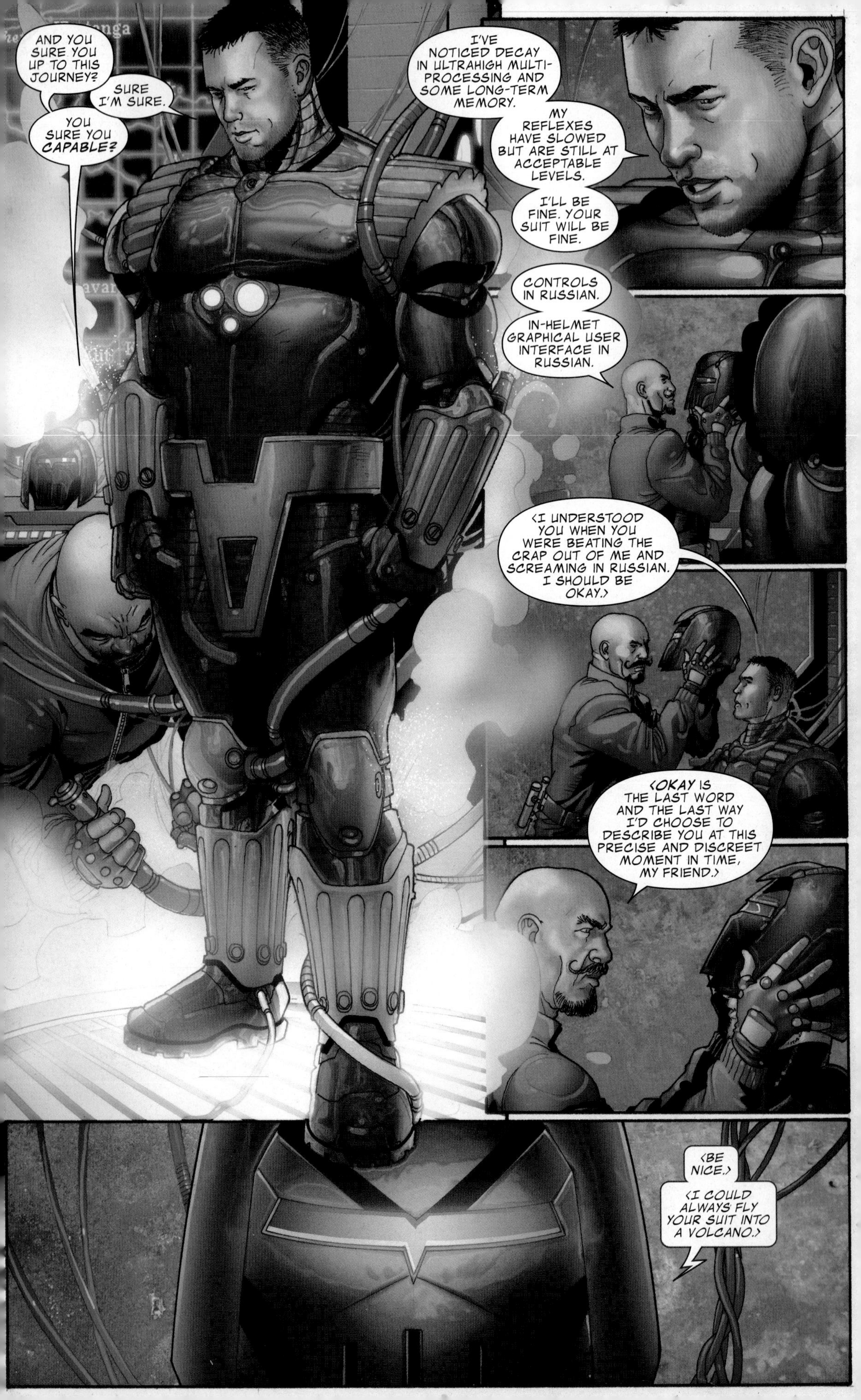
AND YOU SURE YOU UP TO THIS JOURNEY?
SURE I'M SURE.
YOU SURE YOU CAPABLE?
I'VE NOTICED DECAY IN ULTRAHIGH MULTI-PROCESSING AND SOME LONG-TERM MEMORY.
MY REFLEXES HAVE SLOWED BUT ARE STILL AT ACCEPTABLE LEVELS.
I'LL BE FINE. YOUR SUIT WILL BE FINE.
CONTROLS IN RUSSIAN.
IN-HELMET GRAPHICAL USER INTERFACE IN RUSSIAN.
<I UNDERSTOOD YOU WHEN YOU WERE BEATING THE CRAP OUT OF ME AND SCREAMING IN RUSSIAN. I SHOULD BE OKAY.>
<OKAY IS THE LAST WORD AND THE LAST WAY I'D CHOOSE TO DESCRIBE YOU AT THIS PRECISE AND DISCREET MOMENT IN TIME, MY FRIEND.>
<BE NICE.>
<I COULD ALWAYS FLY YOUR SUIT INTO A VOLCANO.>

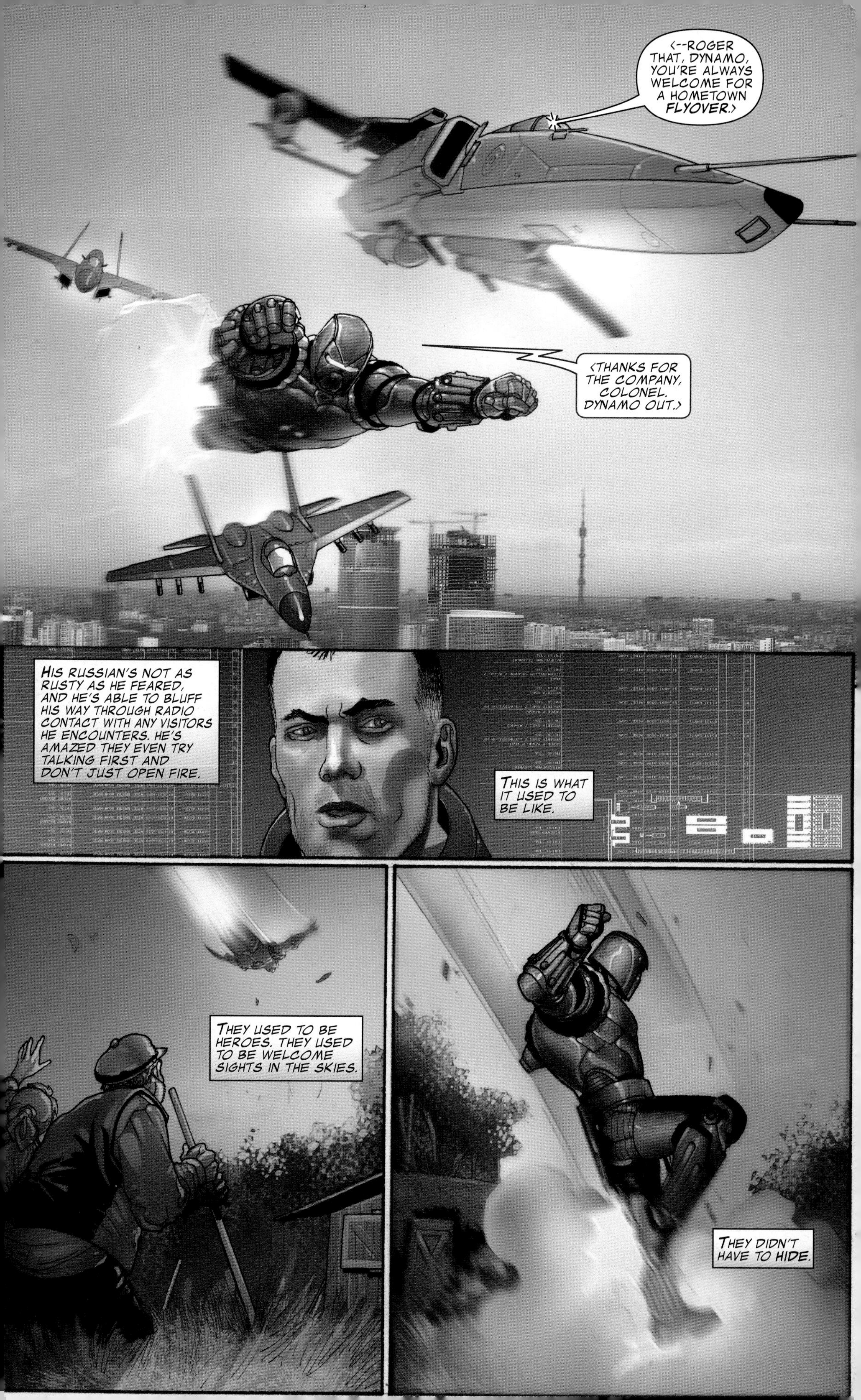
<--ROGER THAT, DYNAMO, YOU'RE ALWAYS WELCOME FOR A HOMETOWN FLYOVER.>
<THANKS FOR THE COMPANY, COLONEL. DYNAMO OUT.>
HIS RUSSIAN'S NOT AS RUSTY AS HE FEARED, AND HE'S ABLE TO BLUFF HIS WAY THROUGH RADIO CONTACT WITH ANY VISITORS HE ENCOUNTERS. HE'S AMAZED THEY EVEN TRY TALKING FIRST AND DON'T JUST OPEN FIRE.
THIS IS WHAT IT USED TO BE LIKE.
THEY USED TO BE HEROES. THEY USED TO BE WELCOME SIGHTS IN THE SKIES.
THEY DIDN'T HAVE TO HIDE.

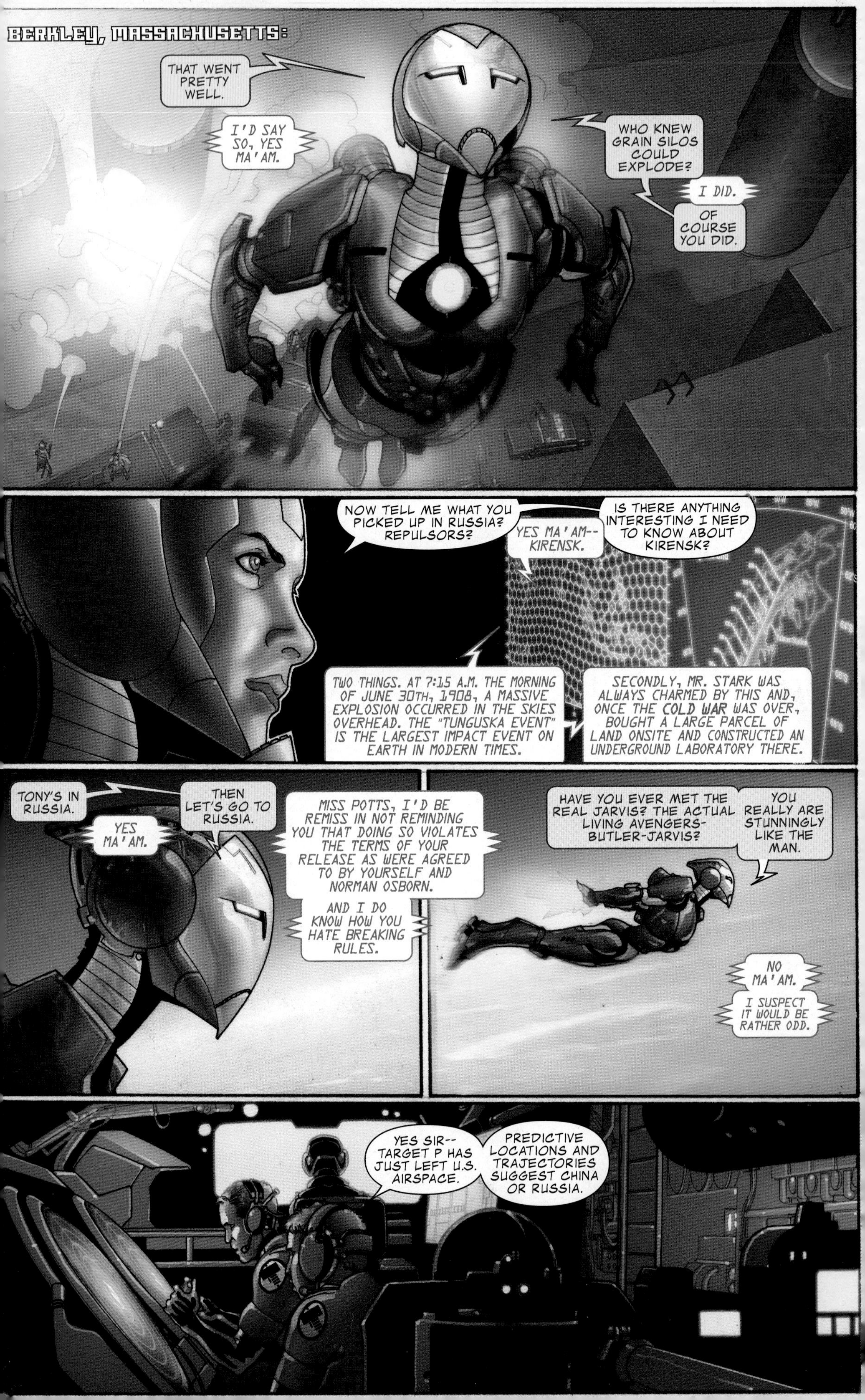
BERKLEY, MASSACHUSETTS:
THAT WENT PRETTY WELL.
I'D SAY SO, YES MA'AM.
WHO KNEW GRAIN SILOS COULD EXPLODE?
I DID.
OF COURSE YOU DID.
NOW TELL ME WHAT YOU PICKED UP IN RUSSIA? REPULSORS?
YES MA'AM--KIRENSK.
IS THERE ANYTHING INTERESTING I NEED TO KNOW ABOUT KIRENSK?
TWO THINGS. AT 7:15 A.M. THE MORNING OF JUNE 30TH, 1908, A MASSIVE EXPLOSION OCCURRED IN THE SKIES OVERHEAD. THE "TUNGUSKA EVENT" IS THE LARGEST IMPACT EVENT ON EARTH IN MODERN TIMES.
SECONDLY, MR. STARK WAS ALWAYS CHARMED BY THIS AND, ONCE THE COLD WAR WAS OVER, BOUGHT A LARGE PARCEL OF LAND ONSITE AND CONSTRUCTED AN UNDERGROUND LABORATORY THERE.
TONY'S IN RUSSIA.
YES MA'AM.
THEN LET'S GO TO RUSSIA.
MISS POTTS, I'D BE REMISS IN NOT REMINDING YOU THAT DOING SO VIOLATES THE TERMS OF YOUR RELEASE AS WERE AGREED TO BY YOURSELF AND NORMAN OSBORN.
AND I DO KNOW HOW YOU HATE BREAKING RULES.
HAVE YOU EVER MET THE REAL JARVIS? THE ACTUAL LIVING AVENGERS-BUTLER-JARVIS?
YOU REALLY ARE STUNNINGLY LIKE THE MAN.
NO MA'AM.
I SUSPECT IT WOULD BE RATHER ODD.
YES SIR--TARGET P HAS JUST LEFT U.S. AIRSPACE.
PREDICTIVE LOCATIONS AND TRAJECTORIES SUGGEST CHINA OR RUSSIA.

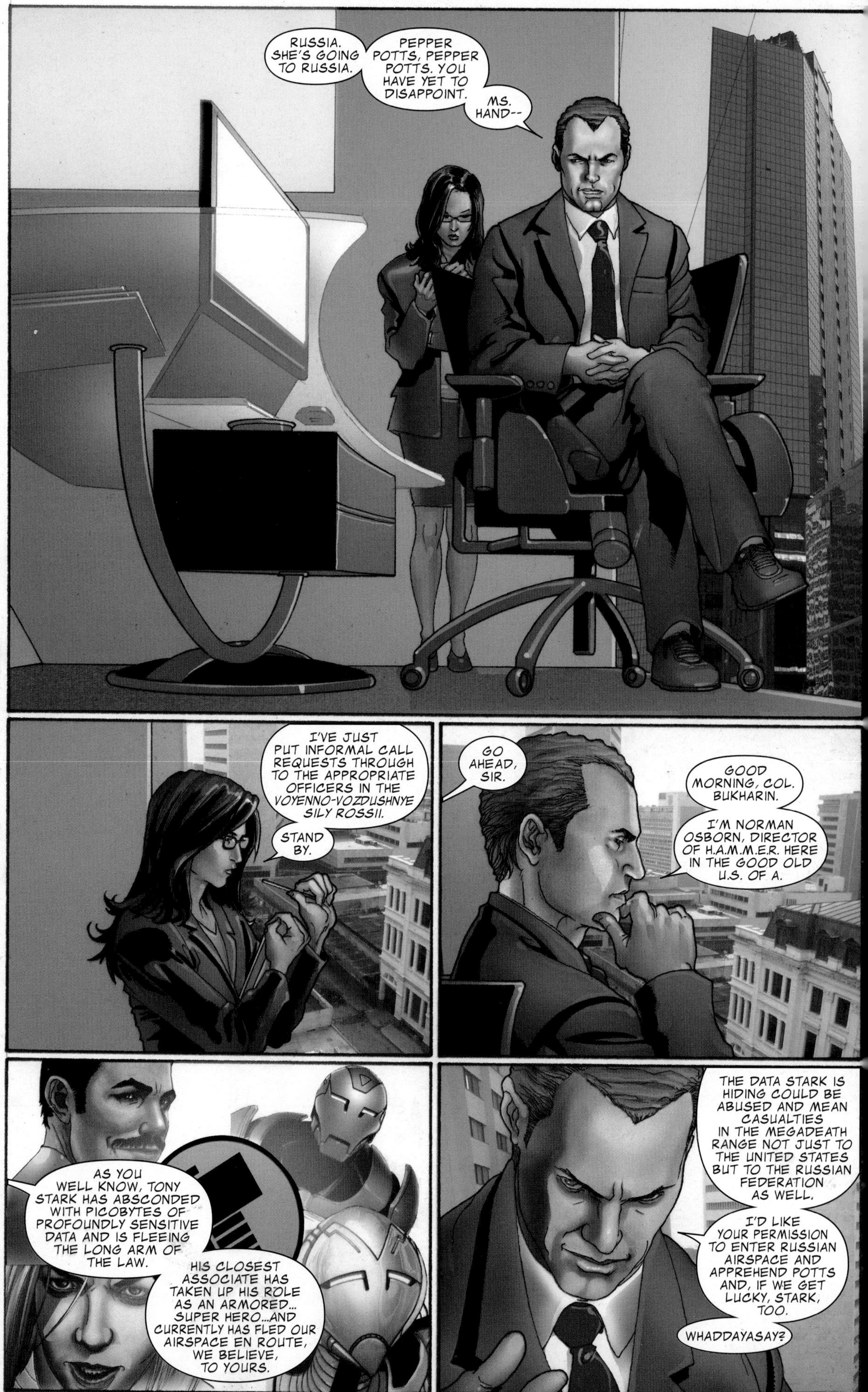
RUSSIA. SHE'S GOING TO RUSSIA.
PEPPER POTTS, PEPPER POTTS. YOU HAVE YET TO DISAPPOINT.
MS. HAND--
I'VE JUST PUT INFORMAL CALL REQUESTS THROUGH TO THE APPROPRIATE OFFICERS IN THE *VOYENNO-VOZDUSHNYE SILY ROSSII.*
STAND BY.
GO AHEAD, SIR.
GOOD MORNING, COL. BUKHARIN.
I'M NORMAN OSBORN, DIRECTOR OF H.A.M.M.E.R. HERE IN THE GOOD OLD U.S. OF A.
AS YOU WELL KNOW, TONY STARK HAS ABSCONDED WITH PICOBYTES OF PROFOUNDLY SENSITIVE DATA AND IS FLEEING THE LONG ARM OF THE LAW.
HIS CLOSEST ASSOCIATE HAS TAKEN UP HIS ROLE AS AN ARMORED... SUPER HERO...AND CURRENTLY HAS FLED OUR AIRSPACE EN ROUTE, WE BELIEVE, TO YOURS.
THE DATA STARK IS HIDING COULD BE ABUSED AND MEAN CASUALTIES IN THE MEGADEATH RANGE NOT JUST TO THE UNITED STATES BUT TO THE RUSSIAN FEDERATION AS WELL.
I'D LIKE YOUR PERMISSION TO ENTER RUSSIAN AIRSPACE AND APPREHEND POTTS AND, IF WE GET LUCKY, STARK, TOO.
WHADDAYASAY?

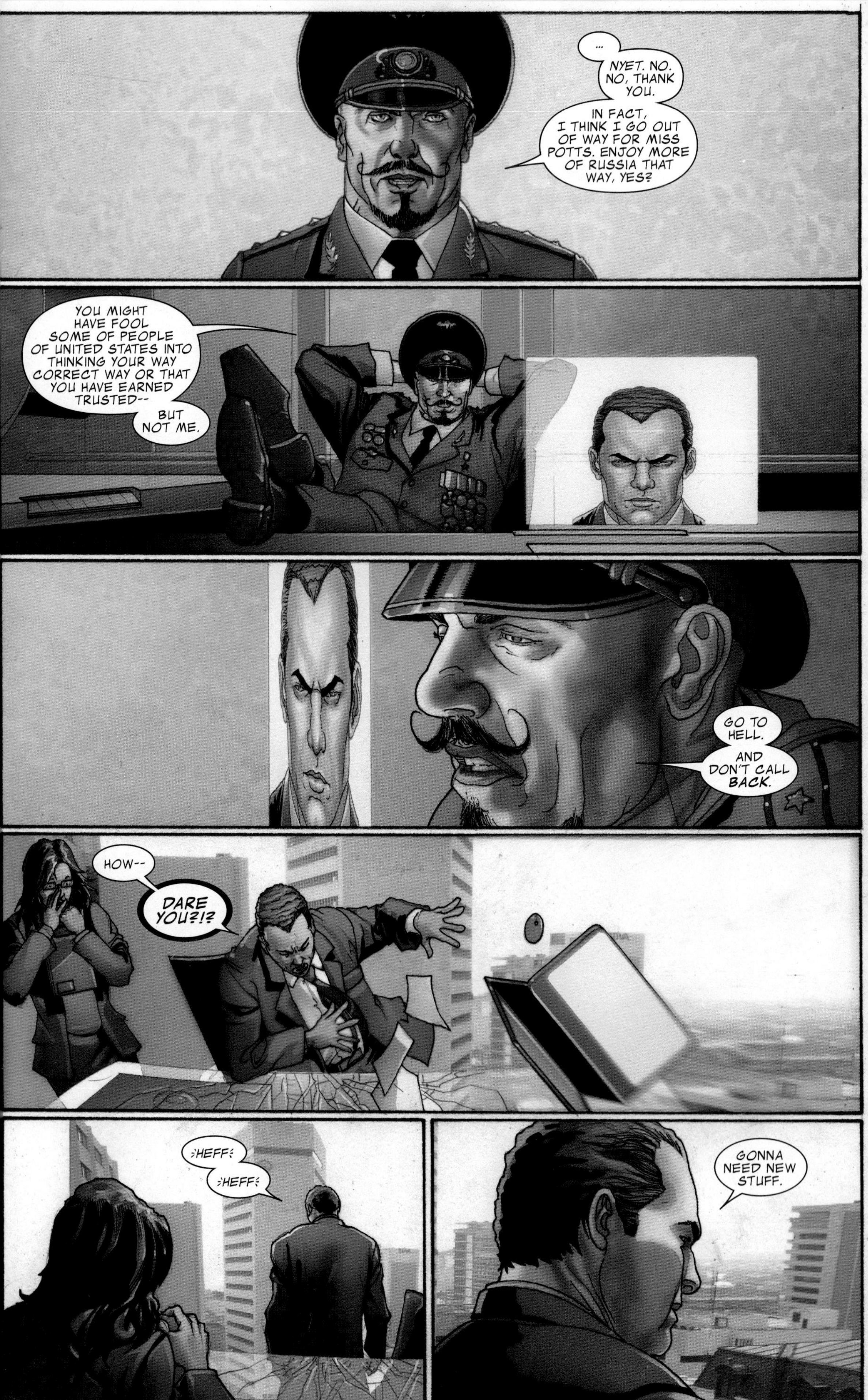
...
NYET. NO. NO, THANK YOU.
IN FACT, I THINK I GO OUT OF WAY FOR MISS POTTS. ENJOY MORE OF RUSSIA THAT WAY, YES?
YOU MIGHT HAVE FOOL SOME OF PEOPLE OF UNITED STATES INTO THINKING YOUR WAY CORRECT WAY OR THAT YOU HAVE EARNED TRUSTED--
BUT NOT ME.
GO TO HELL.
AND DON'T CALL BACK.
HOW--
DARE YOU?!?
HEFF
HEFF
GONNA NEED NEW STUFF.

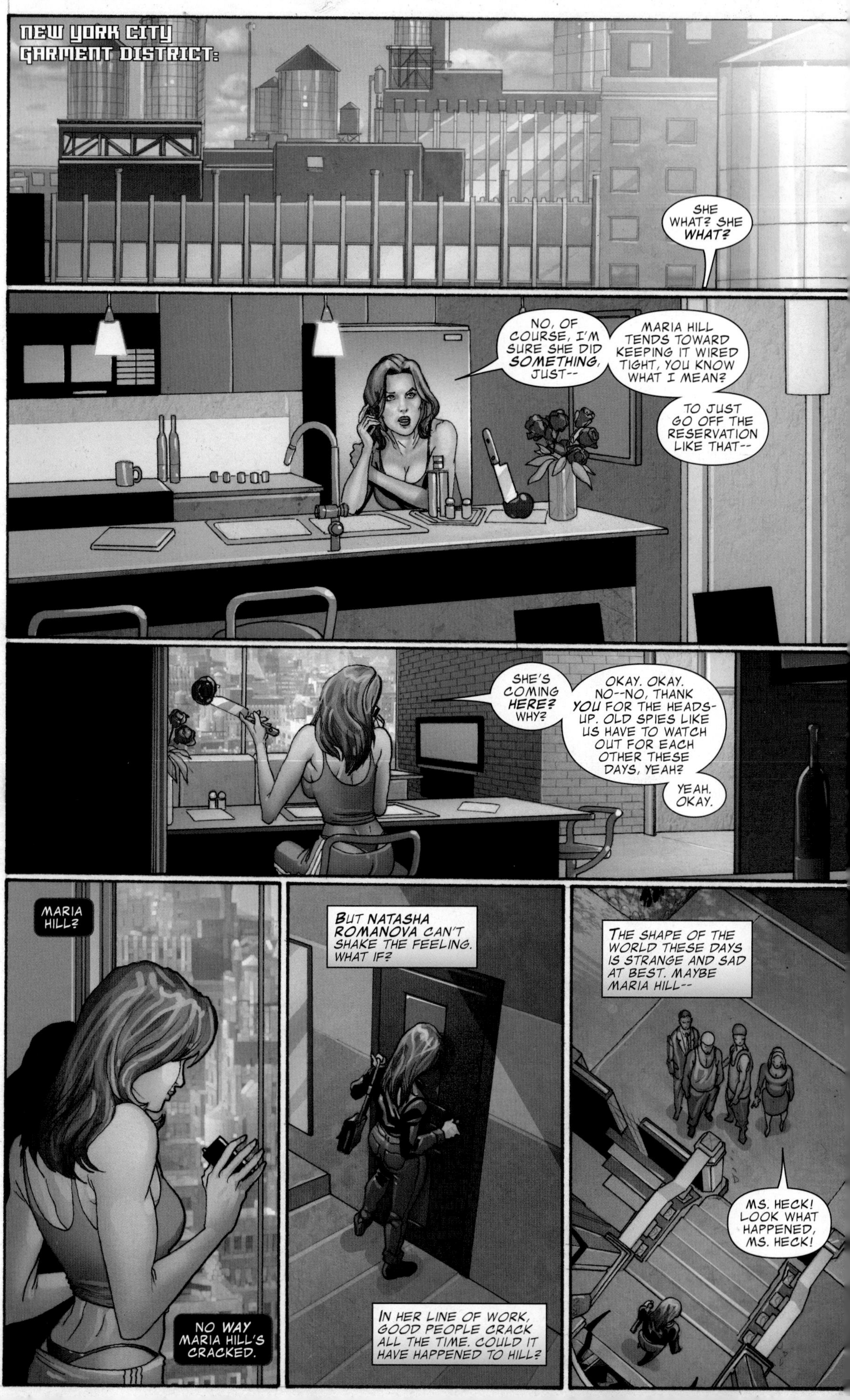
NEW YORK CITY GARMENT DISTRICT:
SHE WHAT? SHE WHAT?
NO, OF COURSE, I'M SURE SHE DID SOMETHING, JUST--
MARIA HILL TENDS TOWARD KEEPING IT WIRED TIGHT, YOU KNOW WHAT I MEAN?
TO JUST GO OFF THE RESERVATION LIKE THAT--
SHE'S COMING HERE? WHY?
OKAY. OKAY. NO--NO, THANK YOU FOR THE HEADS-UP. OLD SPIES LIKE US HAVE TO WATCH OUT FOR EACH OTHER THESE DAYS, YEAH?
YEAH. OKAY.
MARIA HILL?
NO WAY MARIA HILL'S CRACKED.
BUT NATASHA ROMANOVA CAN'T SHAKE THE FEELING. WHAT IF?
IN HER LINE OF WORK, GOOD PEOPLE CRACK ALL THE TIME. COULD IT HAVE HAPPENED TO HILL?
THE SHAPE OF THE WORLD THESE DAYS IS STRANGE AND SAD AT BEST. MAYBE MARIA HILL--
MS. HECK! LOOK WHAT HAPPENED, MS. HECK!

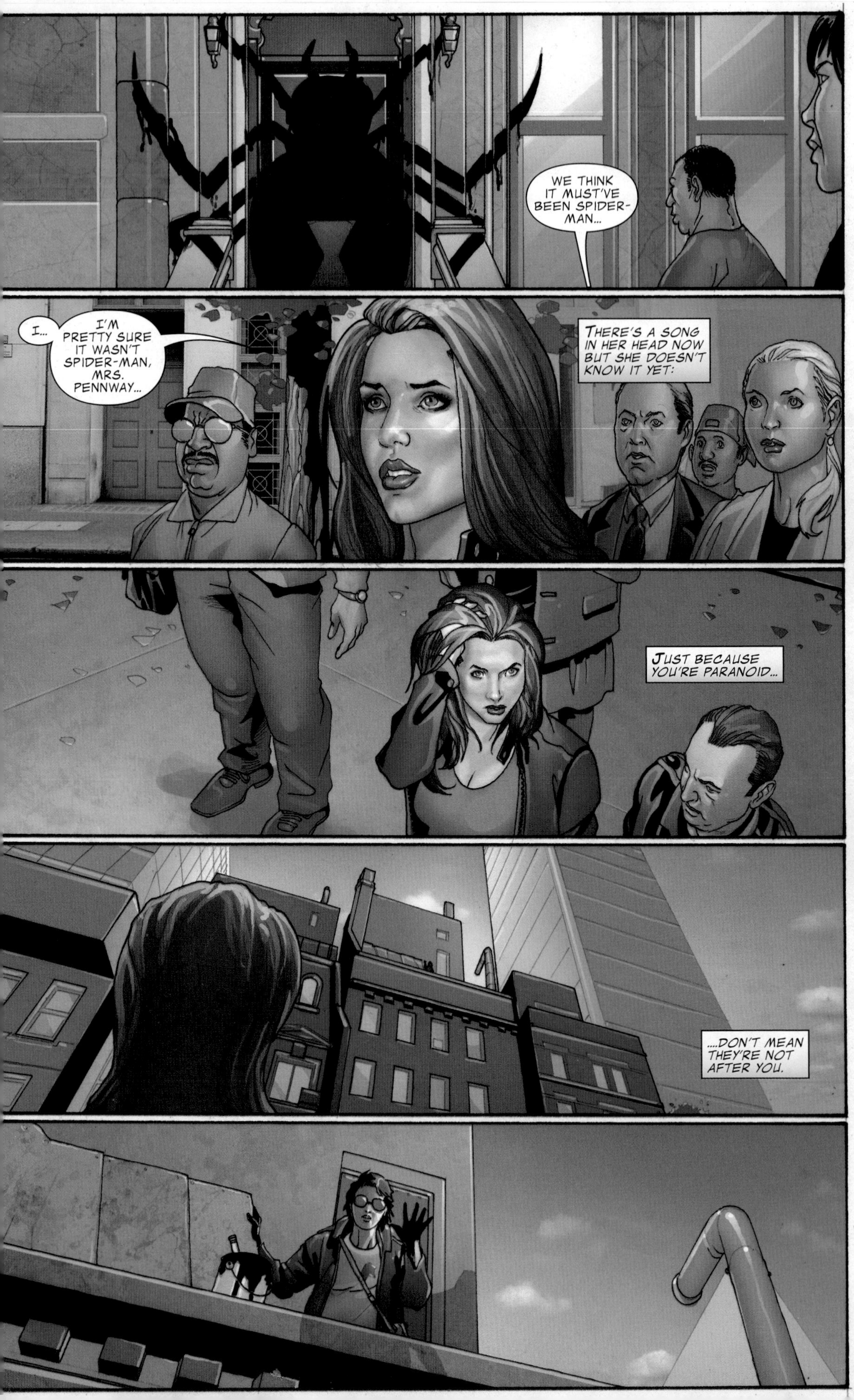
WE THINK IT MUST'VE BEEN SPIDER-MAN...
I...
I'M PRETTY SURE IT WASN'T SPIDER-MAN, MRS. PENNWAY...
THERE'S A SONG IN HER HEAD NOW BUT SHE DOESN'T KNOW IT YET:
JUST BECAUSE YOU'RE PARANOID...
...DON'T MEAN THEY'RE NOT AFTER YOU.

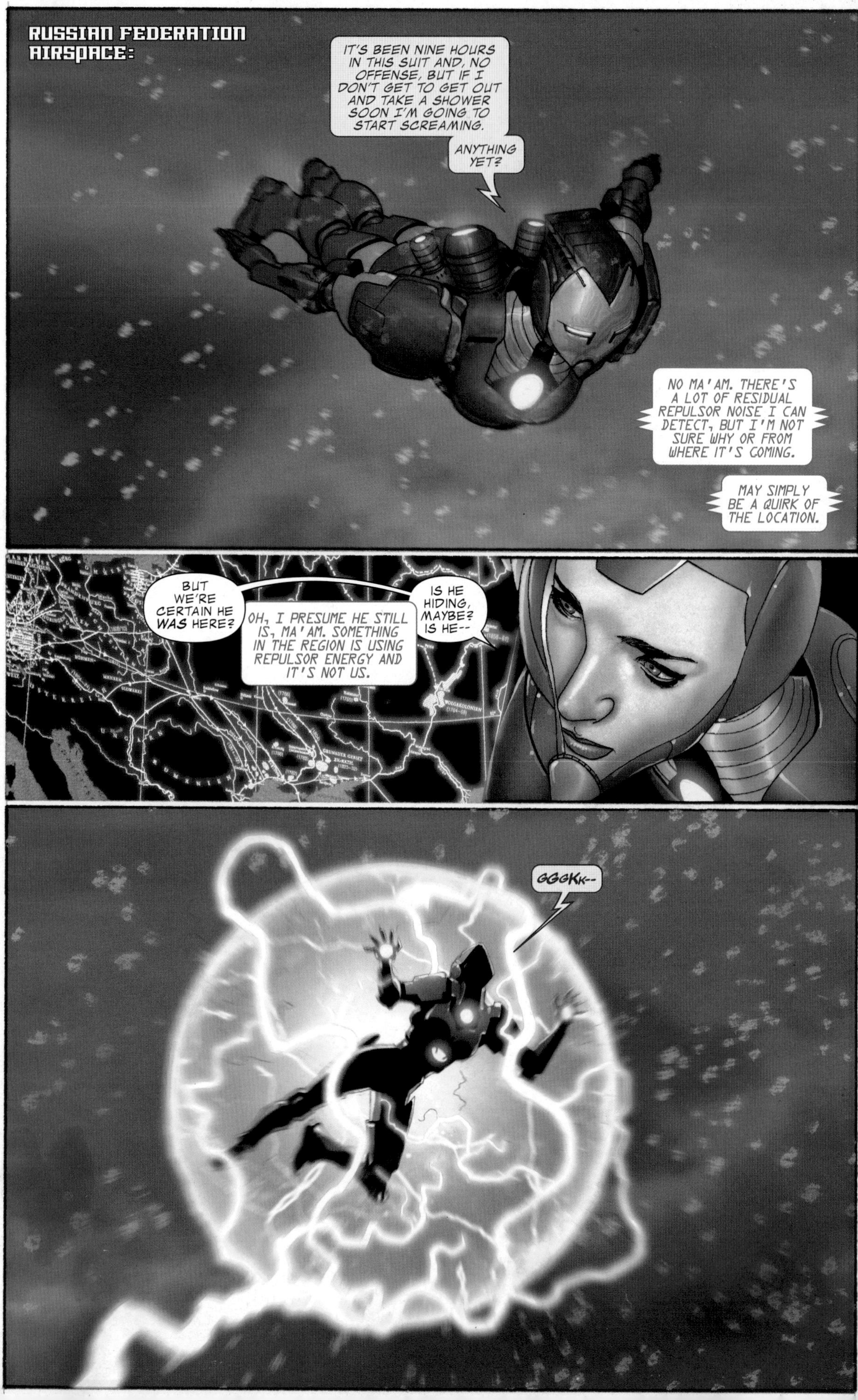
RUSSIAN FEDERATION AIRSPACE:
IT'S BEEN NINE HOURS IN THIS SUIT AND, NO OFFENSE, BUT IF I DON'T GET TO GET OUT AND TAKE A SHOWER SOON I'M GOING TO START SCREAMING.
ANYTHING YET?
NO MA'AM. THERE'S A LOT OF RESIDUAL REPULSOR NOISE I CAN DETECT, BUT I'M NOT SURE WHY OR FROM WHERE IT'S COMING.
MAY SIMPLY BE A QUIRK OF THE LOCATION.
BUT WE'RE CERTAIN HE WAS HERE?
OH, I PRESUME HE STILL IS, MA'AM. SOMETHING IN THE REGION IS USING REPULSOR ENERGY AND IT'S NOT US.
IS HE HIDING, MAYBE? IS HE--
GGGKk--

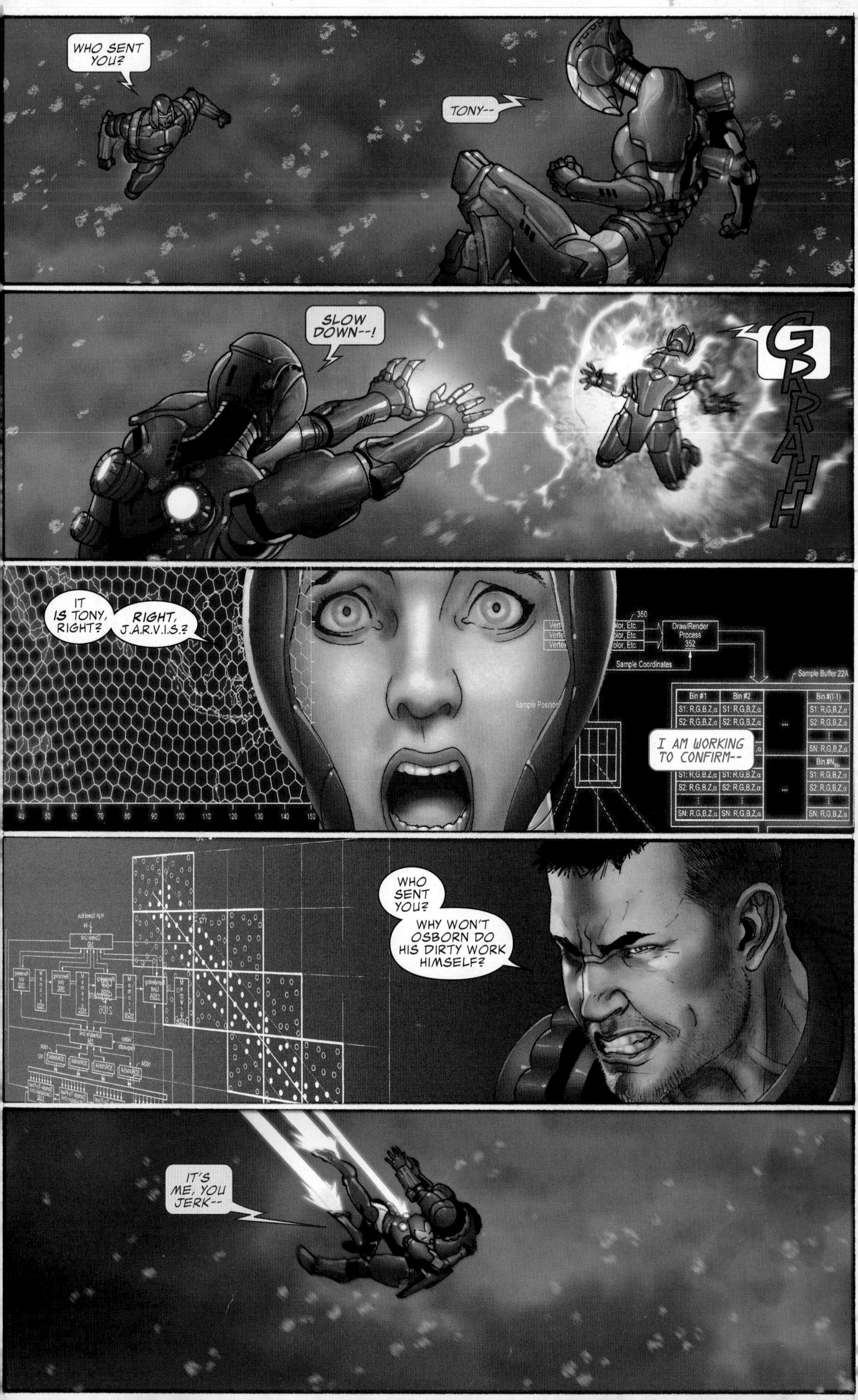
WHO SENT YOU?
TONY--
SLOW DOWN--!
GRAAHH
IT IS TONY, RIGHT?
RIGHT, J.A.R.V.I.S.?
Draw/Render Process 352
Sample Coordinates
Sample Buffer 22A
I AM WORKING TO CONFIRM--
WHO SENT YOU?
WHY WON'T OSBORN DO HIS DIRTY WORK HIMSELF?
IT'S ME, YOU JERK--

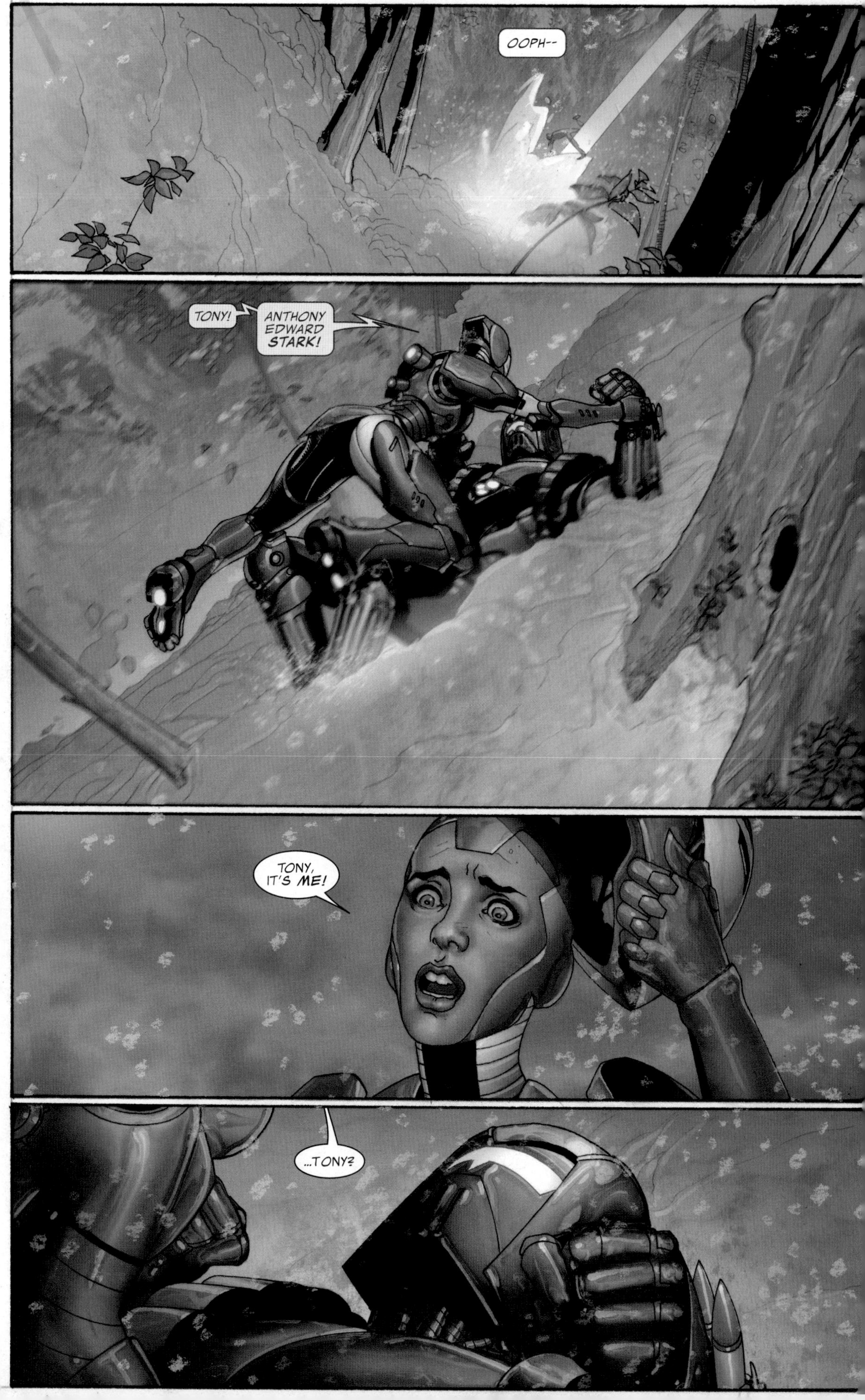
OOPH--
TONY!
ANTHONY EDWARD STARK!
TONY, IT'S ME!
...TONY?

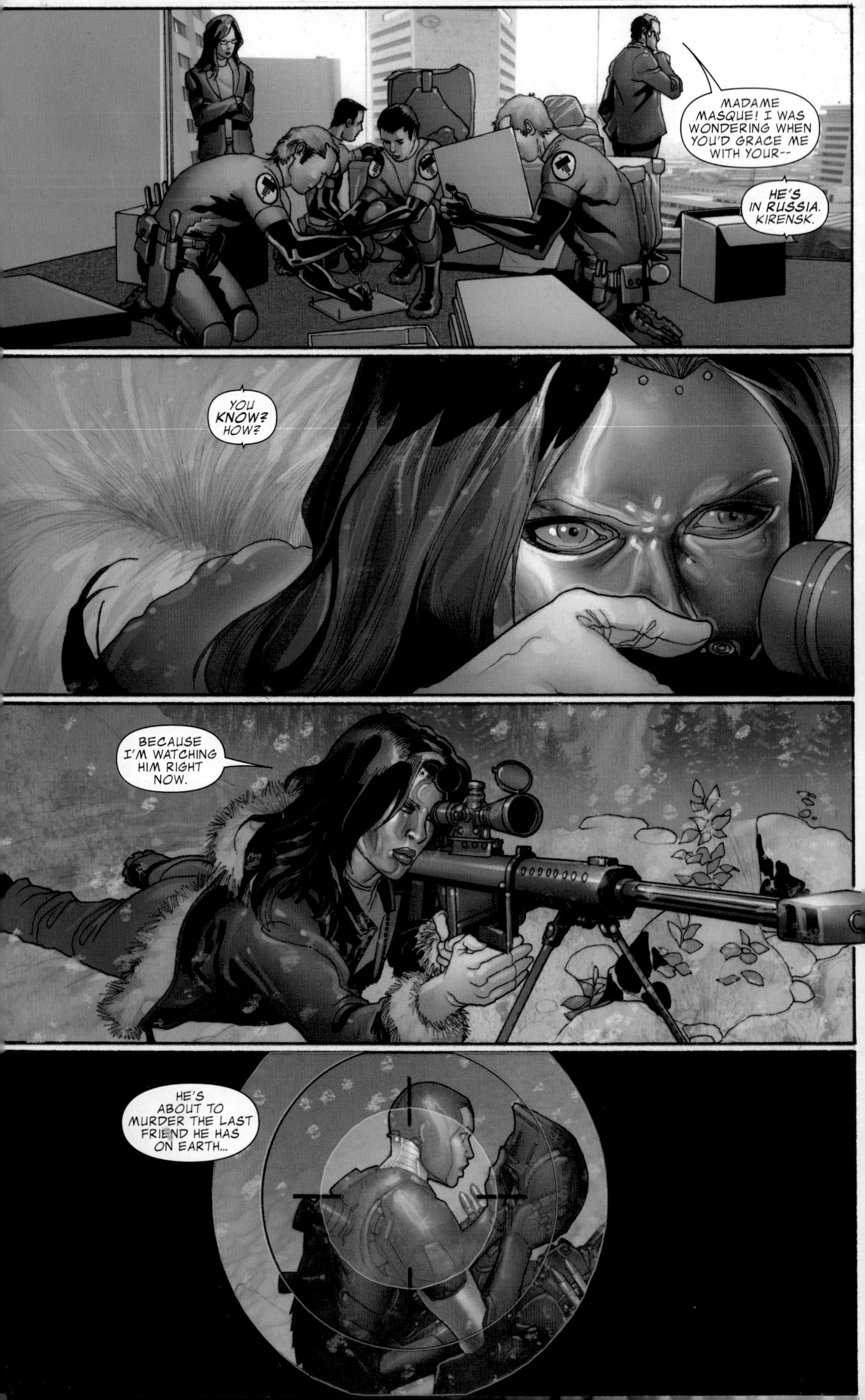
MADAME MASQUE! I WAS WONDERING WHEN YOU'D GRACE ME WITH YOUR--
HE'S IN RUSSIA. KIRENSK.
YOU KNOW? HOW?
BECAUSE I'M WATCHING HIM RIGHT NOW.
HE'S ABOUT TO MURDER THE LAST FRIEND HE HAS ON EARTH...

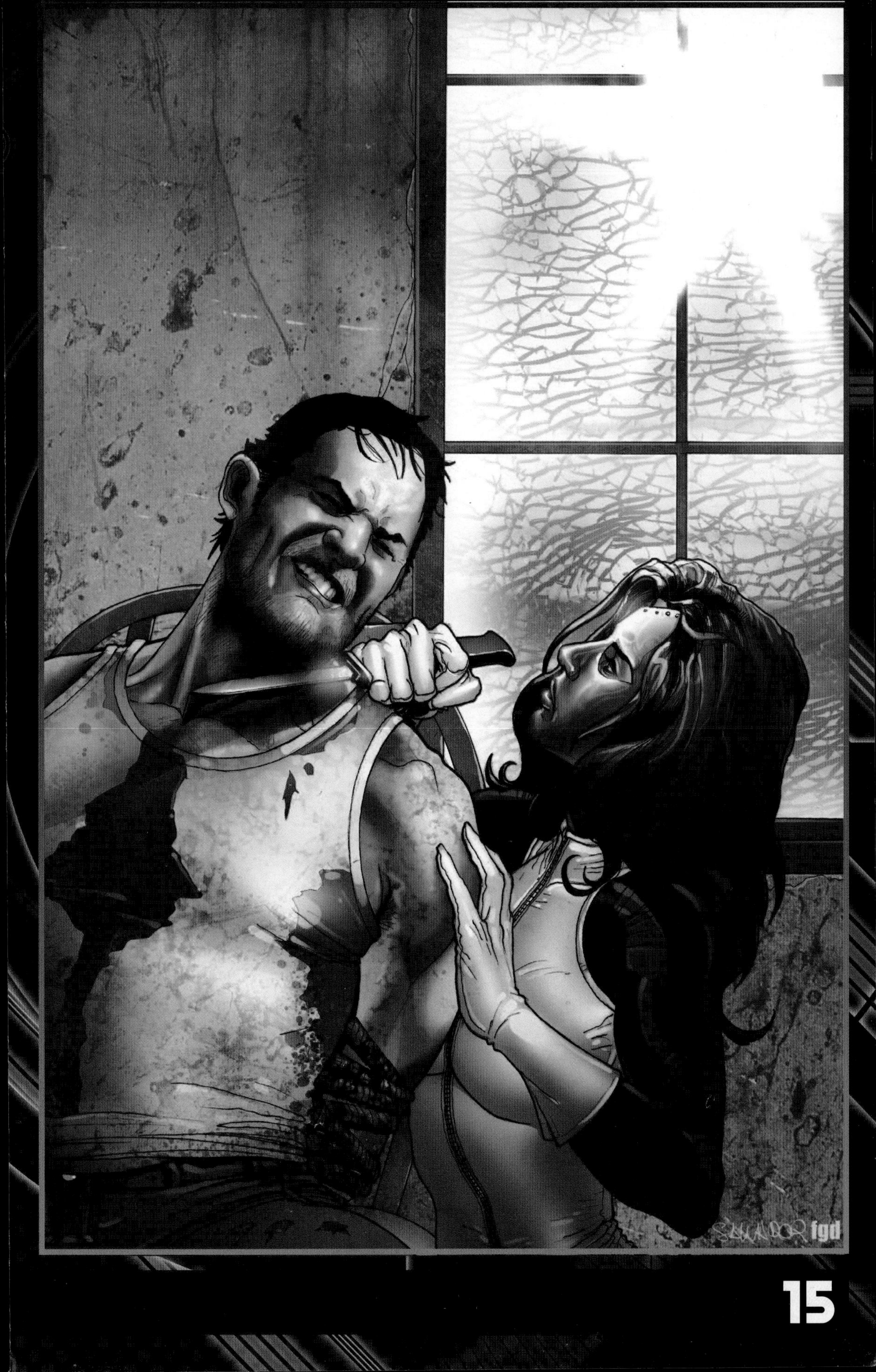

15

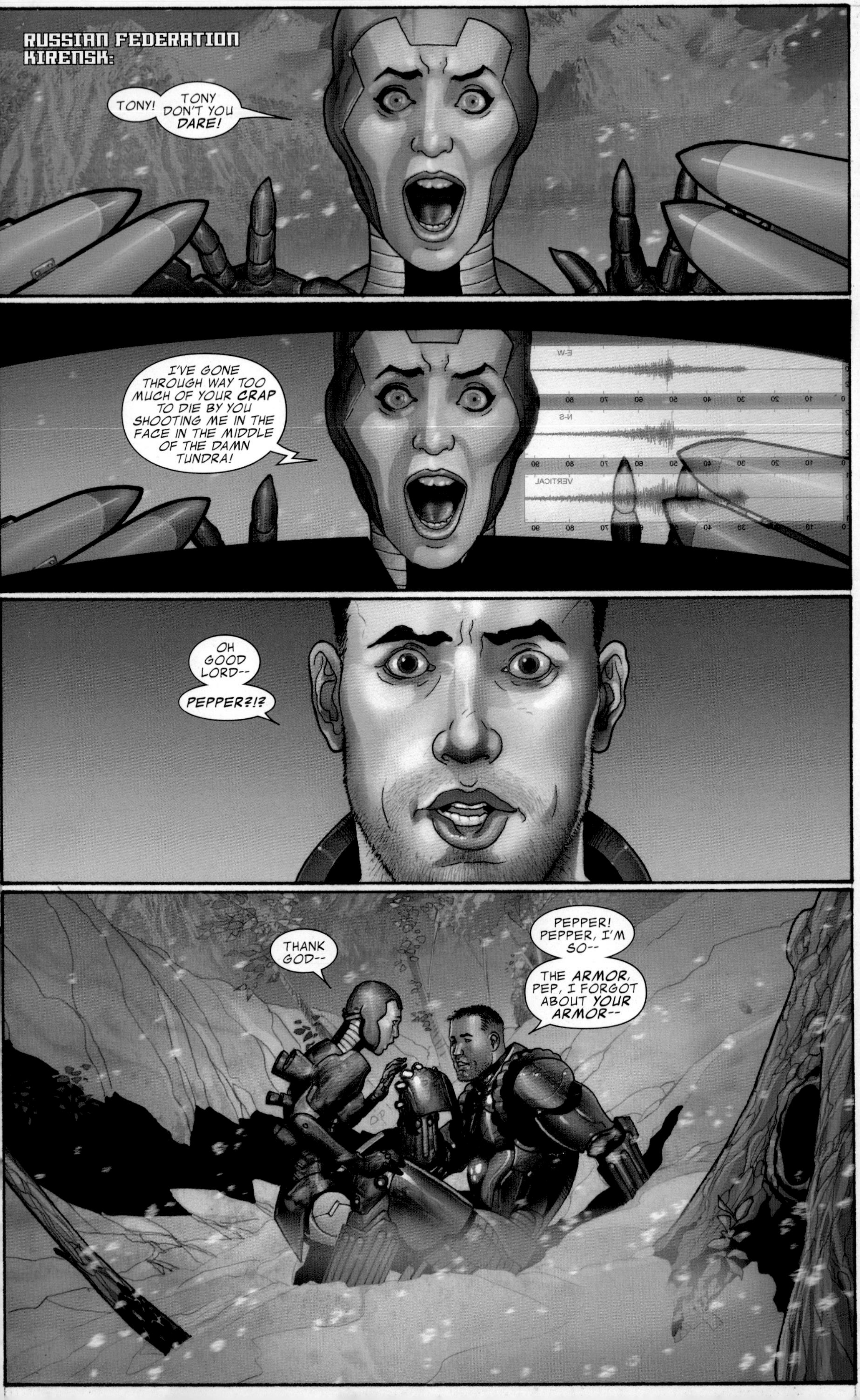
RUSSIAN FEDERATION
KIRENSK:
TONY!
TONY DON'T YOU DARE!
I'VE GONE THROUGH WAY TOO MUCH OF YOUR CRAP TO DIE BY YOU SHOOTING ME IN THE FACE IN THE MIDDLE OF THE DAMN TUNDRA!
OH GOOD LORD--
PEPPER?!?
THANK GOD--
PEPPER! PEPPER, I'M SO--
THE ARMOR, PEP, I FORGOT ABOUT YOUR ARMOR--

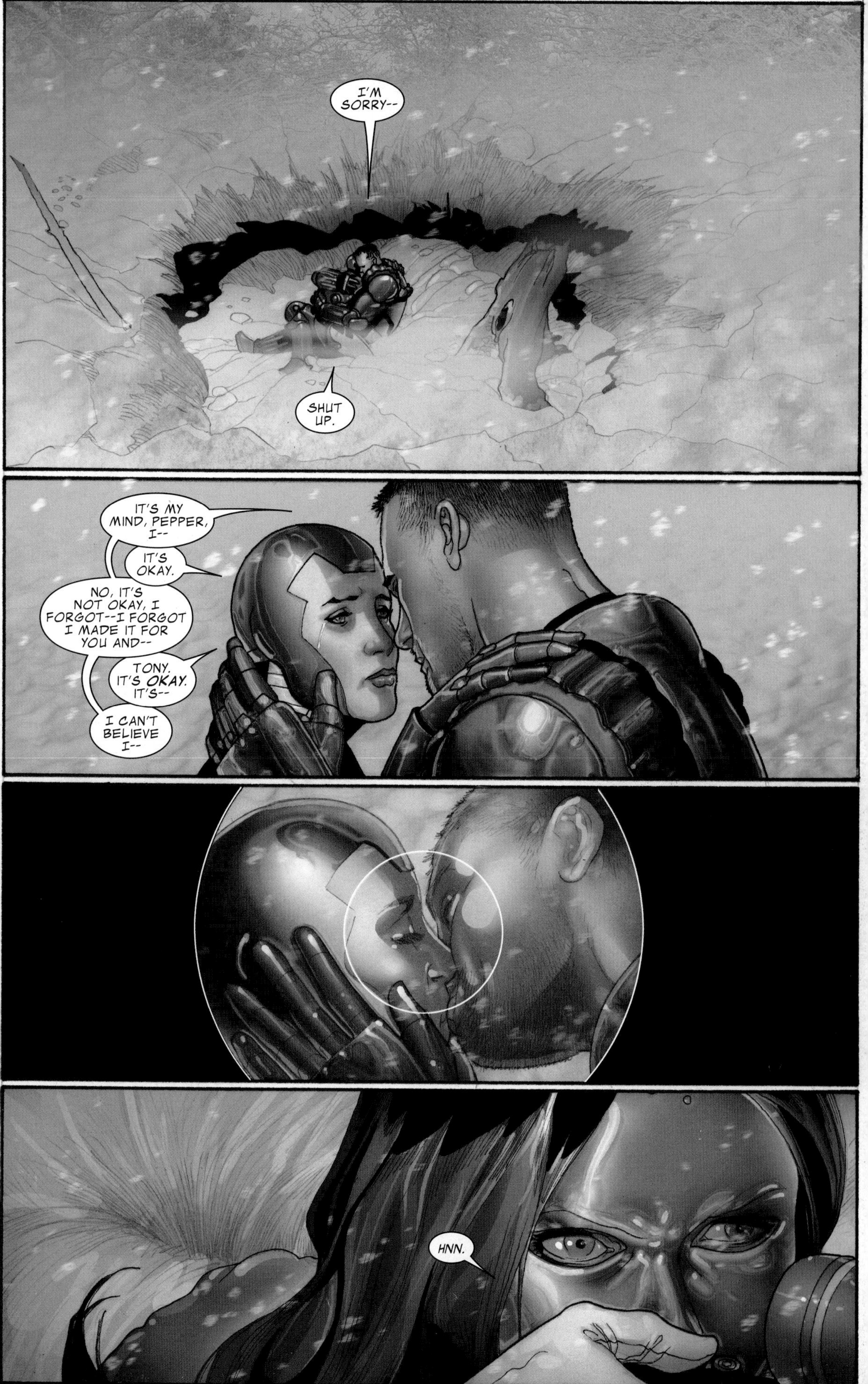
I'M SORRY--
SHUT UP.
IT'S MY MIND, PEPPER, I--
IT'S OKAY.
NO, IT'S NOT OKAY, I FORGOT--I FORGOT I MADE IT FOR YOU AND--
TONY. IT'S *OKAY.* IT'S--
I CAN'T BELIEVE I--
HNN.

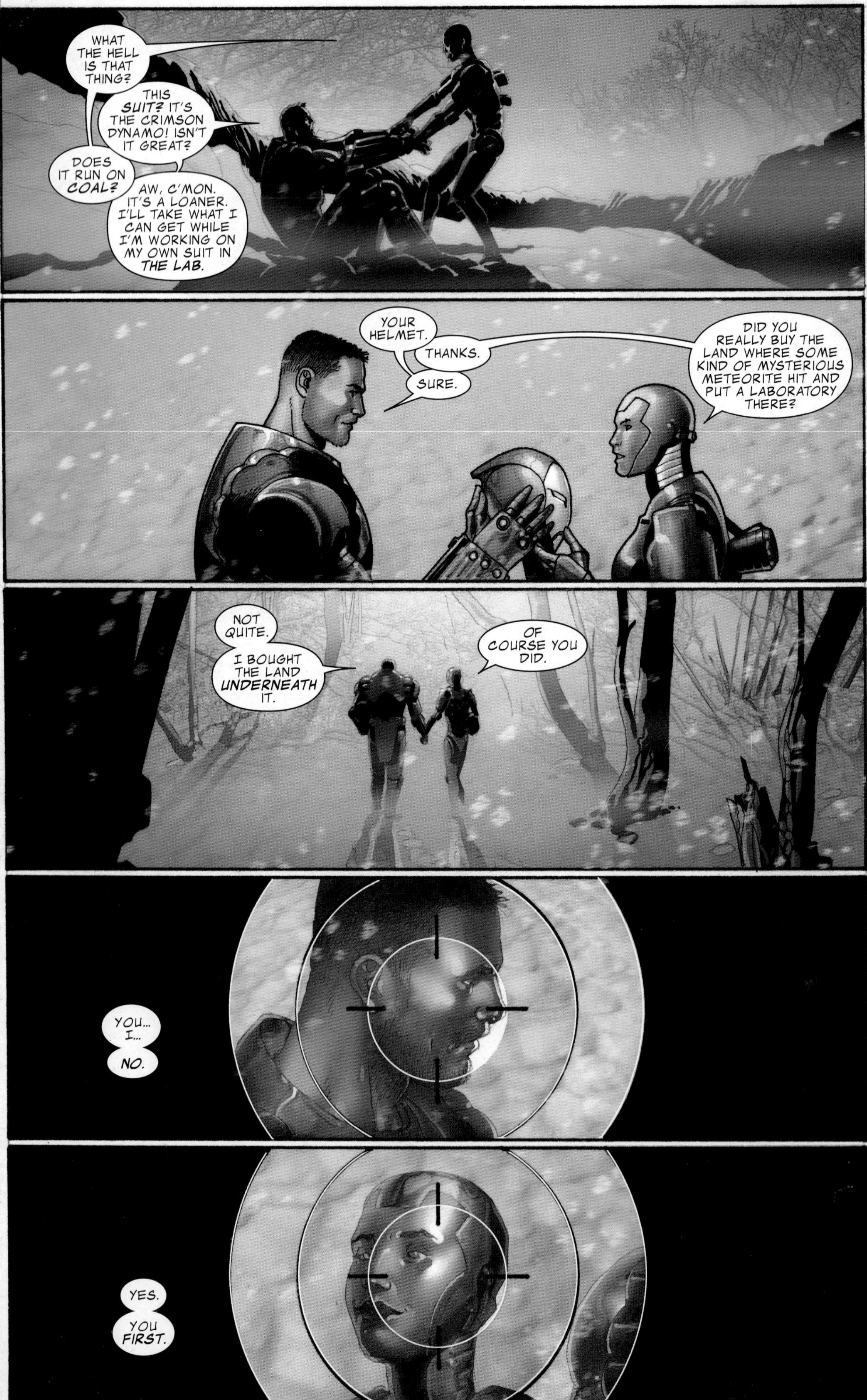
WHAT THE HELL IS THAT THING?
THIS SUIT? IT'S THE CRIMSON DYNAMO! ISN'T IT GREAT?
DOES IT RUN ON COAL?
AW, C'MON. IT'S A LOANER. I'LL TAKE WHAT I CAN GET WHILE I'M WORKING ON MY OWN SUIT IN THE LAB.
YOUR HELMET.
THANKS.
SURE.
DID YOU REALLY BUY THE LAND WHERE SOME KIND OF MYSTERIOUS METEORITE HIT AND PUT A LABORATORY THERE?
NOT QUITE.
I BOUGHT THE LAND UNDERNEATH IT.
OF COURSE YOU DID.
YOU...
I...
NO.
YES.
YOU FIRST.

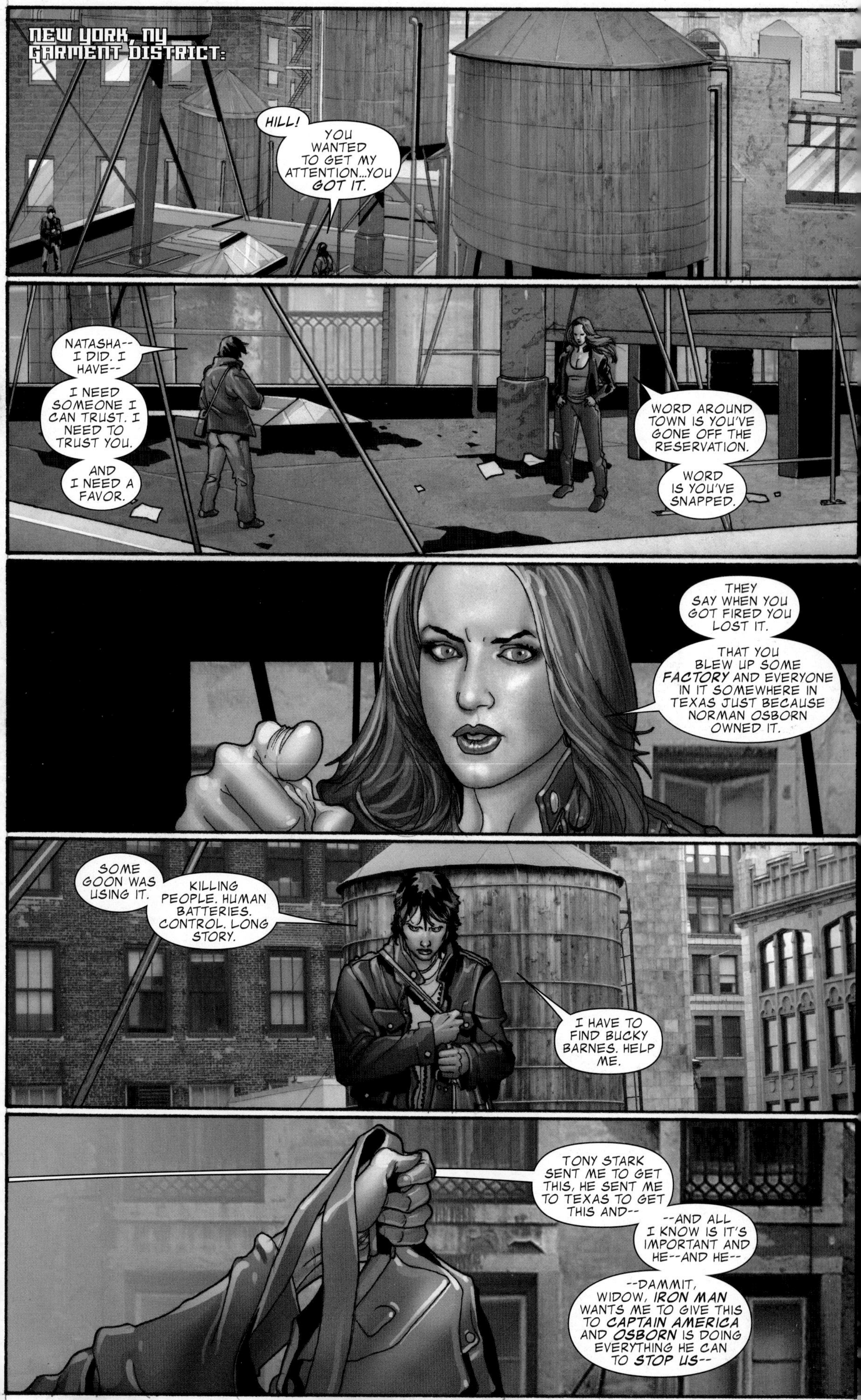
NEW YORK, NY
GARMENT DISTRICT:
HILL!
YOU WANTED TO GET MY ATTENTION...YOU GOT IT.
NATASHA-- I DID. I HAVE--
I NEED SOMEONE I CAN TRUST. I NEED TO TRUST YOU.
AND I NEED A FAVOR.
WORD AROUND TOWN IS YOU'VE GONE OFF THE RESERVATION.
WORD IS YOU'VE SNAPPED.
THEY SAY WHEN YOU GOT FIRED YOU LOST IT.
THAT YOU BLEW UP SOME FACTORY AND EVERYONE IN IT SOMEWHERE IN TEXAS JUST BECAUSE NORMAN OSBORN OWNED IT.
SOME GOON WAS USING IT.
KILLING PEOPLE. HUMAN BATTERIES. CONTROL. LONG STORY.
I HAVE TO FIND BUCKY BARNES. HELP ME.
TONY STARK SENT ME TO GET THIS, HE SENT ME TO TEXAS TO GET THIS AND--
--AND ALL I KNOW IS IT'S IMPORTANT AND HE--AND HE--
--DAMMIT, WIDOW, IRON MAN WANTS ME TO GIVE THIS TO CAPTAIN AMERICA AND OSBORN IS DOING EVERYTHING HE CAN TO STOP US--

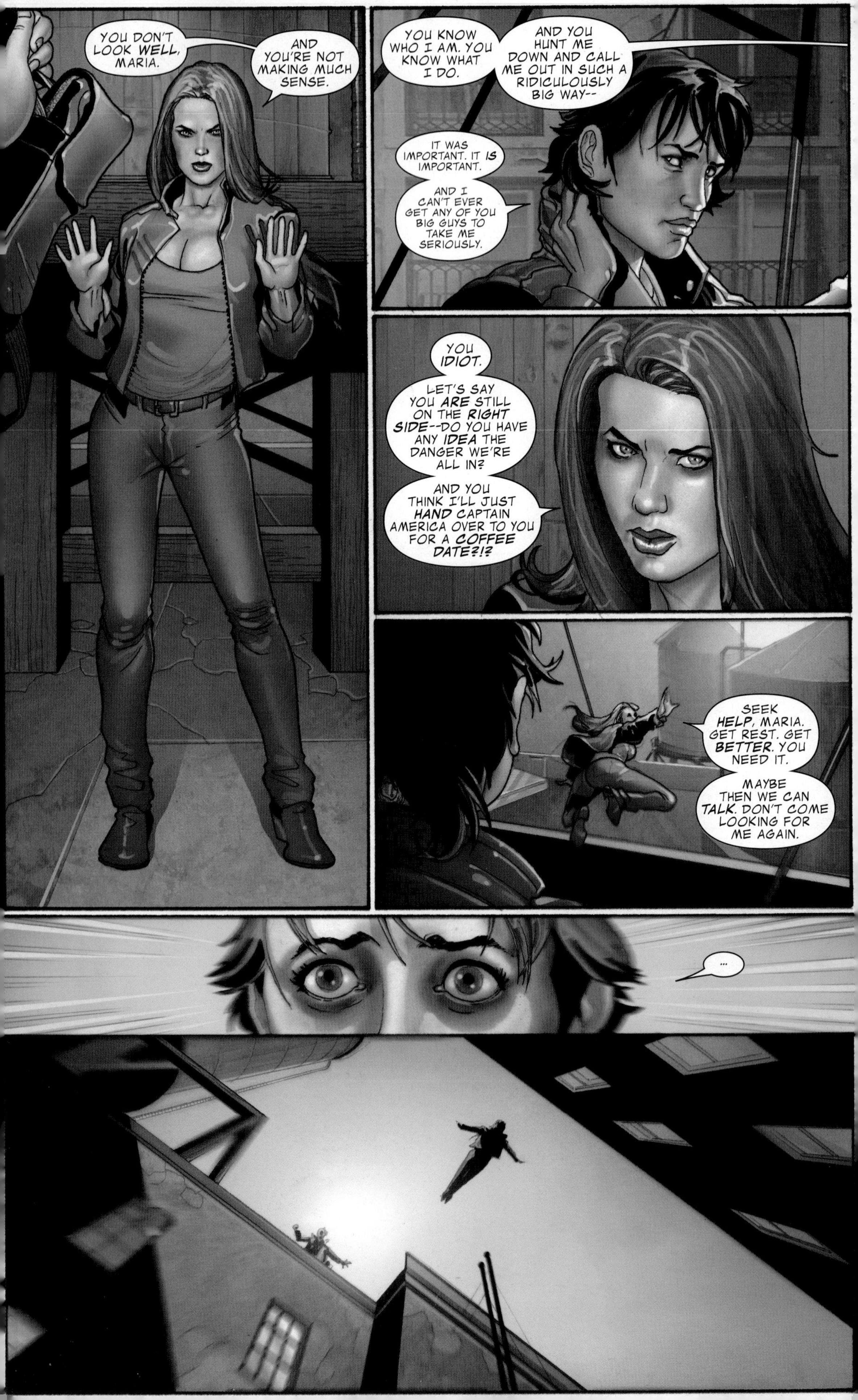
YOU DON'T LOOK WELL, MARIA.
AND YOU'RE NOT MAKING MUCH SENSE.
YOU KNOW WHO I AM. YOU KNOW WHAT I DO.
AND YOU HUNT ME DOWN AND CALL ME OUT IN SUCH A RIDICULOUSLY BIG WAY--
IT WAS IMPORTANT. IT IS IMPORTANT.
AND I CAN'T EVER GET ANY OF YOU BIG GUYS TO TAKE ME SERIOUSLY.
YOU IDIOT.
LET'S SAY YOU ARE STILL ON THE RIGHT SIDE--DO YOU HAVE ANY IDEA THE DANGER WE'RE ALL IN?
AND YOU THINK I'LL JUST HAND CAPTAIN AMERICA OVER TO YOU FOR A COFFEE DATE?!?
SEEK HELP, MARIA. GET REST. GET BETTER. YOU NEED IT.
MAYBE THEN WE CAN TALK. DON'T COME LOOKING FOR ME AGAIN.
...

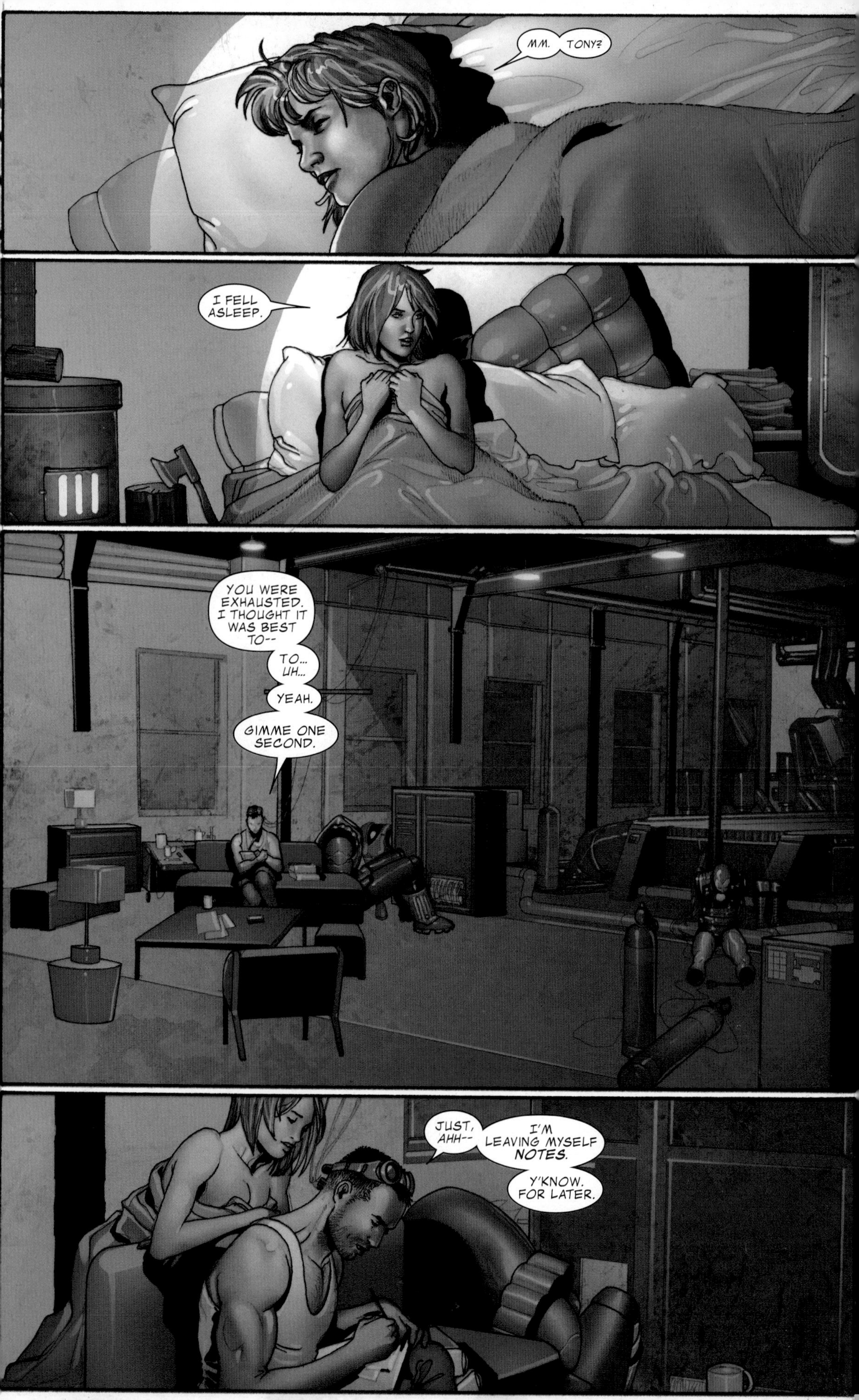
MM. TONY?
I FELL ASLEEP.
YOU WERE EXHAUSTED. I THOUGHT IT WAS BEST TO--
TO... UH...
YEAH.
GIMME ONE SECOND.
JUST, AHH--
I'M LEAVING MYSELF NOTES.
Y'KNOW. FOR LATER.

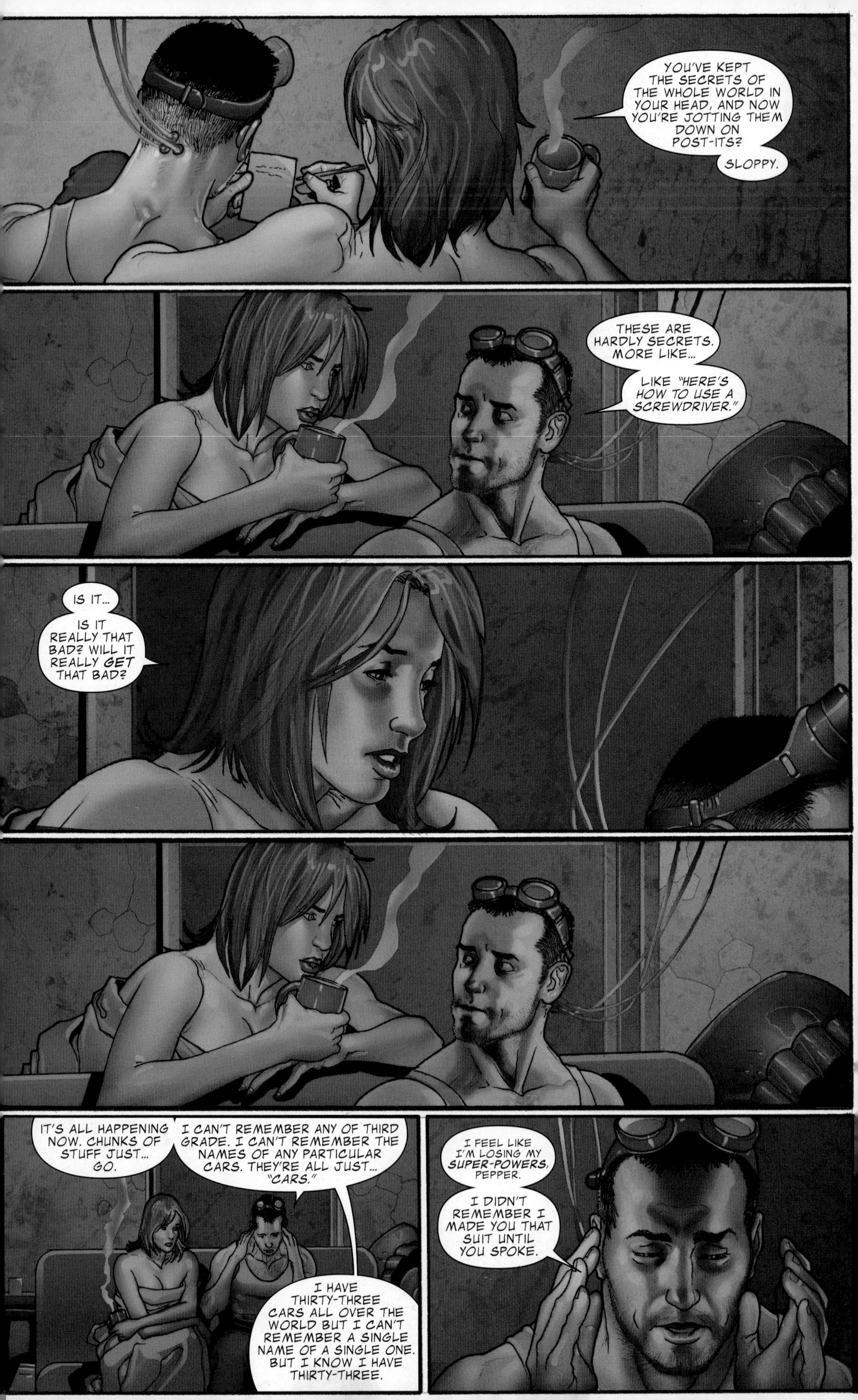
YOU'VE KEPT THE SECRETS OF THE WHOLE WORLD IN YOUR HEAD, AND NOW YOU'RE JOTTING THEM DOWN ON POST-ITS?
SLOPPY.
THESE ARE HARDLY SECRETS. MORE LIKE...
LIKE "HERE'S HOW TO USE A SCREWDRIVER."
IS IT...
IS IT REALLY THAT BAD? WILL IT REALLY GET THAT BAD?
IT'S ALL HAPPENING NOW. CHUNKS OF STUFF JUST... GO.
I CAN'T REMEMBER ANY OF THIRD GRADE. I CAN'T REMEMBER THE NAMES OF ANY PARTICULAR CARS. THEY'RE ALL JUST... "CARS."
I HAVE THIRTY-THREE CARS ALL OVER THE WORLD BUT I CAN'T REMEMBER A SINGLE NAME OF A SINGLE ONE. BUT I KNOW I HAVE THIRTY-THREE.
I FEEL LIKE I'M LOSING MY SUPER-POWERS, PEPPER.
I DIDN'T REMEMBER I MADE YOU THAT SUIT UNTIL YOU SPOKE.

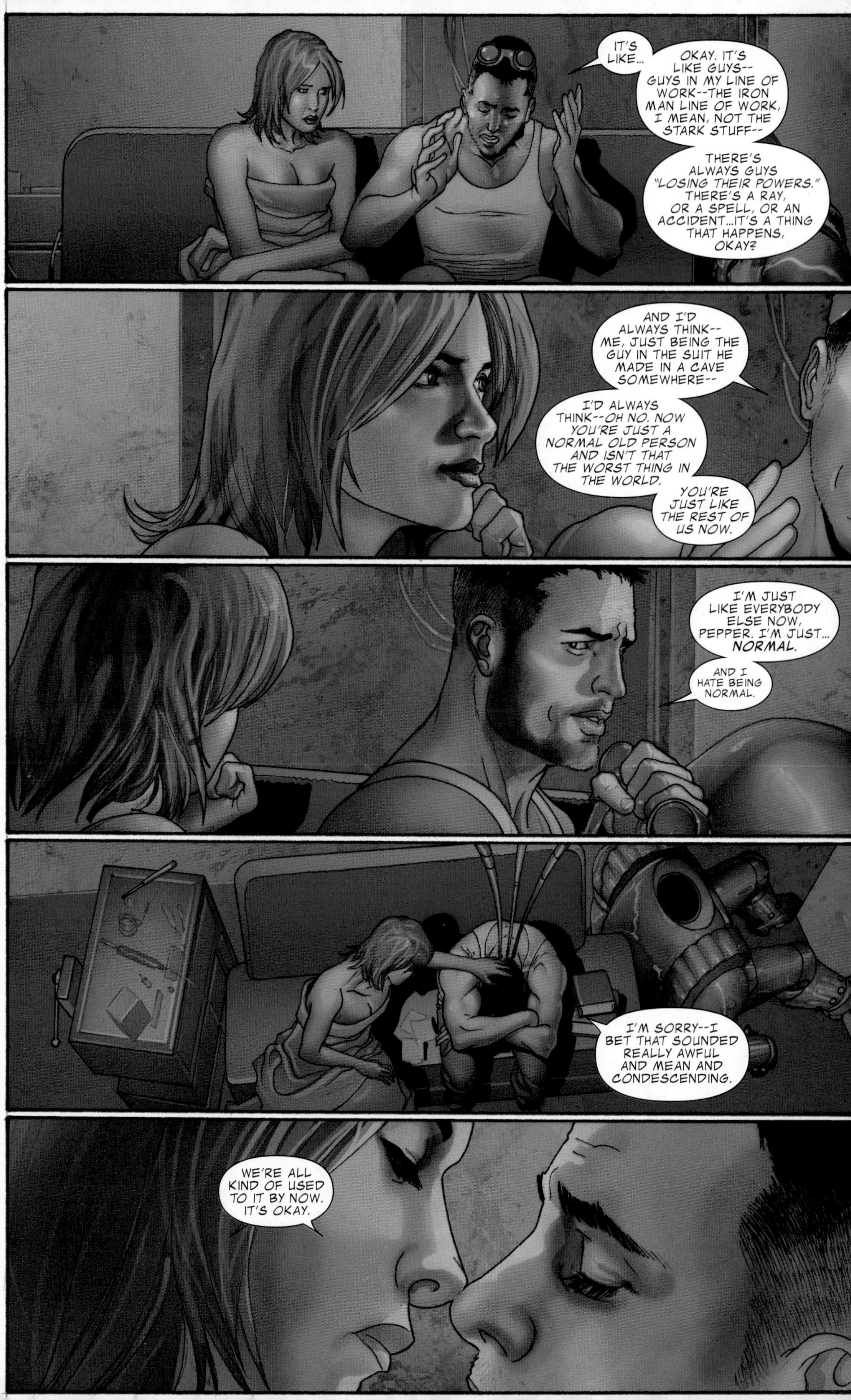
IT'S LIKE...
OKAY. IT'S LIKE GUYS-- GUYS IN MY LINE OF WORK--THE IRON MAN LINE OF WORK, I MEAN, NOT THE STARK STUFF--
THERE'S ALWAYS GUYS "LOSING THEIR POWERS." THERE'S A RAY, OR A SPELL, OR AN ACCIDENT...IT'S A THING THAT HAPPENS, OKAY?
AND I'D ALWAYS THINK-- ME, JUST BEING THE GUY IN THE SUIT HE MADE IN A CAVE SOMEWHERE--
I'D ALWAYS THINK--OH NO. NOW YOU'RE JUST A NORMAL OLD PERSON AND ISN'T THAT THE WORST THING IN THE WORLD.
YOU'RE JUST LIKE THE REST OF US NOW.
I'M JUST LIKE EVERYBODY ELSE NOW, PEPPER. I'M JUST... **NORMAL.**
AND I HATE BEING NORMAL.
I'M SORRY--I BET THAT SOUNDED REALLY AWFUL AND MEAN AND CONDESCENDING.
WE'RE ALL KIND OF USED TO IT BY NOW. IT'S OKAY.

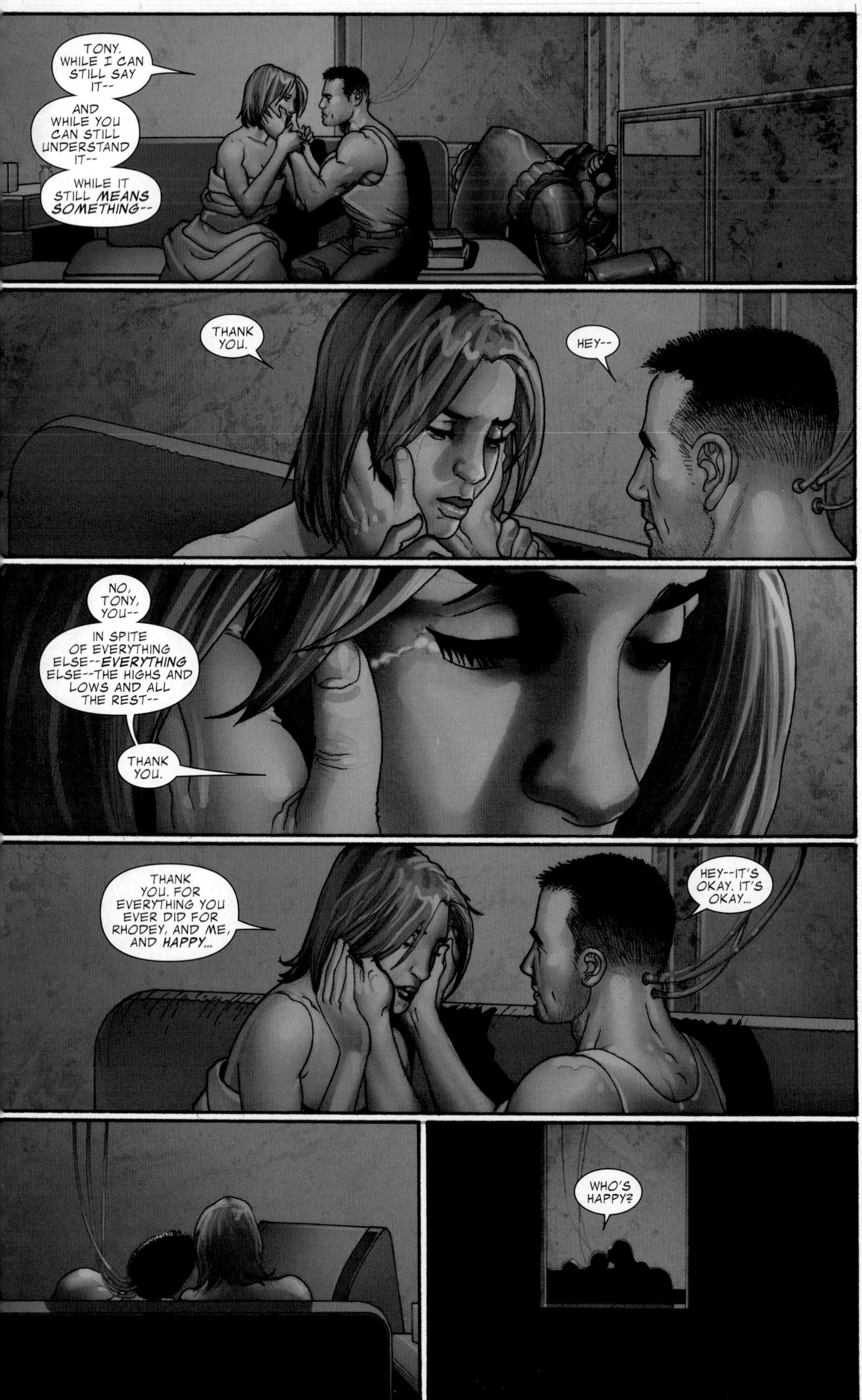
TONY. WHILE I CAN STILL SAY IT--
AND WHILE YOU CAN STILL UNDERSTAND IT--
WHILE IT STILL MEANS SOMETHING--
THANK YOU.
HEY--
NO, TONY, YOU--
IN SPITE OF EVERYTHING ELSE--EVERYTHING ELSE--THE HIGHS AND LOWS AND ALL THE REST--
THANK YOU.
THANK YOU. FOR EVERYTHING YOU EVER DID FOR RHODEY, AND ME, AND HAPPY...
HEY--IT'S OKAY. IT'S OKAY...
WHO'S HAPPY?

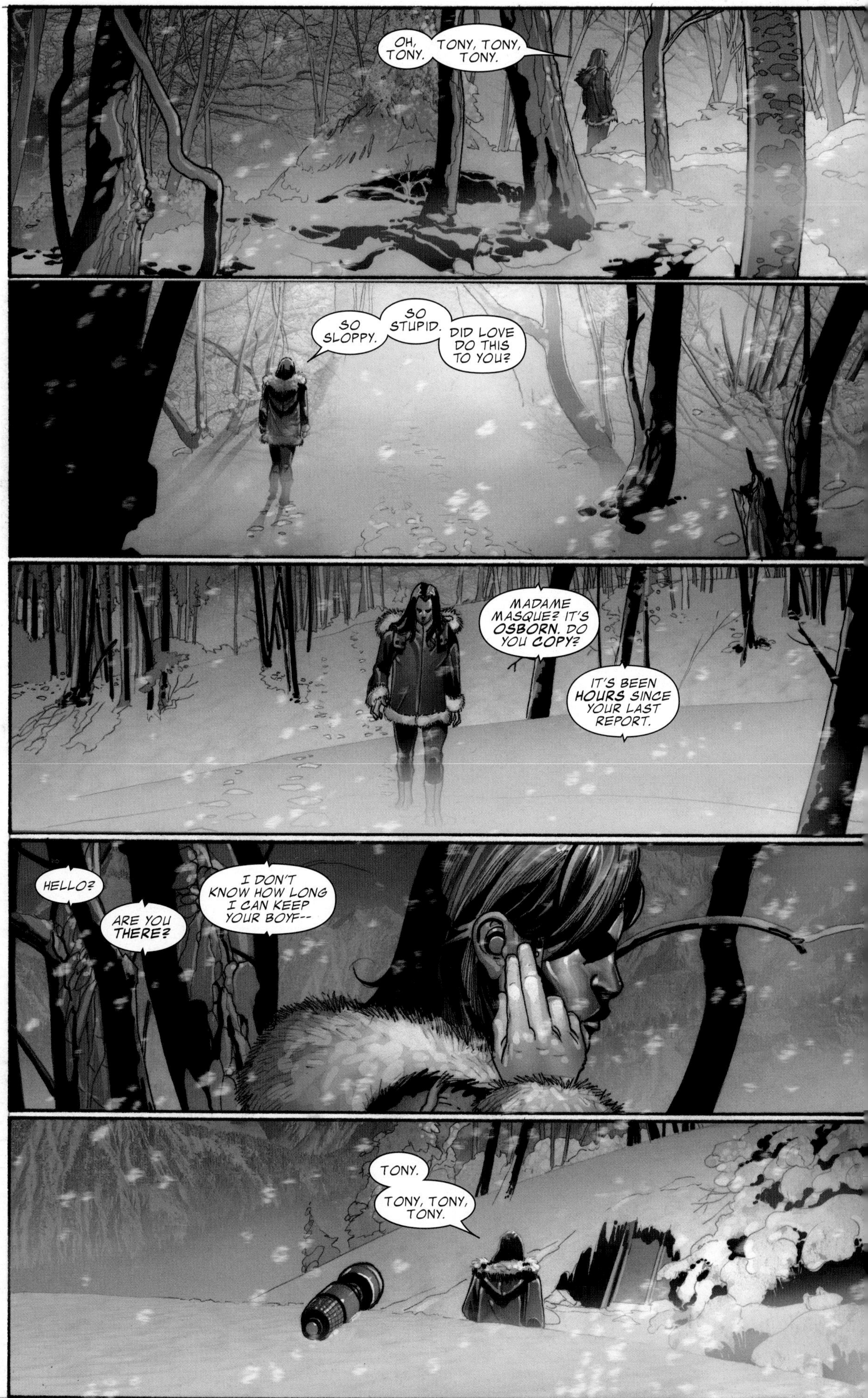
OH, TONY.
TONY, TONY, TONY.
SO SLOPPY.
SO STUPID.
DID LOVE DO THIS TO YOU?
MADAME MASQUE? IT'S OSBORN. DO YOU COPY?
IT'S BEEN HOURS SINCE YOUR LAST REPORT.
HELLO?
ARE YOU THERE?
I DON'T KNOW HOW LONG I CAN KEEP YOUR BOYF--
TONY.
TONY, TONY, TONY.

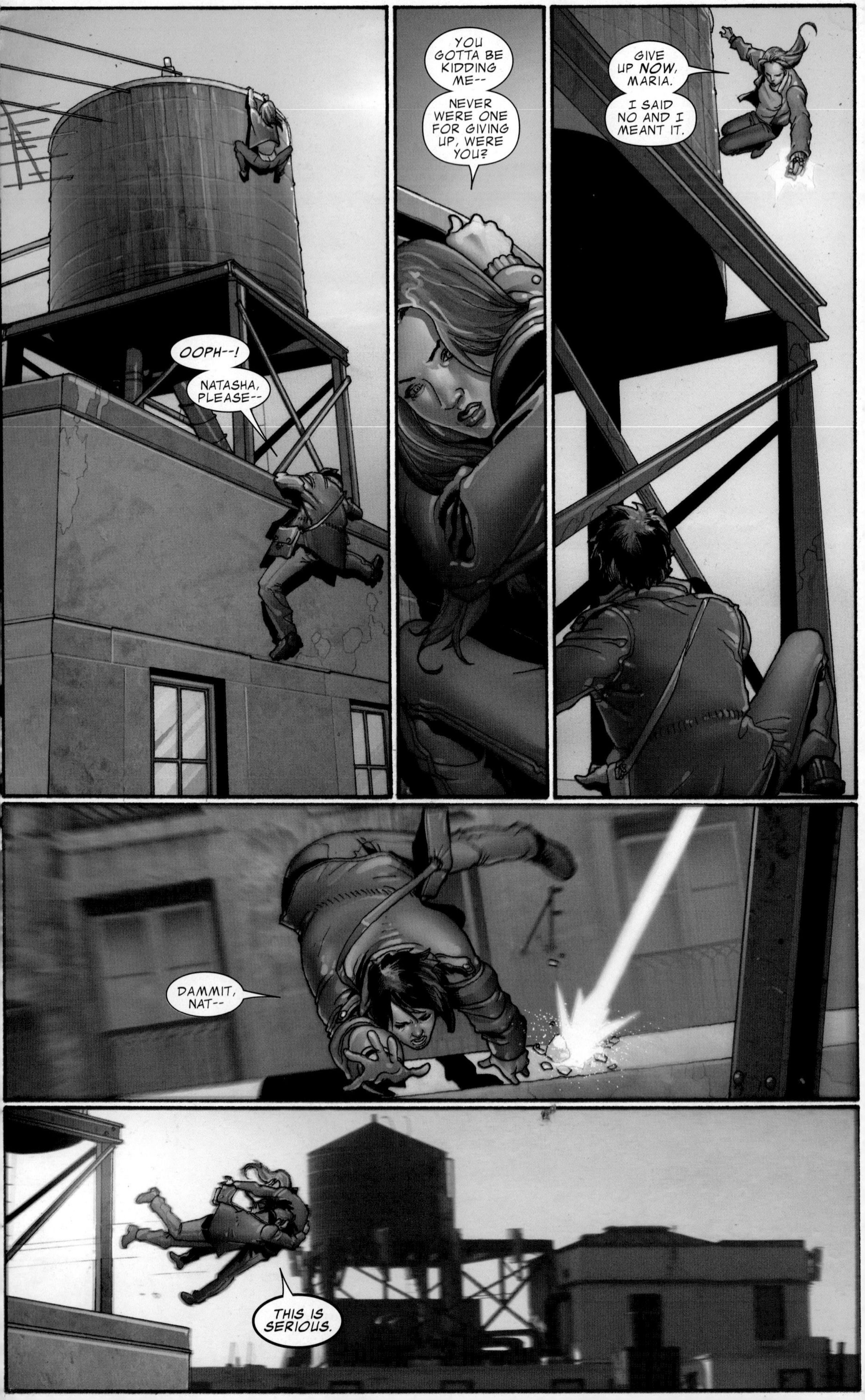
OOPH--!
NATASHA, PLEASE--
YOU GOTTA BE KIDDING ME--
NEVER WERE ONE FOR GIVING UP, WERE YOU?
GIVE UP NOW, MARIA.
I SAID NO AND I MEANT IT.
DAMMIT, NAT--
THIS IS SERIOUS.

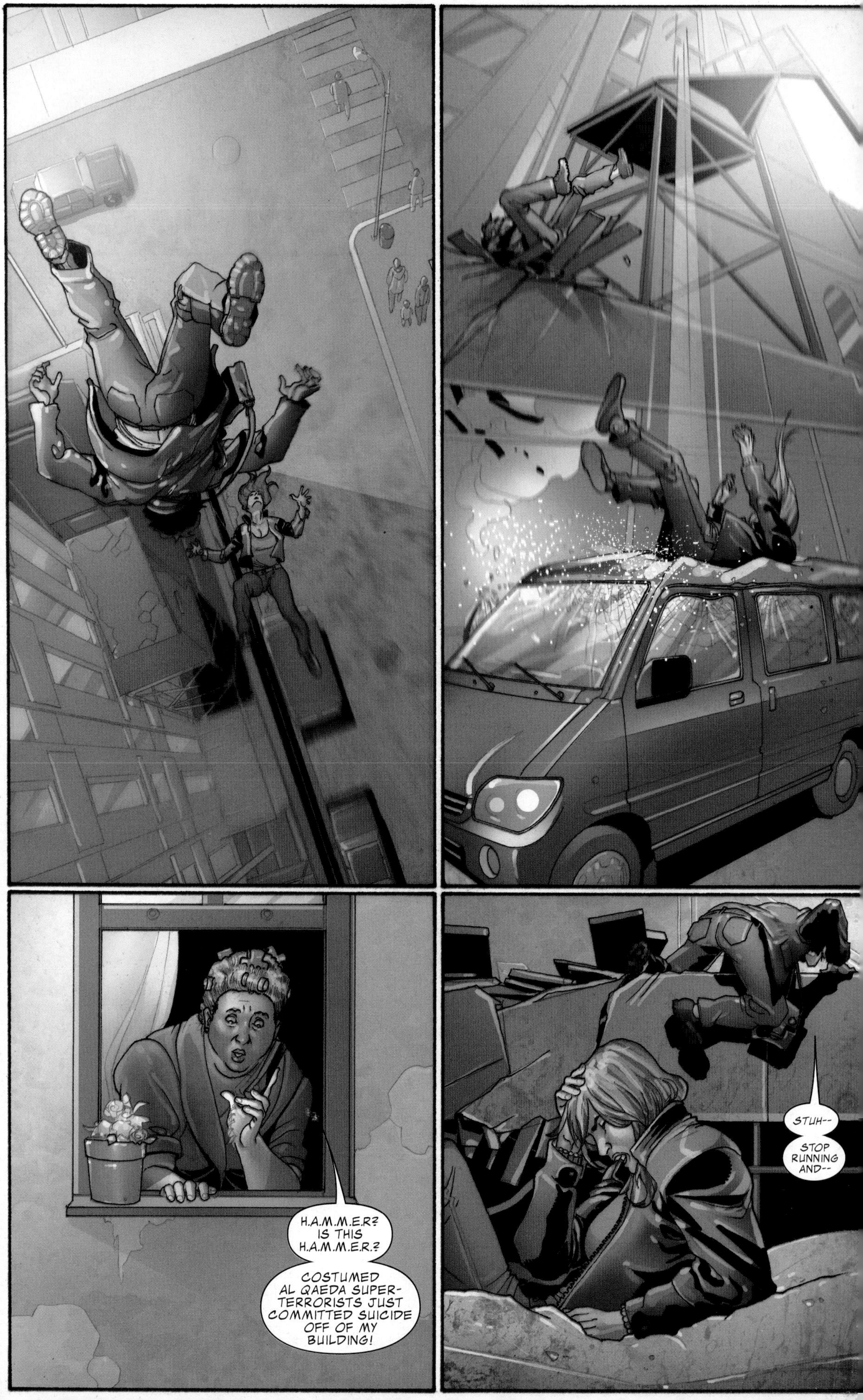
H.A.M.M.E.R.? IS THIS H.A.M.M.E.R.?
COSTUMED AL QAEDA SUPER-TERRORISTS JUST COMMITTED SUICIDE OFF OF MY BUILDING!
STUH--
STOP RUNNING AND--

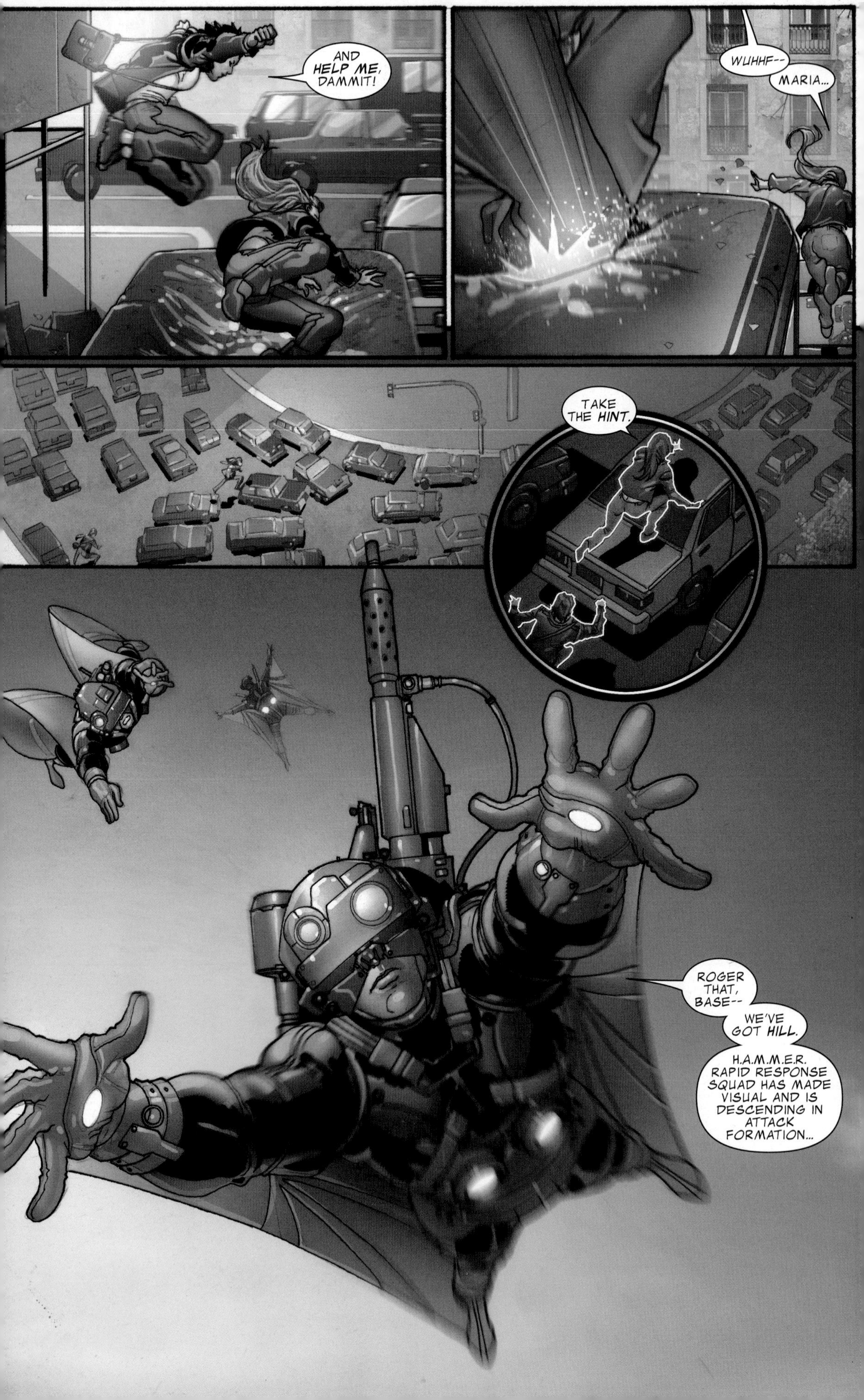
AND HELP ME, DAMMIT!
WUHHF--
MARIA...
TAKE THE HINT.
ROGER THAT, BASE--
WE'VE GOT HILL.
H.A.M.M.E.R. RAPID RESPONSE SQUAD HAS MADE VISUAL AND IS DESCENDING IN ATTACK FORMATION...

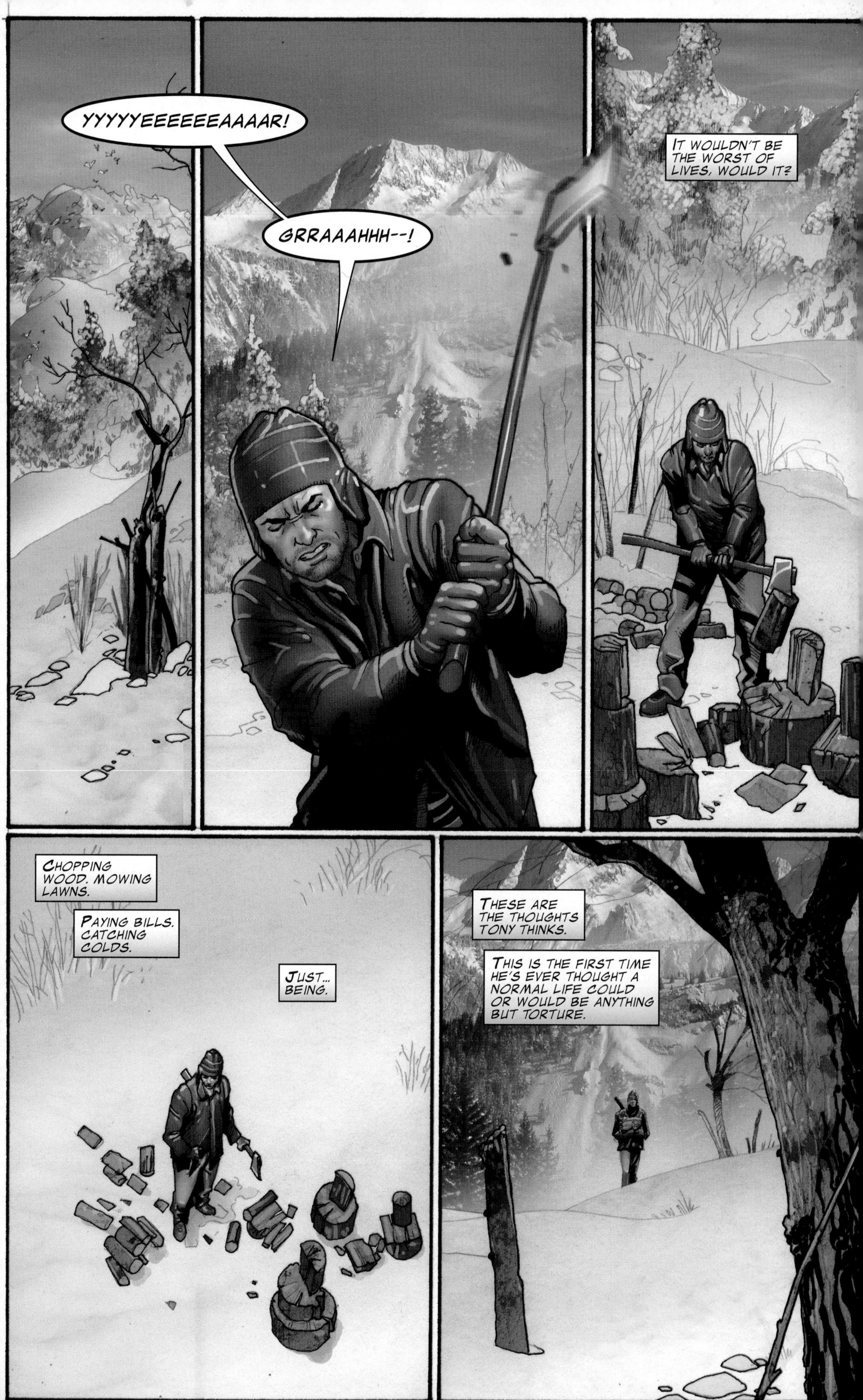
YYYYYEEEEEEAAAAR!
GRRAAAHHH--!
IT WOULDN'T BE THE WORST OF LIVES, WOULD IT?
CHOPPING WOOD. MOWING LAWNS.
PAYING BILLS. CATCHING COLDS.
JUST... BEING.
THESE ARE THE THOUGHTS TONY THINKS.
THIS IS THE FIRST TIME HE'S EVER THOUGHT A NORMAL LIFE COULD OR WOULD BE ANYTHING BUT TORTURE.

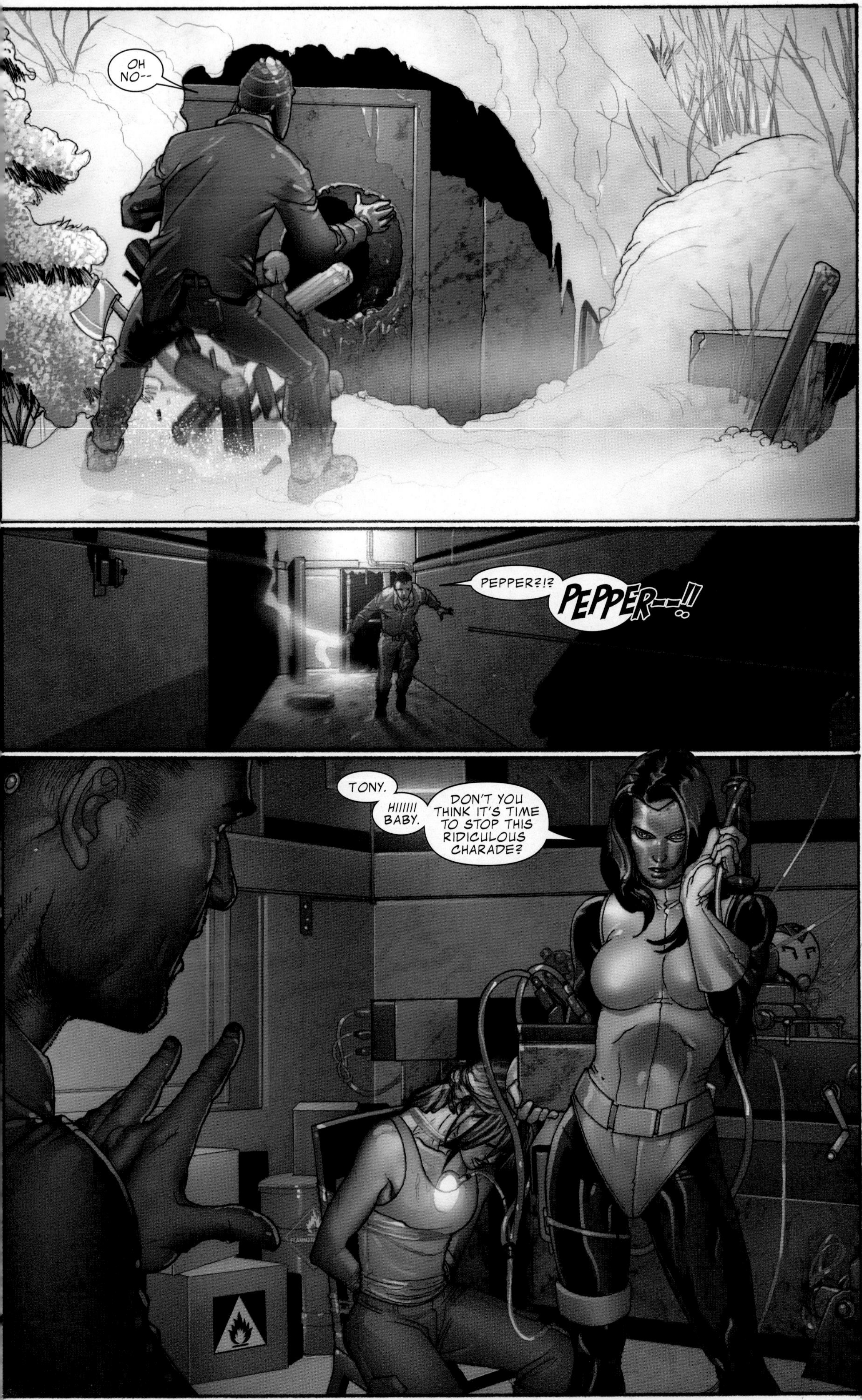
OH NO--
PEPPER?!?
PEPPER--!!
TONY.
HI!!!!! BABY.
DON'T YOU THINK IT'S TIME TO STOP THIS RIDICULOUS CHARADE?

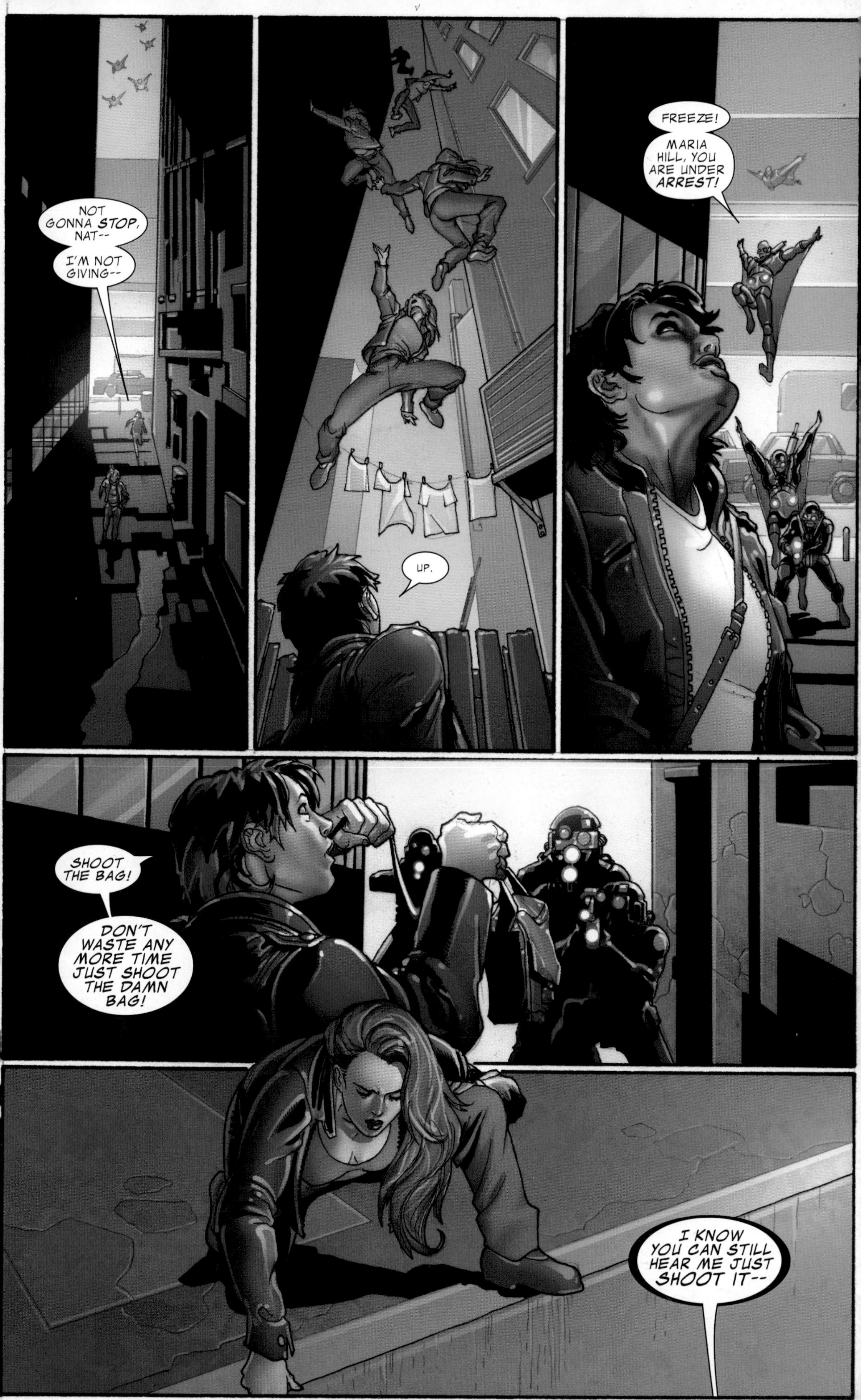
NOT GONNA STOP, NAT--
I'M NOT GIVING--
UP.
FREEZE!
MARIA HILL, YOU ARE UNDER ARREST!
SHOOT THE BAG!
DON'T WASTE ANY MORE TIME JUST SHOOT THE DAMN BAG!
I KNOW YOU CAN STILL HEAR ME JUST SHOOT IT--

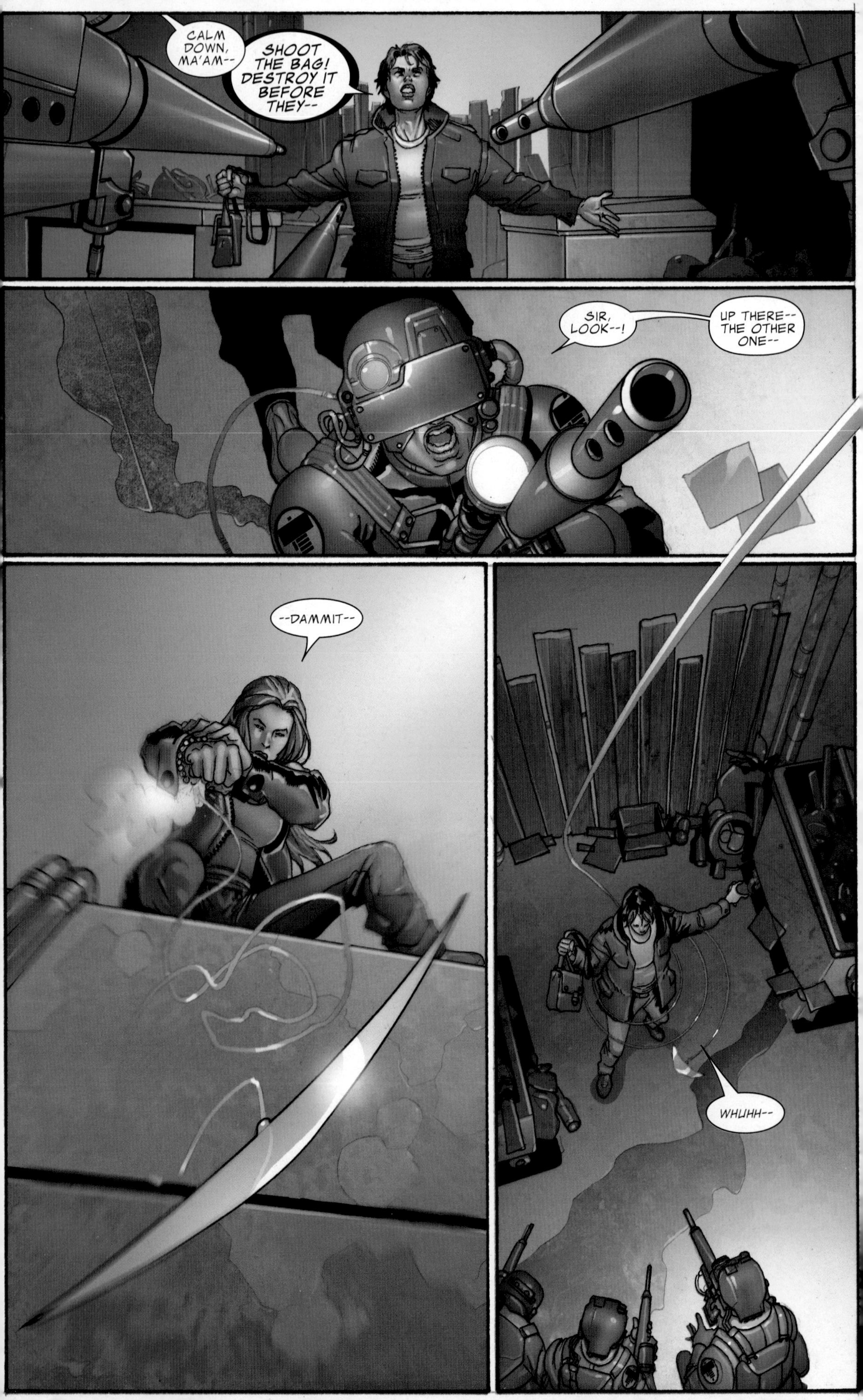
CALM DOWN, MA'AM--
SHOOT THE BAG! DESTROY IT BEFORE THEY--
SIR, LOOK--!
UP THERE-- THE OTHER ONE--
--DAMMIT--
WHUHH--

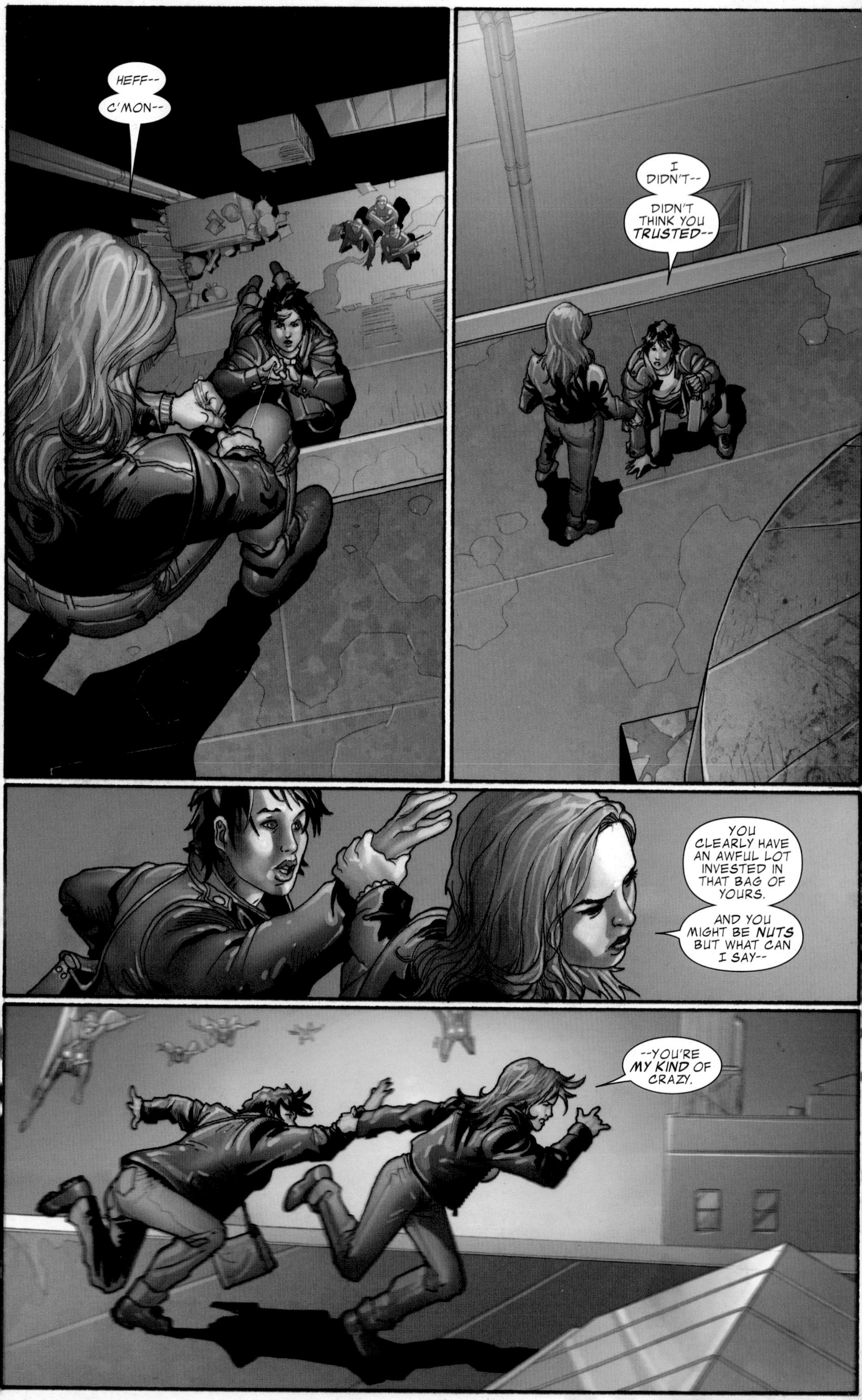
HEFF--
C'MON--
I DIDN'T--
DIDN'T THINK YOU TRUSTED--
YOU CLEARLY HAVE AN AWFUL LOT INVESTED IN THAT BAG OF YOURS.
AND YOU MIGHT BE NUTS BUT WHAT CAN I SAY--
--YOU'RE MY KIND OF CRAZY.

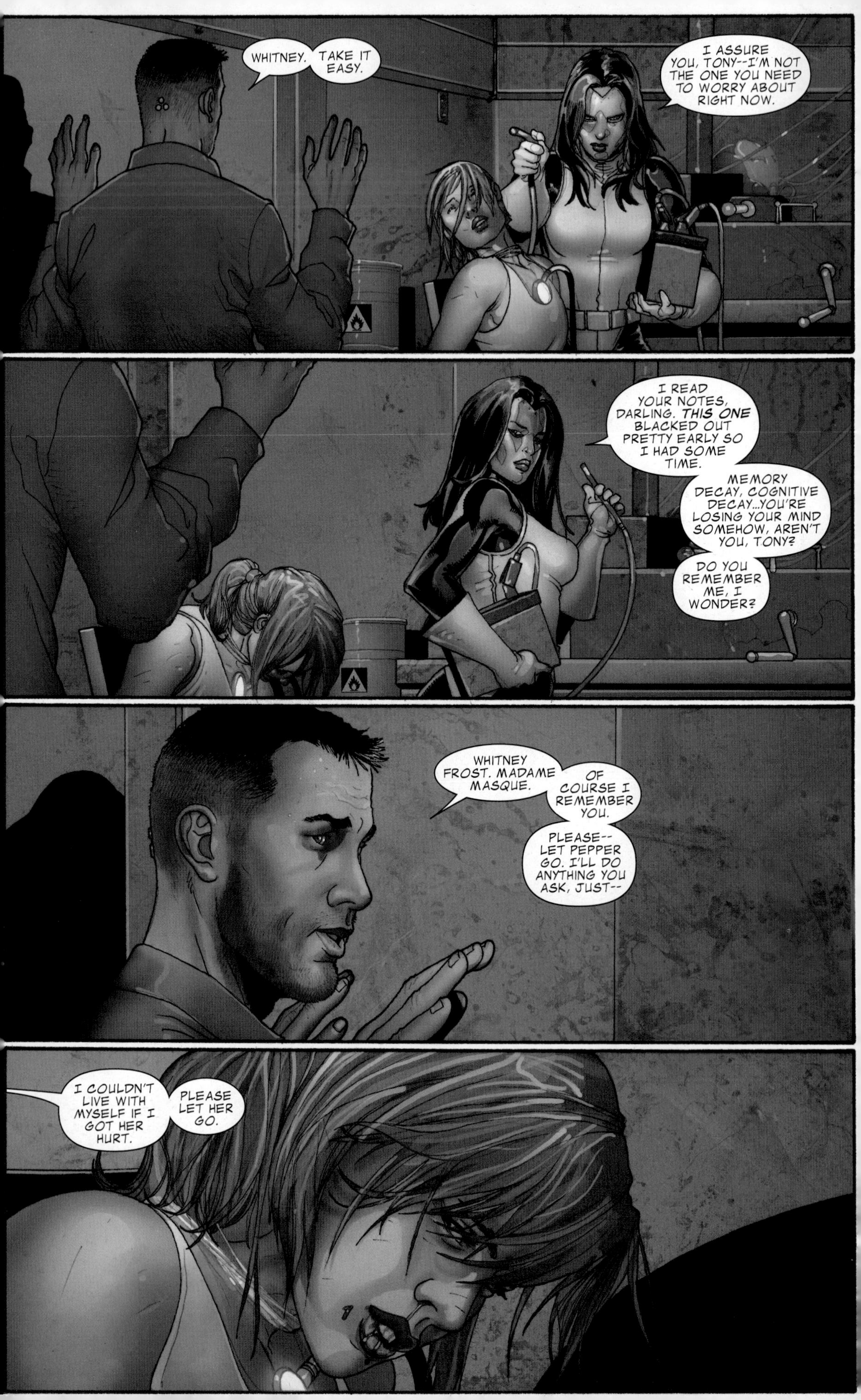
WHITNEY.
TAKE IT EASY.
I ASSURE YOU, TONY--I'M NOT THE ONE YOU NEED TO WORRY ABOUT RIGHT NOW.
I READ YOUR NOTES, DARLING. THIS ONE BLACKED OUT PRETTY EARLY SO I HAD SOME TIME.
MEMORY DECAY, COGNITIVE DECAY...YOU'RE LOSING YOUR MIND SOMEHOW, AREN'T YOU, TONY?
DO YOU REMEMBER ME, I WONDER?
WHITNEY FROST. MADAME MASQUE.
OF COURSE I REMEMBER YOU.
PLEASE--LET PEPPER GO. I'LL DO ANYTHING YOU ASK, JUST--
I COULDN'T LIVE WITH MYSELF IF I GOT HER HURT.
PLEASE LET HER GO.

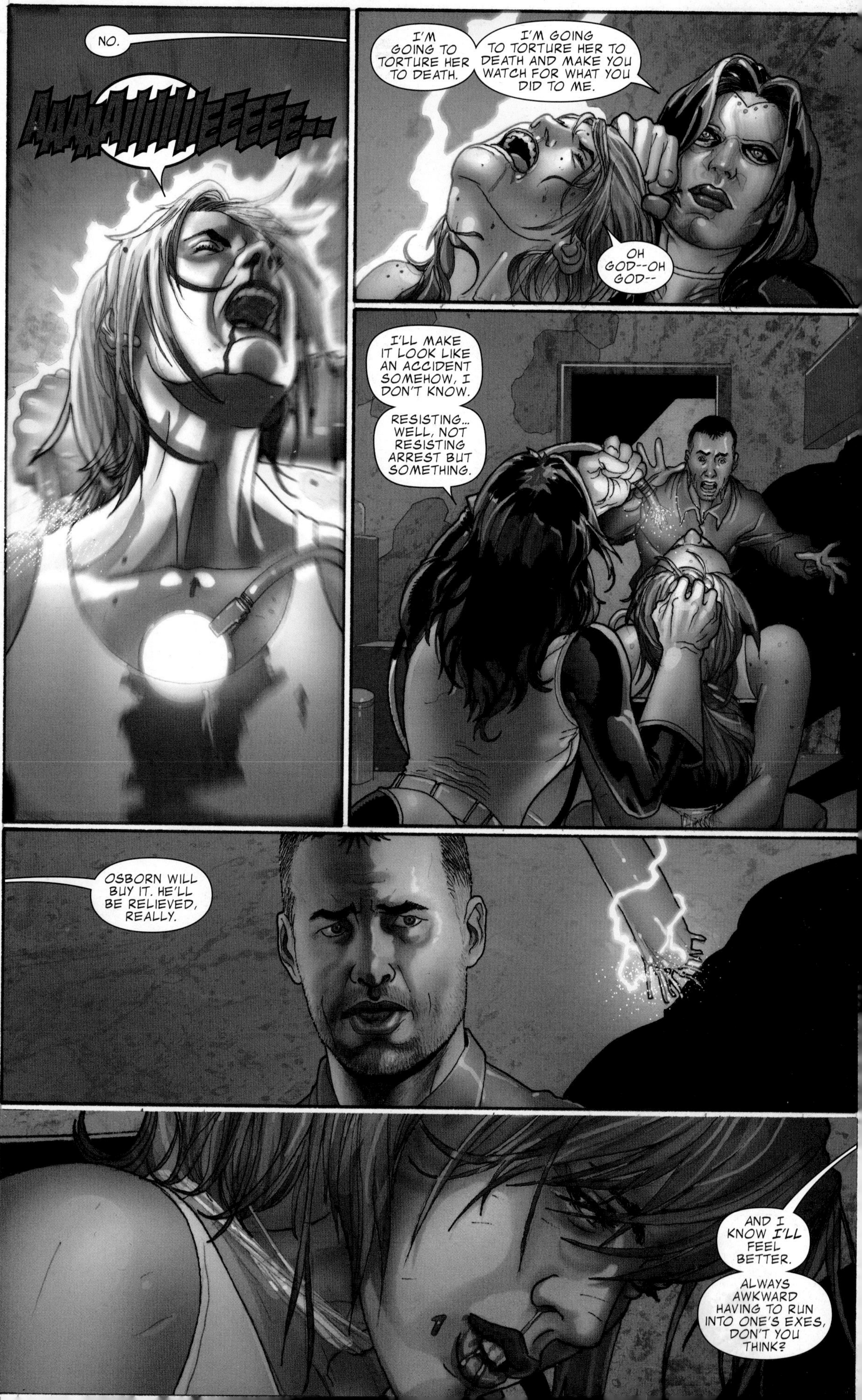
NO.
AAAAAIIIIIIEEEEE...
I'M GOING TO TORTURE HER TO DEATH.
I'M GOING TO TORTURE HER TO DEATH AND MAKE YOU WATCH FOR WHAT YOU DID TO ME.
OH GOD--OH GOD--
I'LL MAKE IT LOOK LIKE AN ACCIDENT SOMEHOW, I DON'T KNOW.
RESISTING... WELL, NOT RESISTING ARREST BUT SOMETHING.
OSBORN WILL BUY IT. HE'LL BE RELIEVED, REALLY.
AND I KNOW I'LL FEEL BETTER.
ALWAYS AWKWARD HAVING TO RUN INTO ONE'S EXES, DON'T YOU THINK?

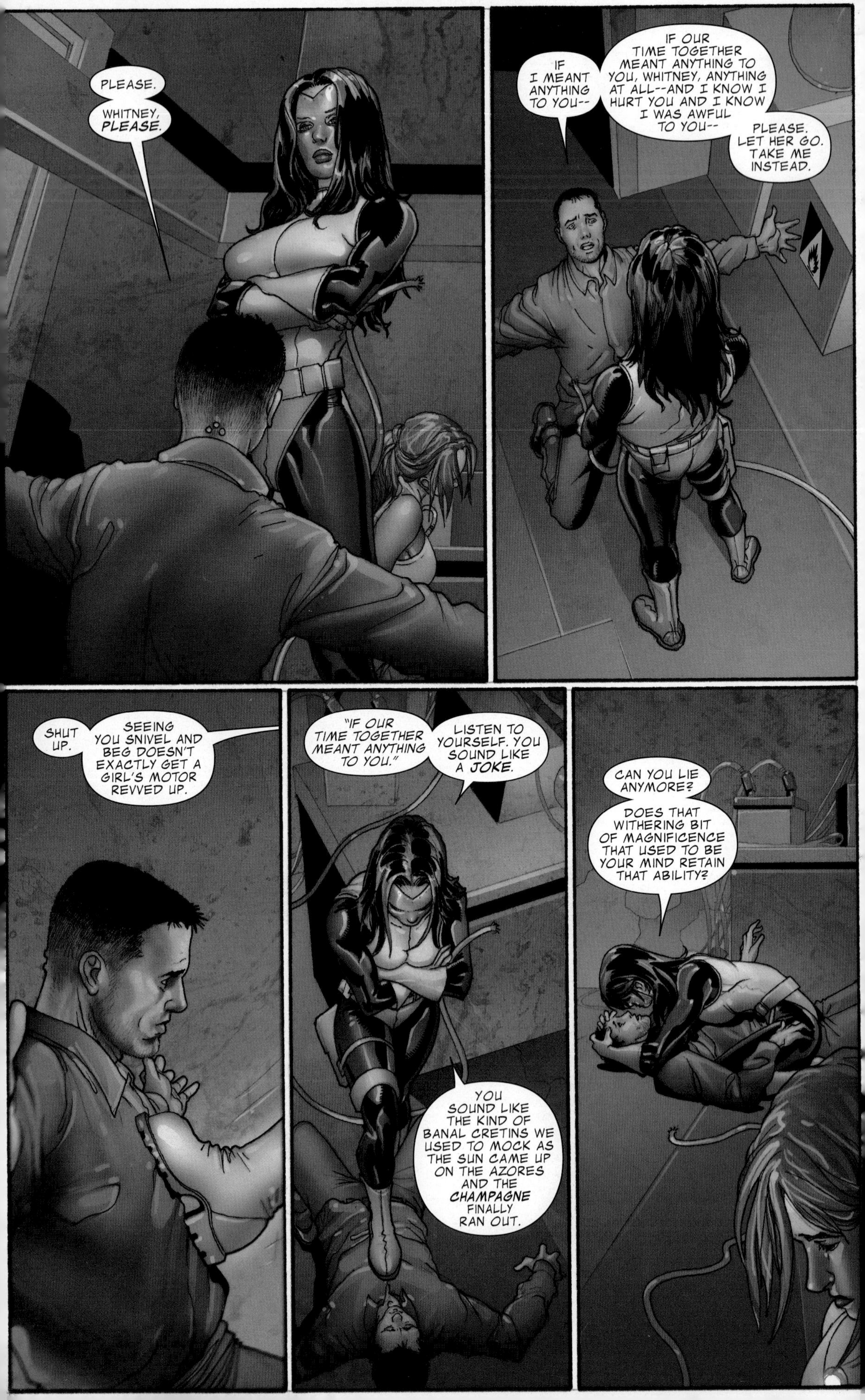
PLEASE.
WHITNEY, *PLEASE.*
IF I MEANT ANYTHING TO YOU--
IF OUR TIME TOGETHER MEANT ANYTHING TO YOU, WHITNEY, ANYTHING AT ALL--AND I KNOW I HURT YOU AND I KNOW I WAS AWFUL TO YOU--
PLEASE. LET HER GO. TAKE ME INSTEAD.
SHUT UP.
SEEING YOU SNIVEL AND BEG DOESN'T EXACTLY GET A GIRL'S MOTOR REVVED UP.
"IF OUR TIME TOGETHER MEANT ANYTHING TO YOU."
LISTEN TO YOURSELF. YOU SOUND LIKE A *JOKE*.
YOU SOUND LIKE THE KIND OF BANAL CRETINS WE USED TO MOCK AS THE SUN CAME UP ON THE AZORES AND THE *CHAMPAGNE* FINALLY RAN OUT.
CAN YOU LIE ANYMORE?
DOES THAT WITHERING BIT OF MAGNIFICENCE THAT USED TO BE YOUR MIND RETAIN THAT ABILITY?

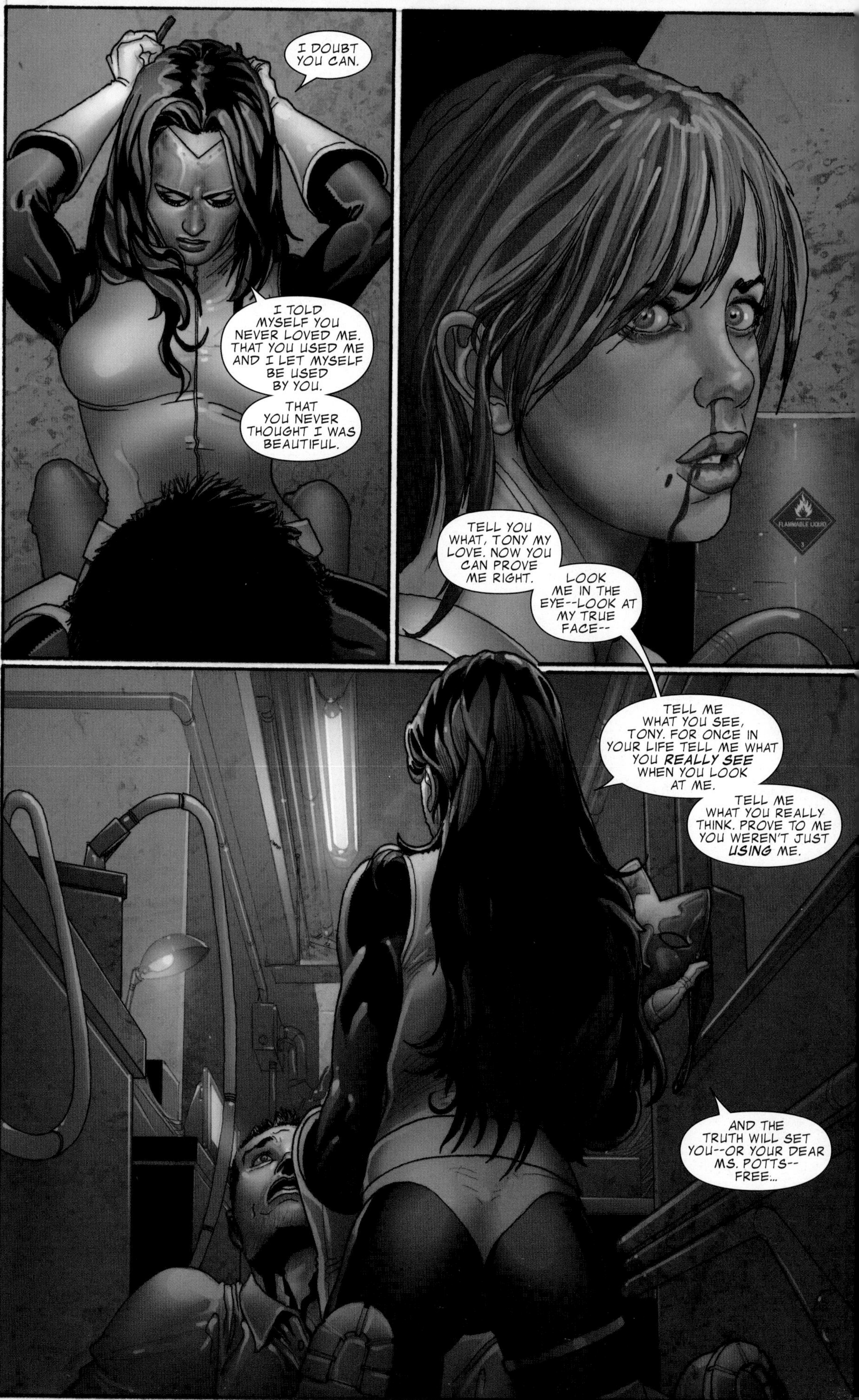
I DOUBT YOU CAN.
I TOLD MYSELF YOU NEVER LOVED ME. THAT YOU USED ME AND I LET MYSELF BE USED BY YOU.
THAT YOU NEVER THOUGHT I WAS BEAUTIFUL.
FLAMMABLE LIQUID
TELL YOU WHAT, TONY MY LOVE. NOW YOU CAN PROVE ME RIGHT.
LOOK ME IN THE EYE--LOOK AT MY TRUE FACE--
TELL ME WHAT YOU SEE, TONY. FOR ONCE IN YOUR LIFE TELL ME WHAT YOU **REALLY SEE** WHEN YOU LOOK AT ME.
TELL ME WHAT YOU REALLY THINK. PROVE TO ME YOU WEREN'T JUST **USING** ME.
AND THE TRUTH WILL SET YOU--OR YOUR DEAR MS. POTTS--FREE...

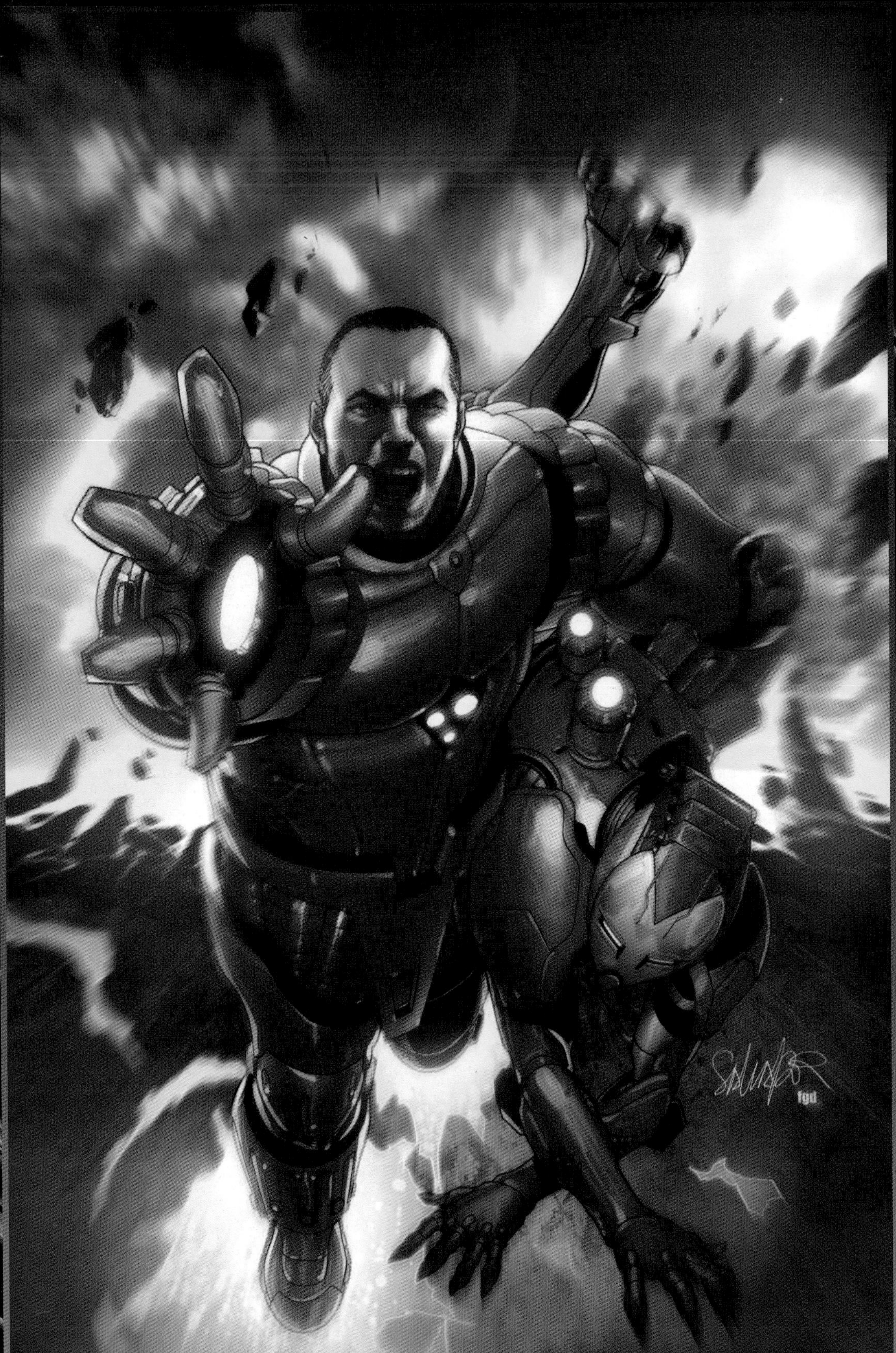

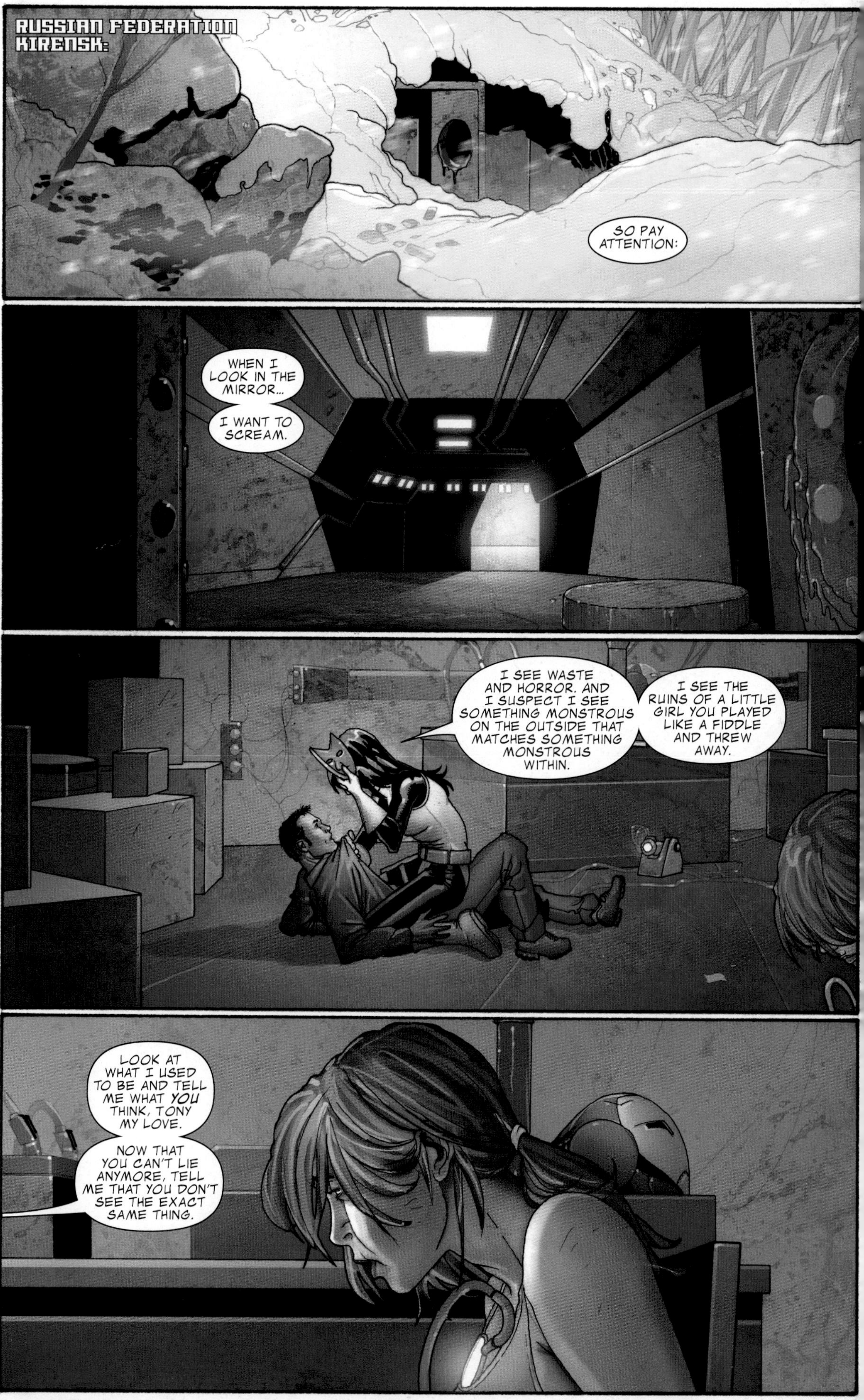
RUSSIAN FEDERATION
KIRENSK:
SO PAY ATTENTION:
WHEN I LOOK IN THE MIRROR...
I WANT TO SCREAM.
I SEE WASTE AND HORROR. AND I SUSPECT I SEE SOMETHING MONSTROUS ON THE OUTSIDE THAT MATCHES SOMETHING MONSTROUS WITHIN.
I SEE THE RUINS OF A LITTLE GIRL YOU PLAYED LIKE A FIDDLE AND THREW AWAY.
LOOK AT WHAT I USED TO BE AND TELL ME WHAT YOU THINK, TONY MY LOVE.
NOW THAT YOU CAN'T LIE ANYMORE, TELL ME THAT YOU DON'T SEE THE EXACT SAME THING.

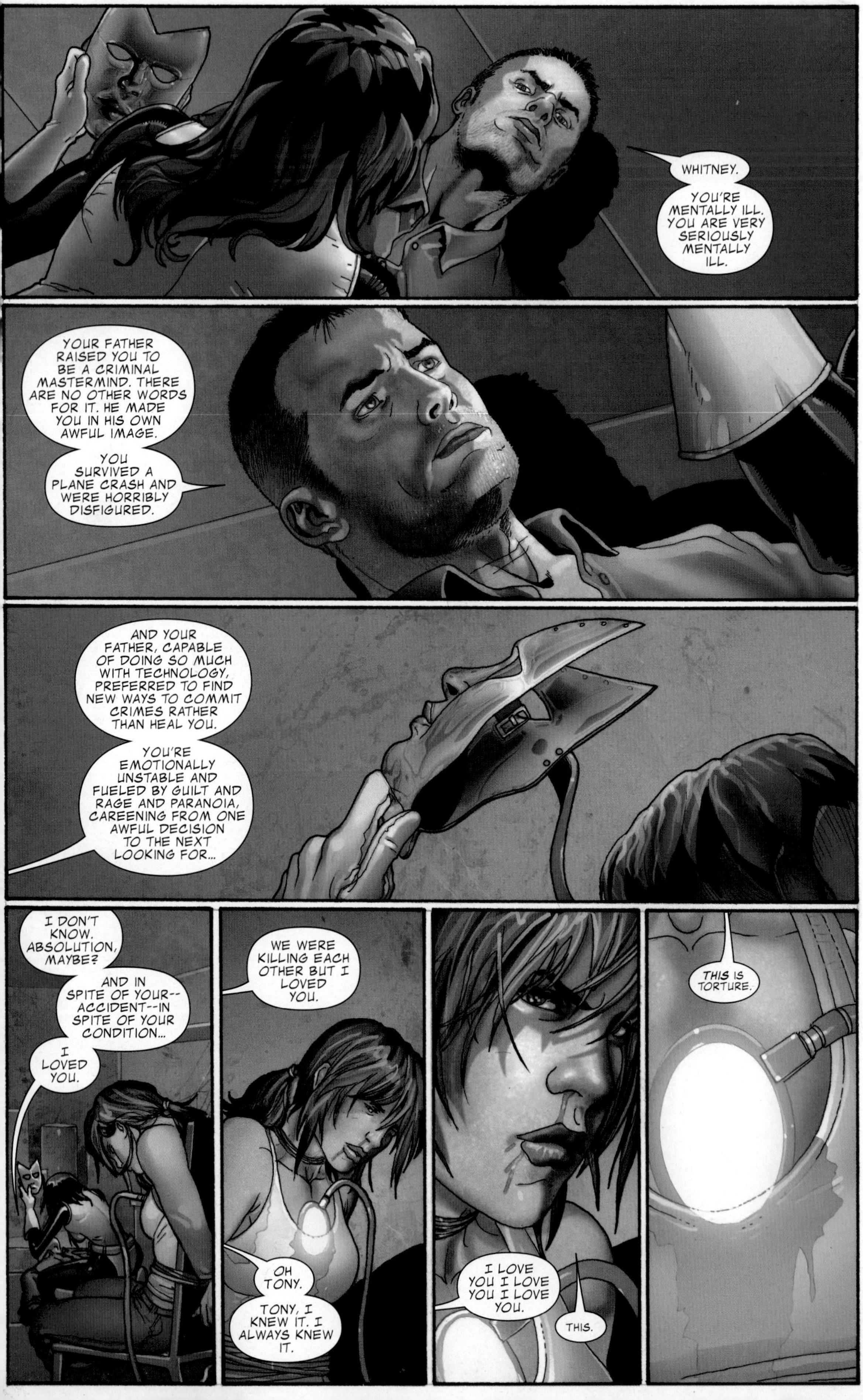
WHITNEY.
YOU'RE MENTALLY ILL. YOU ARE VERY SERIOUSLY MENTALLY ILL.
YOUR FATHER RAISED YOU TO BE A CRIMINAL MASTERMIND. THERE ARE NO OTHER WORDS FOR IT. HE MADE YOU IN HIS OWN AWFUL IMAGE.
YOU SURVIVED A PLANE CRASH AND WERE HORRIBLY DISFIGURED.
AND YOUR FATHER, CAPABLE OF DOING SO MUCH WITH TECHNOLOGY, PREFERRED TO FIND NEW WAYS TO COMMIT CRIMES RATHER THAN HEAL YOU.
YOU'RE EMOTIONALLY UNSTABLE AND FUELED BY GUILT AND RAGE AND PARANOIA, CAREENING FROM ONE AWFUL DECISION TO THE NEXT LOOKING FOR...
I DON'T KNOW. ABSOLUTION, MAYBE?
AND IN SPITE OF YOUR--ACCIDENT--IN SPITE OF YOUR CONDITION...
I LOVED YOU.
WE WERE KILLING EACH OTHER BUT I LOVED YOU.
OH TONY.
TONY, I KNEW IT. I ALWAYS KNEW IT.
I LOVE YOU I LOVE YOU I LOVE YOU.
THIS.
THIS IS TORTURE.

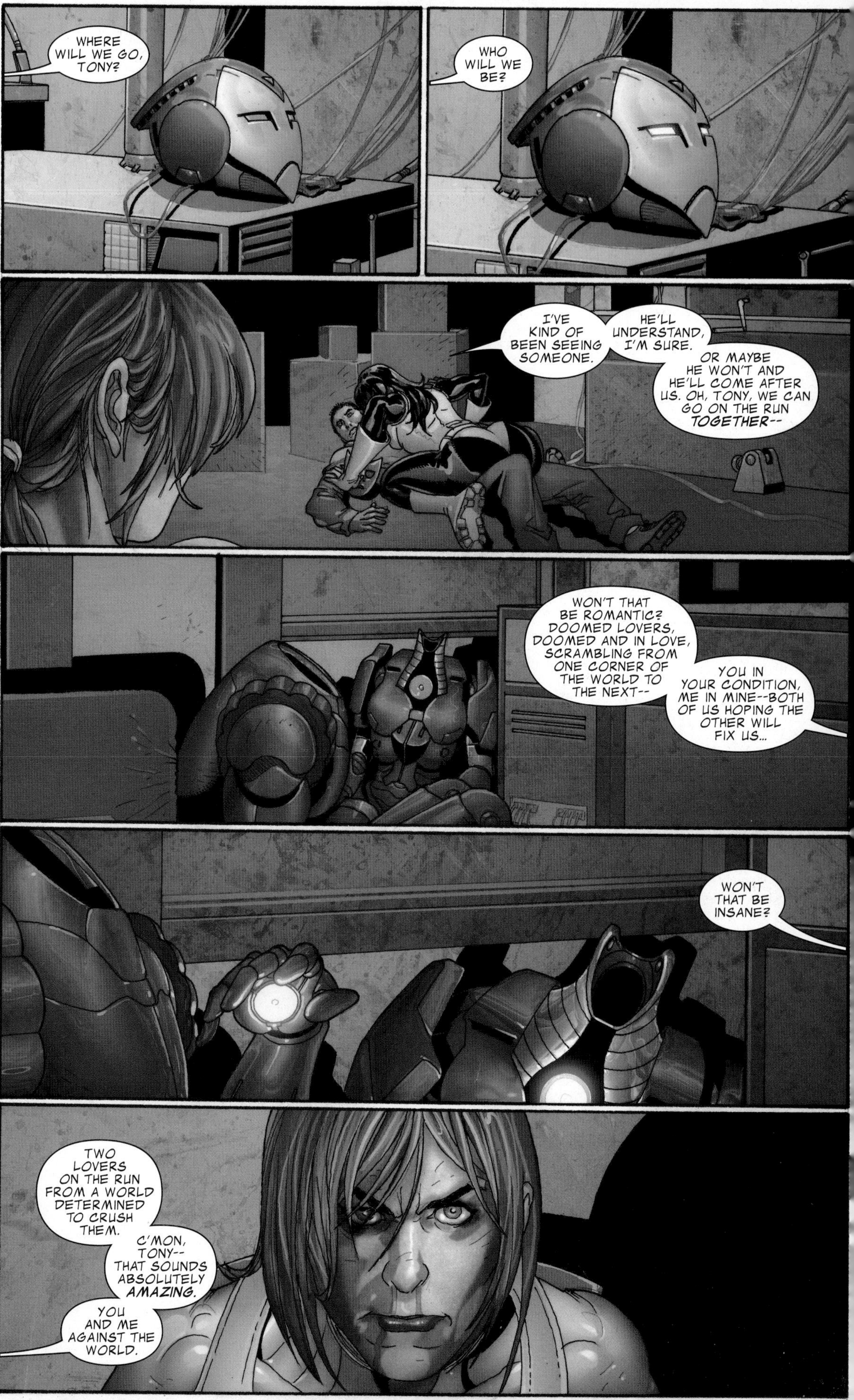

WHERE WILL WE GO, TONY?
WHO WILL WE BE?
I'VE KIND OF BEEN SEEING SOMEONE.
HE'LL UNDERSTAND, I'M SURE.
OR MAYBE HE WON'T AND HE'LL COME AFTER US. OH, TONY, WE CAN GO ON THE RUN *TOGETHER*--
WON'T THAT BE ROMANTIC? DOOMED LOVERS, DOOMED AND IN LOVE, SCRAMBLING FROM ONE CORNER OF THE WORLD TO THE NEXT--
YOU IN YOUR CONDITION, ME IN MINE--BOTH OF US HOPING THE OTHER WILL FIX US...
WON'T THAT BE INSANE?
TWO LOVERS ON THE RUN FROM A WORLD DETERMINED TO CRUSH THEM.
C'MON, TONY-- THAT SOUNDS ABSOLUTELY *AMAZING*.
YOU AND ME AGAINST THE WORLD.

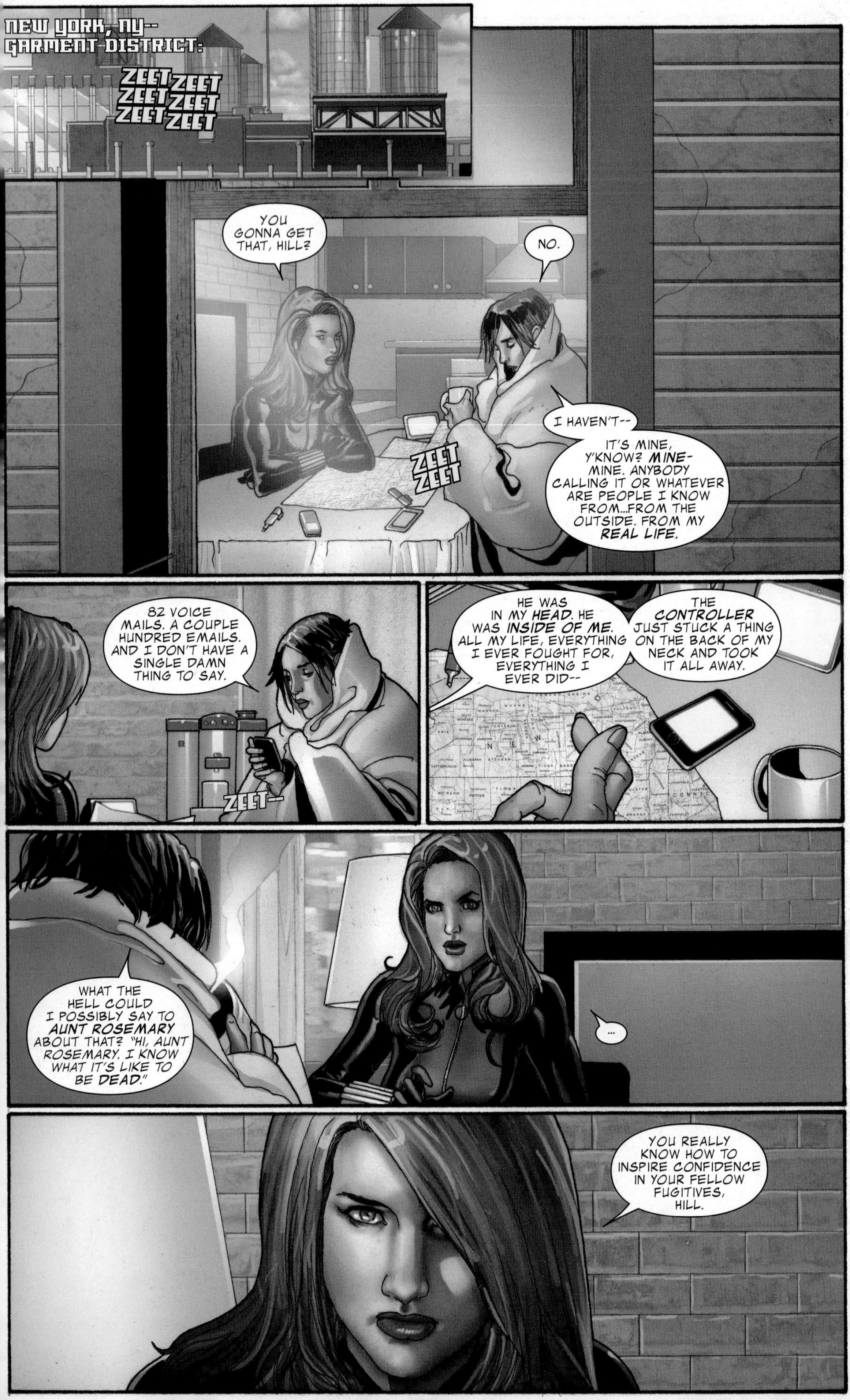
NEW YORK, NY--
GARMENT DISTRICT:
ZEET ZEET
ZEET ZEET
ZEET ZEET
YOU GONNA GET THAT, HILL?
NO.
I HAVEN'T--
IT'S MINE, Y'KNOW? MINE-MINE. ANYBODY CALLING IT OR WHATEVER ARE PEOPLE I KNOW FROM...FROM THE OUTSIDE. FROM MY REAL LIFE.
ZEET
ZEET
82 VOICE MAILS. A COUPLE HUNDRED EMAILS. AND I DON'T HAVE A SINGLE DAMN THING TO SAY.
ZEET--
HE WAS IN MY HEAD. HE WAS INSIDE OF ME. ALL MY LIFE, EVERYTHING I EVER FOUGHT FOR, EVERYTHING I EVER DID--
THE CONTROLLER JUST STUCK A THING ON THE BACK OF MY NECK AND TOOK IT ALL AWAY.
WHAT THE HELL COULD I POSSIBLY SAY TO AUNT ROSEMARY ABOUT THAT? "HI, AUNT ROSEMARY. I KNOW WHAT IT'S LIKE TO BE DEAD."
...
YOU REALLY KNOW HOW TO INSPIRE CONFIDENCE IN YOUR FELLOW FUGITIVES, HILL.

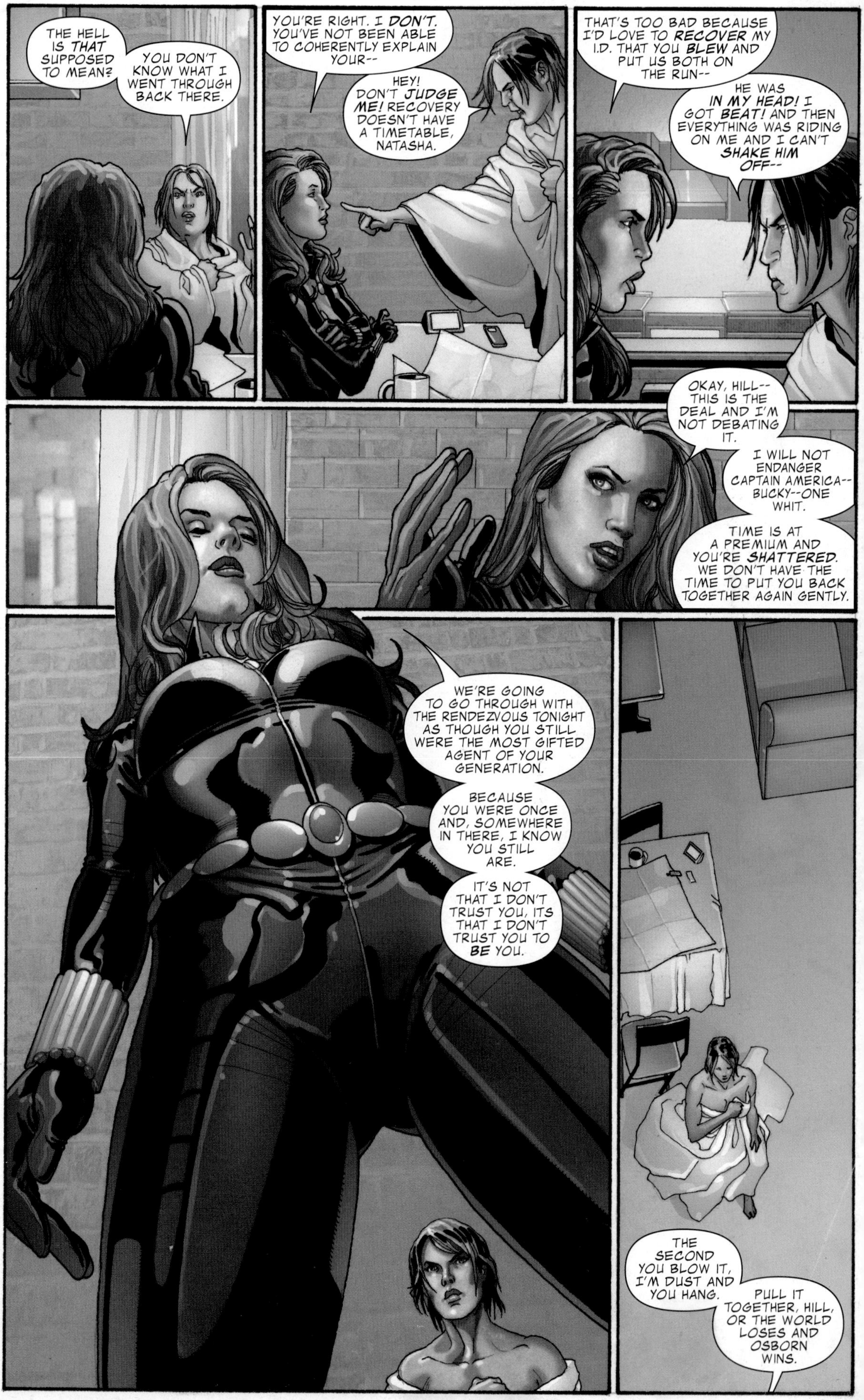
THE HELL IS THAT SUPPOSED TO MEAN?
YOU DON'T KNOW WHAT I WENT THROUGH BACK THERE.
YOU'RE RIGHT. I DON'T. YOU'VE NOT BEEN ABLE TO COHERENTLY EXPLAIN YOUR--
HEY! DON'T JUDGE ME! RECOVERY DOESN'T HAVE A TIMETABLE, NATASHA.
THAT'S TOO BAD BECAUSE I'D LOVE TO RECOVER MY I.D. THAT YOU BLEW AND PUT US BOTH ON THE RUN--
HE WAS IN MY HEAD! I GOT BEAT! AND THEN EVERYTHING WAS RIDING ON ME AND I CAN'T SHAKE HIM OFF--
OKAY, HILL-- THIS IS THE DEAL AND I'M NOT DEBATING IT.
I WILL NOT ENDANGER CAPTAIN AMERICA-- BUCKY--ONE WHIT.
TIME IS AT A PREMIUM AND YOU'RE SHATTERED. WE DON'T HAVE THE TIME TO PUT YOU BACK TOGETHER AGAIN GENTLY.
WE'RE GOING TO GO THROUGH WITH THE RENDEZVOUS TONIGHT AS THOUGH YOU STILL WERE THE MOST GIFTED AGENT OF YOUR GENERATION.
BECAUSE YOU WERE ONCE AND, SOMEWHERE IN THERE, I KNOW YOU STILL ARE.
IT'S NOT THAT I DON'T TRUST YOU, ITS THAT I DON'T TRUST YOU TO BE YOU.
THE SECOND YOU BLOW IT, I'M DUST AND YOU HANG.
PULL IT TOGETHER, HILL, OR THE WORLD LOSES AND OSBORN WINS.

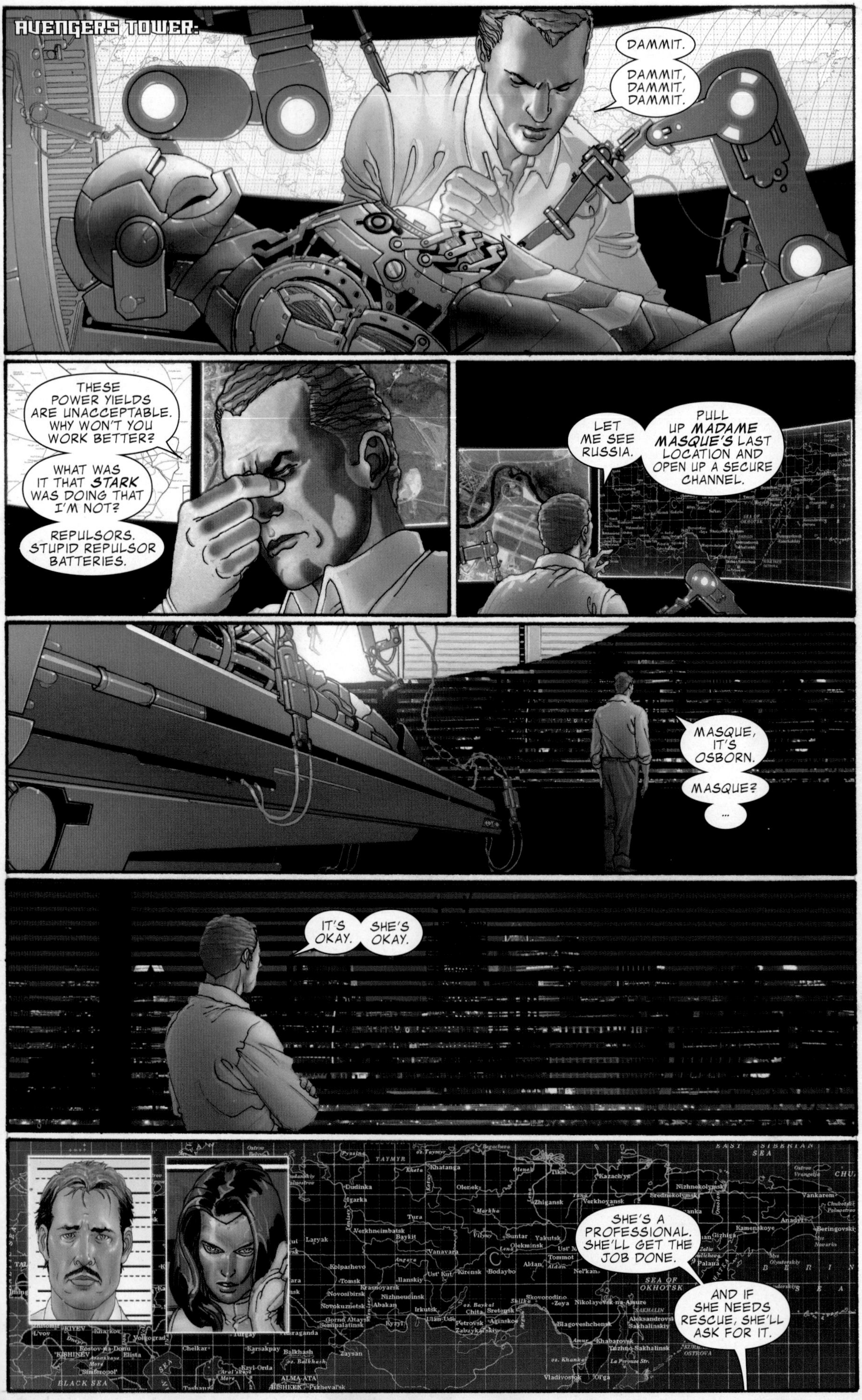
AVENGERS TOWER:
DAMMIT.
DAMMIT, DAMMIT, DAMMIT.
THESE POWER YIELDS ARE UNACCEPTABLE. WHY WON'T YOU WORK BETTER?
WHAT WAS IT THAT STARK WAS DOING THAT I'M NOT?
REPULSORS. STUPID REPULSOR BATTERIES.
LET ME SEE RUSSIA.
PULL UP MADAME MASQUE'S LAST LOCATION AND OPEN UP A SECURE CHANNEL.
MASQUE, IT'S OSBORN.
MASQUE?
...
IT'S OKAY.
SHE'S OKAY.
SHE'S A PROFESSIONAL. SHE'LL GET THE JOB DONE.
AND IF SHE NEEDS RESCUE, SHE'LL ASK FOR IT.

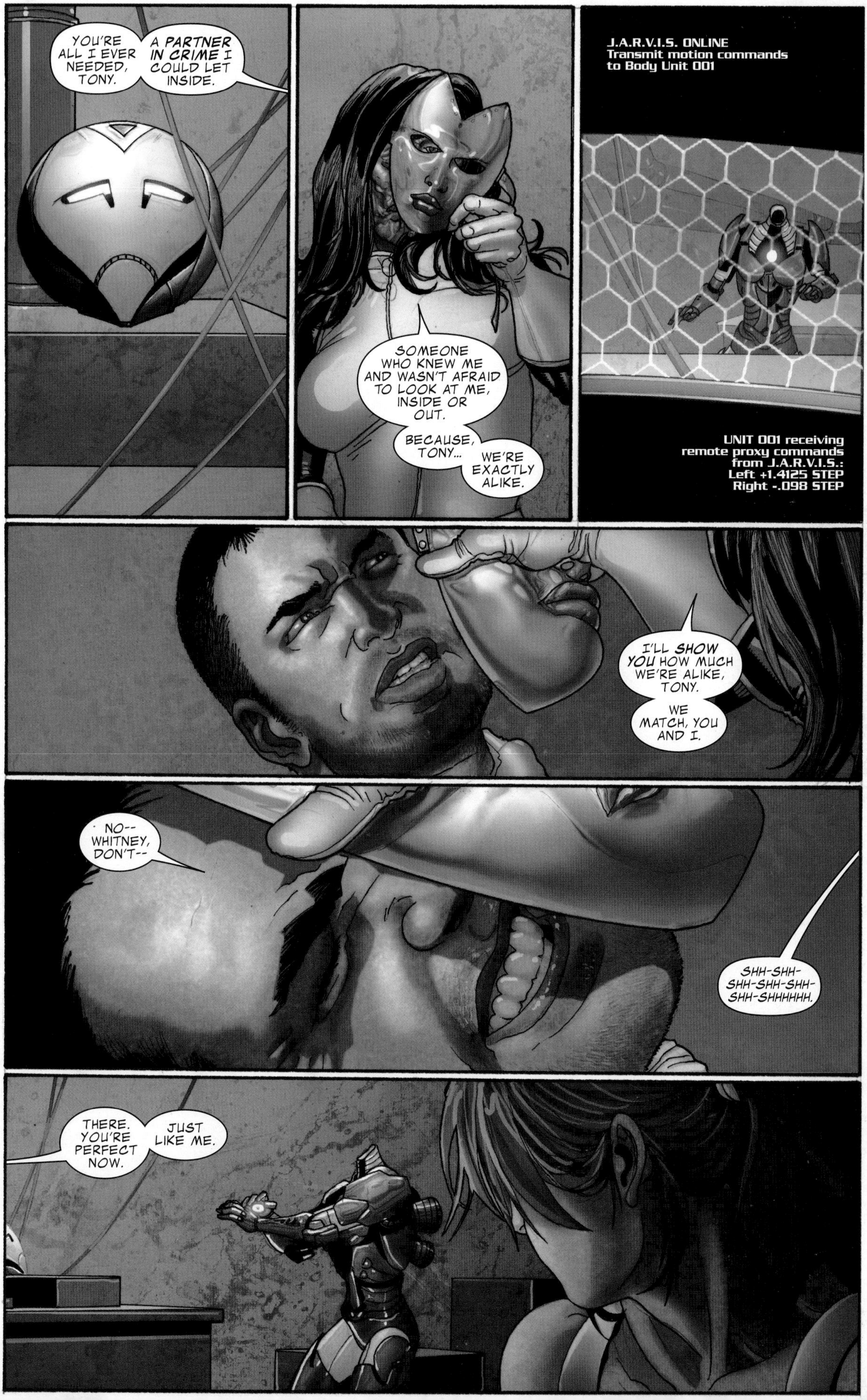
YOU'RE ALL I EVER NEEDED, TONY.
A PARTNER IN CRIME I COULD LET INSIDE.
SOMEONE WHO KNEW ME AND WASN'T AFRAID TO LOOK AT ME, INSIDE OR OUT.
BECAUSE, TONY...
WE'RE EXACTLY ALIKE.
J.A.R.V.I.S. ONLINE
Transmit motion commands
to Body Unit 001
UNIT 001 receiving
remote proxy commands
from J.A.R.V.I.S.:
Left +1.4125 STEP
Right -.098 STEP
I'LL SHOW YOU HOW MUCH WE'RE ALIKE, TONY.
WE MATCH, YOU AND I.
NO-- WHITNEY, DON'T--
SHH-SHH-SHH-SHH-SHH-SHH-SHHHHHH.
THERE. YOU'RE PERFECT NOW.
JUST LIKE ME.

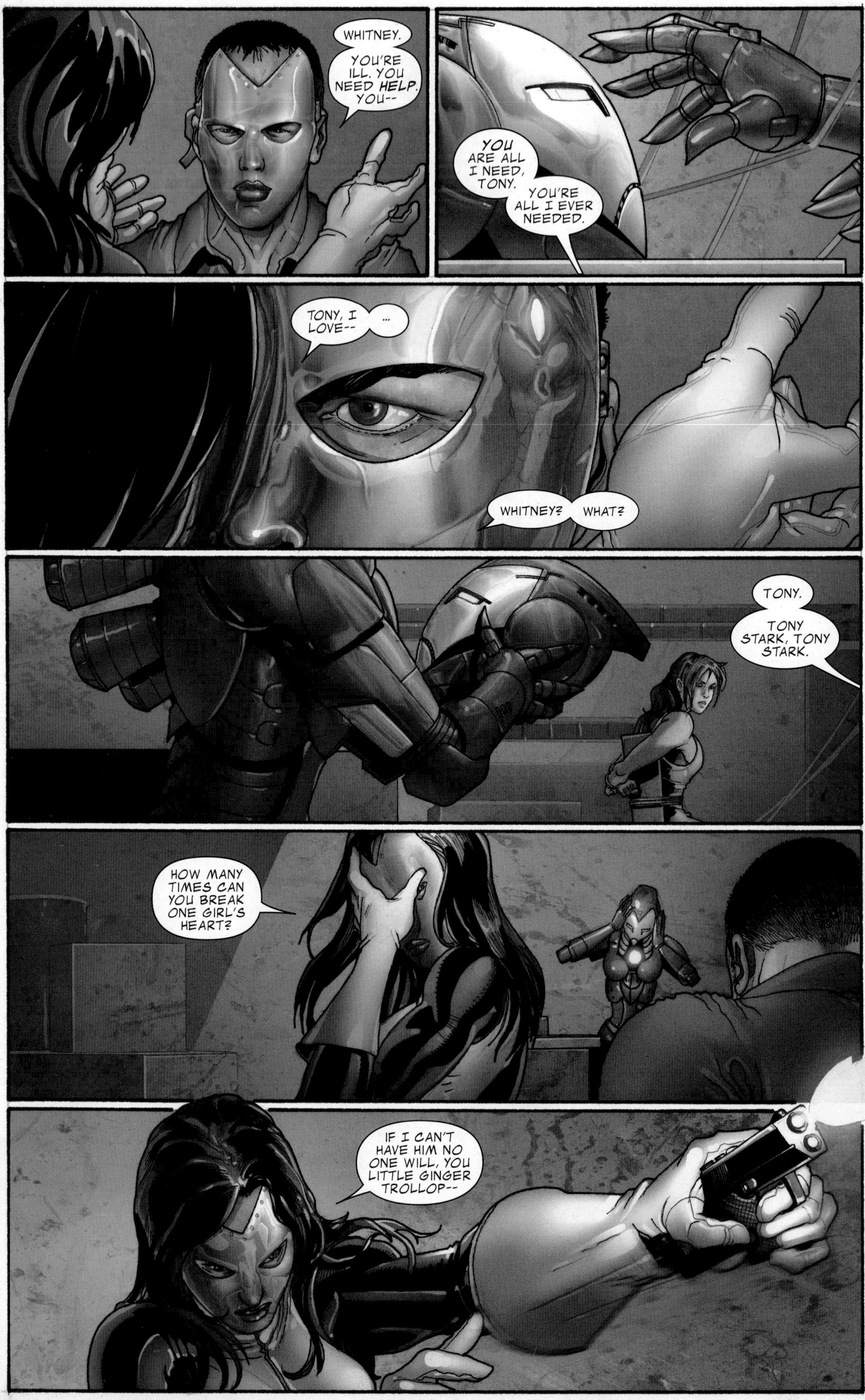
WHITNEY.
YOU'RE ILL. YOU NEED HELP. YOU--
YOU ARE ALL I NEED, TONY.
YOU'RE ALL I EVER NEEDED.
TONY, I LOVE--
...
WHITNEY?
WHAT?
TONY.
TONY STARK, TONY STARK.
HOW MANY TIMES CAN YOU BREAK ONE GIRL'S HEART?
IF I CAN'T HAVE HIM NO ONE WILL, YOU LITTLE GINGER TROLLOP--

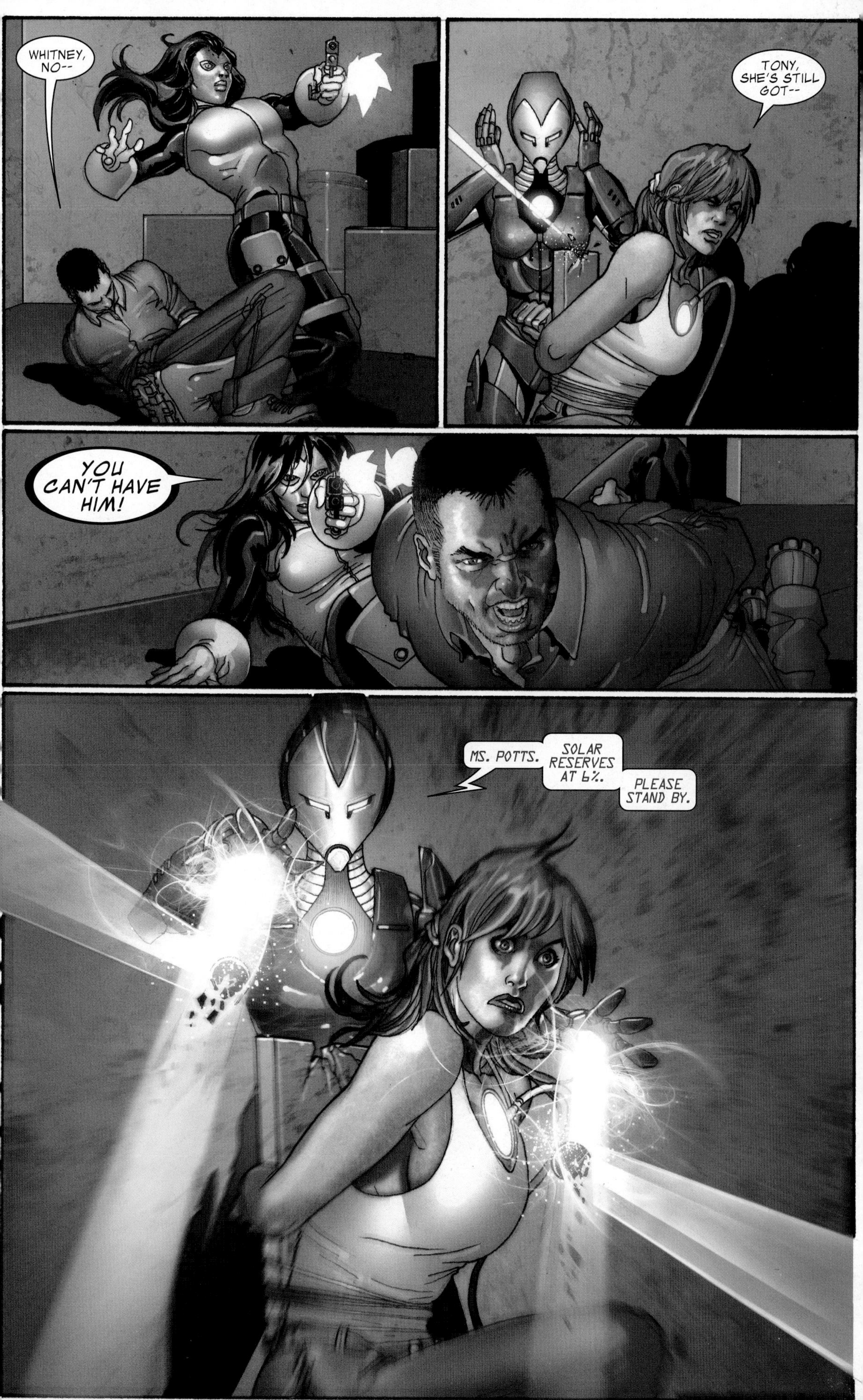
WHITNEY, NO--
TONY, SHE'S STILL GOT--
YOU CAN'T HAVE HIM!
MS. POTTS.
SOLAR RESERVES AT 6%.
PLEASE STAND BY.

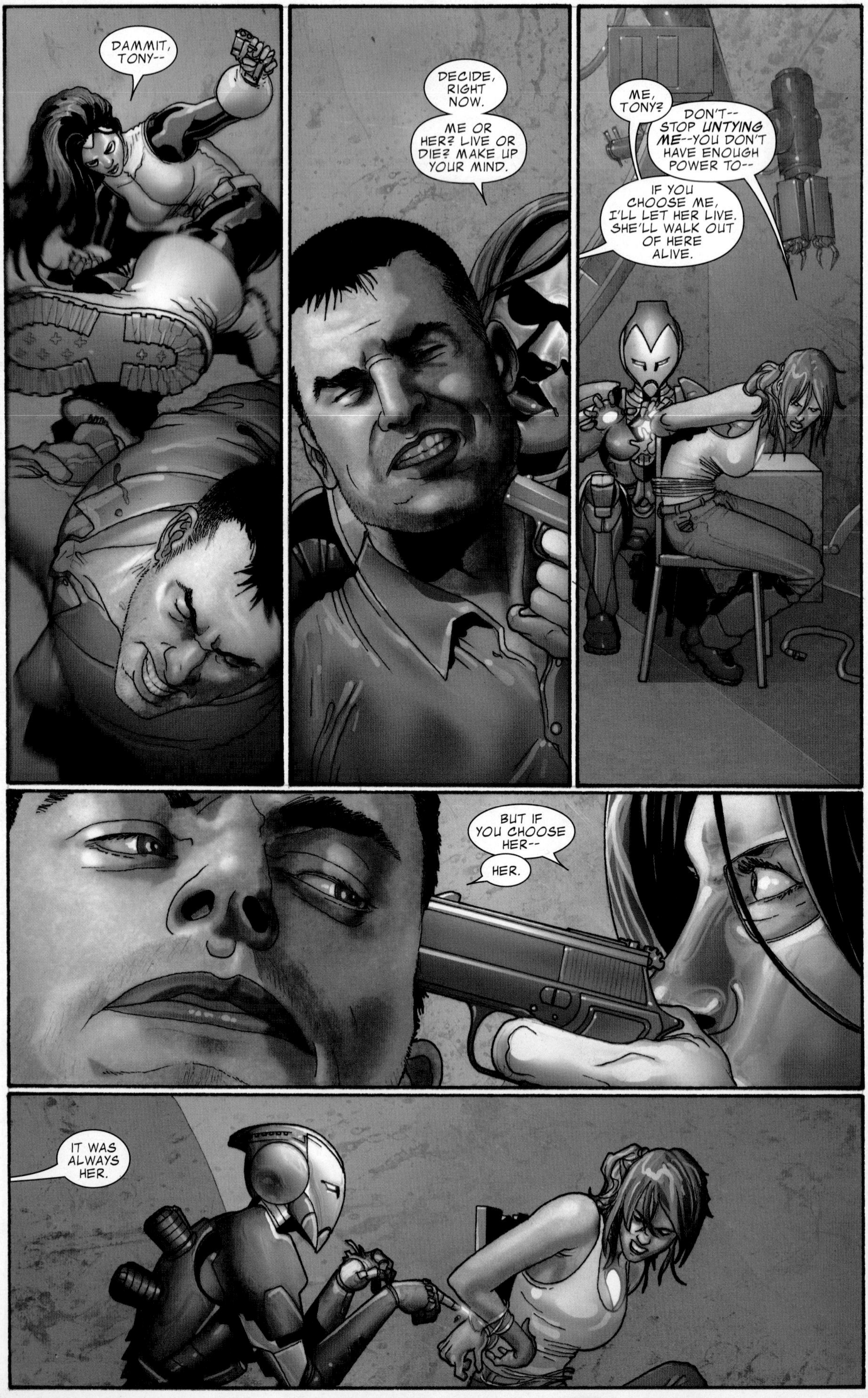
DAMMIT, TONY--
DECIDE, RIGHT NOW.
ME OR HER? LIVE OR DIE? MAKE UP YOUR MIND.
ME, TONY?
DON'T-- STOP UNTYING ME--YOU DON'T HAVE ENOUGH POWER TO--
IF YOU CHOOSE ME, I'LL LET HER LIVE. SHE'LL WALK OUT OF HERE ALIVE.
BUT IF YOU CHOOSE HER--
HER.
IT WAS ALWAYS HER.

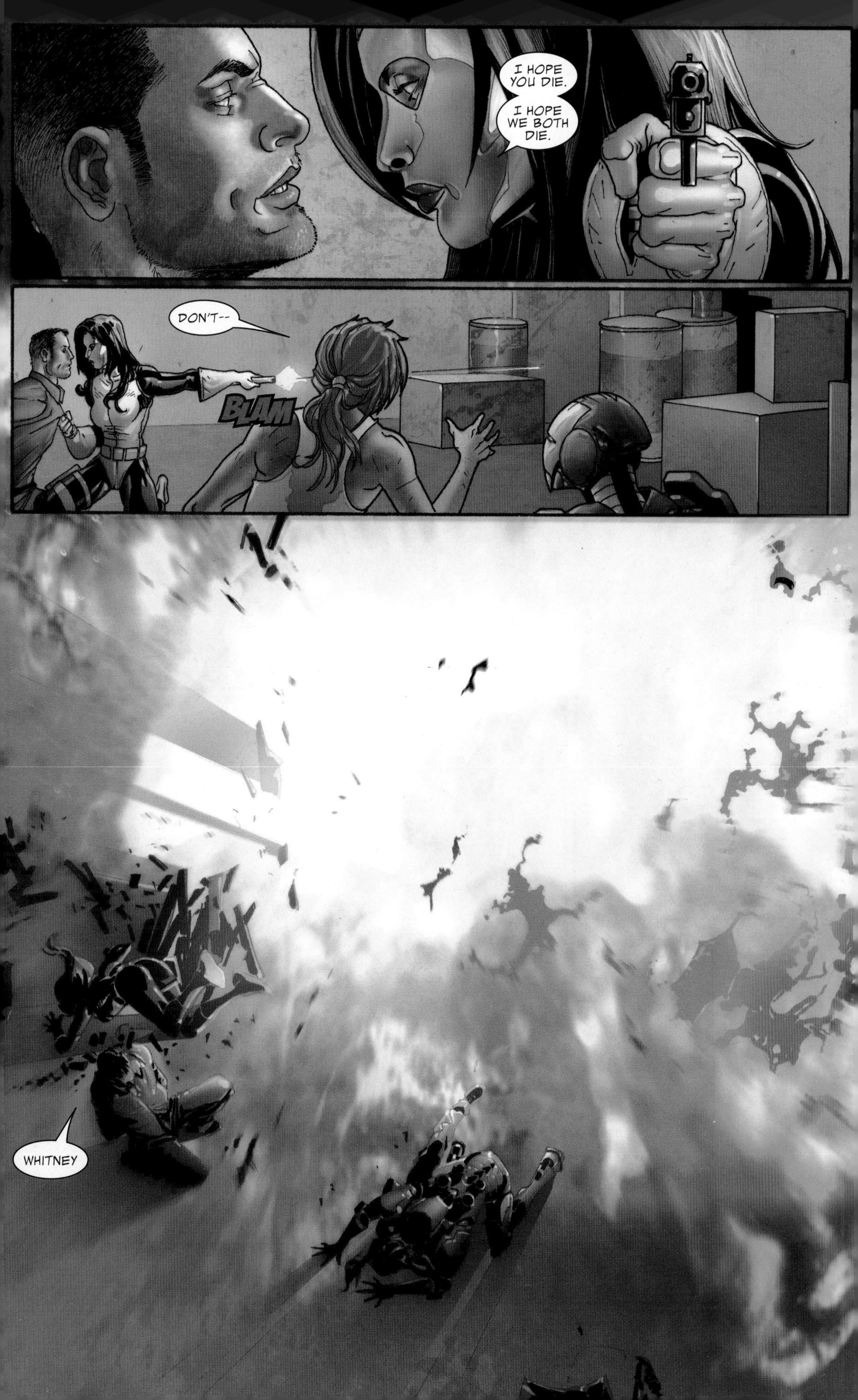
I HOPE YOU DIE.
I HOPE WE BOTH DIE.
DON'T--
BLAM
WHITNEY

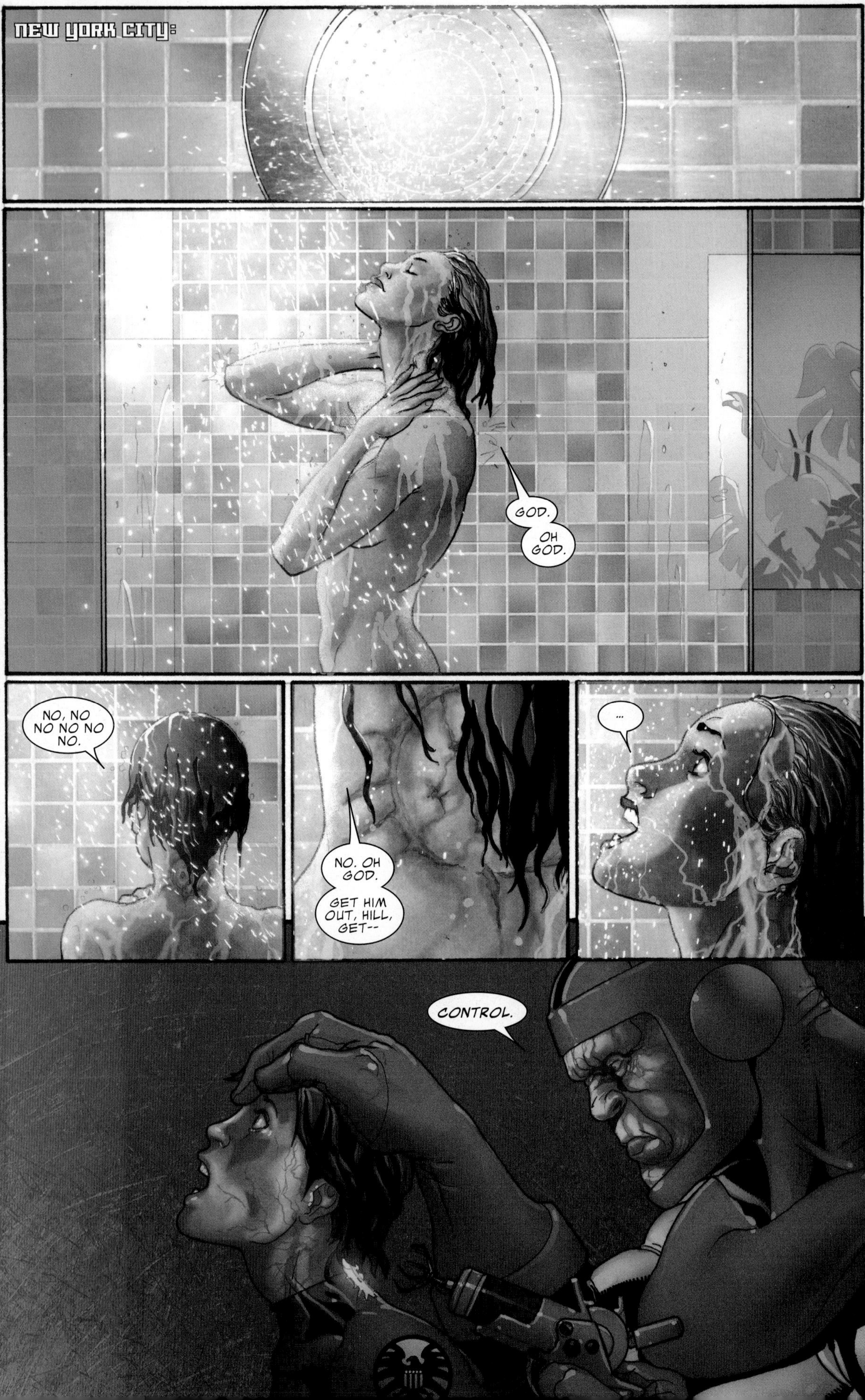
NEW YORK CITY:
GOD.
OH GOD.
NO, NO NO NO NO NO.
NO. OH GOD.
GET HIM OUT, HILL, GET--
...
CONTROL.

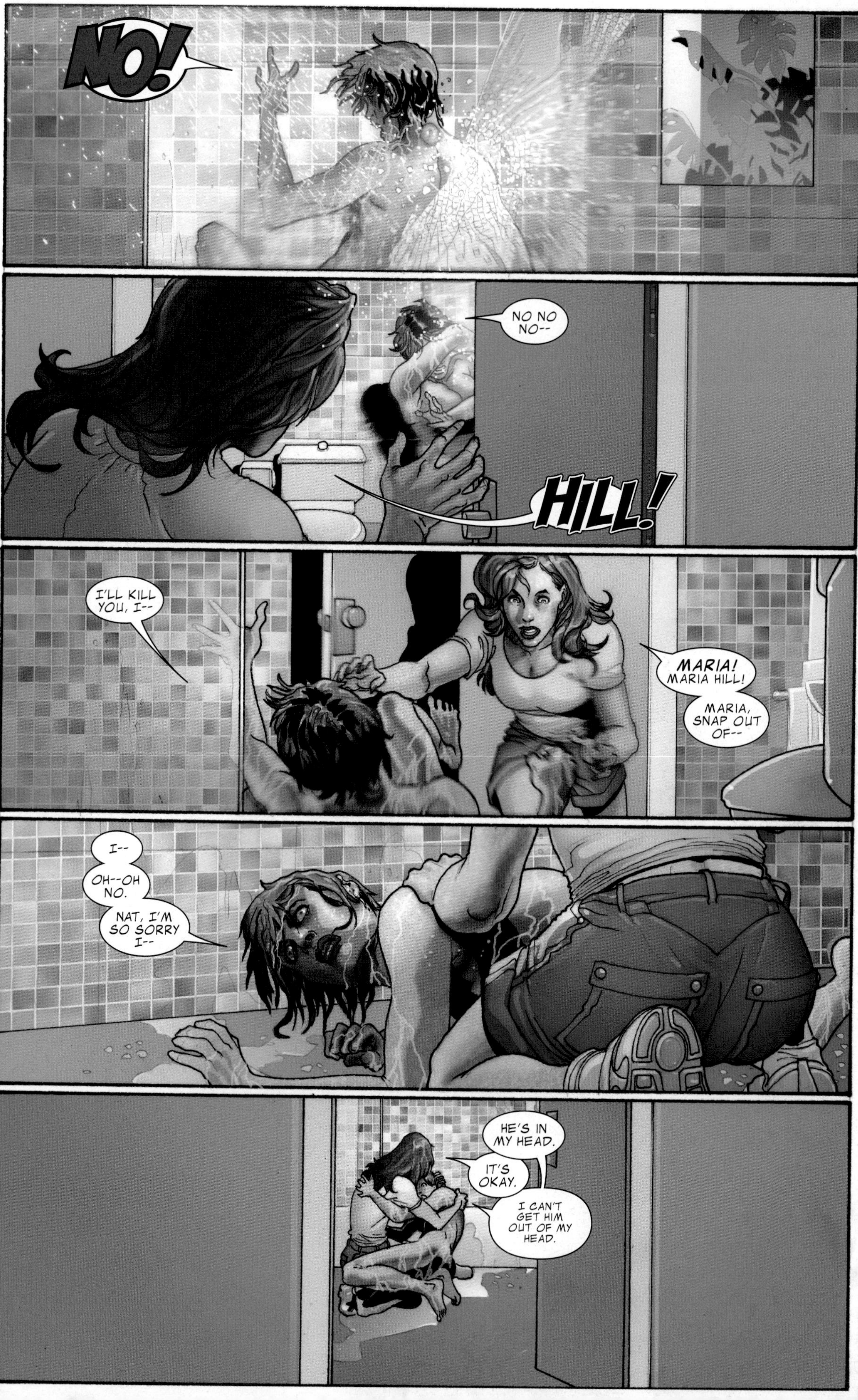
NO!
NO NO NO--
HILL!
I'LL KILL YOU, I--
MARIA! MARIA HILL!
MARIA, SNAP OUT OF--
I--
OH--OH NO.
NAT, I'M SO SORRY I--
HE'S IN MY HEAD.
IT'S OKAY.
I CAN'T GET HIM OUT OF MY HEAD.

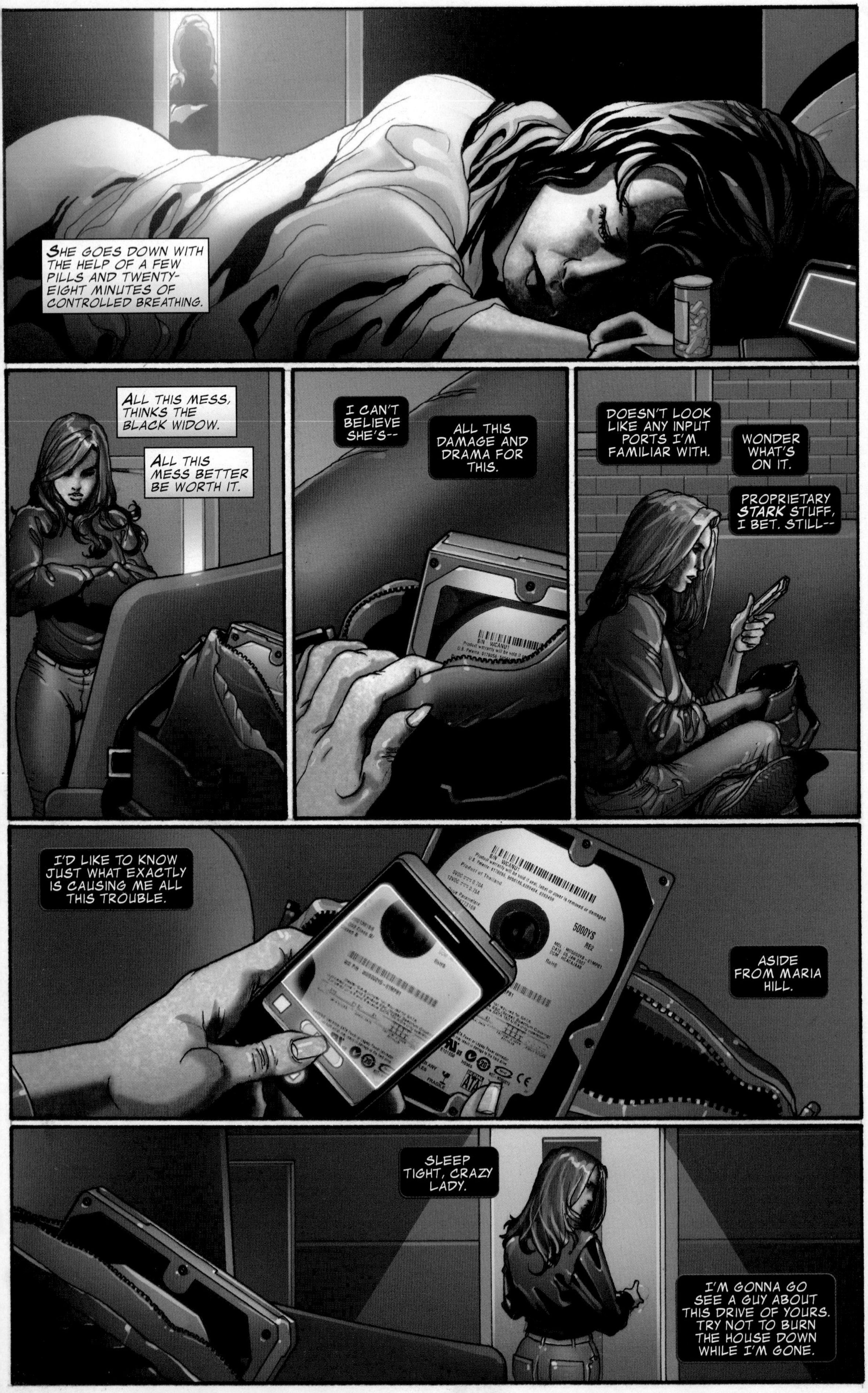
SHE GOES DOWN WITH THE HELP OF A FEW PILLS AND TWENTY-EIGHT MINUTES OF CONTROLLED BREATHING.
ALL THIS MESS, THINKS THE BLACK WIDOW.
ALL THIS MESS BETTER BE WORTH IT.
I CAN'T BELIEVE SHE'S--
ALL THIS DAMAGE AND DRAMA FOR THIS.
DOESN'T LOOK LIKE ANY INPUT PORTS I'M FAMILIAR WITH.
WONDER WHAT'S ON IT.
PROPRIETARY STARK STUFF, I BET. STILL--
I'D LIKE TO KNOW JUST WHAT EXACTLY IS CAUSING ME ALL THIS TROUBLE.
ASIDE FROM MARIA HILL.
SLEEP TIGHT, CRAZY LADY.
I'M GONNA GO SEE A GUY ABOUT THIS DRIVE OF YOURS. TRY NOT TO BURN THE HOUSE DOWN WHILE I'M GONE.

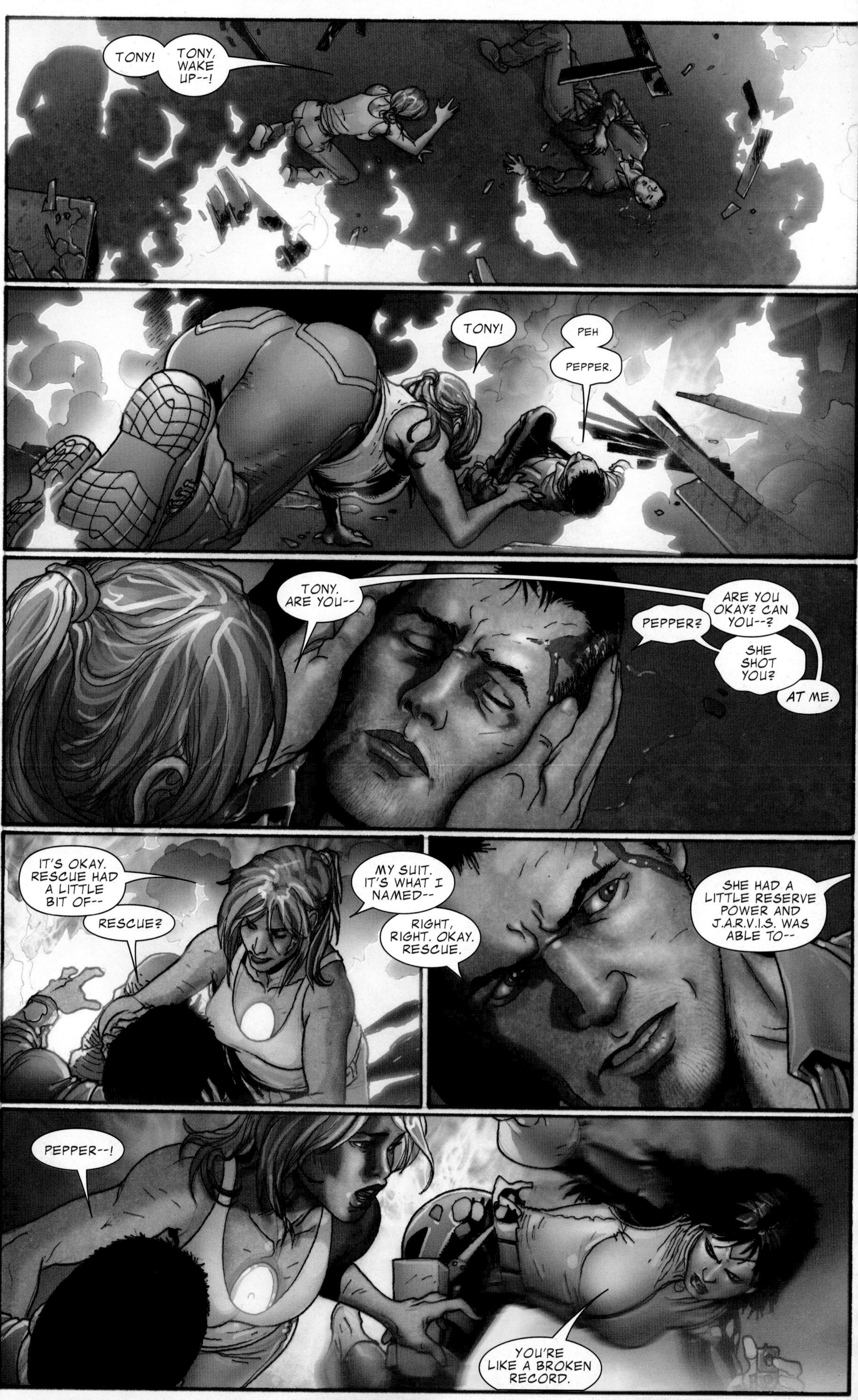
TONY!
TONY, WAKE UP--!
TONY!
PEH
PEPPER.
TONY. ARE YOU--
PEPPER?
ARE YOU OKAY? CAN YOU--?
SHE SHOT YOU?
AT ME.
IT'S OKAY. RESCUE HAD A LITTLE BIT OF--
RESCUE?
MY SUIT. IT'S WHAT I NAMED--
RIGHT, RIGHT. OKAY. RESCUE.
SHE HAD A LITTLE RESERVE POWER AND J.A.R.V.I.S. WAS ABLE TO--
PEPPER--!
YOU'RE LIKE A BROKEN RECORD.

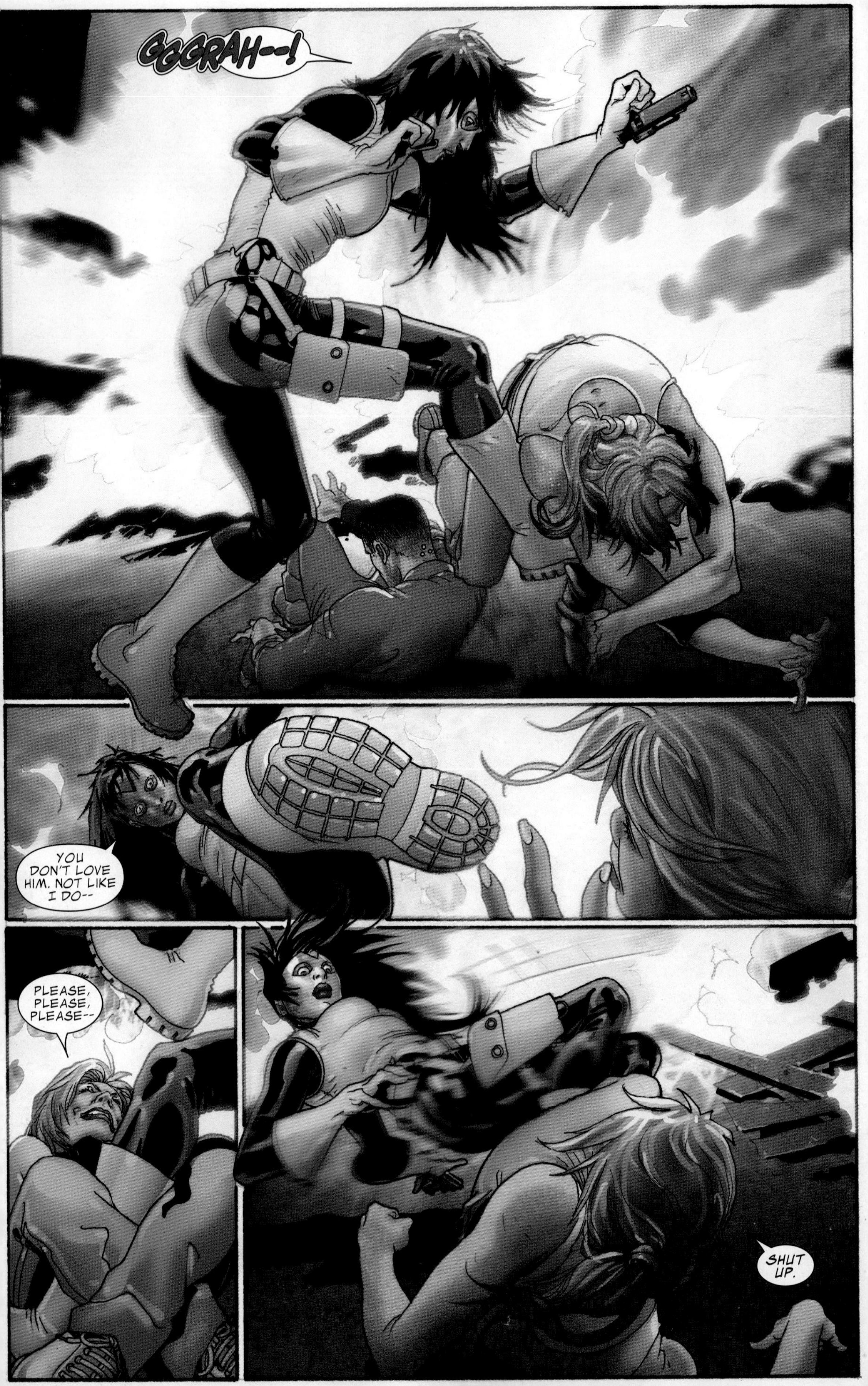
GGGRAH--!
YOU DON'T LOVE HIM. NOT LIKE I DO--
PLEASE, PLEASE, PLEASE--
SHUT UP.

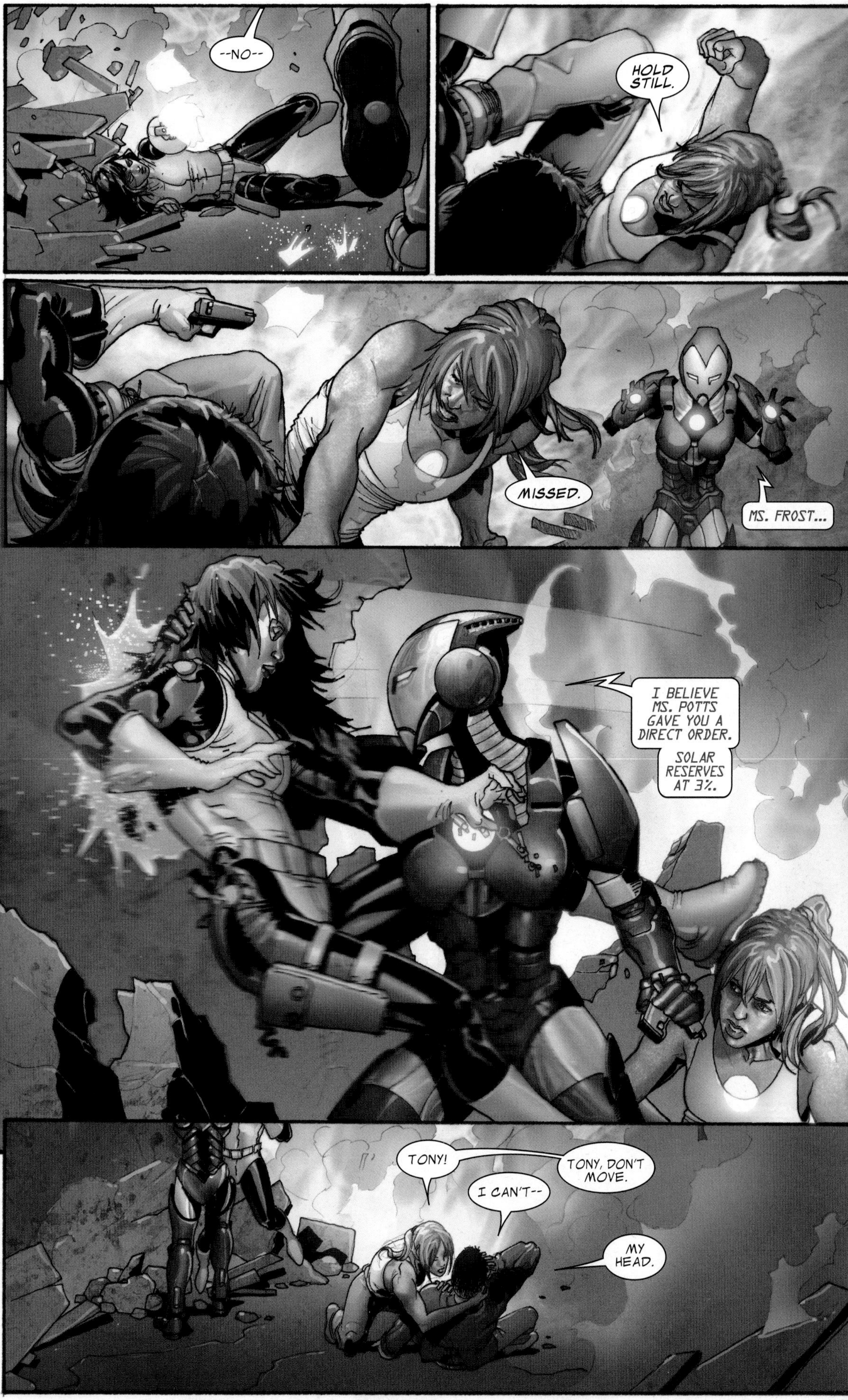
--NO--
HOLD STILL.
MISSED.
MS. FROST...
I BELIEVE MS. POTTS GAVE YOU A DIRECT ORDER.
SOLAR RESERVES AT 3%.
TONY!
TONY, DON'T MOVE.
I CAN'T--
MY HEAD.

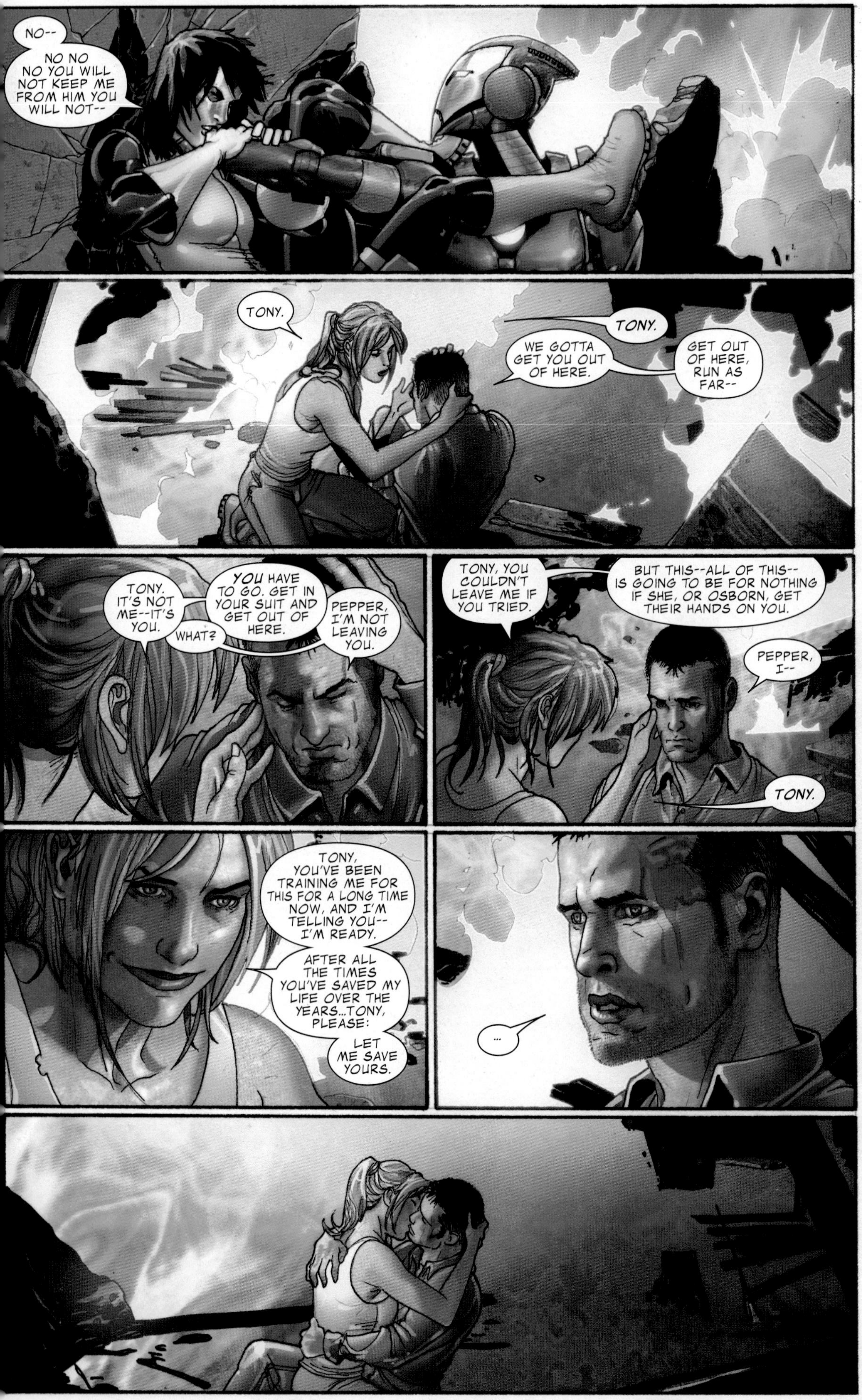

NO--
NO NO NO YOU WILL NOT KEEP ME FROM HIM YOU WILL NOT--
TONY.
TONY.
WE GOTTA GET YOU OUT OF HERE.
GET OUT OF HERE, RUN AS FAR--
TONY. IT'S NOT ME--IT'S YOU.
WHAT?
YOU HAVE TO GO. GET IN YOUR SUIT AND GET OUT OF HERE.
PEPPER, I'M NOT LEAVING YOU.
TONY, YOU COULDN'T LEAVE ME IF YOU TRIED.
BUT THIS--ALL OF THIS--IS GOING TO BE FOR NOTHING IF SHE, OR OSBORN, GET THEIR HANDS ON YOU.
PEPPER, I--
TONY.
TONY, YOU'VE BEEN TRAINING ME FOR THIS FOR A LONG TIME NOW, AND I'M TELLING YOU--I'M READY.
AFTER ALL THE TIMES YOU'VE SAVED MY LIFE OVER THE YEARS...TONY, PLEASE:
LET ME SAVE YOURS.
...

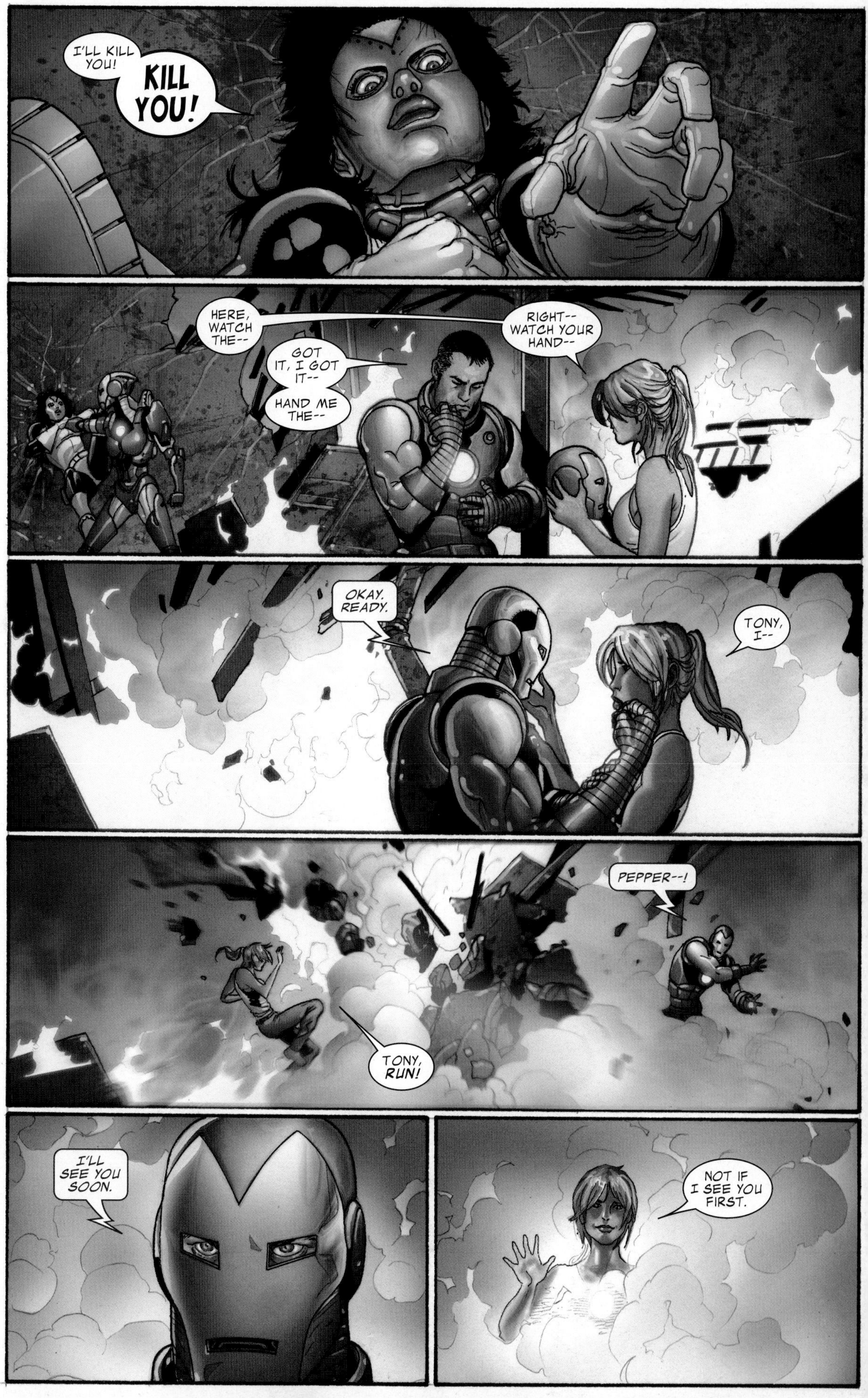
I'LL KILL YOU!
KILL YOU!
HERE, WATCH THE--
RIGHT-- WATCH YOUR HAND--
GOT IT, I GOT IT--
HAND ME THE--
OKAY. READY.
TONY, I--
PEPPER--!
TONY, RUN!
I'LL SEE YOU SOON.
NOT IF I SEE YOU FIRST.

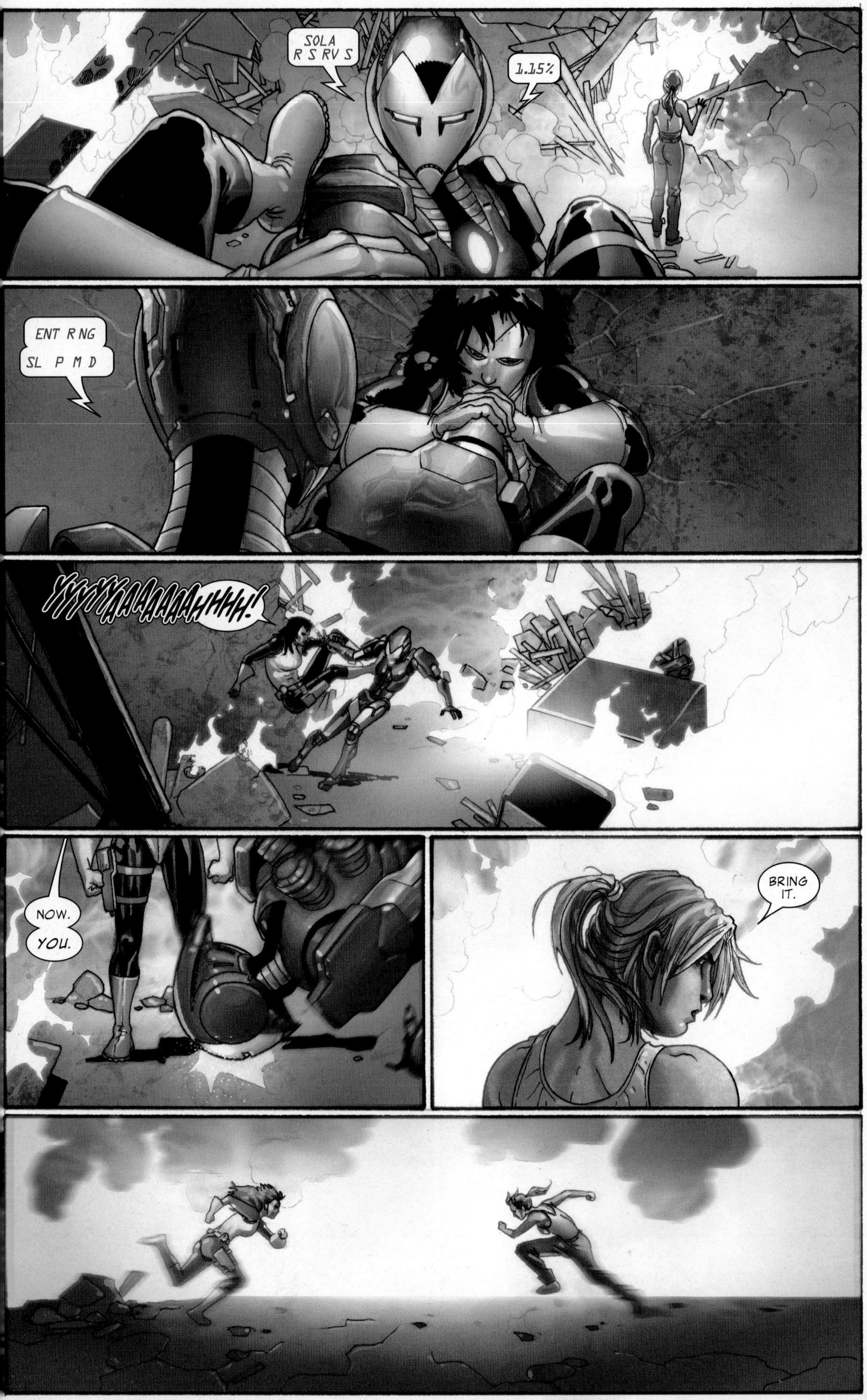
SOLA
R S RV S
1.15%
ENT R NG
SL P M D
YYYYYAAAAAAAHHHH!
NOW.
YOU.
BRING IT.

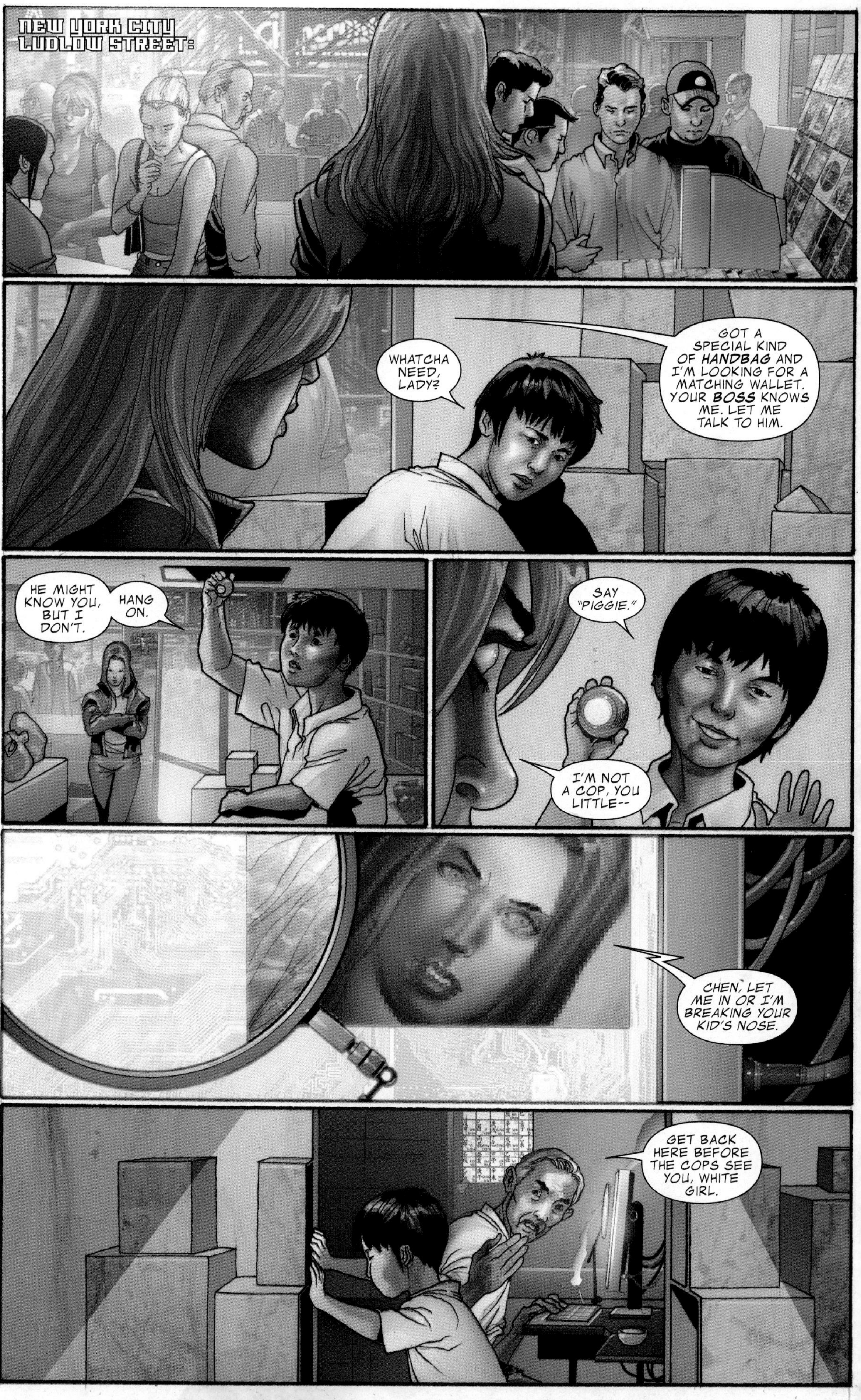
NEW YORK CITY
LUDLOW STREET:
WHATCHA NEED, LADY?
GOT A SPECIAL KIND OF HANDBAG AND I'M LOOKING FOR A MATCHING WALLET. YOUR BOSS KNOWS ME. LET ME TALK TO HIM.
HE MIGHT KNOW YOU, BUT I DON'T.
HANG ON.
SAY "PIGGIE."
I'M NOT A COP, YOU LITTLE--
CHEN, LET ME IN OR I'M BREAKING YOUR KID'S NOSE.
GET BACK HERE BEFORE THE COPS SEE YOU, WHITE GIRL.

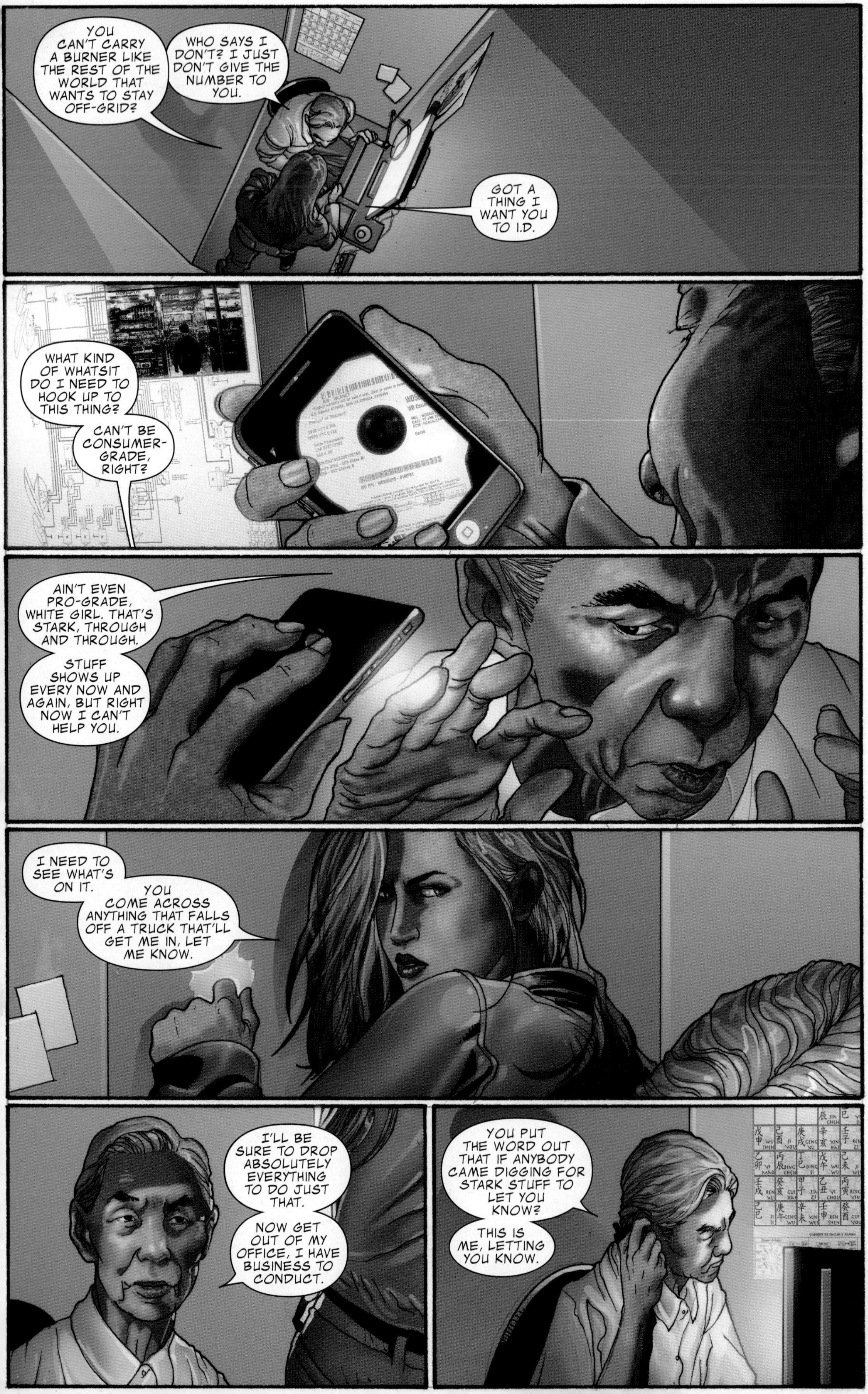
YOU CAN'T CARRY A BURNER LIKE THE REST OF THE WORLD THAT WANTS TO STAY OFF-GRID?
WHO SAYS I DON'T? I JUST DON'T GIVE THE NUMBER TO YOU.
GOT A THING I WANT YOU TO I.D.
WHAT KIND OF WHATSIT DO I NEED TO HOOK UP TO THIS THING?
CAN'T BE CONSUMER-GRADE, RIGHT?
AIN'T EVEN PRO-GRADE, WHITE GIRL. THAT'S STARK, THROUGH AND THROUGH.
STUFF SHOWS UP EVERY NOW AND AGAIN, BUT RIGHT NOW I CAN'T HELP YOU.
I NEED TO SEE WHAT'S ON IT.
YOU COME ACROSS ANYTHING THAT FALLS OFF A TRUCK THAT'LL GET ME IN, LET ME KNOW.
I'LL BE SURE TO DROP ABSOLUTELY EVERYTHING TO DO JUST THAT.
NOW GET OUT OF MY OFFICE, I HAVE BUSINESS TO CONDUCT.
YOU PUT THE WORD OUT THAT IF ANYBODY CAME DIGGING FOR STARK STUFF TO LET YOU KNOW?
THIS IS ME, LETTING YOU KNOW.

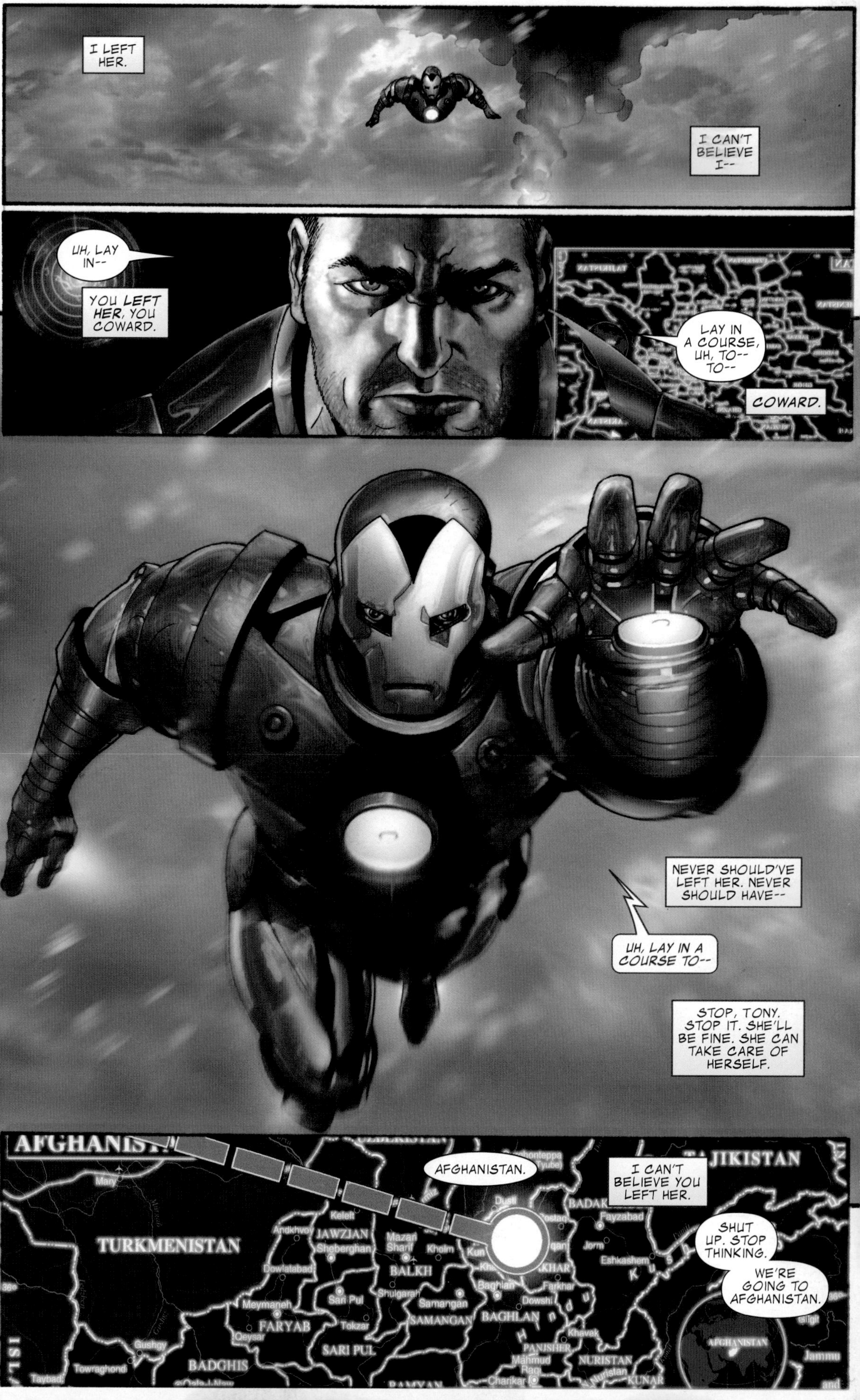

I LEFT HER.
I CAN'T BELIEVE I--
UH, LAY IN--
YOU LEFT HER, YOU COWARD.
LAY IN A COURSE, UH, TO-- TO--
COWARD.
NEVER SHOULD'VE LEFT HER. NEVER SHOULD HAVE--
UH, LAY IN A COURSE TO--
STOP, TONY. STOP IT. SHE'LL BE FINE. SHE CAN TAKE CARE OF HERSELF.
AFGHANISTAN.
I CAN'T BELIEVE YOU LEFT HER.
SHUT UP. STOP THINKING.
WE'RE GOING TO AFGHANISTAN.
TURKMENISTAN
TAJIKISTAN
JAWZJAN
BALKH
FARYAB
SAMANGAN
BAGHLAN
SARI PUL
BADGHIS
NURISTAN
KUNAR

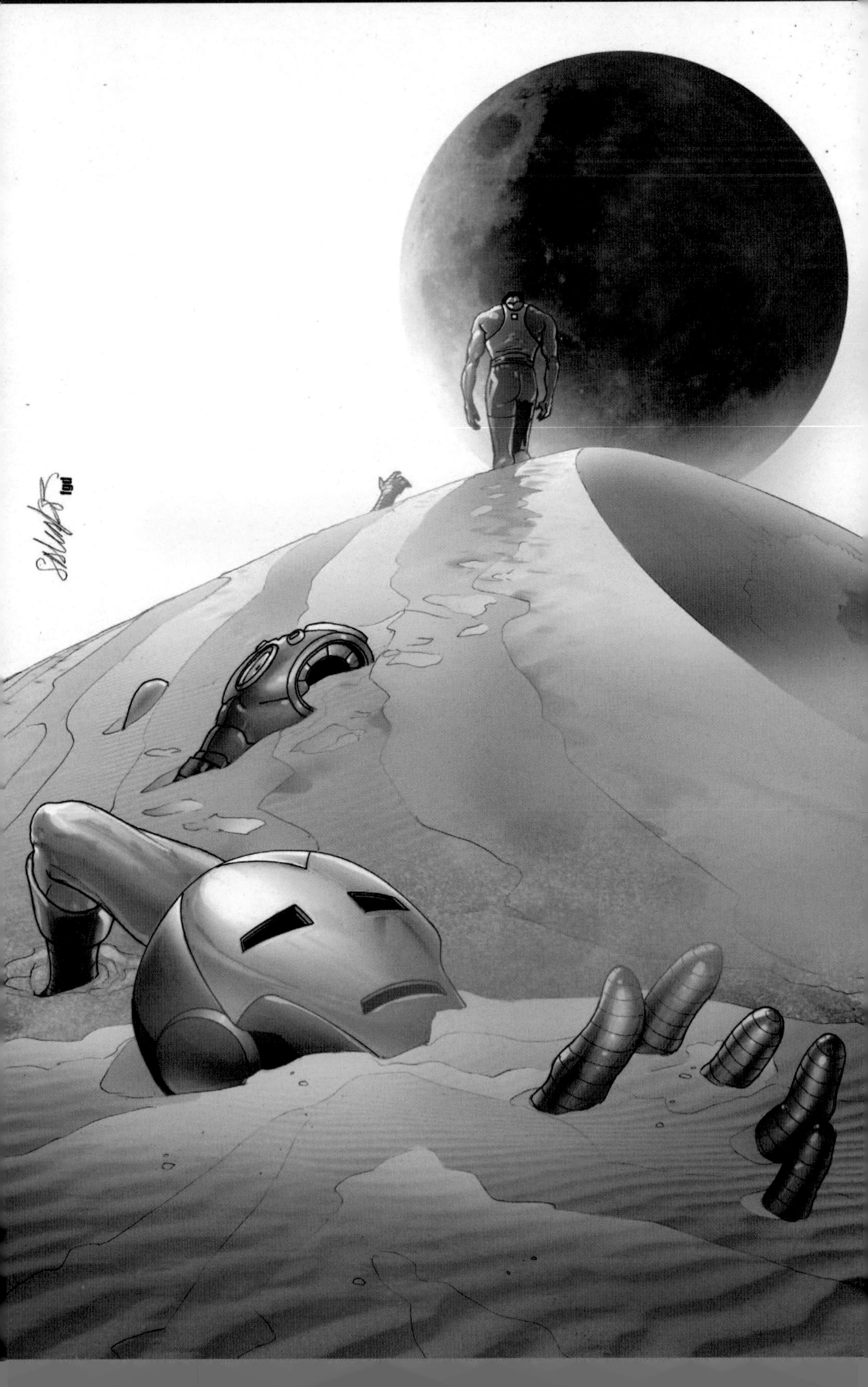

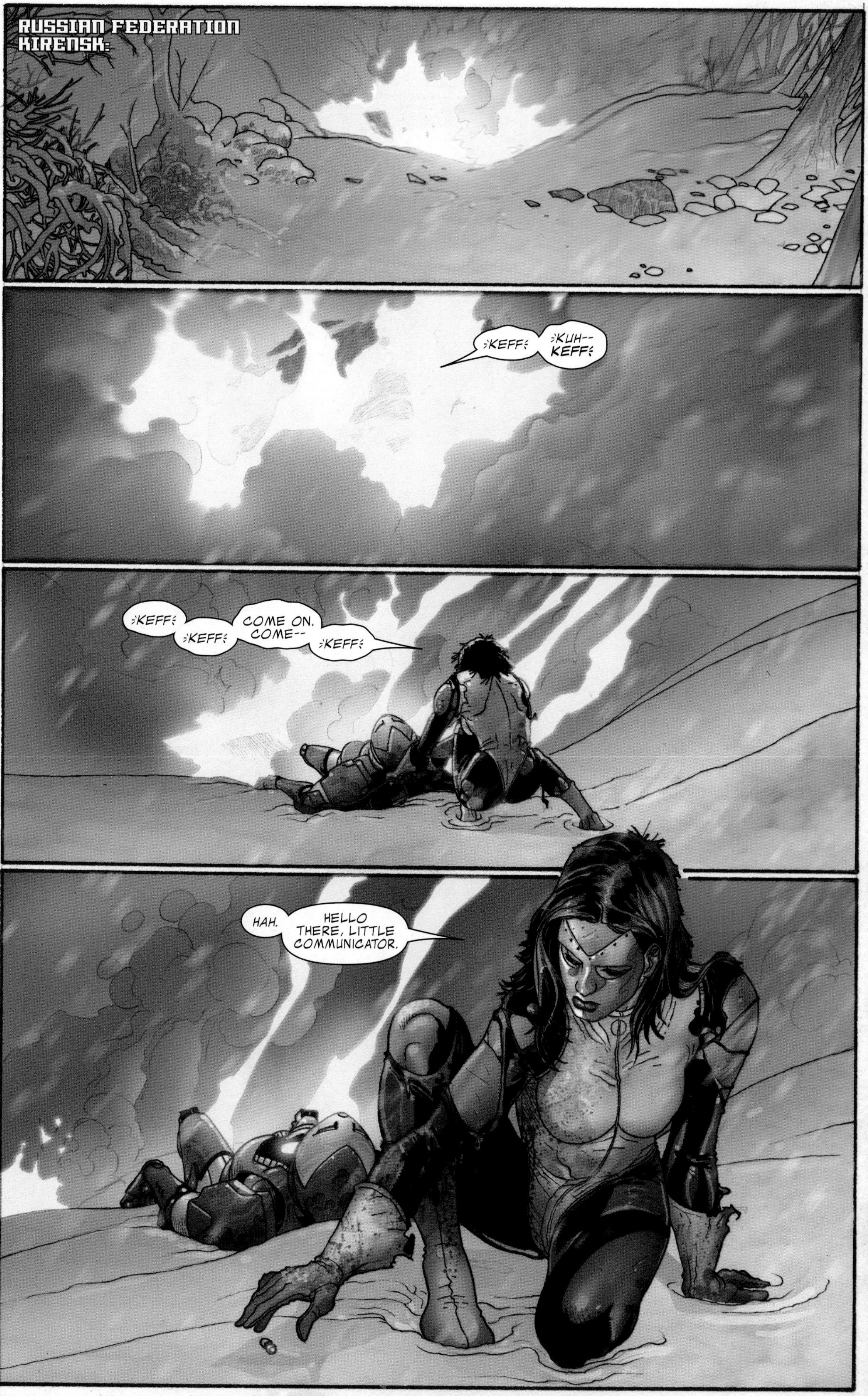
RUSSIAN FEDERATION
KIRENSK:
KEFF
KUH--
KEFF
KEFF
KEFF
COME ON.
COME--
KEFF
HAH.
HELLO
THERE, LITTLE
COMMUNICATOR.

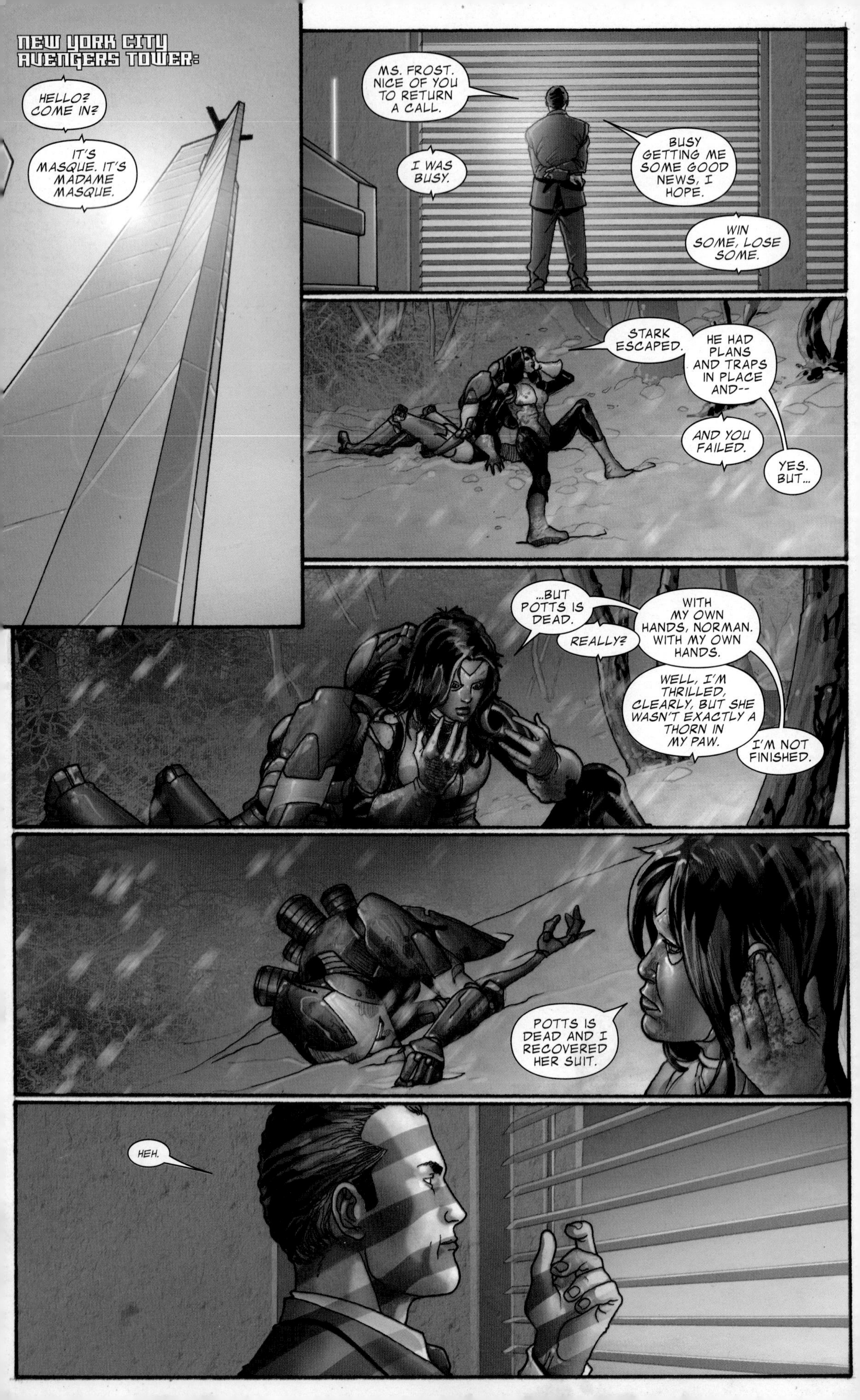
NEW YORK CITY
AVENGERS TOWER:
HELLO? COME IN?
IT'S MASQUE. IT'S MADAME MASQUE.
MS. FROST. NICE OF YOU TO RETURN A CALL.
I WAS BUSY.
BUSY GETTING ME SOME GOOD NEWS, I HOPE.
WIN SOME, LOSE SOME.
STARK ESCAPED.
HE HAD PLANS AND TRAPS IN PLACE AND--
AND YOU FAILED.
YES. BUT...
...BUT POTTS IS DEAD.
REALLY?
WITH MY OWN HANDS, NORMAN. WITH MY OWN HANDS.
WELL, I'M THRILLED, CLEARLY, BUT SHE WASN'T EXACTLY A THORN IN MY PAW.
I'M NOT FINISHED.
POTTS IS DEAD AND I RECOVERED HER SUIT.
HEH.

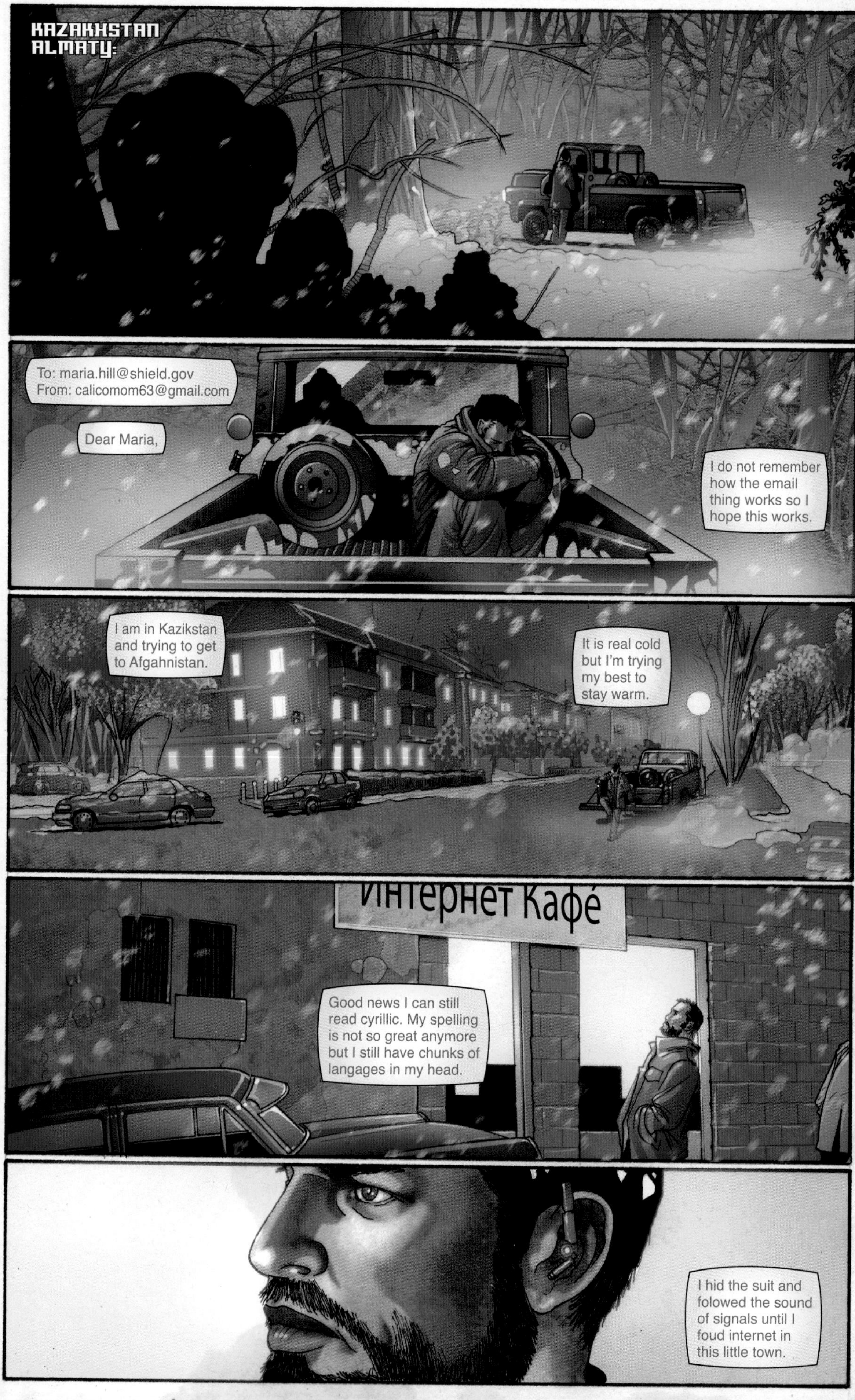
KAZAKHSTAN
ALMATY:
To: maria.hill@shield.gov
From: calicomom63@gmail.com
Dear Maria,
I do not remember how the email thing works so I hope this works.
I am in Kazikstan and trying to get to Afgahnistan.
It is real cold but I'm trying my best to stay warm.
Интернет Кафé
Good news I can still read cyrillic. My spelling is not so great anymore but I still have chunks of langages in my head.
I hid the suit and folowed the sound of signals until I foud internet in this little town.

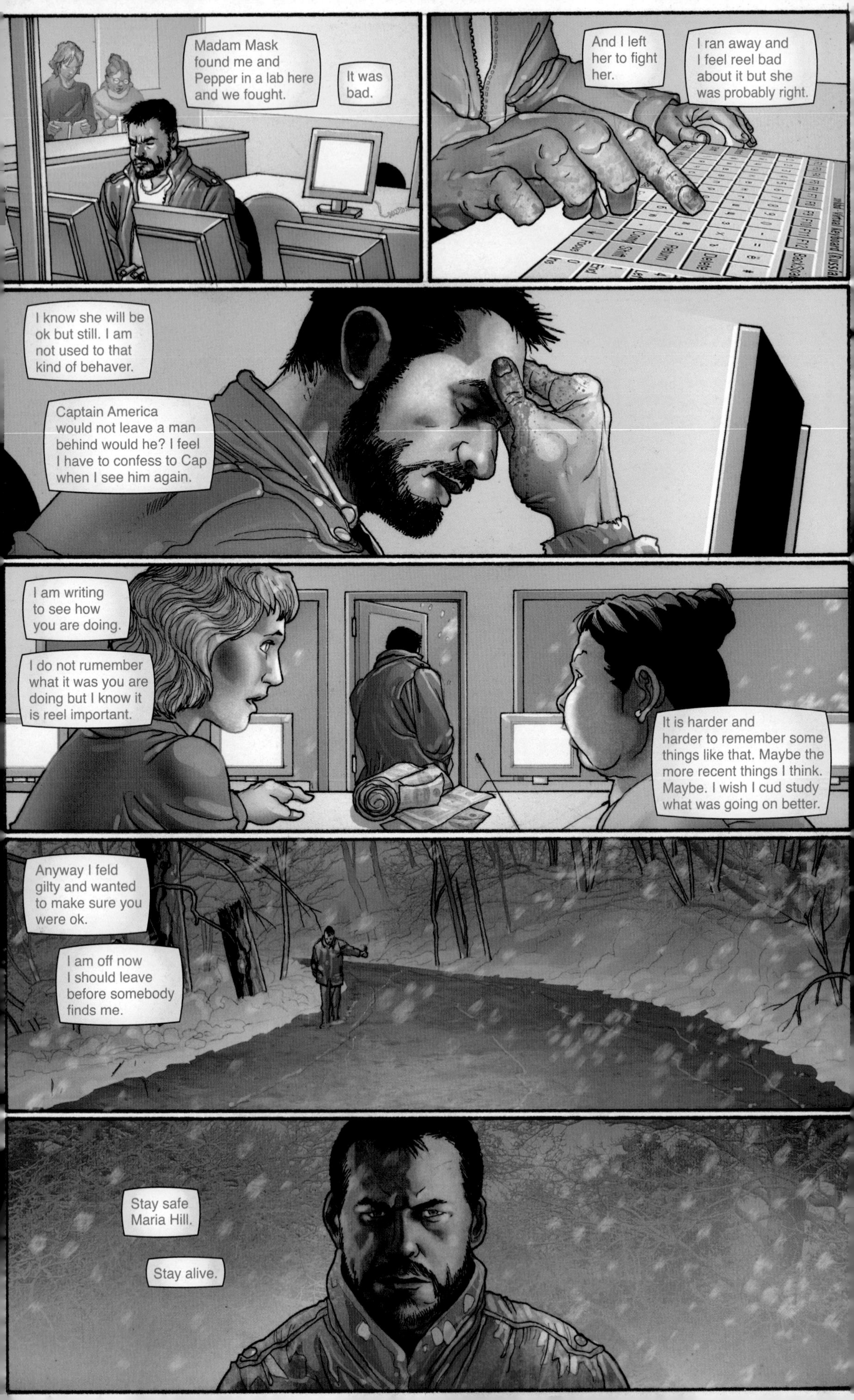
Madam Mask found me and Pepper in a lab here and we fought.
It was bad.
And I left her to fight her.
I ran away and I feel reel bad about it but she was probably right.
I know she will be ok but still. I am not used to that kind of behaver.
Captain America would not leave a man behind would he? I feel I have to confess to Cap when I see him again.
I am writing to see how you are doing.
I do not rumember what it was you are doing but I know it is reel important.
It is harder and harder to remember some things like that. Maybe the more recent things I think. Maybe. I wish I cud study what was going on better.
Anyway I feld gilty and wanted to make sure you were ok.
I am off now I should leave before somebody finds me.
Stay safe Maria Hill.
Stay alive.

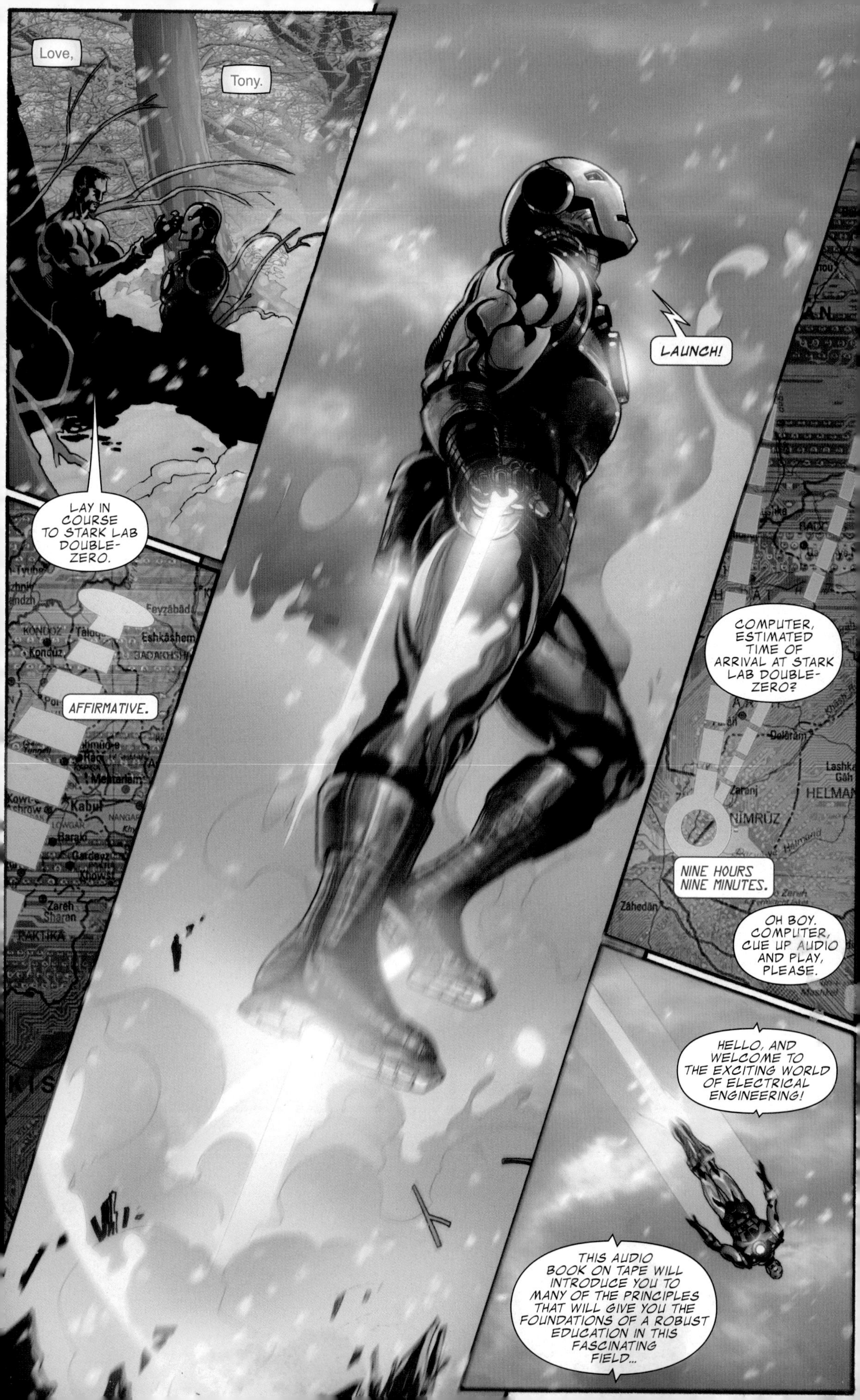
Love,
Tony.
LAY IN COURSE TO STARK LAB DOUBLE-ZERO.
AFFIRMATIVE.
LAUNCH!
COMPUTER, ESTIMATED TIME OF ARRIVAL AT STARK LAB DOUBLE-ZERO?
NINE HOURS NINE MINUTES.
OH BOY. COMPUTER, CUE UP AUDIO AND PLAY, PLEASE.
HELLO, AND WELCOME TO THE EXCITING WORLD OF ELECTRICAL ENGINEERING!
THIS AUDIO BOOK ON TAPE WILL INTRODUCE YOU TO MANY OF THE PRINCIPLES THAT WILL GIVE YOU THE FOUNDATIONS OF A ROBUST EDUCATION IN THIS FASCINATING FIELD...

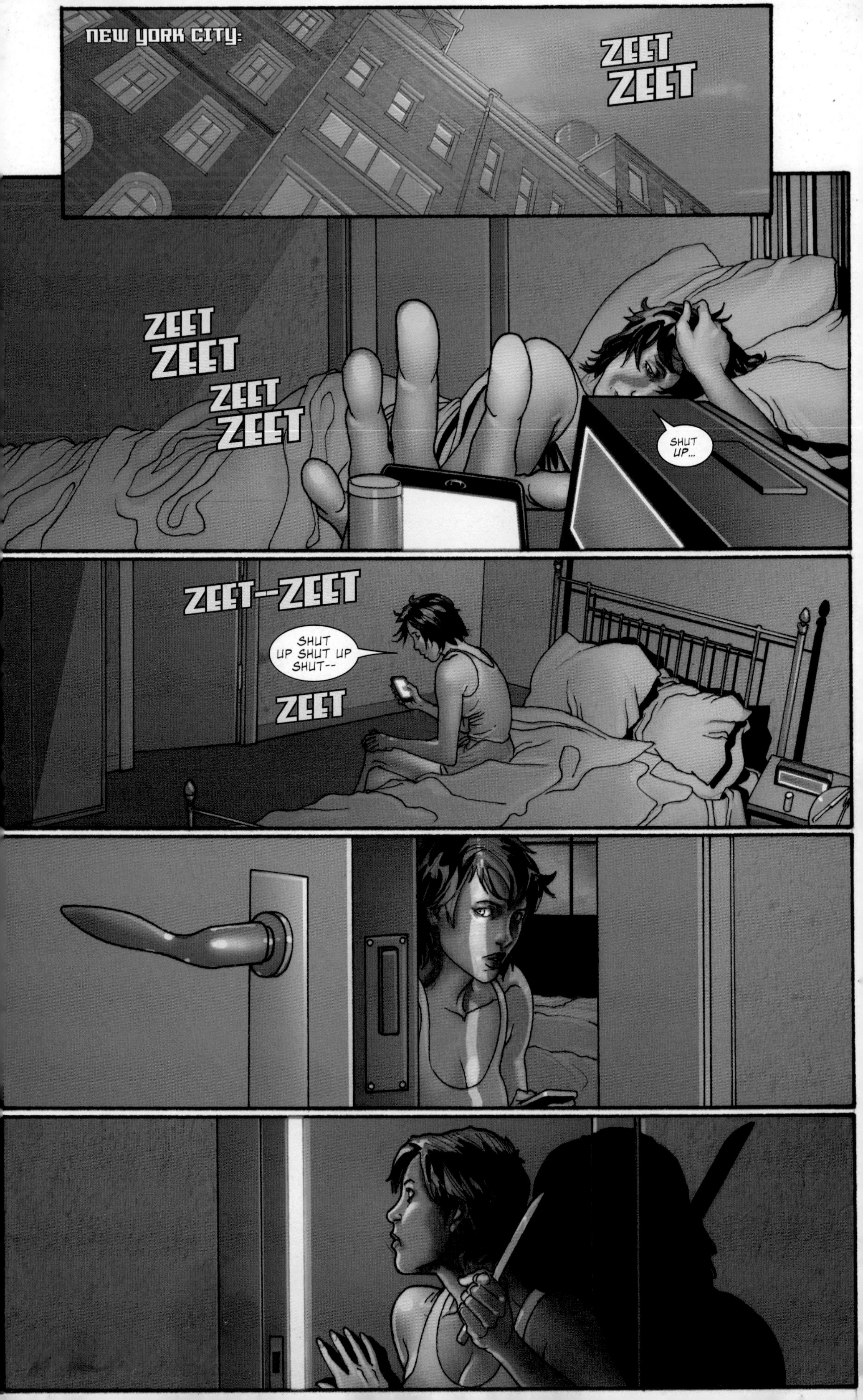
NEW YORK CITY:
ZEET
ZEET
ZEET
ZEET
ZEET
ZEET
SHUT UP...
ZEET--ZEET
SHUT UP SHUT UP SHUT--
ZEET

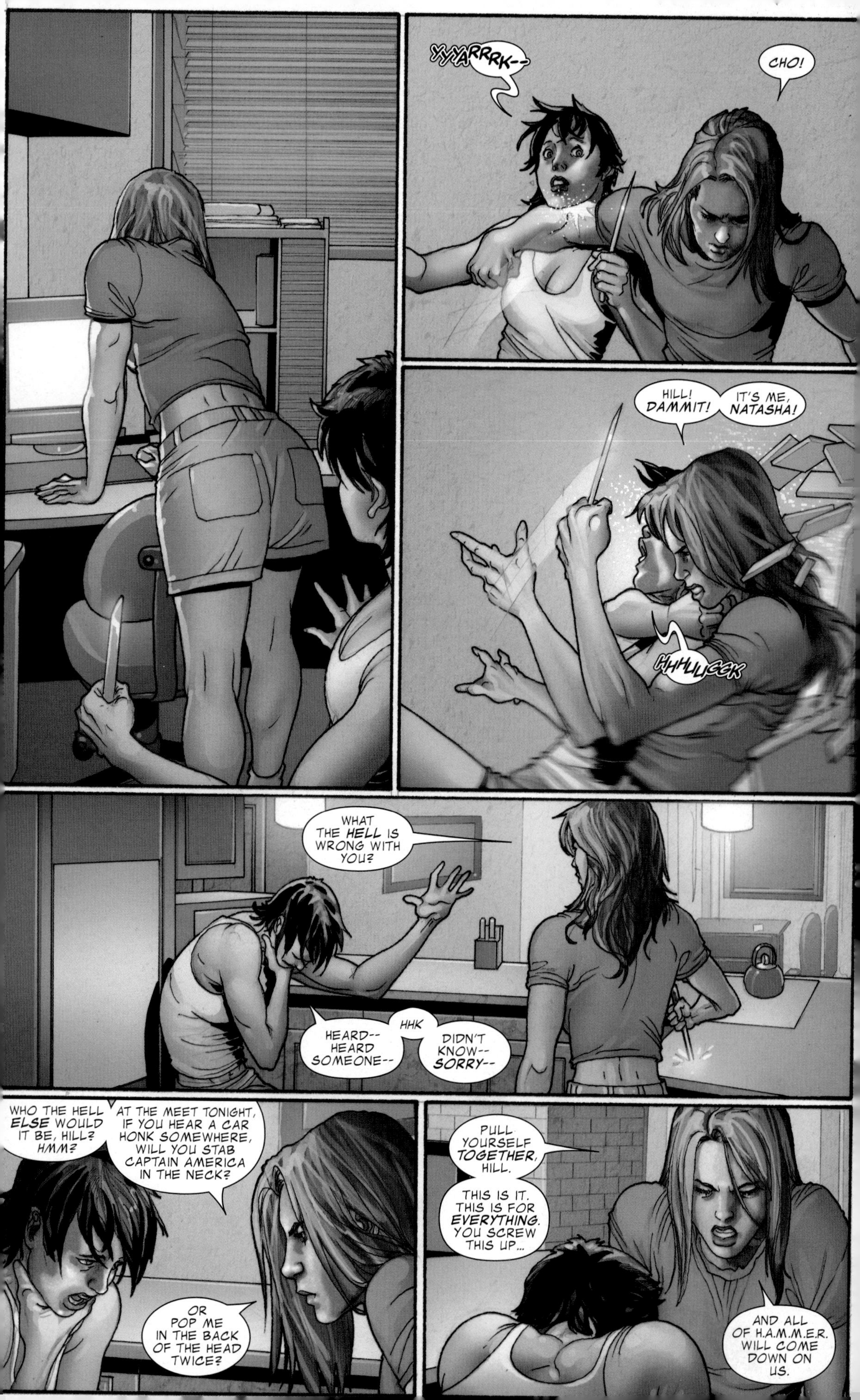
YYYARRRK--
CHO!
HILL! DAMMIT!
IT'S ME, NATASHA!
HHHUUGGK
WHAT THE HELL IS WRONG WITH YOU?
HEARD-- HEARD SOMEONE--
HHK
DIDN'T KNOW-- SORRY--
WHO THE HELL ELSE WOULD IT BE, HILL? HMM?
AT THE MEET TONIGHT, IF YOU HEAR A CAR HONK SOMEWHERE, WILL YOU STAB CAPTAIN AMERICA IN THE NECK?
OR POP ME IN THE BACK OF THE HEAD TWICE?
PULL YOURSELF TOGETHER, HILL.
THIS IS IT. THIS IS FOR EVERYTHING. YOU SCREW THIS UP...
AND ALL OF H.A.M.M.E.R. WILL COME DOWN ON US.

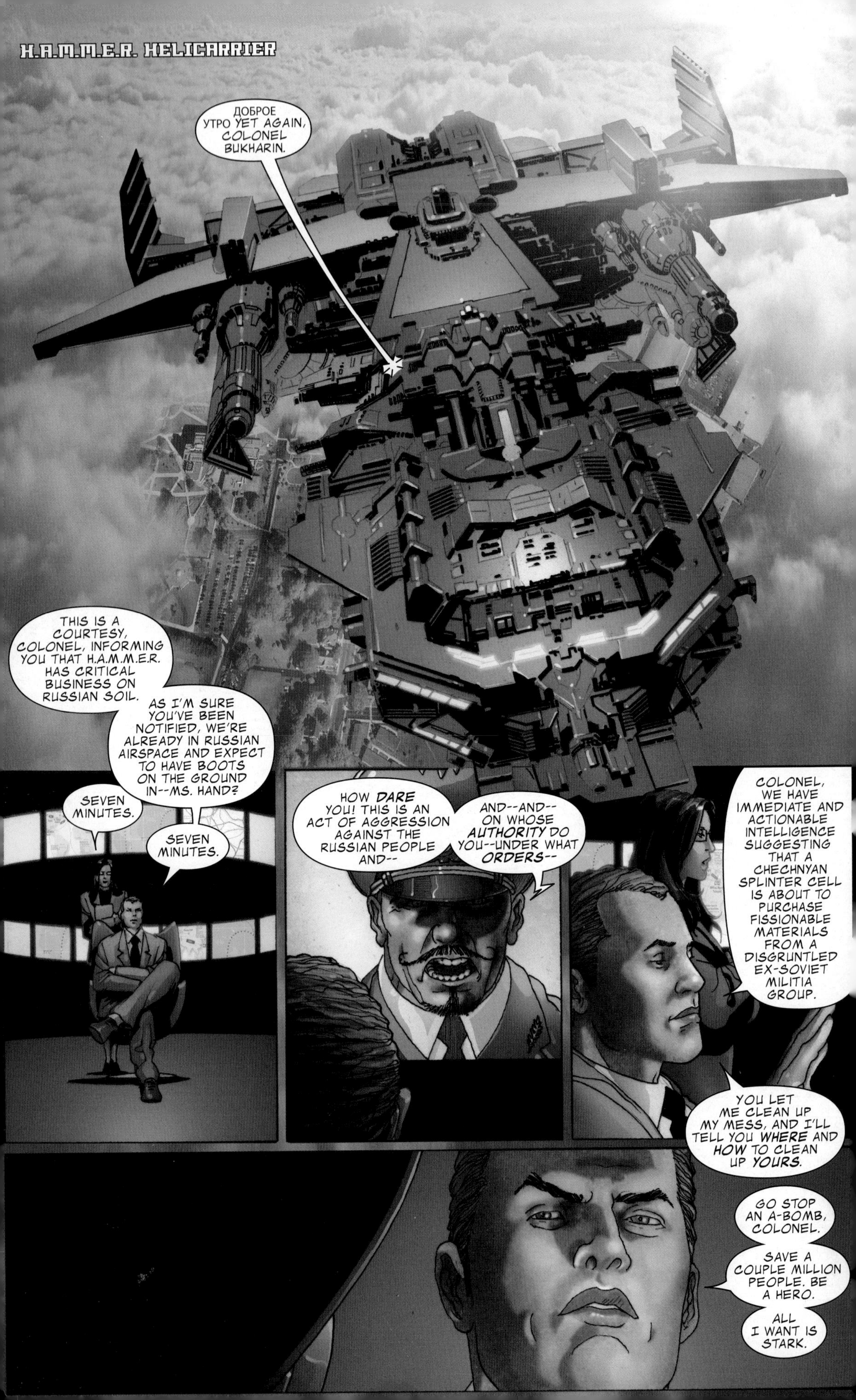
H.A.M.M.E.R. HELICARRIER
ДОБРОЕ УТРО YET AGAIN, COLONEL BUKHARIN.
THIS IS A COURTESY, COLONEL, INFORMING YOU THAT H.A.M.M.E.R. HAS CRITICAL BUSINESS ON RUSSIAN SOIL.
AS I'M SURE YOU'VE BEEN NOTIFIED, WE'RE ALREADY IN RUSSIAN AIRSPACE AND EXPECT TO HAVE BOOTS ON THE GROUND IN--MS. HAND?
SEVEN MINUTES.
SEVEN MINUTES.
HOW DARE YOU! THIS IS AN ACT OF AGGRESSION AGAINST THE RUSSIAN PEOPLE AND--
AND--AND-- ON WHOSE AUTHORITY DO YOU--UNDER WHAT ORDERS--
COLONEL, WE HAVE IMMEDIATE AND ACTIONABLE INTELLIGENCE SUGGESTING THAT A CHECHNYAN SPLINTER CELL IS ABOUT TO PURCHASE FISSIONABLE MATERIALS FROM A DISGRUNTLED EX-SOVIET MILITIA GROUP.
YOU LET ME CLEAN UP MY MESS, AND I'LL TELL YOU WHERE AND HOW TO CLEAN UP YOURS.
GO STOP AN A-BOMB, COLONEL.
SAVE A COUPLE MILLION PEOPLE. BE A HERO.
ALL I WANT IS STARK.

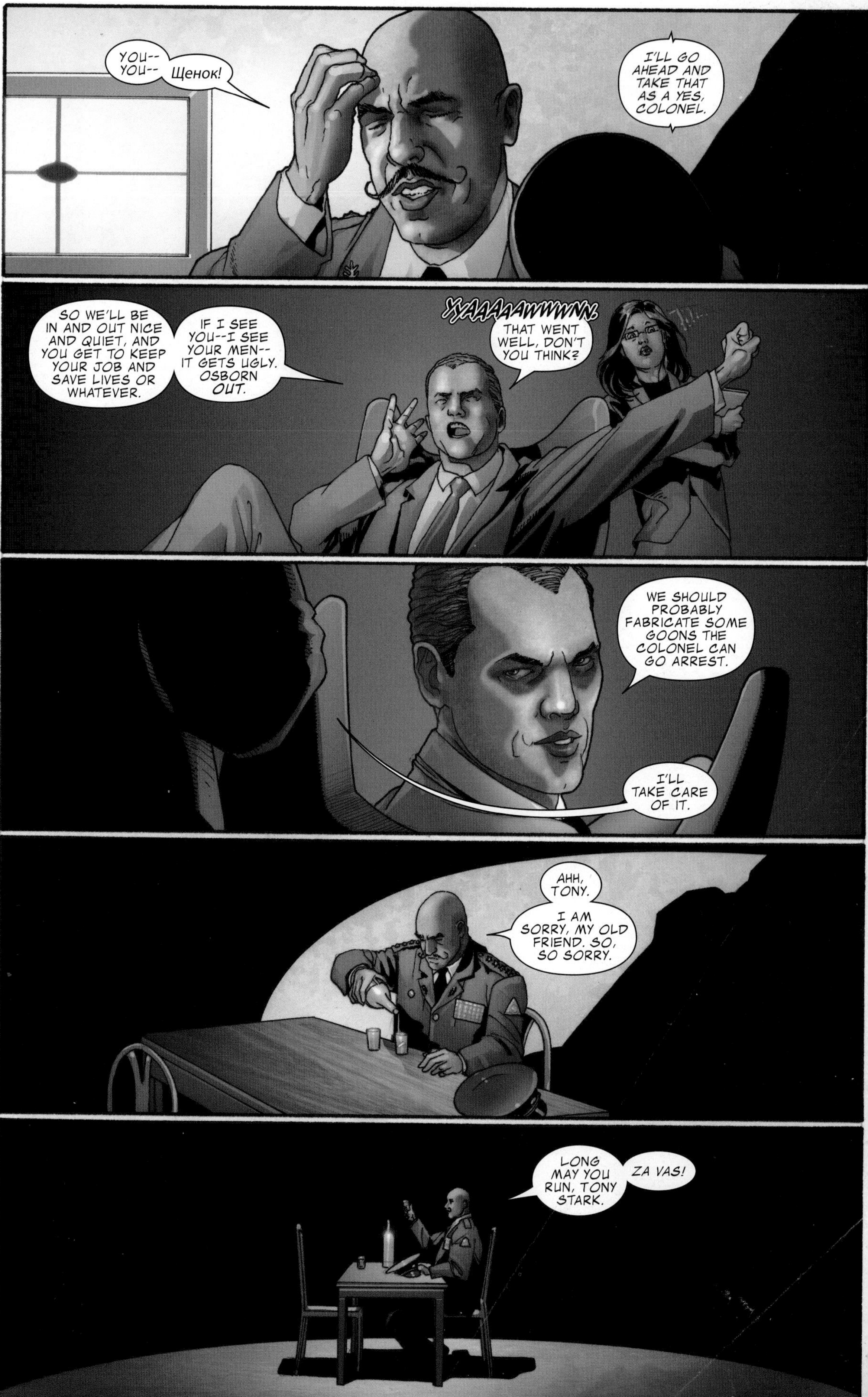
YOU-- YOU--
Щенок!
I'LL GO AHEAD AND TAKE THAT AS A YES, COLONEL.
SO WE'LL BE IN AND OUT NICE AND QUIET, AND YOU GET TO KEEP YOUR JOB AND SAVE LIVES OR WHATEVER.
IF I SEE YOU--I SEE YOUR MEN--IT GETS UGLY. OSBORN OUT.
YYAAAAAAWWWNN.
THAT WENT WELL, DON'T YOU THINK?
WE SHOULD PROBABLY FABRICATE SOME GOONS THE COLONEL CAN GO ARREST.
I'LL TAKE CARE OF IT.
AHH, TONY.
I AM SORRY, MY OLD FRIEND. SO, SO SORRY.
LONG MAY YOU RUN, TONY STARK.
ZA VAS!

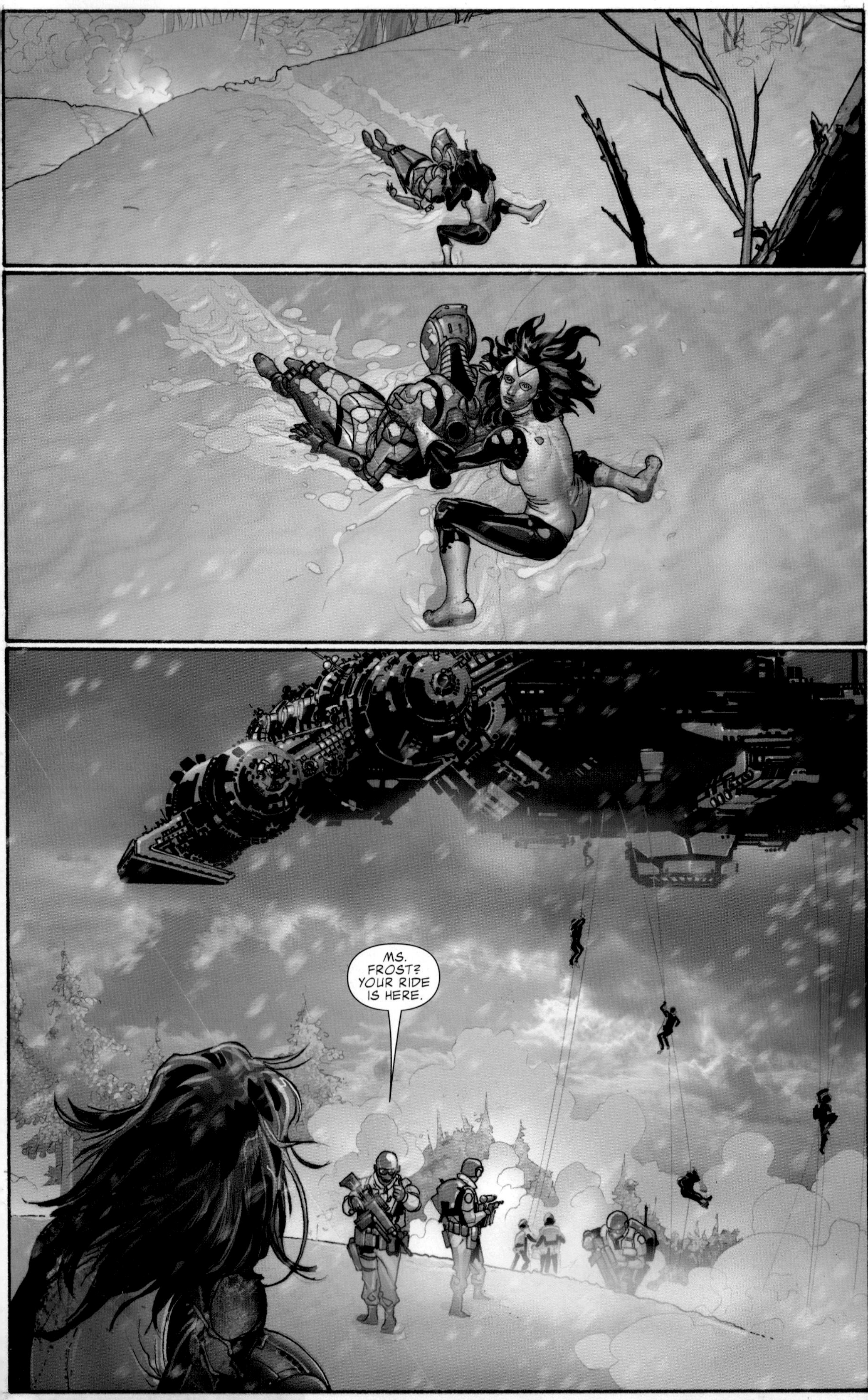
MS. FROST? YOUR RIDE IS HERE.

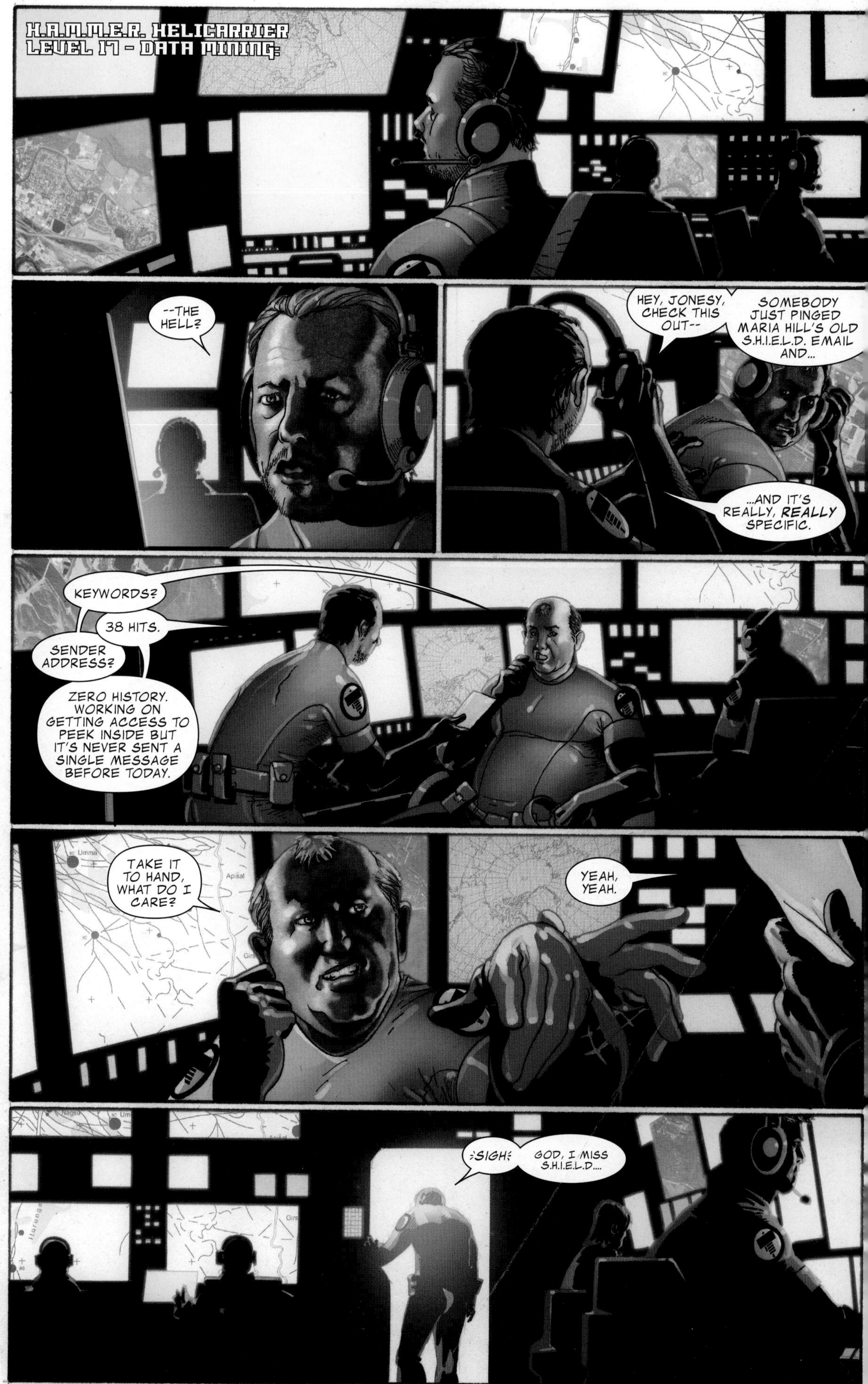
H.A.M.M.E.R. HELICARRIER
LEVEL 17 - DATA MINING:
--THE HELL?
HEY, JONESY, CHECK THIS OUT--
SOMEBODY JUST PINGED MARIA HILL'S OLD S.H.I.E.L.D. EMAIL AND...
...AND IT'S REALLY, REALLY SPECIFIC.
KEYWORDS?
38 HITS.
SENDER ADDRESS?
ZERO HISTORY. WORKING ON GETTING ACCESS TO PEEK INSIDE BUT IT'S NEVER SENT A SINGLE MESSAGE BEFORE TODAY.
TAKE IT TO HAND, WHAT DO I CARE?
YEAH, YEAH.
SIGH
GOD, I MISS S.H.I.E.L.D....

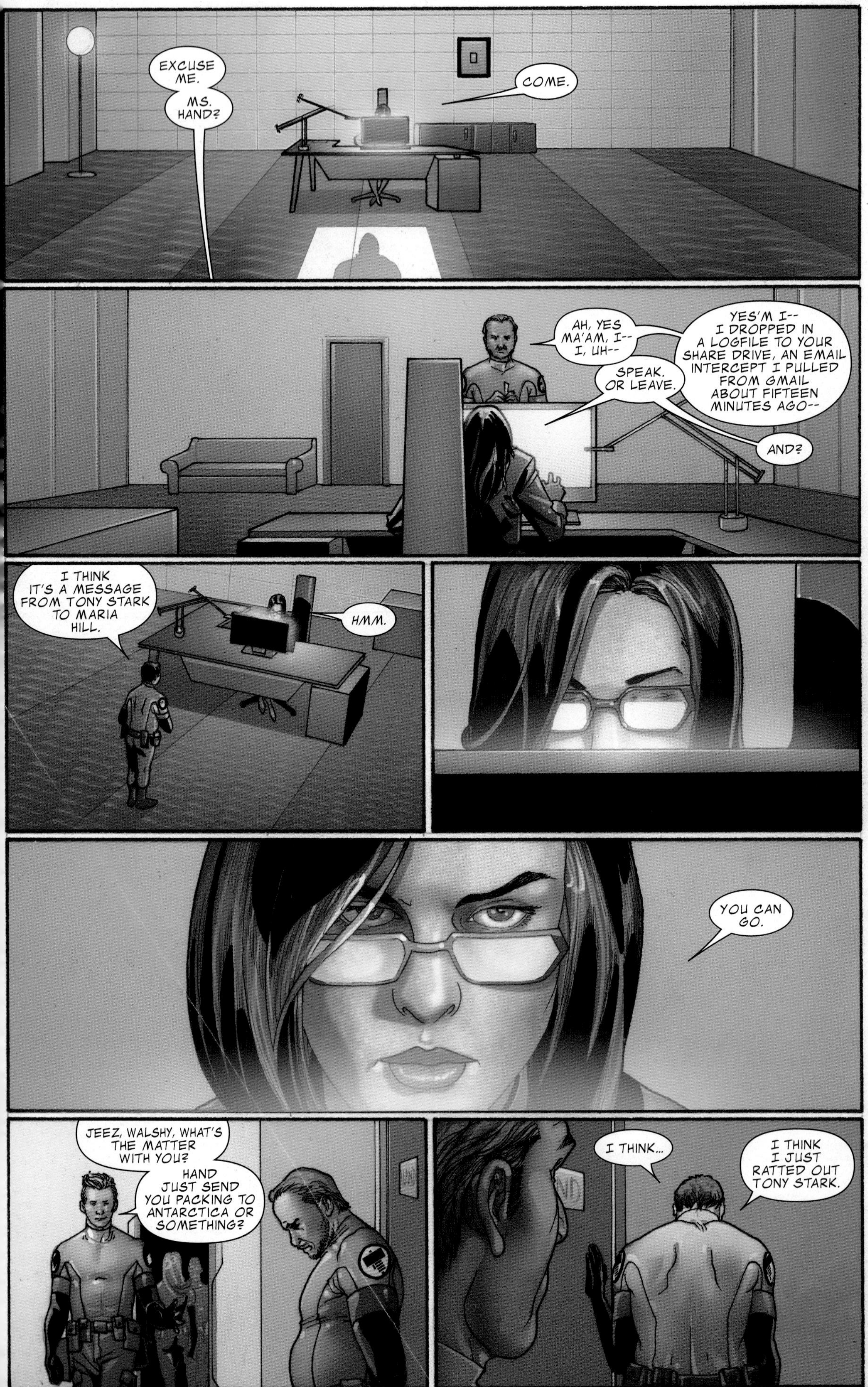
EXCUSE ME.
MS. HAND?
COME.
AH, YES MA'AM, I-- I, UH--
SPEAK. OR LEAVE.
YES'M I-- I DROPPED IN A LOGFILE TO YOUR SHARE DRIVE, AN EMAIL INTERCEPT I PULLED FROM GMAIL ABOUT FIFTEEN MINUTES AGO--
AND?
I THINK IT'S A MESSAGE FROM TONY STARK TO MARIA HILL.
HMM.
YOU CAN GO.
JEEZ, WALSHY, WHAT'S THE MATTER WITH YOU?
HAND JUST SEND YOU PACKING TO ANTARCTICA OR SOMETHING?
I THINK...
I THINK I JUST RATTED OUT TONY STARK.

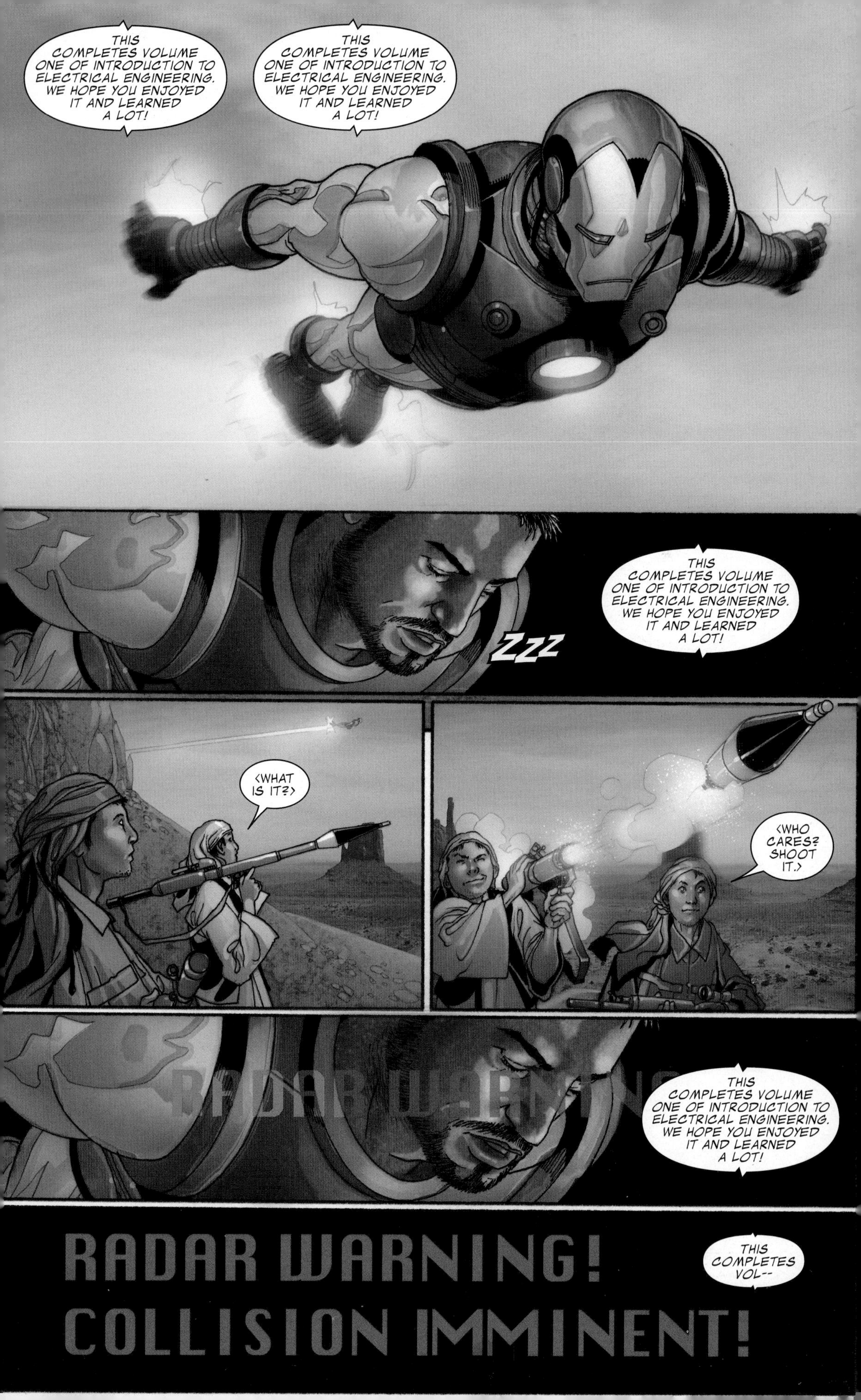
THIS COMPLETES VOLUME ONE OF INTRODUCTION TO ELECTRICAL ENGINEERING. WE HOPE YOU ENJOYED IT AND LEARNED A LOT!
THIS COMPLETES VOLUME ONE OF INTRODUCTION TO ELECTRICAL ENGINEERING. WE HOPE YOU ENJOYED IT AND LEARNED A LOT!
THIS COMPLETES VOLUME ONE OF INTRODUCTION TO ELECTRICAL ENGINEERING. WE HOPE YOU ENJOYED IT AND LEARNED A LOT!
ZZZ
<WHAT IS IT?>
<WHO CARES? SHOOT IT.>
THIS COMPLETES VOLUME ONE OF INTRODUCTION TO ELECTRICAL ENGINEERING. WE HOPE YOU ENJOYED IT AND LEARNED A LOT!
RADAR WARNING!
COLLISION IMMINENT!
THIS COMPLETES VOL--

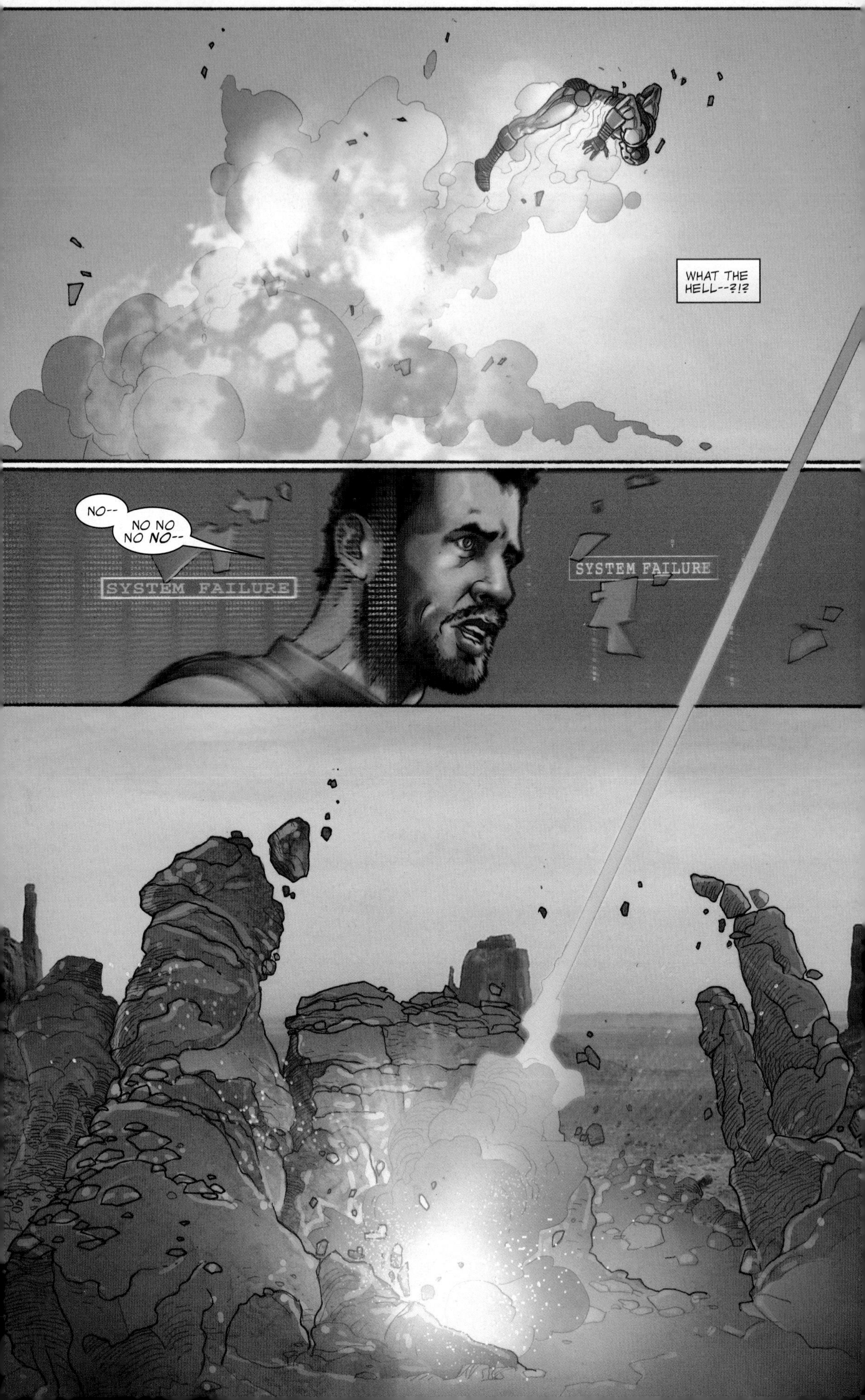
WHAT THE HELL--?!?
NO--
NO NO NO NO--
SYSTEM FAILURE
SYSTEM FAILURE

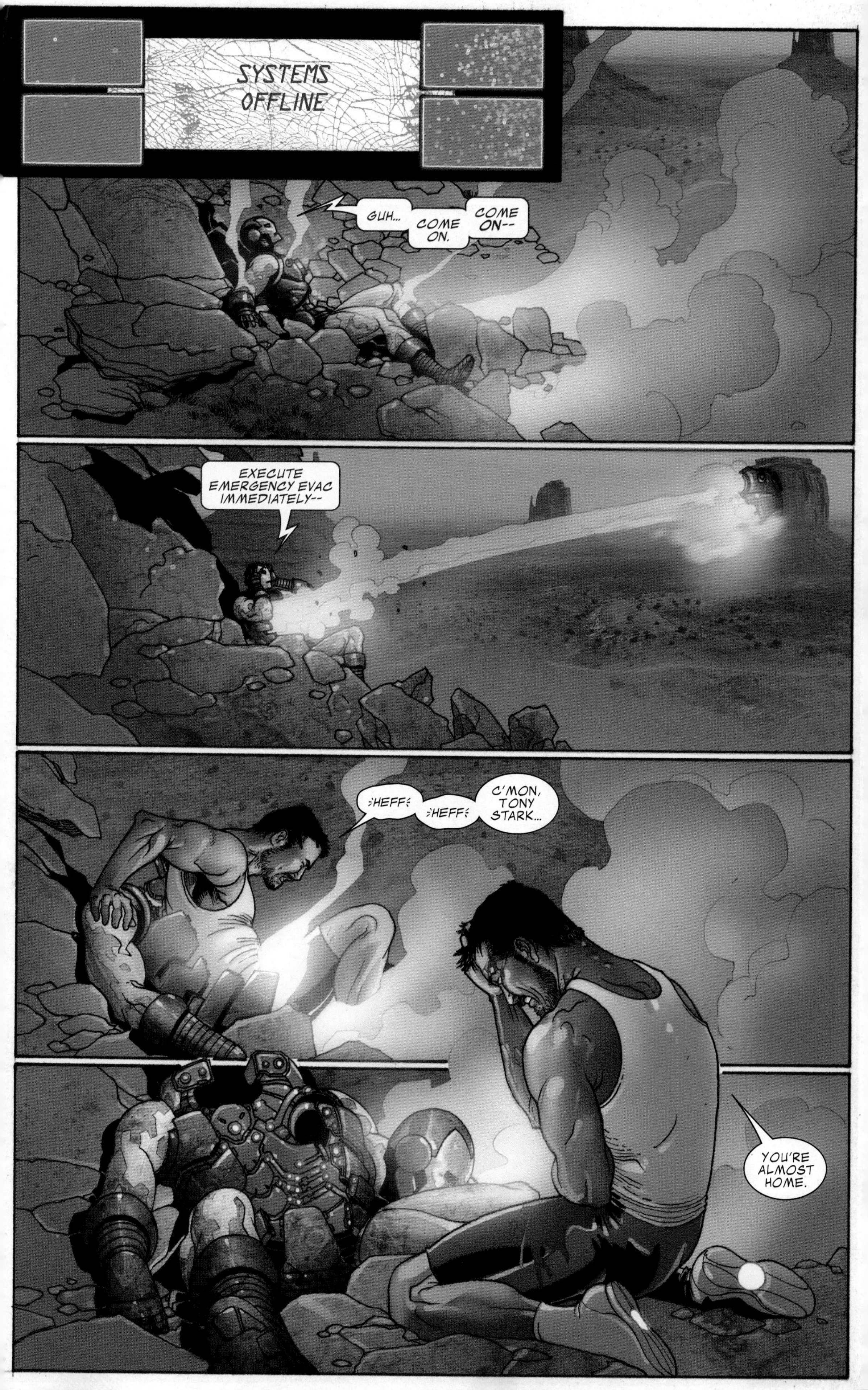
SYSTEMS OFFLINE
GUH...
COME ON.
COME ON--
EXECUTE EMERGENCY EVAC IMMEDIATELY--
HEFF
HEFF
C'MON, TONY STARK...
YOU'RE ALMOST HOME.

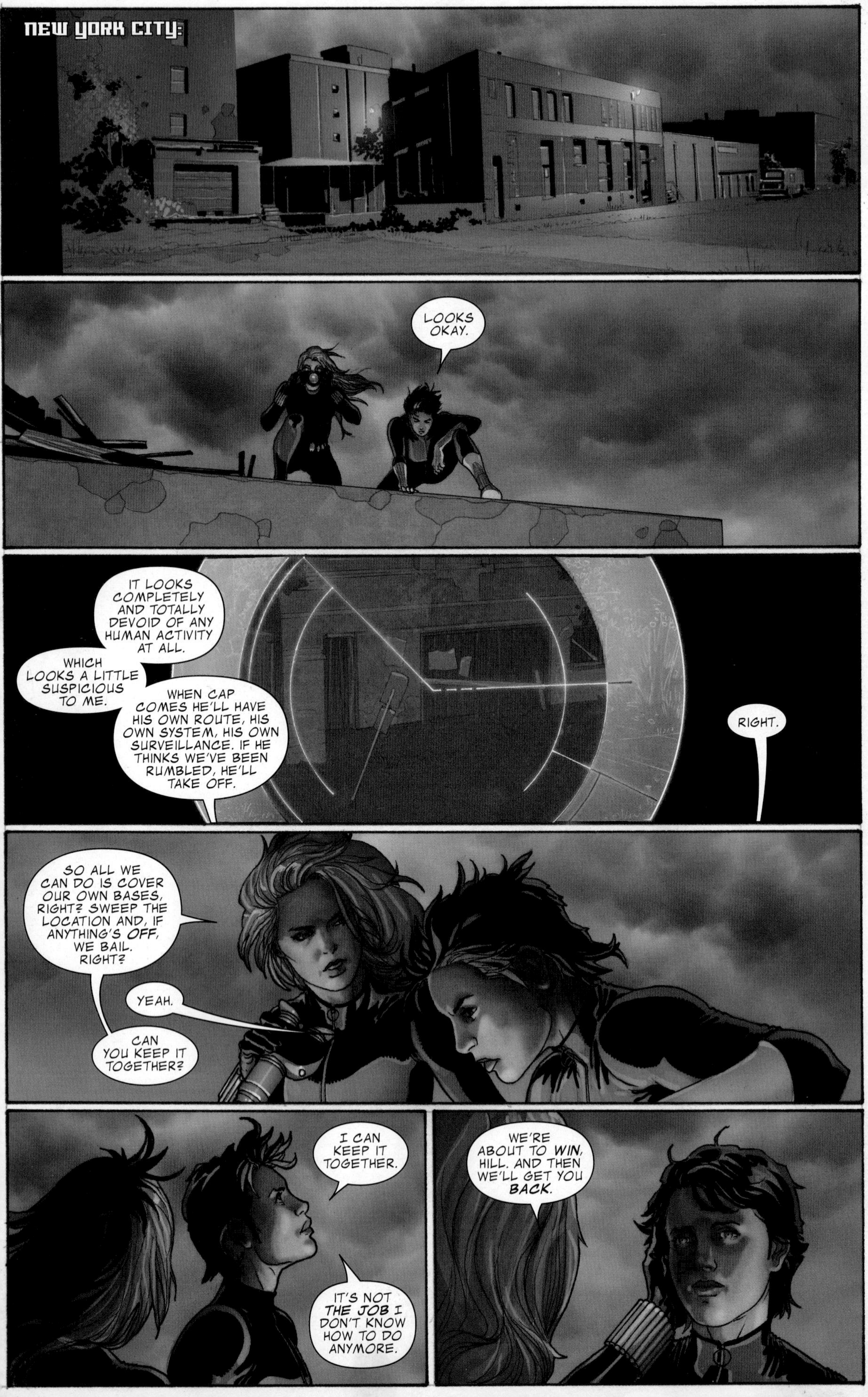
NEW YORK CITY:
LOOKS OKAY.
IT LOOKS COMPLETELY AND TOTALLY DEVOID OF ANY HUMAN ACTIVITY AT ALL.
WHICH LOOKS A LITTLE SUSPICIOUS TO ME.
WHEN CAP COMES HE'LL HAVE HIS OWN ROUTE, HIS OWN SYSTEM, HIS OWN SURVEILLANCE. IF HE THINKS WE'VE BEEN RUMBLED, HE'LL TAKE OFF.
RIGHT.
SO ALL WE CAN DO IS COVER OUR OWN BASES, RIGHT? SWEEP THE LOCATION AND, IF ANYTHING'S OFF, WE BAIL. RIGHT?
YEAH.
CAN YOU KEEP IT TOGETHER?
I CAN KEEP IT TOGETHER.
IT'S NOT THE JOB I DON'T KNOW HOW TO DO ANYMORE.
WE'RE ABOUT TO WIN, HILL. AND THEN WE'LL GET YOU BACK.

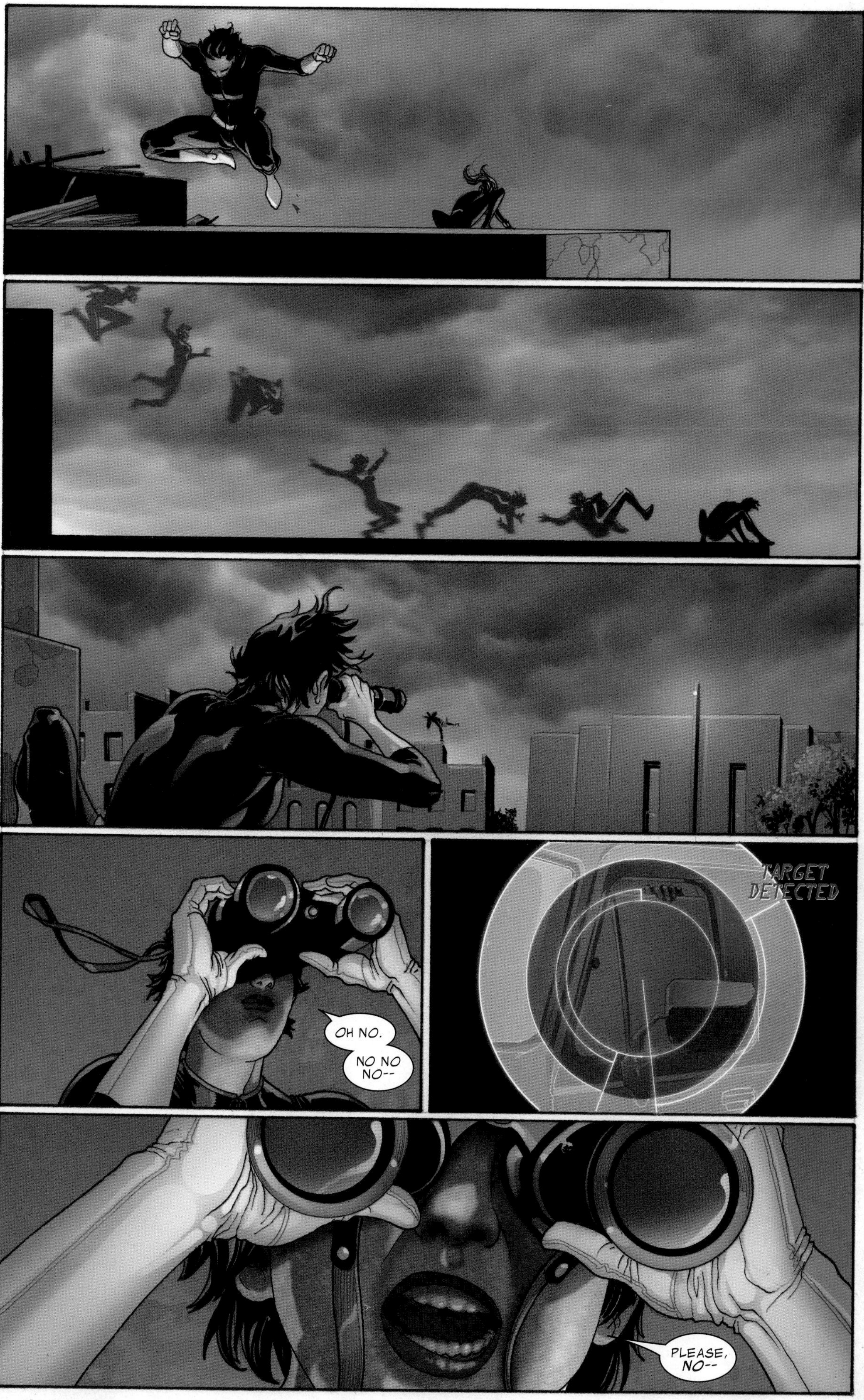
TARGET DETECTED
OH NO.
NO NO NO--
PLEASE, NO--

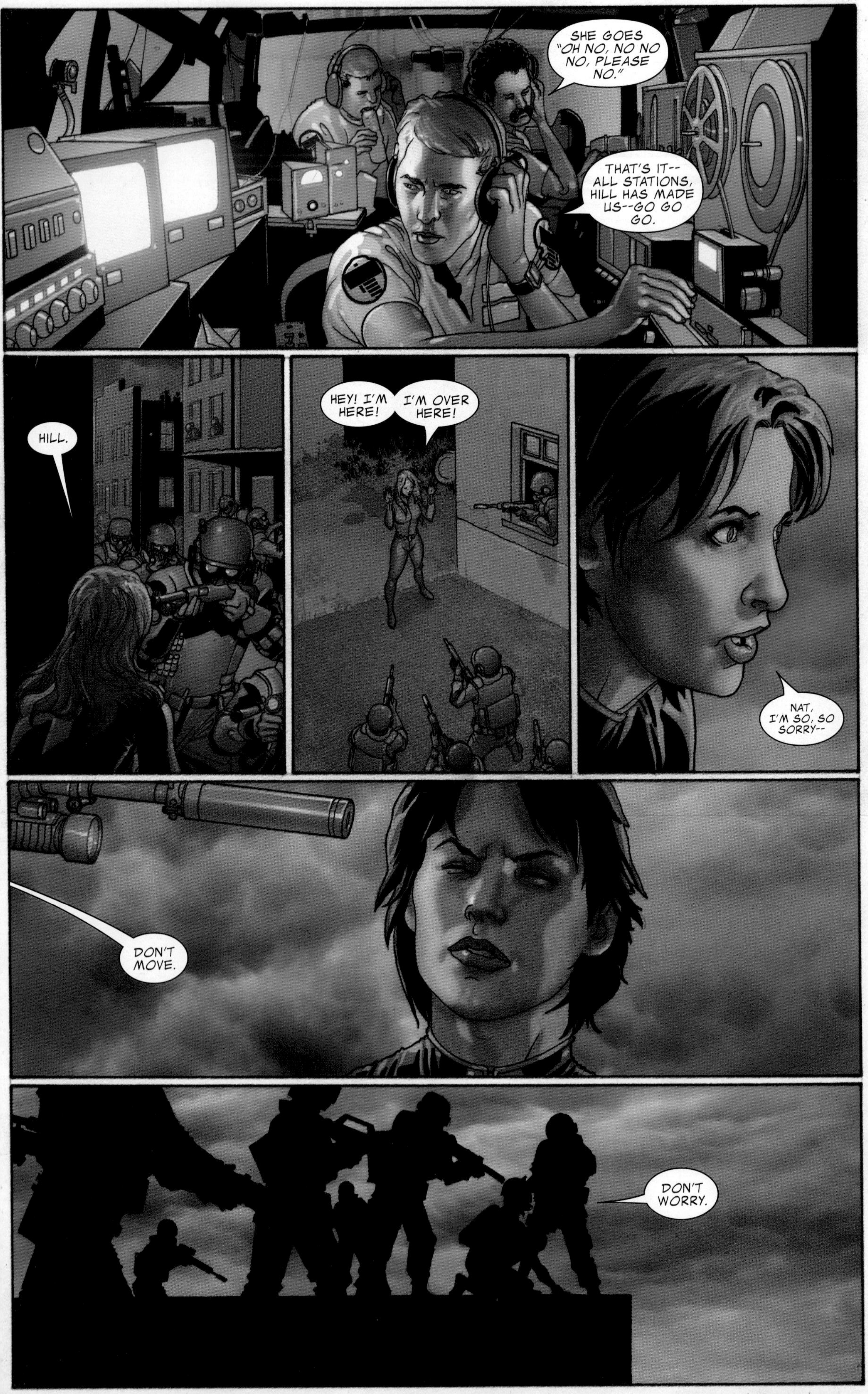
SHE GOES "OH NO, NO NO NO, PLEASE NO."
THAT'S IT-- ALL STATIONS, HILL HAS MADE US--GO GO GO.
HILL.
HEY! I'M HERE!
I'M OVER HERE!
NAT, I'M SO, SO SORRY--
DON'T MOVE.
DON'T WORRY.

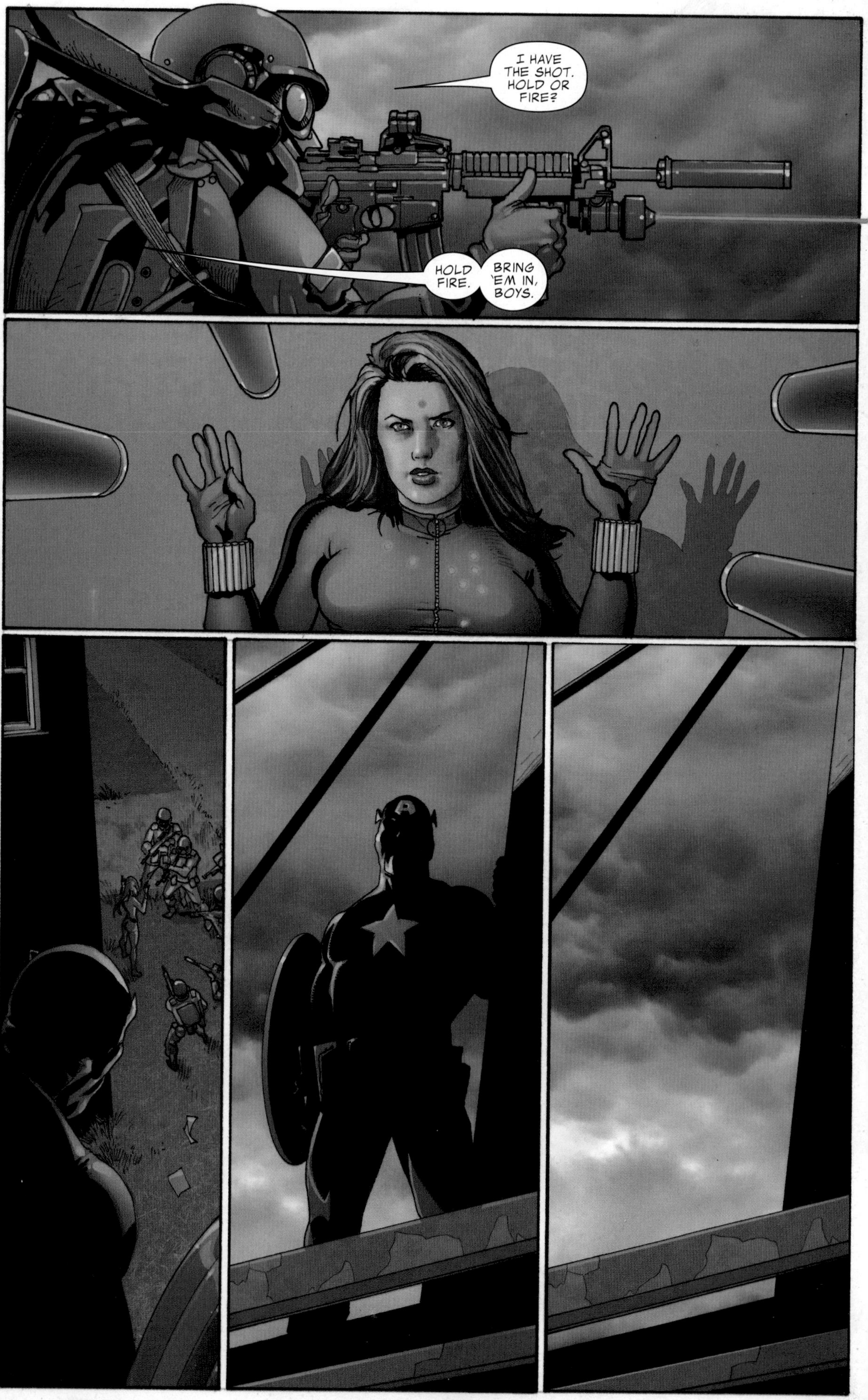
I HAVE THE SHOT. HOLD OR FIRE?
HOLD FIRE.
BRING 'EM IN, BOYS.

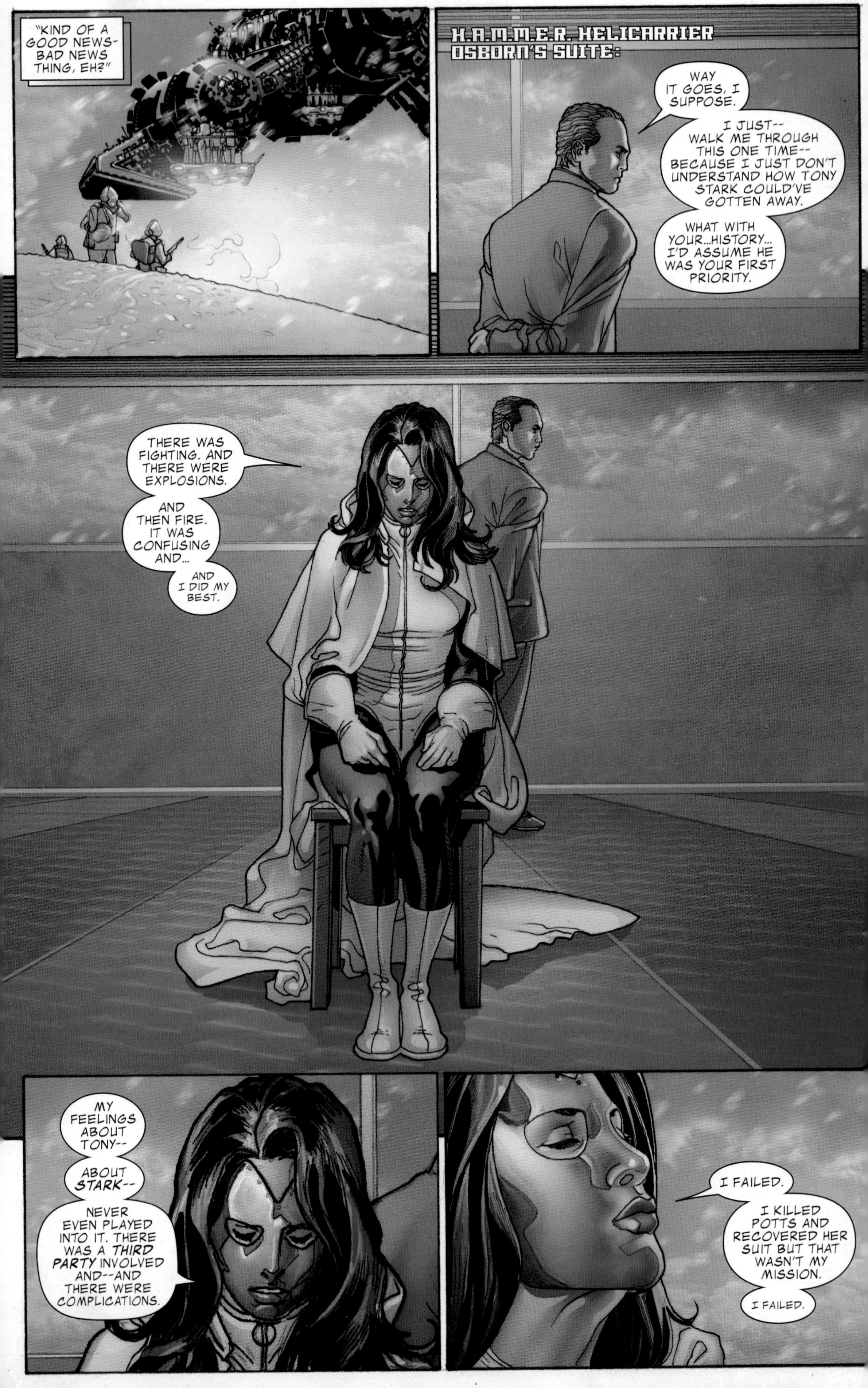
"KIND OF A GOOD NEWS-BAD NEWS THING, EH?"
H.A.M.M.E.R. HELICARRIER OSBORN'S SUITE:
WAY IT GOES, I SUPPOSE.
I JUST-- WALK ME THROUGH THIS ONE TIME-- BECAUSE I JUST DON'T UNDERSTAND HOW TONY STARK COULD'VE GOTTEN AWAY.
WHAT WITH YOUR...HISTORY... I'D ASSUME HE WAS YOUR FIRST PRIORITY.
THERE WAS FIGHTING. AND THERE WERE EXPLOSIONS.
AND THEN FIRE. IT WAS CONFUSING AND...
AND I DID MY BEST.
MY FEELINGS ABOUT TONY--
ABOUT STARK--
NEVER EVEN PLAYED INTO IT. THERE WAS A THIRD PARTY INVOLVED AND--AND THERE WERE COMPLICATIONS.
I FAILED.
I KILLED POTTS AND RECOVERED HER SUIT BUT THAT WASN'T MY MISSION.
I FAILED.

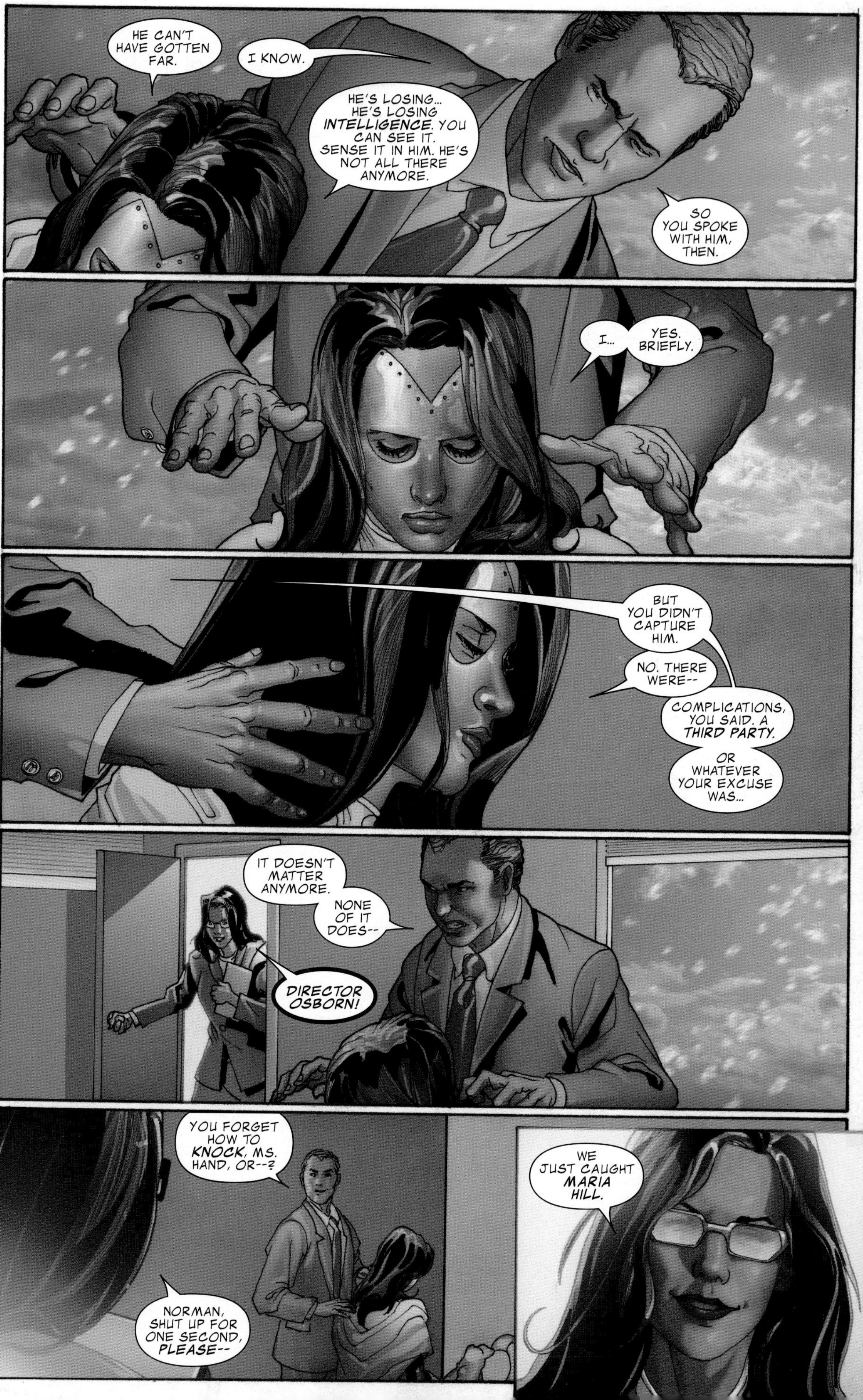
HE CAN'T HAVE GOTTEN FAR.
I KNOW.
HE'S LOSING... HE'S LOSING INTELLIGENCE. YOU CAN SEE IT. SENSE IT IN HIM. HE'S NOT ALL THERE ANYMORE.
SO YOU SPOKE WITH HIM, THEN.
I... YES. BRIEFLY.
BUT YOU DIDN'T CAPTURE HIM.
NO. THERE WERE--
COMPLICATIONS, YOU SAID. A THIRD PARTY.
OR WHATEVER YOUR EXCUSE WAS...
IT DOESN'T MATTER ANYMORE.
NONE OF IT DOES--
DIRECTOR OSBORN!
YOU FORGET HOW TO KNOCK, MS. HAND, OR--?
NORMAN, SHUT UP FOR ONE SECOND, PLEASE--
WE JUST CAUGHT MARIA HILL.

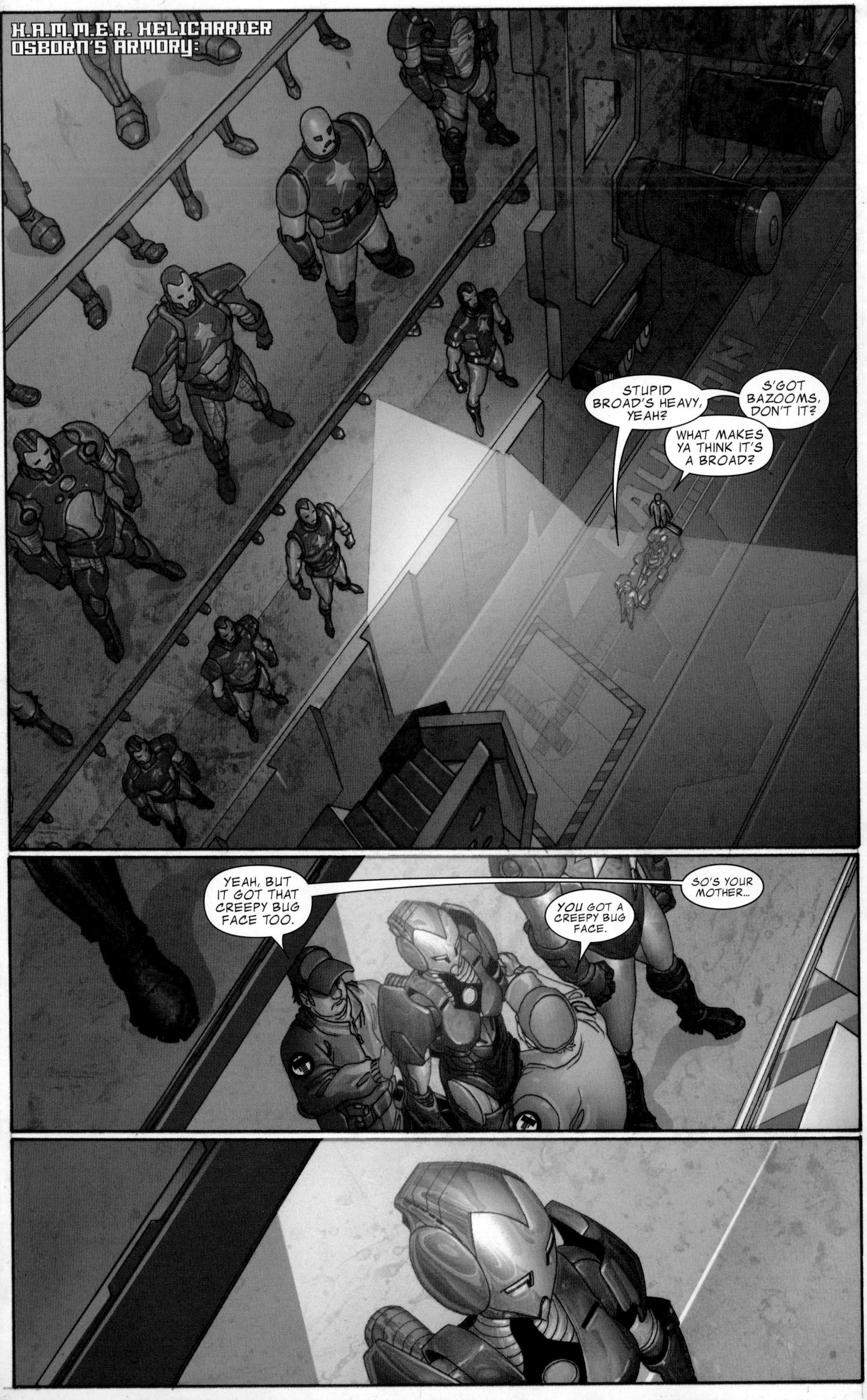
H.A.M.M.E.R. HELICARRIER
OSBORN'S ARMORY:
STUPID BROAD'S HEAVY, YEAH?
S'GOT BAZOOMS, DON'T IT?
WHAT MAKES YA THINK IT'S A BROAD?
YEAH, BUT IT GOT THAT CREEPY BUG FACE TOO.
SO'S YOUR MOTHER...
YOU GOT A CREEPY BUG FACE.

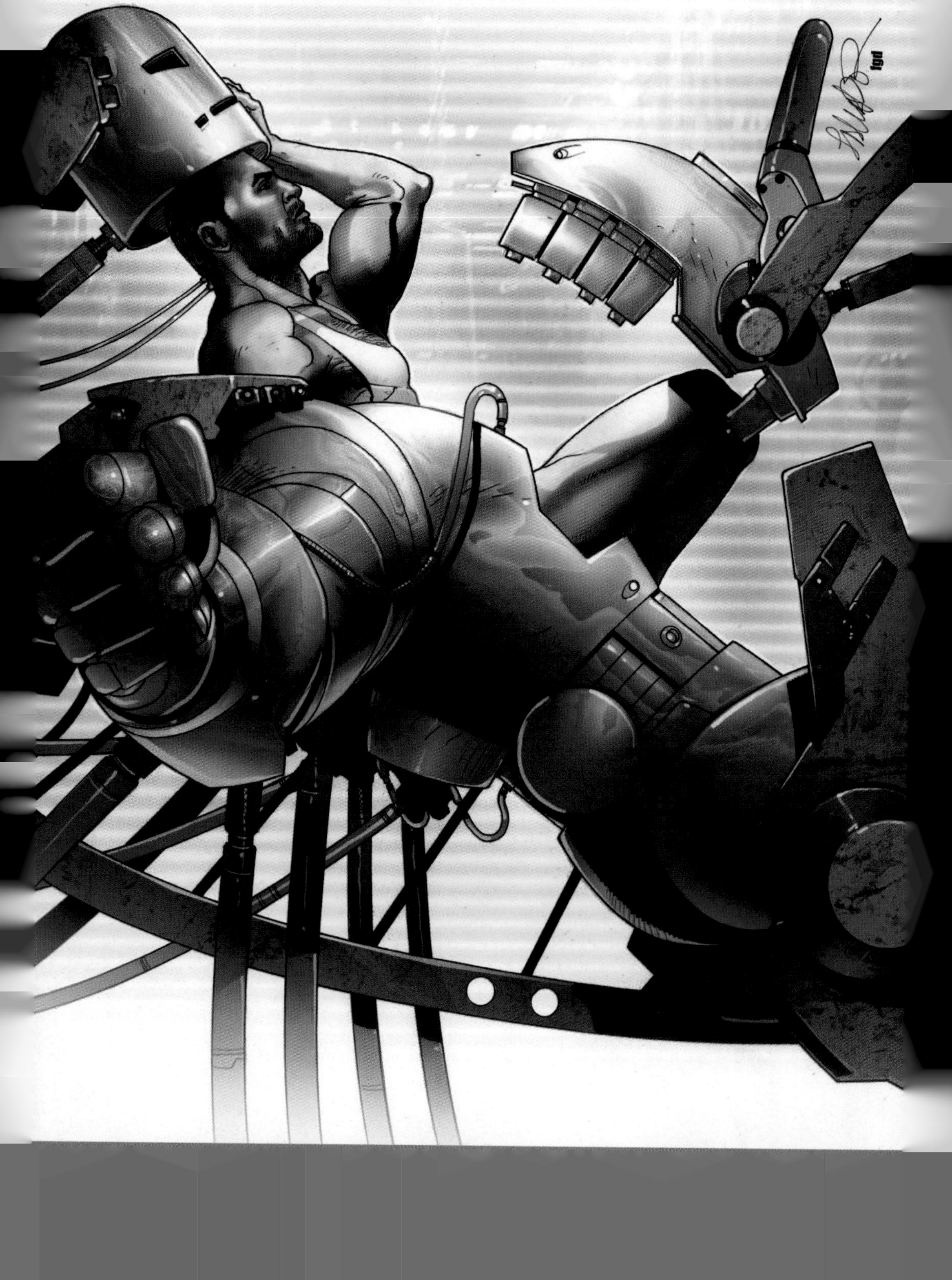

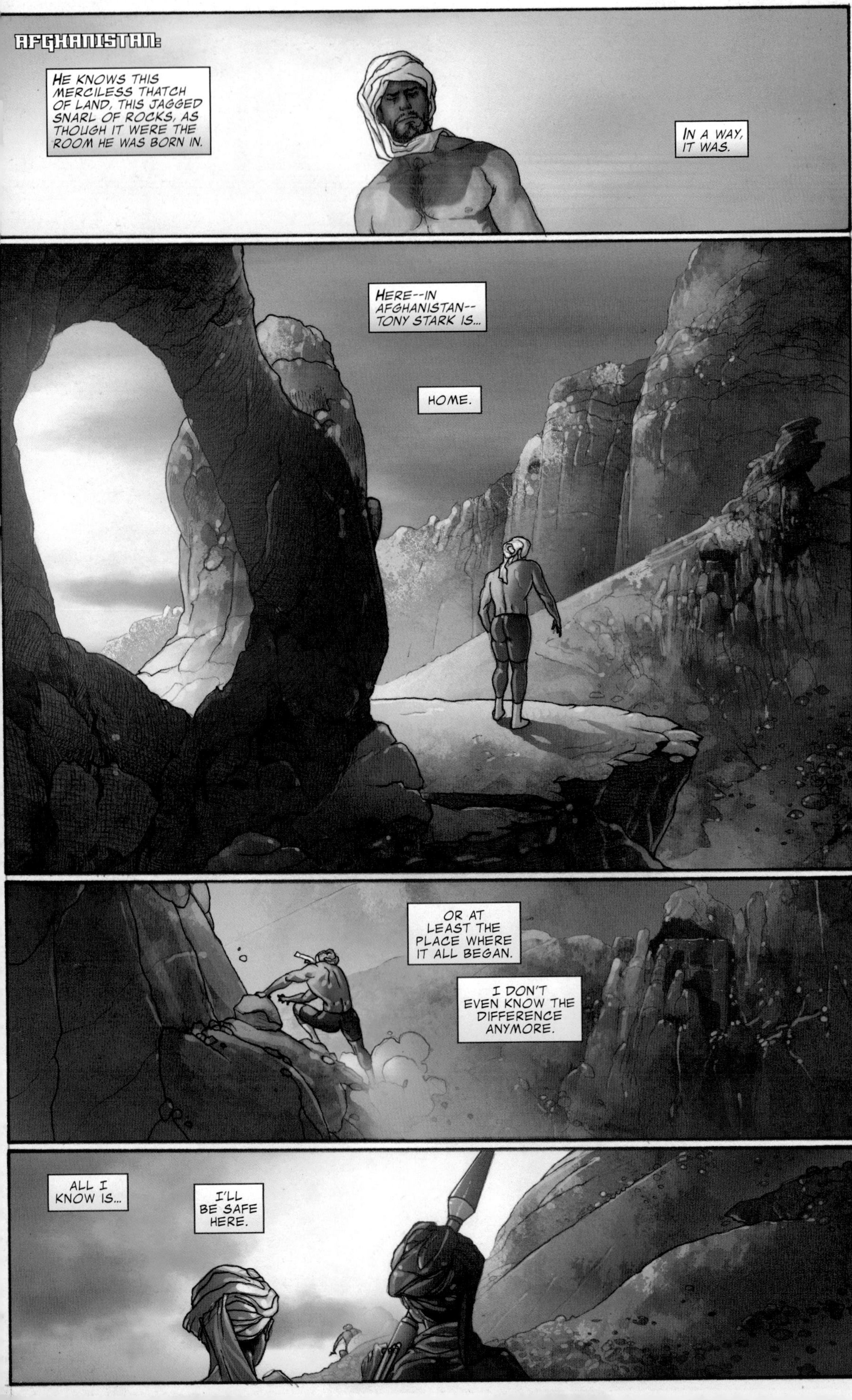
AFGHANISTAN:
HE KNOWS THIS MERCILESS THATCH OF LAND, THIS JAGGED SNARL OF ROCKS, AS THOUGH IT WERE THE ROOM HE WAS BORN IN.
IN A WAY, IT WAS.
HERE--IN AFGHANISTAN--TONY STARK IS...
HOME.
OR AT LEAST THE PLACE WHERE IT ALL BEGAN.
I DON'T EVEN KNOW THE DIFFERENCE ANYMORE.
ALL I KNOW IS...
I'LL BE SAFE HERE.

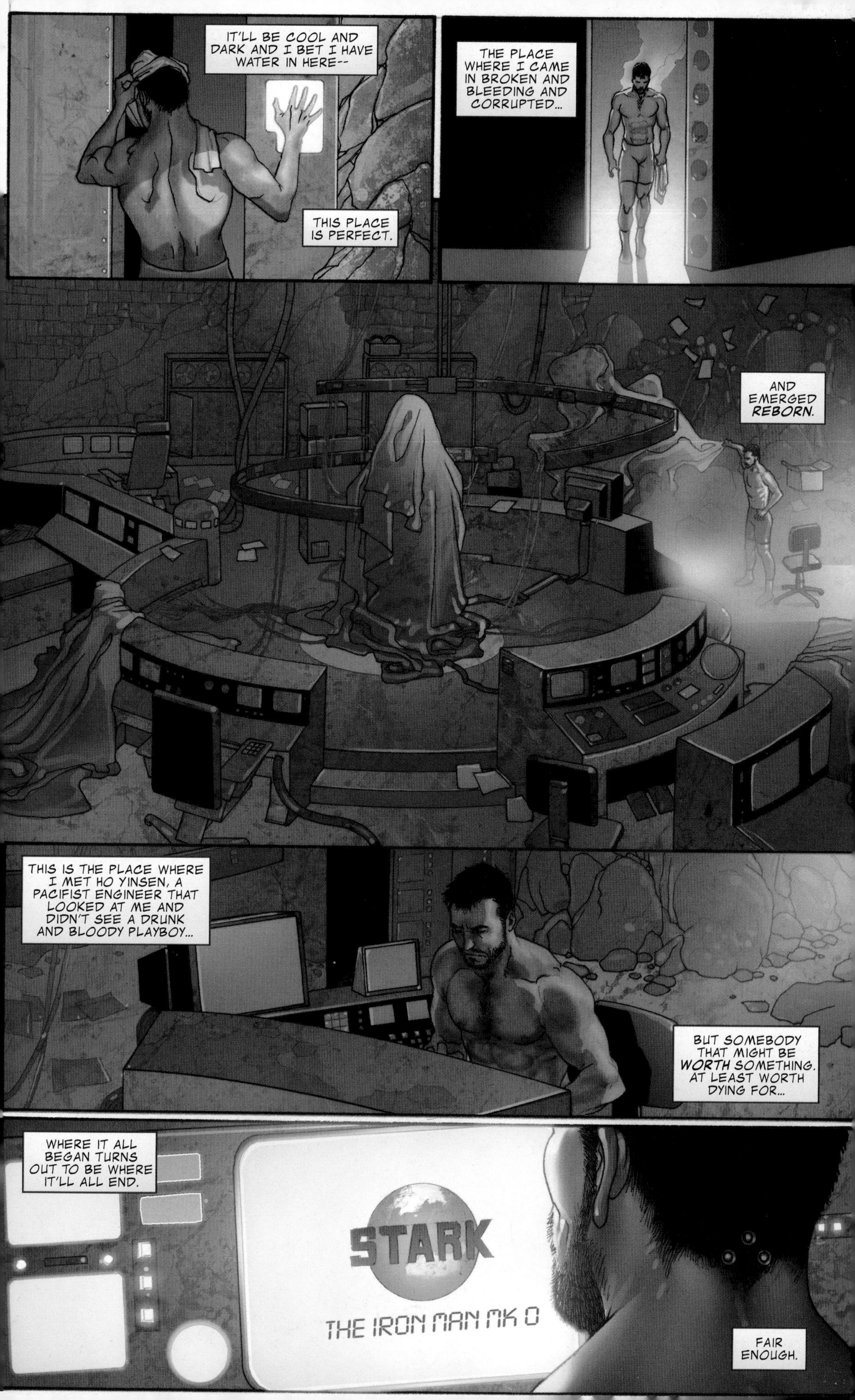
IT'LL BE COOL AND DARK AND I BET I HAVE WATER IN HERE--
THIS PLACE IS PERFECT.
THE PLACE WHERE I CAME IN BROKEN AND BLEEDING AND CORRUPTED...
AND EMERGED *REBORN.*
THIS IS THE PLACE WHERE I MET HO YINSEN, A PACIFIST ENGINEER THAT LOOKED AT ME AND DIDN'T SEE A DRUNK AND BLOODY PLAYBOY...
BUT SOMEBODY THAT MIGHT BE *WORTH* SOMETHING. AT LEAST WORTH DYING FOR...
WHERE IT ALL BEGAN TURNS OUT TO BE WHERE IT'LL ALL END.
STARK
THE IRON MAN MK 0
FAIR ENOUGH.

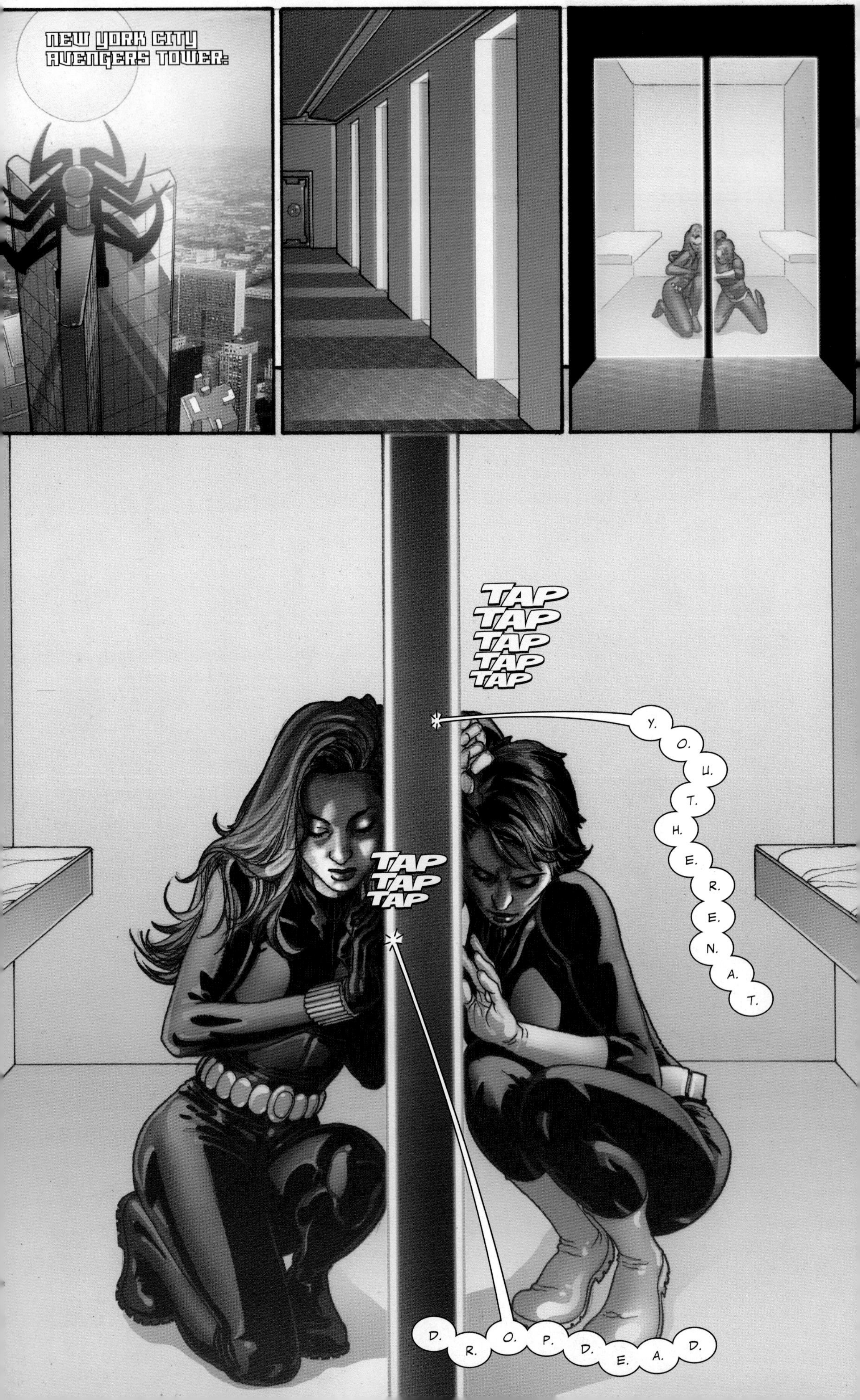
NEW YORK CITY
AVENGERS TOWER:
TAP TAP TAP TAP TAP
Y. O. U. T. H. E. R. E. N. A. T.
TAP TAP TAP
D. R. O. P. D. E. A. D.

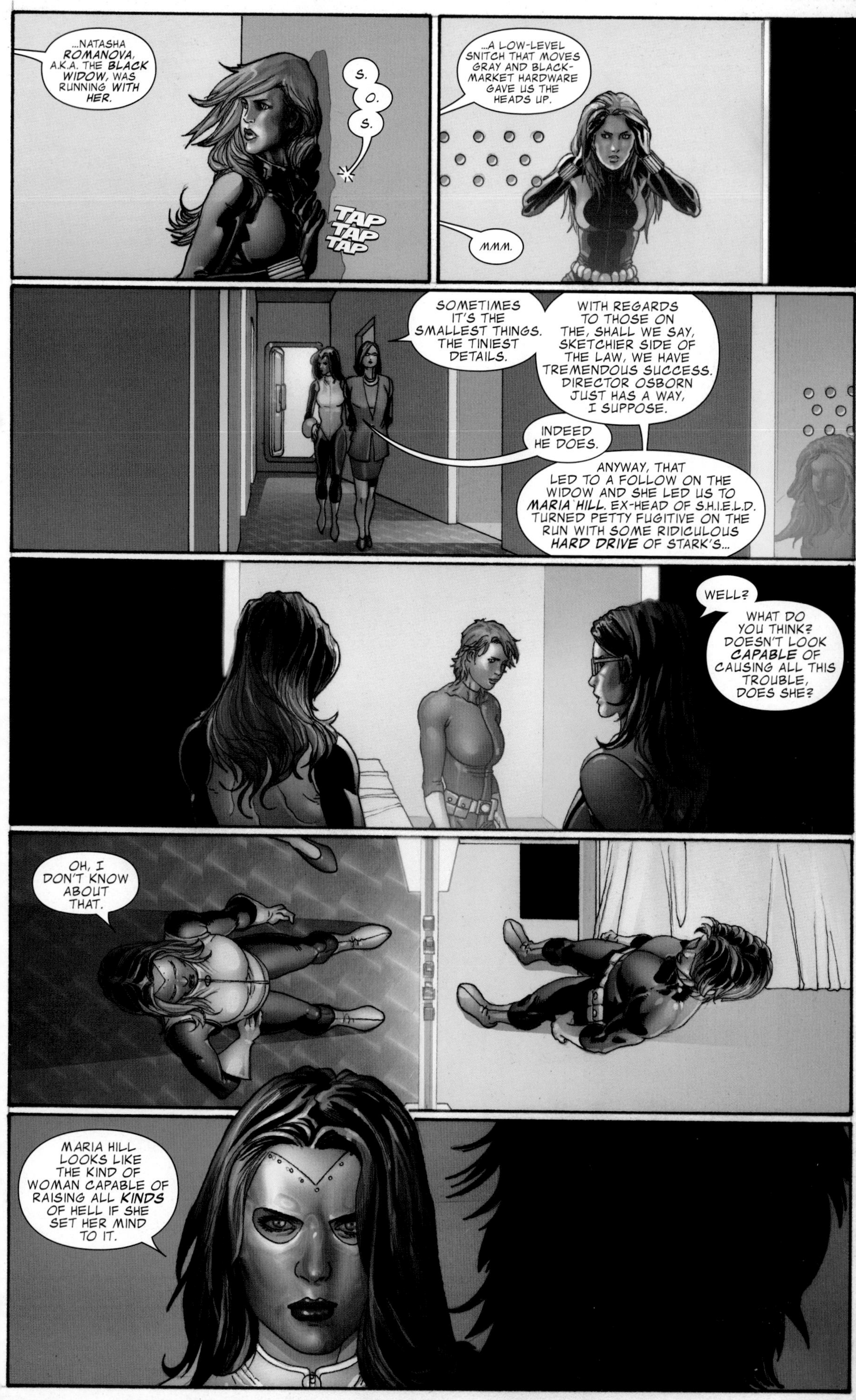
...NATASHA ROMANOVA, A.K.A. THE BLACK WIDOW, WAS RUNNING WITH HER.
S.
O.
S.
TAP TAP TAP
...A LOW-LEVEL SNITCH THAT MOVES GRAY AND BLACK-MARKET HARDWARE GAVE US THE HEADS UP.
MMM.
SOMETIMES IT'S THE SMALLEST THINGS. THE TINIEST DETAILS.
WITH REGARDS TO THOSE ON THE, SHALL WE SAY, SKETCHIER SIDE OF THE LAW, WE HAVE TREMENDOUS SUCCESS. DIRECTOR OSBORN JUST HAS A WAY, I SUPPOSE.
INDEED HE DOES.
ANYWAY, THAT LED TO A FOLLOW ON THE WIDOW AND SHE LED US TO MARIA HILL. EX-HEAD OF S.H.I.E.L.D. TURNED PETTY FUGITIVE ON THE RUN WITH SOME RIDICULOUS HARD DRIVE OF STARK'S...
WELL?
WHAT DO YOU THINK? DOESN'T LOOK CAPABLE OF CAUSING ALL THIS TROUBLE, DOES SHE?
OH, I DON'T KNOW ABOUT THAT.
MARIA HILL LOOKS LIKE THE KIND OF WOMAN CAPABLE OF RAISING ALL KINDS OF HELL IF SHE SET HER MIND TO IT.

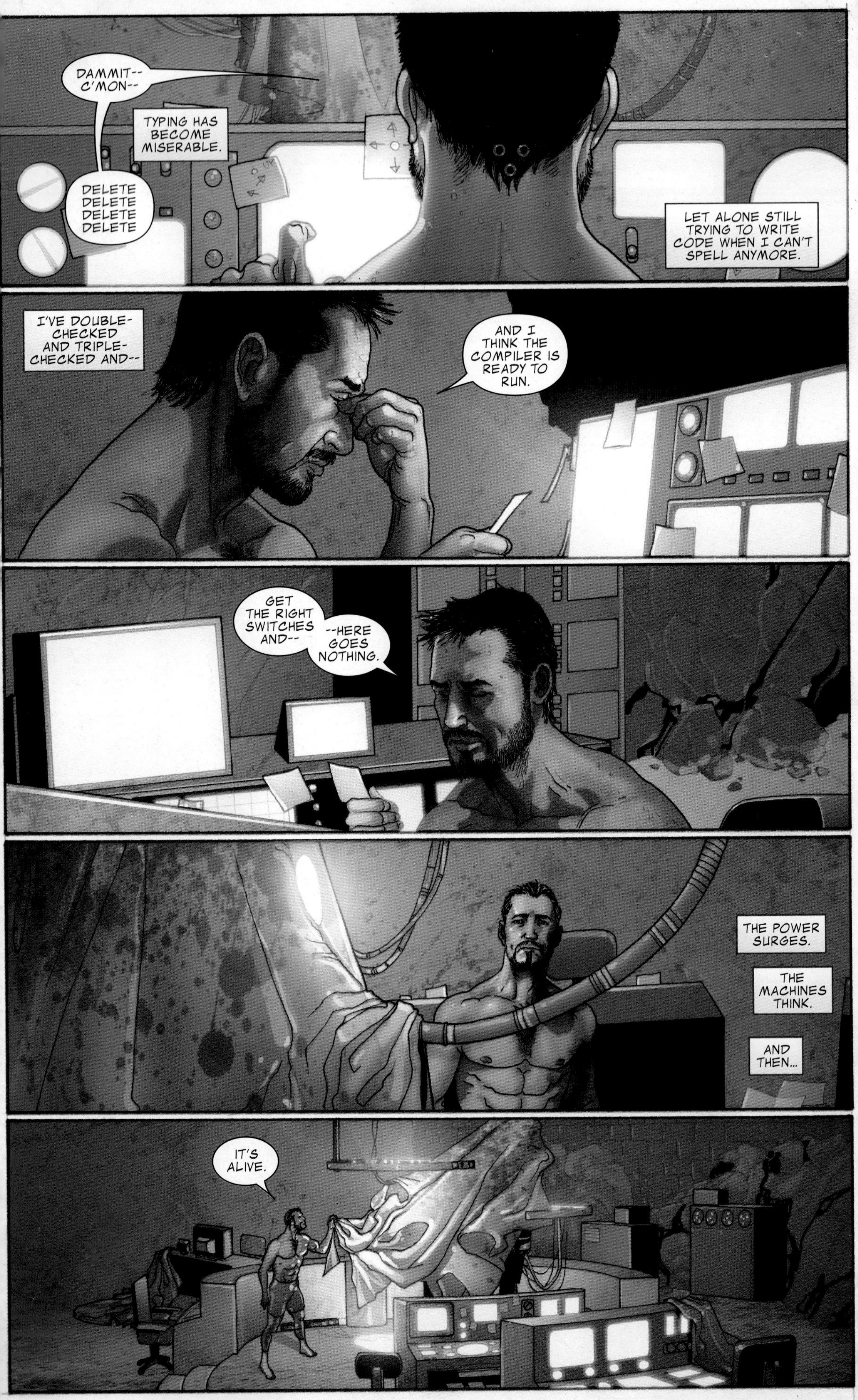
DAMMIT-- C'MON--
TYPING HAS BECOME MISERABLE.
DELETE DELETE DELETE DELETE
LET ALONE STILL TRYING TO WRITE CODE WHEN I CAN'T SPELL ANYMORE.
I'VE DOUBLE-CHECKED AND TRIPLE-CHECKED AND--
AND I THINK THE COMPILER IS READY TO RUN.
GET THE RIGHT SWITCHES AND--
--HERE GOES NOTHING.
THE POWER SURGES.
THE MACHINES THINK.
AND THEN...
IT'S ALIVE.

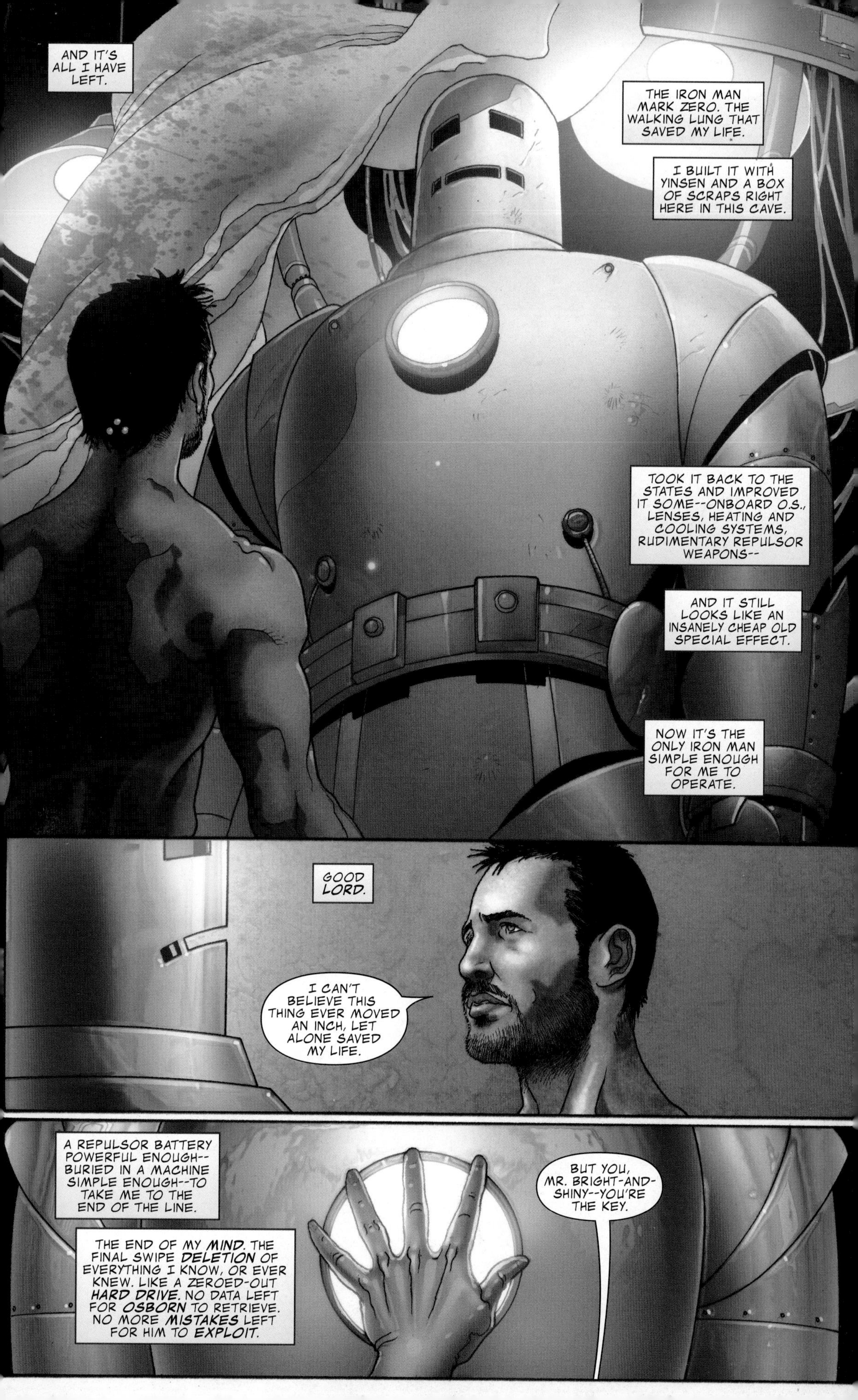
AND IT'S ALL I HAVE LEFT.
THE IRON MAN MARK ZERO. THE WALKING LUNG THAT SAVED MY LIFE.
I BUILT IT WITH YINSEN AND A BOX OF SCRAPS RIGHT HERE IN THIS CAVE.
TOOK IT BACK TO THE STATES AND IMPROVED IT SOME--ONBOARD O.S., LENSES, HEATING AND COOLING SYSTEMS, RUDIMENTARY REPULSOR WEAPONS--
AND IT STILL LOOKS LIKE AN INSANELY CHEAP OLD SPECIAL EFFECT.
NOW IT'S THE ONLY IRON MAN SIMPLE ENOUGH FOR ME TO OPERATE.
GOOD LORD.
I CAN'T BELIEVE THIS THING EVER MOVED AN INCH, LET ALONE SAVED MY LIFE.
A REPULSOR BATTERY POWERFUL ENOUGH-- BURIED IN A MACHINE SIMPLE ENOUGH--TO TAKE ME TO THE END OF THE LINE.
THE END OF MY MIND. THE FINAL SWIPE DELETION OF EVERYTHING I KNOW, OR EVER KNEW. LIKE A ZEROED-OUT HARD DRIVE. NO DATA LEFT FOR OSBORN TO RETRIEVE. NO MORE MISTAKES LEFT FOR HIM TO EXPLOIT.
BUT YOU, MR. BRIGHT-AND-SHINY--YOU'RE THE KEY.

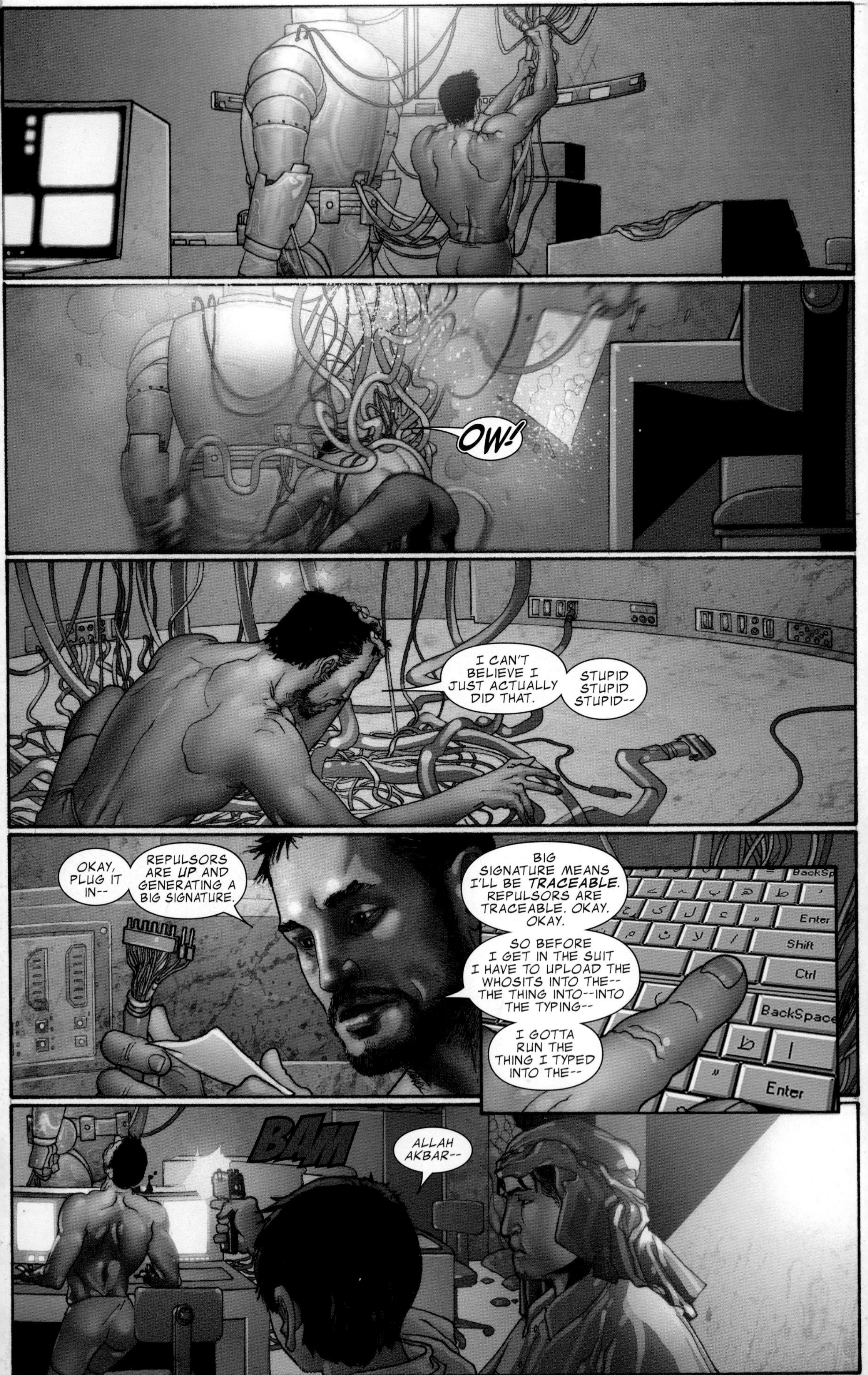
OW!
I CAN'T BELIEVE I JUST ACTUALLY DID THAT.
STUPID STUPID STUPID--
OKAY, PLUG IT IN--
REPULSORS ARE *UP* AND GENERATING A BIG SIGNATURE.
BIG SIGNATURE MEANS I'LL BE ***TRACEABLE***. REPULSORS ARE TRACEABLE. OKAY. OKAY.
SO BEFORE I GET IN THE SUIT I HAVE TO UPLOAD THE WHOSITS INTO THE-- THE THING INTO--INTO THE TYPING--
I GOTTA RUN THE THING I TYPED INTO THE--
BackSp
Enter
Shift
Ctrl
BackSpace
Enter
BAM
ALLAH AKBAR--

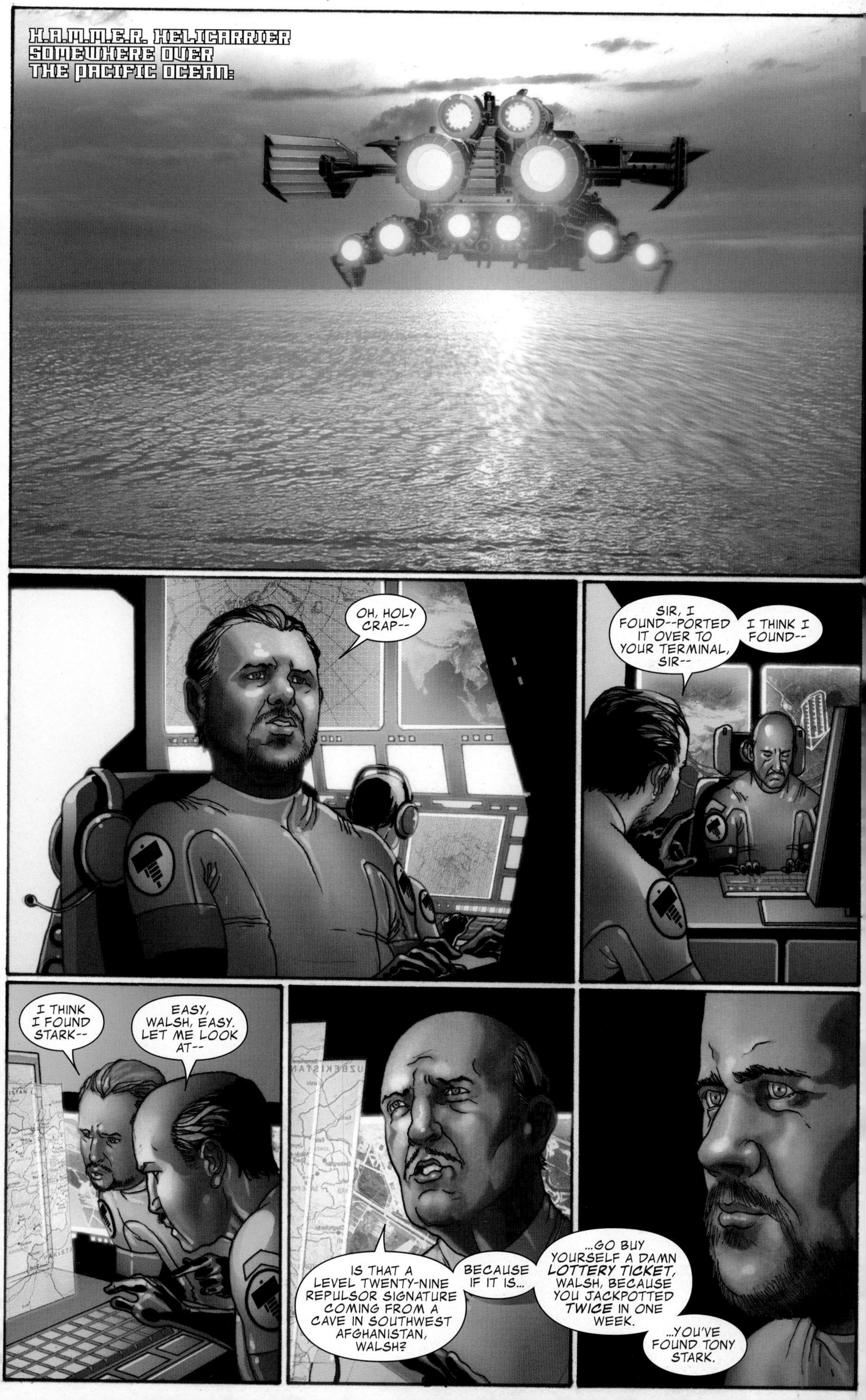
H.A.M.M.E.R. HELICARRIER SOMEWHERE OVER THE PACIFIC OCEAN:
OH, HOLY CRAP--
SIR, I FOUND--PORTED IT OVER TO YOUR TERMINAL, SIR--
I THINK I FOUND--
I THINK I FOUND STARK--
EASY, WALSH, EASY. LET ME LOOK AT--
IS THAT A LEVEL TWENTY-NINE REPULSOR SIGNATURE COMING FROM A CAVE IN SOUTHWEST AFGHANISTAN, WALSH?
BECAUSE IF IT IS...
...GO BUY YOURSELF A DAMN LOTTERY TICKET, WALSH, BECAUSE YOU JACKPOTTED TWICE IN ONE WEEK.
...YOU'VE FOUND TONY STARK.

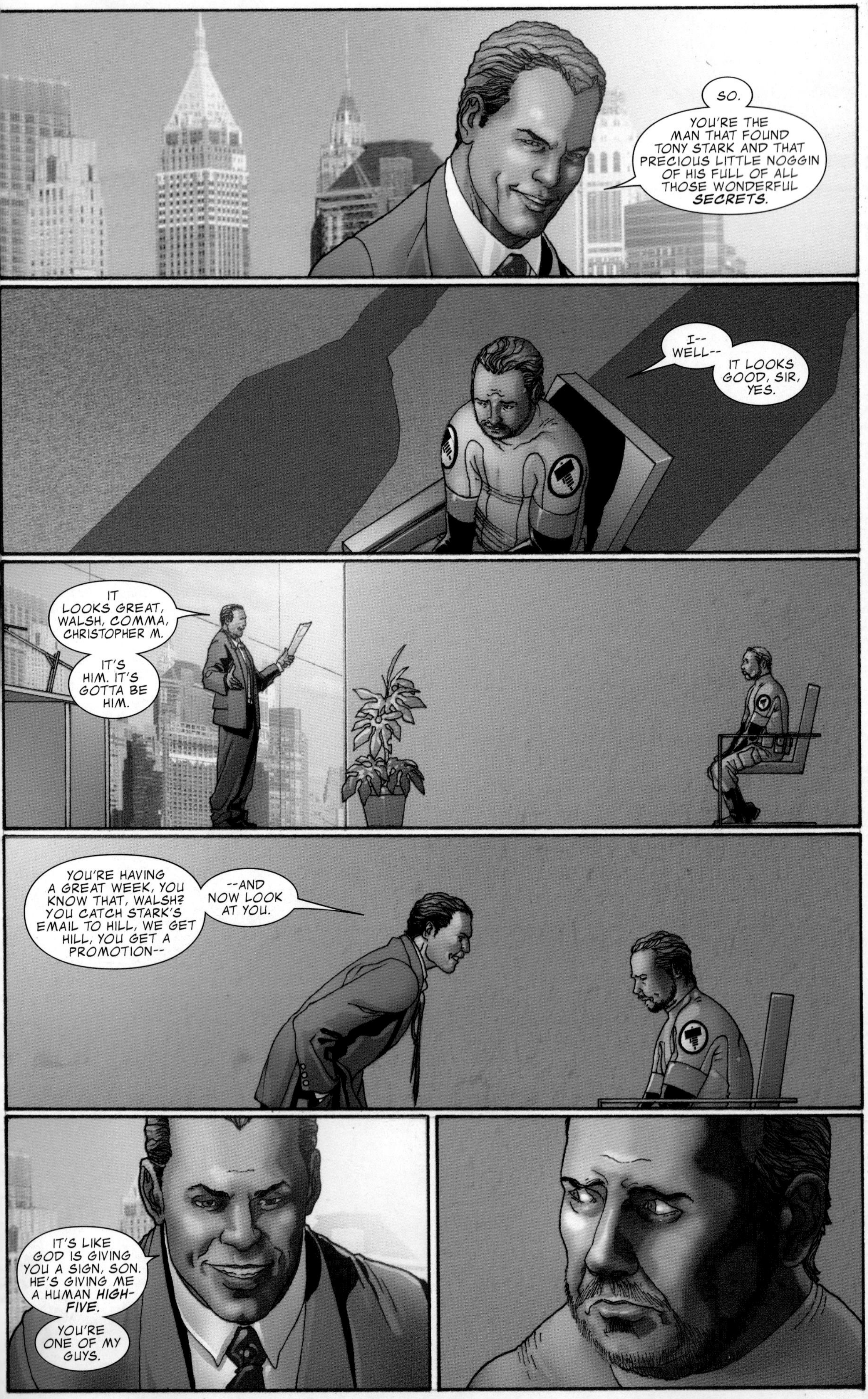
SO.
YOU'RE THE MAN THAT FOUND TONY STARK AND THAT PRECIOUS LITTLE NOGGIN OF HIS FULL OF ALL THOSE WONDERFUL **SECRETS**.
I-- WELL--
IT LOOKS GOOD, SIR, YES.
IT LOOKS GREAT, WALSH, COMMA, CHRISTOPHER M.
IT'S HIM. IT'S GOTTA BE HIM.
YOU'RE HAVING A GREAT WEEK, YOU KNOW THAT, WALSH? YOU CATCH STARK'S EMAIL TO HILL, WE GET HILL, YOU GET A PROMOTION--
--AND NOW LOOK AT YOU.
IT'S LIKE GOD IS GIVING YOU A SIGN, SON. HE'S GIVING ME A HUMAN **HIGH-FIVE.**
YOU'RE ONE OF MY GUYS.

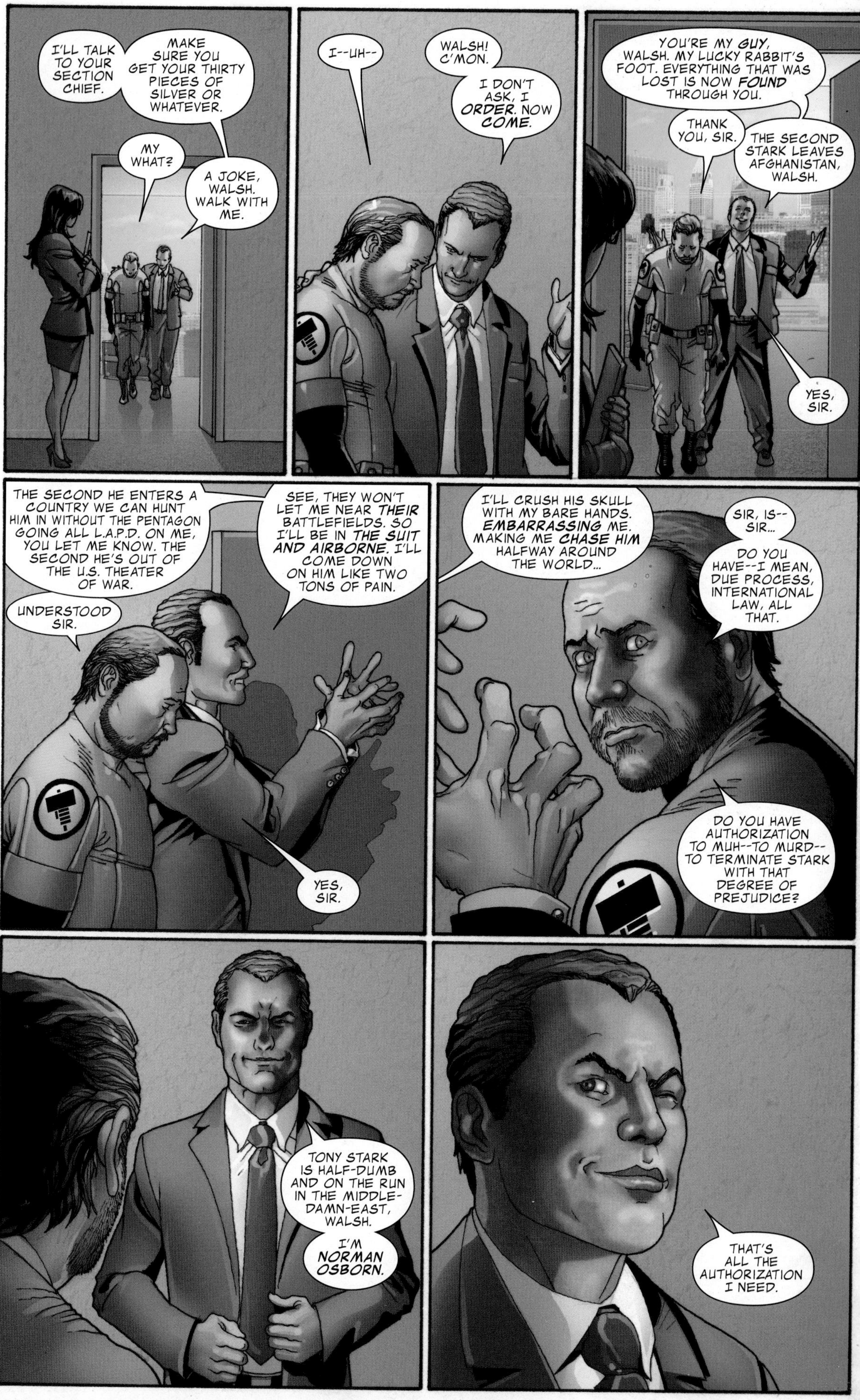

I'LL TALK TO YOUR SECTION CHIEF.
MAKE SURE YOU GET YOUR THIRTY PIECES OF SILVER OR WHATEVER.
MY WHAT?
A JOKE, WALSH. WALK WITH ME.
I--UH--
WALSH! C'MON.
I DON'T ASK, I ORDER. NOW COME.
YOU'RE MY GUY, WALSH. MY LUCKY RABBIT'S FOOT. EVERYTHING THAT WAS LOST IS NOW FOUND THROUGH YOU.
THANK YOU, SIR.
THE SECOND STARK LEAVES AFGHANISTAN, WALSH.
YES, SIR.
THE SECOND HE ENTERS A COUNTRY WE CAN HUNT HIM IN WITHOUT THE PENTAGON GOING ALL L.A.P.D. ON ME, YOU LET ME KNOW. THE SECOND HE'S OUT OF THE U.S. THEATER OF WAR.
UNDERSTOOD SIR.
SEE, THEY WON'T LET ME NEAR THEIR BATTLEFIELDS. SO I'LL BE IN THE SUIT AND AIRBORNE. I'LL COME DOWN ON HIM LIKE TWO TONS OF PAIN.
YES, SIR.
I'LL CRUSH HIS SKULL WITH MY BARE HANDS. EMBARRASSING ME. MAKING ME CHASE HIM HALFWAY AROUND THE WORLD...
SIR, IS-- SIR...
DO YOU HAVE--I MEAN, DUE PROCESS, INTERNATIONAL LAW, ALL THAT.
DO YOU HAVE AUTHORIZATION TO MUH--TO MURD-- TO TERMINATE STARK WITH THAT DEGREE OF PREJUDICE?
TONY STARK IS HALF-DUMB AND ON THE RUN IN THE MIDDLE-DAMN-EAST, WALSH.
I'M NORMAN OSBORN.
THAT'S ALL THE AUTHORIZATION I NEED.

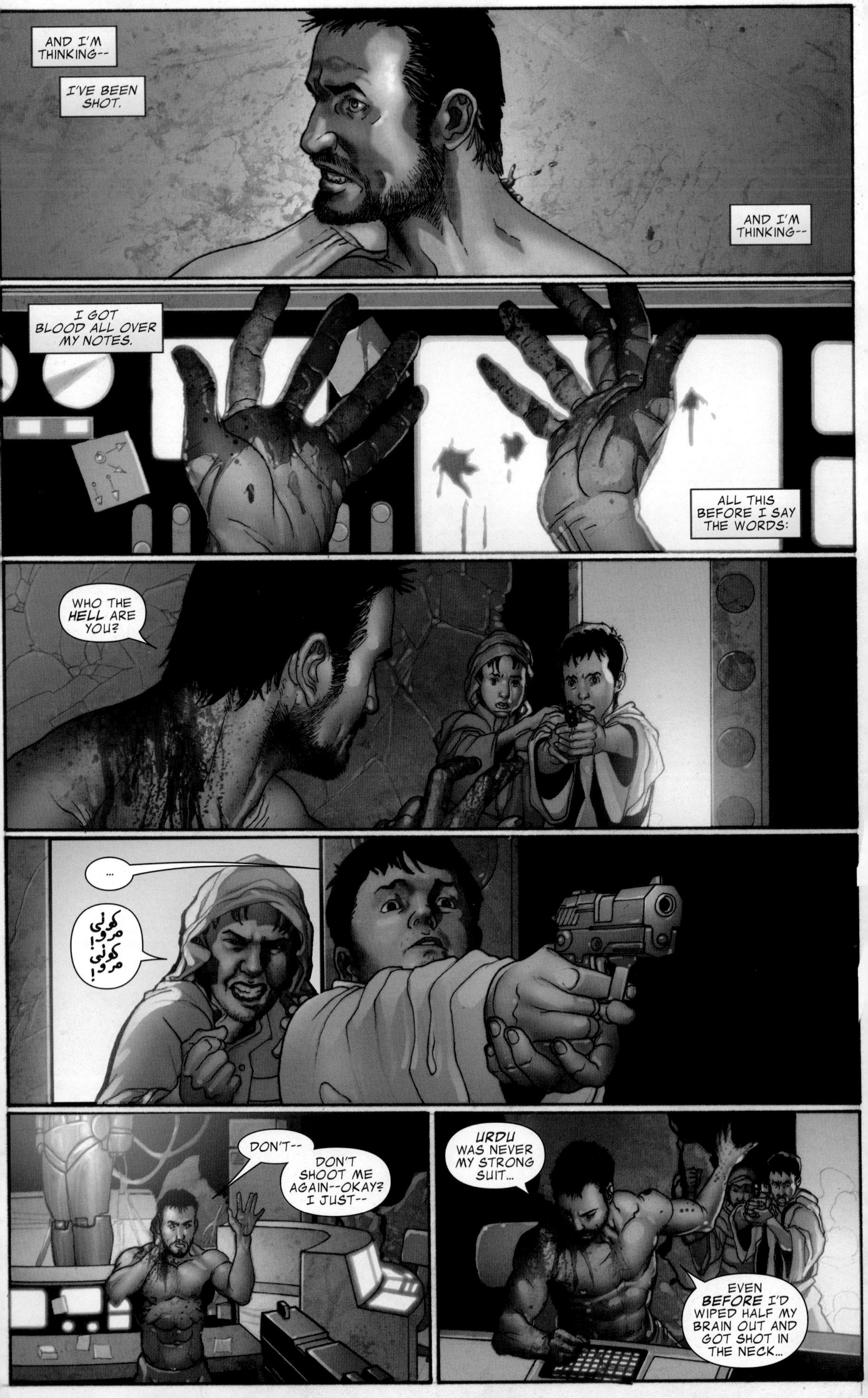
AND I'M THINKING--
I'VE BEEN SHOT.
AND I'M THINKING--
I GOT BLOOD ALL OVER MY NOTES.
ALL THIS BEFORE I SAY THE WORDS:
WHO THE HELL ARE YOU?
...
DON'T--
DON'T SHOOT ME AGAIN--OKAY? I JUST--
URDU WAS NEVER MY STRONG SUIT...
EVEN BEFORE I'D WIPED HALF MY BRAIN OUT AND GOT SHOT IN THE NECK...

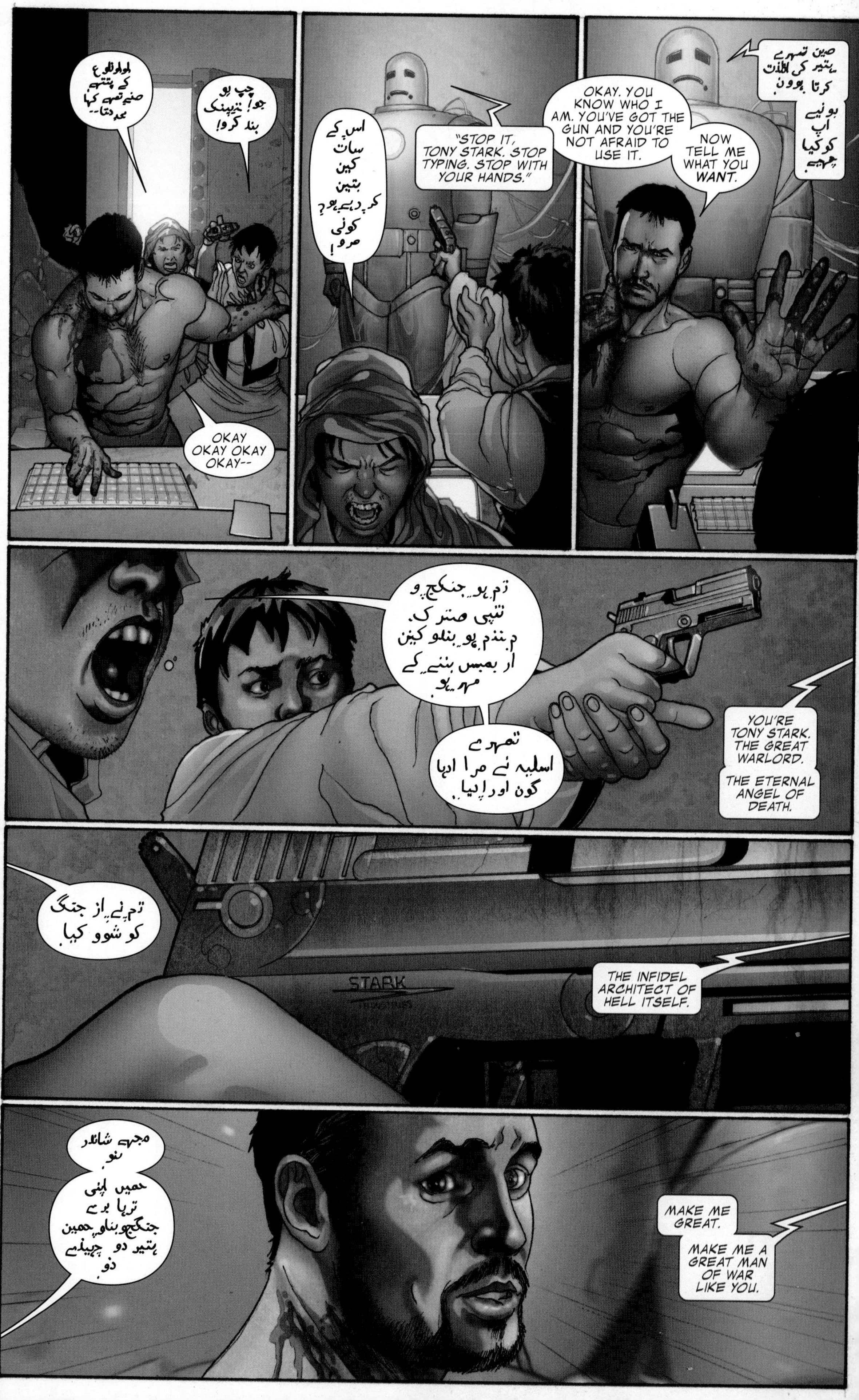

لولولو ع کے پتتھہ صنیہ تمھہ کہا بمہ دتا--
چپ ہو جو! ٹیپنگ بند کرو!
OKAY OKAY OKAY OKAY--
اس پکے سات کین بتین کرپدہیےہو؟ کونی صرو!
"STOP IT, TONY STARK. STOP TYPING. STOP WITH YOUR HANDS."
OKAY. YOU KNOW WHO I AM. YOU'VE GOT THE GUN AND YOU'RE NOT AFRAID TO USE IT.
NOW TELL ME WHAT YOU WANT.
صین تمھرے ہتیر کی الذت کرتا ہوون.
بونیے اپ کوکیا چھیے.
زم ہو جنکج پو تنپی صترک. دم بندم ہو بنلو کین ار بمبس بننے کے مہ ہو.
تمھرے اسلیہ نے مرا ادہا گون اوراپیا..
YOU'RE TONY STARK. THE GREAT WARLORD.
THE ETERNAL ANGEL OF DEATH.
تم نے از جتگ کو شوو کیا.
STARK
THE INFIDEL ARCHITECT OF HELL ITSELF.
مجھے شانلر بنو.
حمیں اپنی ترہا برے جنگجو بناو حمین ہتیر دو چہیذے ذو.
MAKE ME GREAT.
MAKE ME A GREAT MAN OF WAR LIKE YOU.

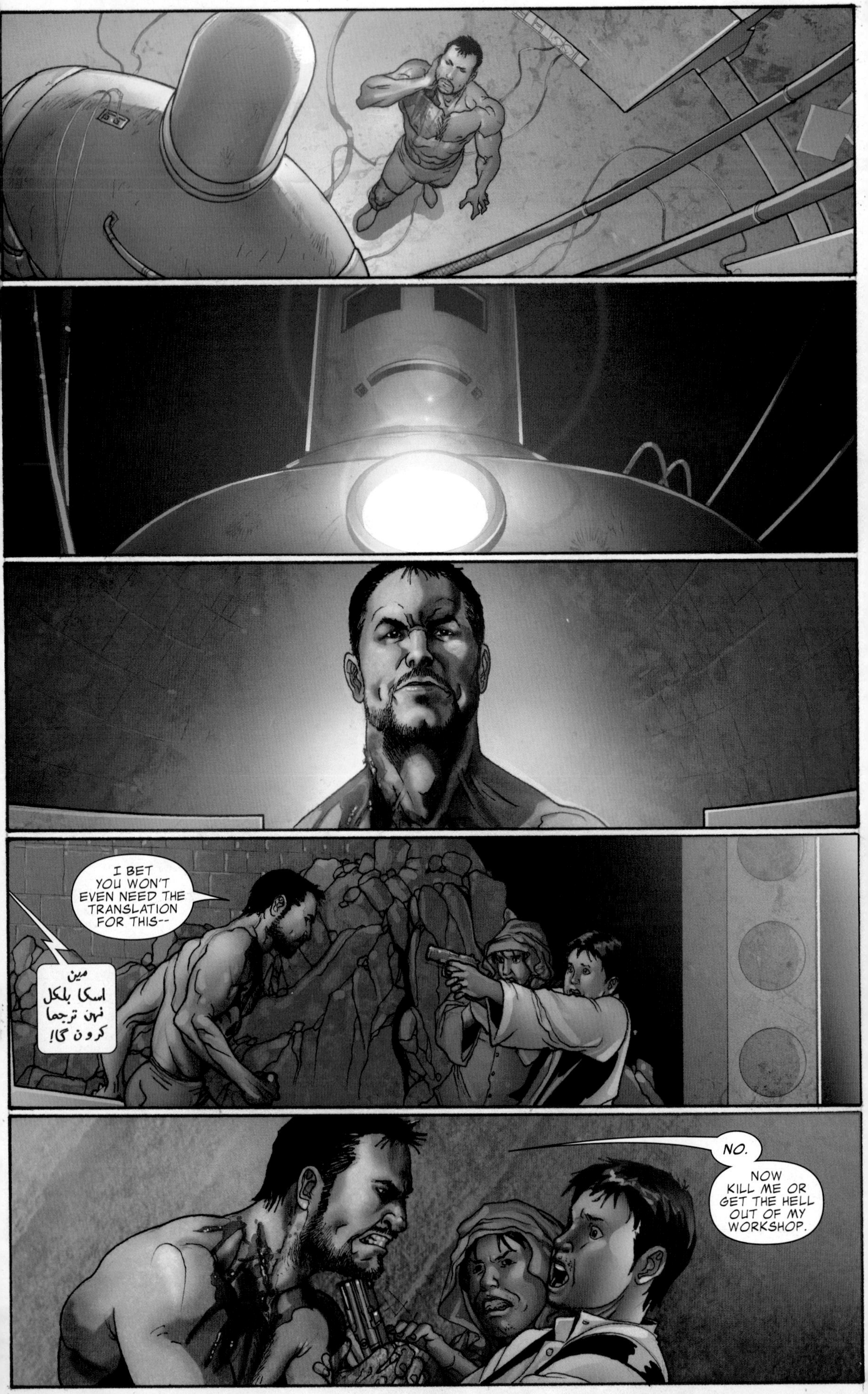
I BET YOU WON'T EVEN NEED THE TRANSLATION FOR THIS--
مین اسکا بلکل نہں ترجما کرون گا!
NO.
NOW KILL ME OR GET THE HELL OUT OF MY WORKSHOP.

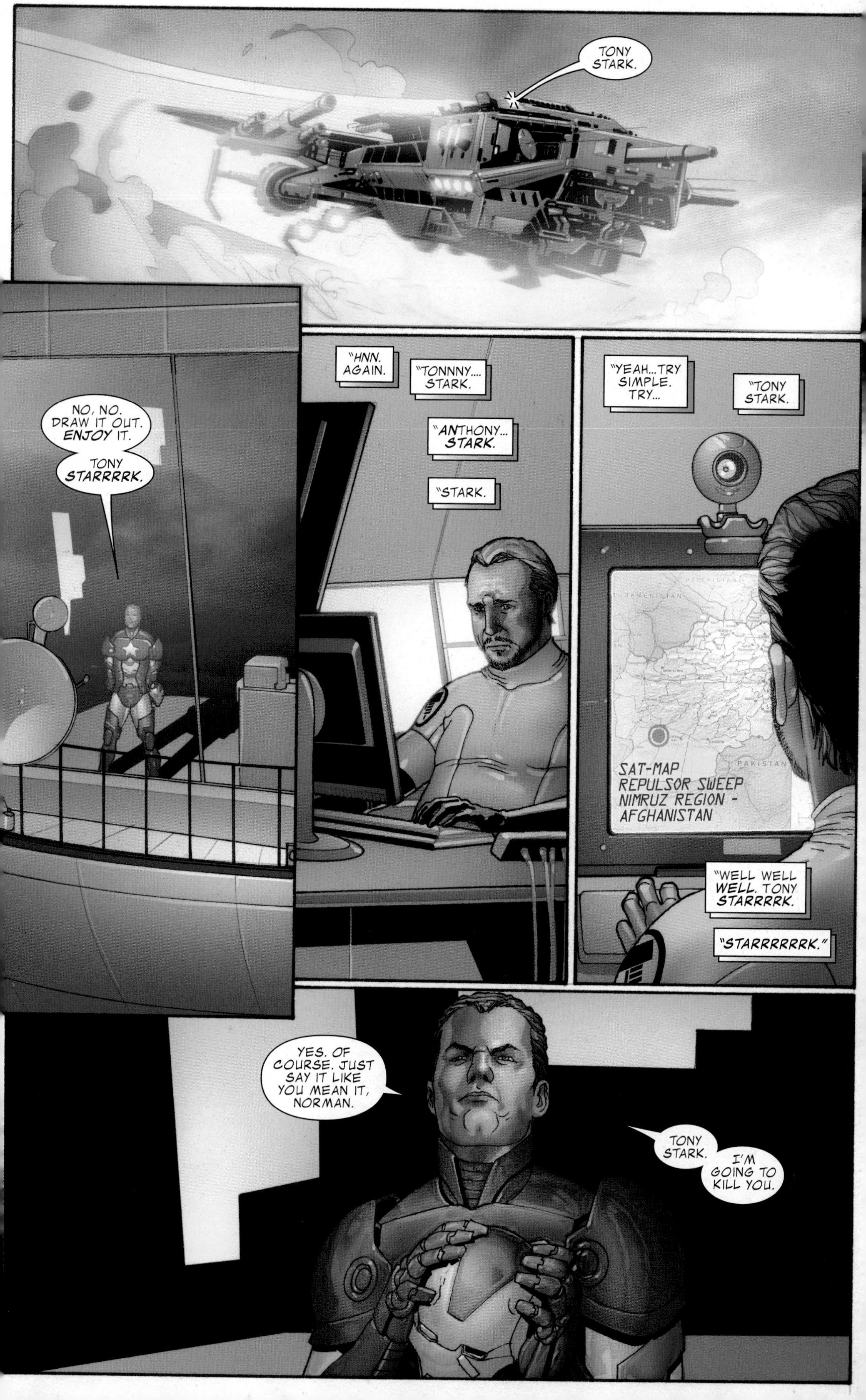
TONY STARK.
NO, NO. DRAW IT OUT. ENJOY IT.
TONY STARRRRK.
"HNN. AGAIN.
"TONNNY.... STARK.
"ANTHONY... STARK.
"STARK.
"YEAH...TRY SIMPLE. TRY...
"TONY STARK.
SAT-MAP REPULSOR SWEEP NIMRUZ REGION - AFGHANISTAN
"WELL WELL WELL. TONY STARRRRK.
"STARRRRRRK."
YES. OF COURSE. JUST SAY IT LIKE YOU MEAN IT, NORMAN.
TONY STARK.
I'M GOING TO KILL YOU.

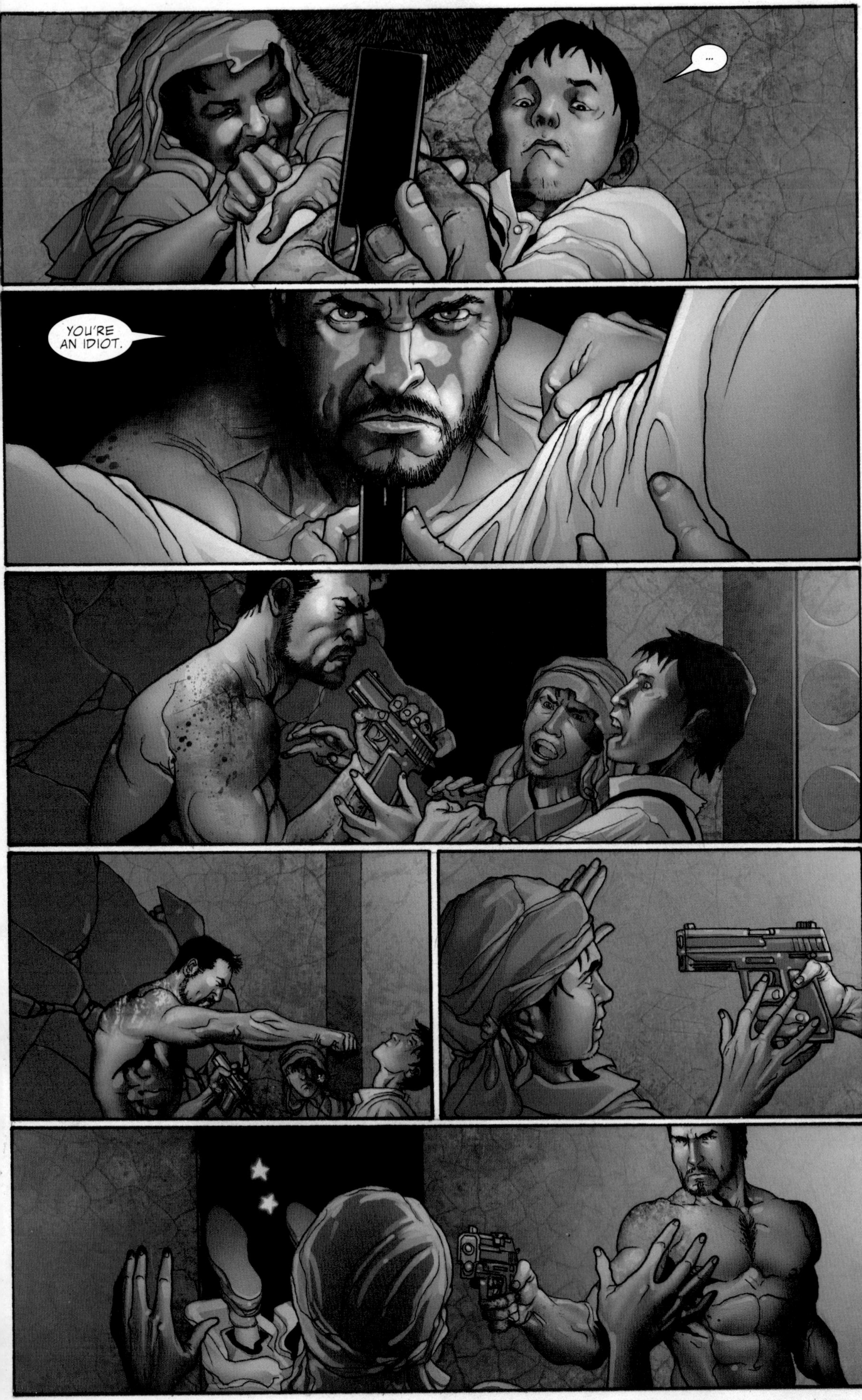
...
YOU'RE AN IDIOT.

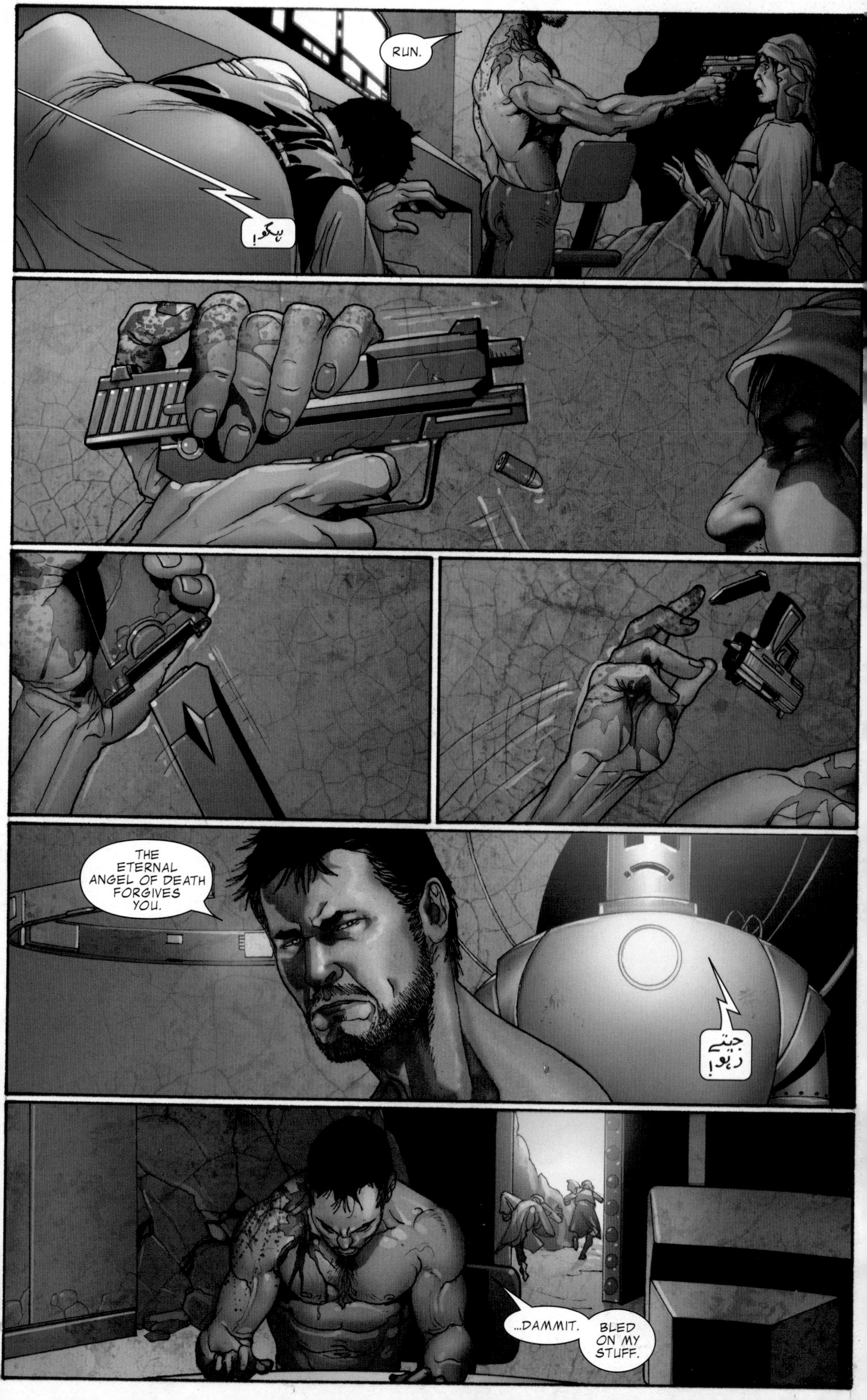
RUN.
ہٹکو!
THE ETERNAL ANGEL OF DEATH FORGIVES YOU.
جیتے رہو!
...DAMMIT.
BLED ON MY STUFF.

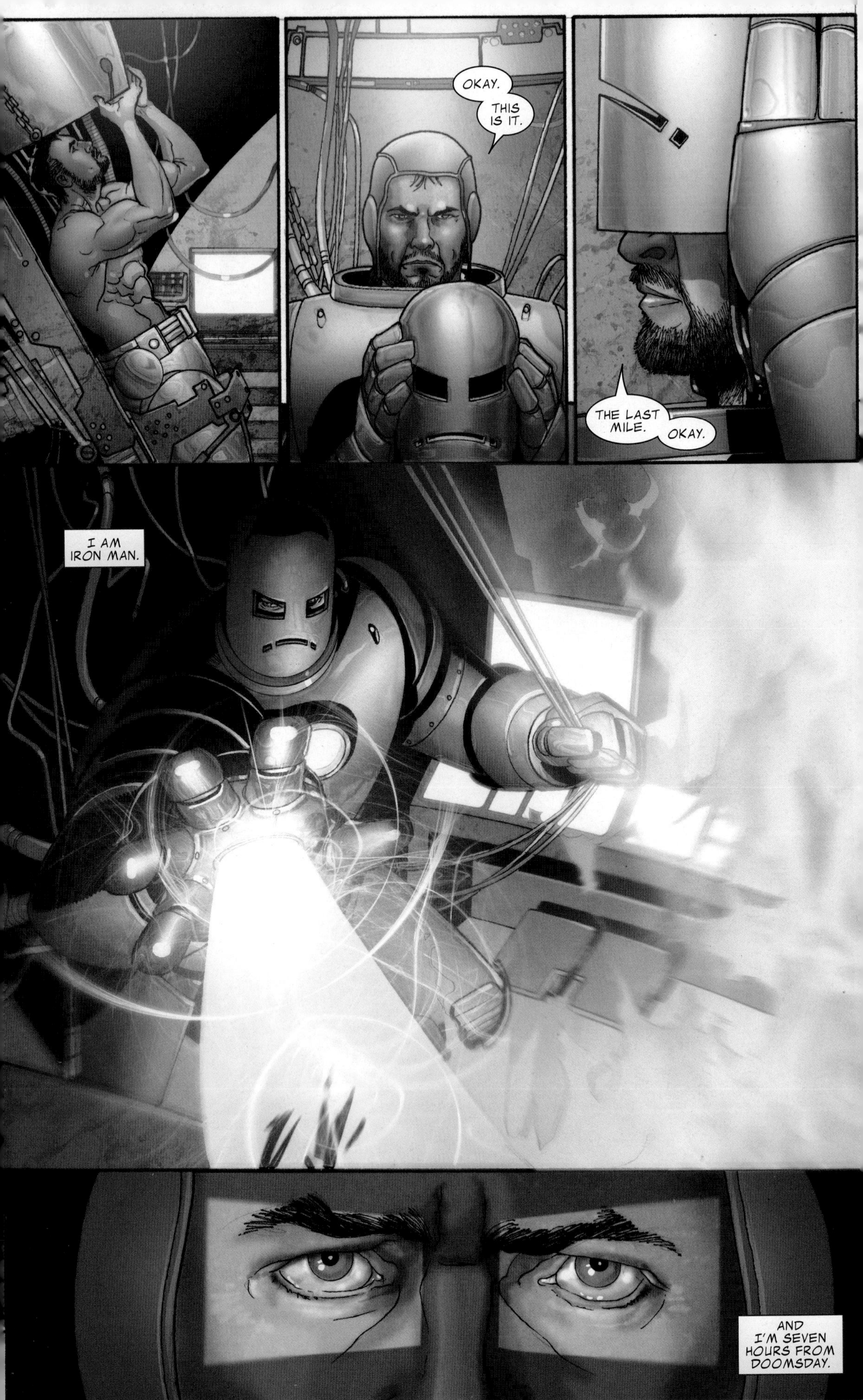
OKAY.
THIS IS IT.
THE LAST MILE.
OKAY.
I AM IRON MAN.
AND I'M SEVEN HOURS FROM DOOMSDAY.

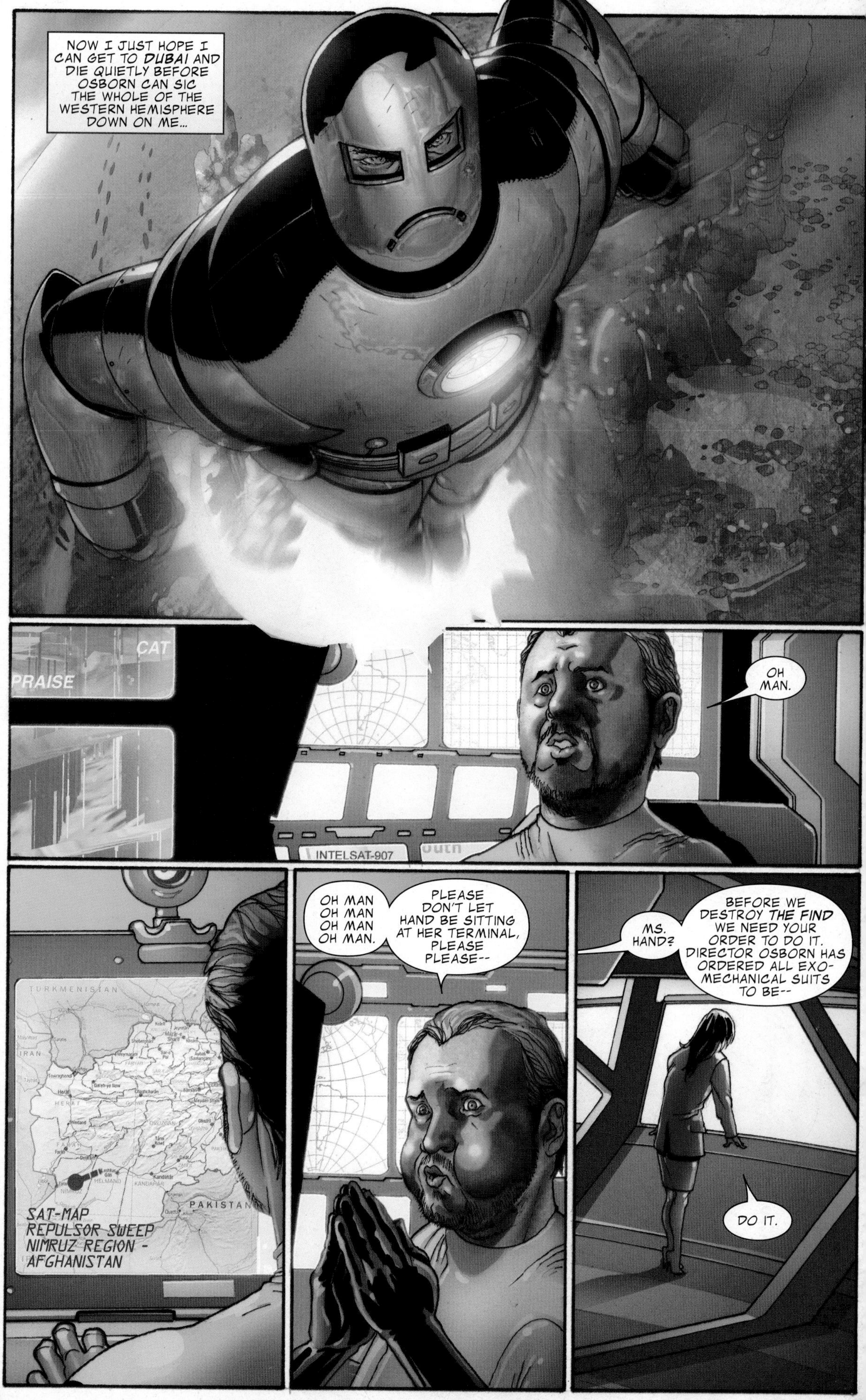
NOW I JUST HOPE I CAN GET TO DUBAI AND DIE QUIETLY BEFORE OSBORN CAN SIC THE WHOLE OF THE WESTERN HEMISPHERE DOWN ON ME...
CAT
PRAISE
OH MAN.
INTELSAT-907
SAT-MAP REPULSOR SWEEP NIMRUZ REGION - AFGHANISTAN
OH MAN OH MAN OH MAN OH MAN.
PLEASE DON'T LET HAND BE SITTING AT HER TERMINAL, PLEASE PLEASE--
MS. HAND?
BEFORE WE DESTROY THE FIND WE NEED YOUR ORDER TO DO IT. DIRECTOR OSBORN HAS ORDERED ALL EXO-MECHANICAL SUITS TO BE--
DO IT.

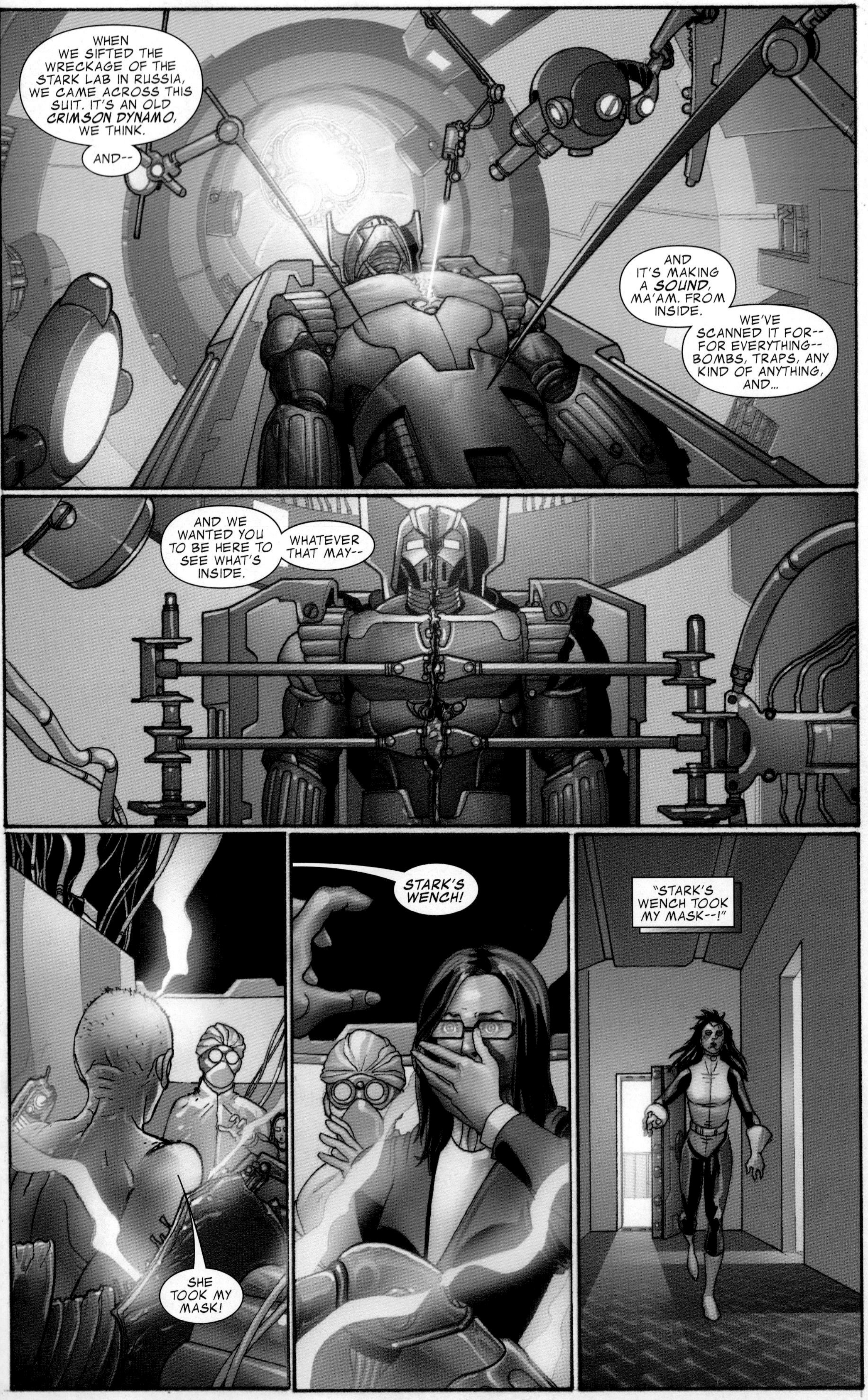
WHEN WE SIFTED THE WRECKAGE OF THE STARK LAB IN RUSSIA, WE CAME ACROSS THIS SUIT. IT'S AN OLD CRIMSON DYNAMO, WE THINK.
AND--
AND IT'S MAKING A SOUND, MA'AM. FROM INSIDE.
WE'VE SCANNED IT FOR-- FOR EVERYTHING-- BOMBS, TRAPS, ANY KIND OF ANYTHING, AND...
AND WE WANTED YOU TO BE HERE TO SEE WHAT'S INSIDE.
WHATEVER THAT MAY--
SHE TOOK MY MASK!
STARK'S WENCH!
"STARK'S WENCH TOOK MY MASK--!"

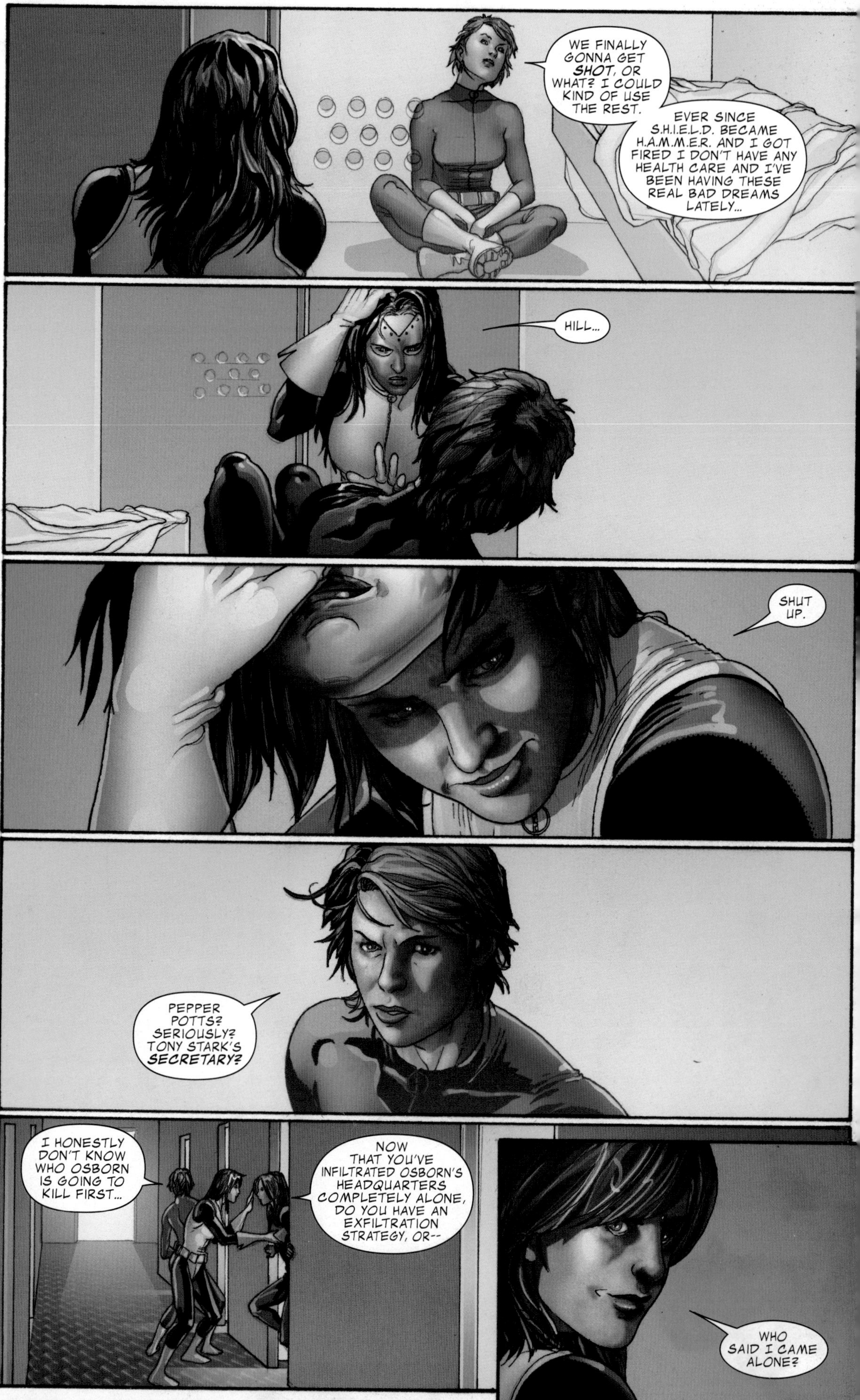
WE FINALLY GONNA GET SHOT, OR WHAT? I COULD KIND OF USE THE REST.
EVER SINCE S.H.I.E.L.D. BECAME H.A.M.M.E.R. AND I GOT FIRED I DON'T HAVE ANY HEALTH CARE AND I'VE BEEN HAVING THESE REAL BAD DREAMS LATELY...
HILL...
SHUT UP.
PEPPER POTTS? SERIOUSLY? TONY STARK'S SECRETARY?
I HONESTLY DON'T KNOW WHO OSBORN IS GOING TO KILL FIRST...
NOW THAT YOU'VE INFILTRATED OSBORN'S HEADQUARTERS COMPLETELY ALONE, DO YOU HAVE AN EXFILTRATION STRATEGY, OR--
WHO SAID I CAME ALONE?

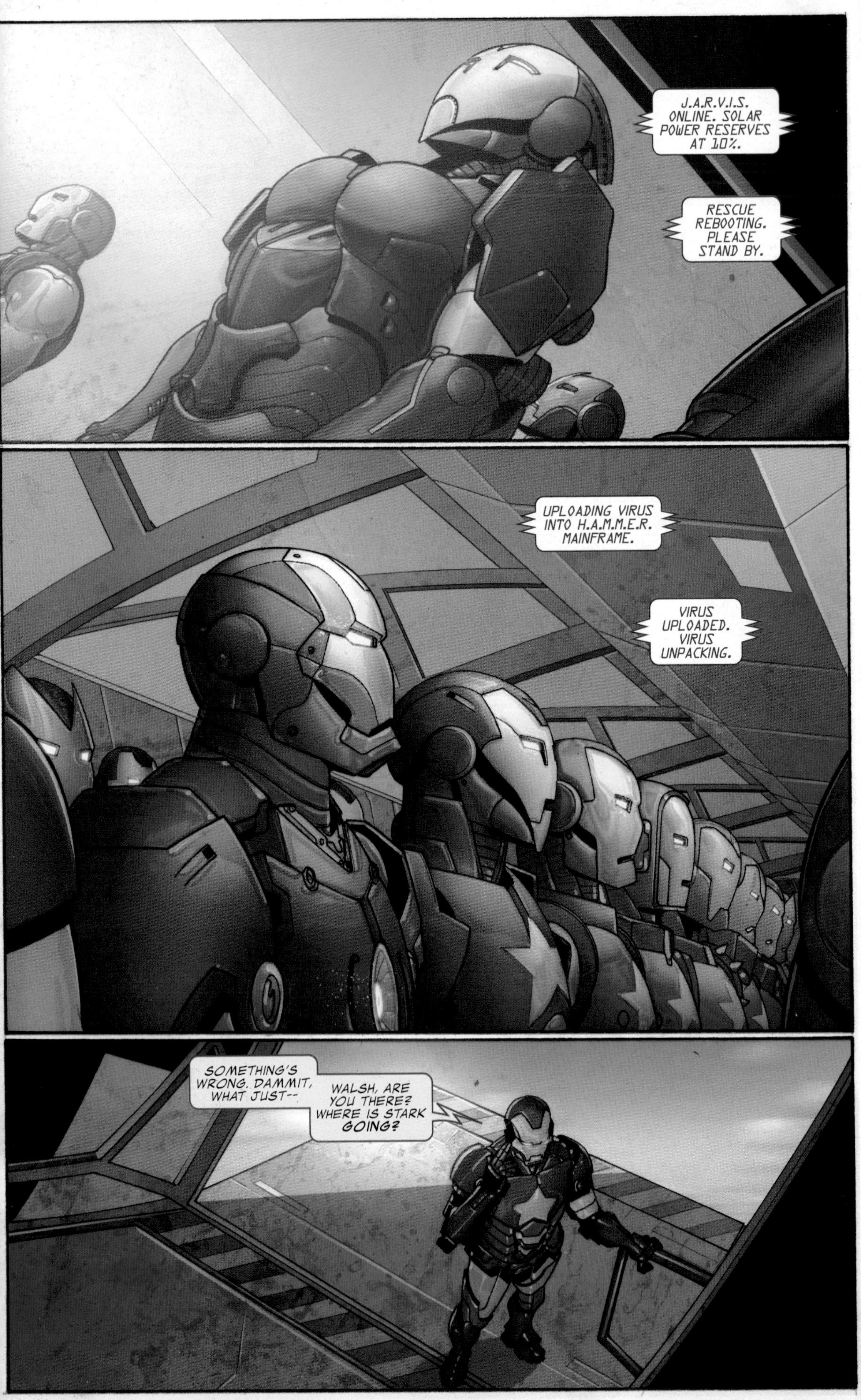
J.A.R.V.I.S. ONLINE. SOLAR POWER RESERVES AT 10%.
RESCUE REBOOTING. PLEASE STAND BY.
UPLOADING VIRUS INTO H.A.M.M.E.R. MAINFRAME.
VIRUS UPLOADED. VIRUS UNPACKING.
SOMETHING'S WRONG. DAMMIT, WHAT JUST--
WALSH, ARE YOU THERE? WHERE IS STARK GOING?

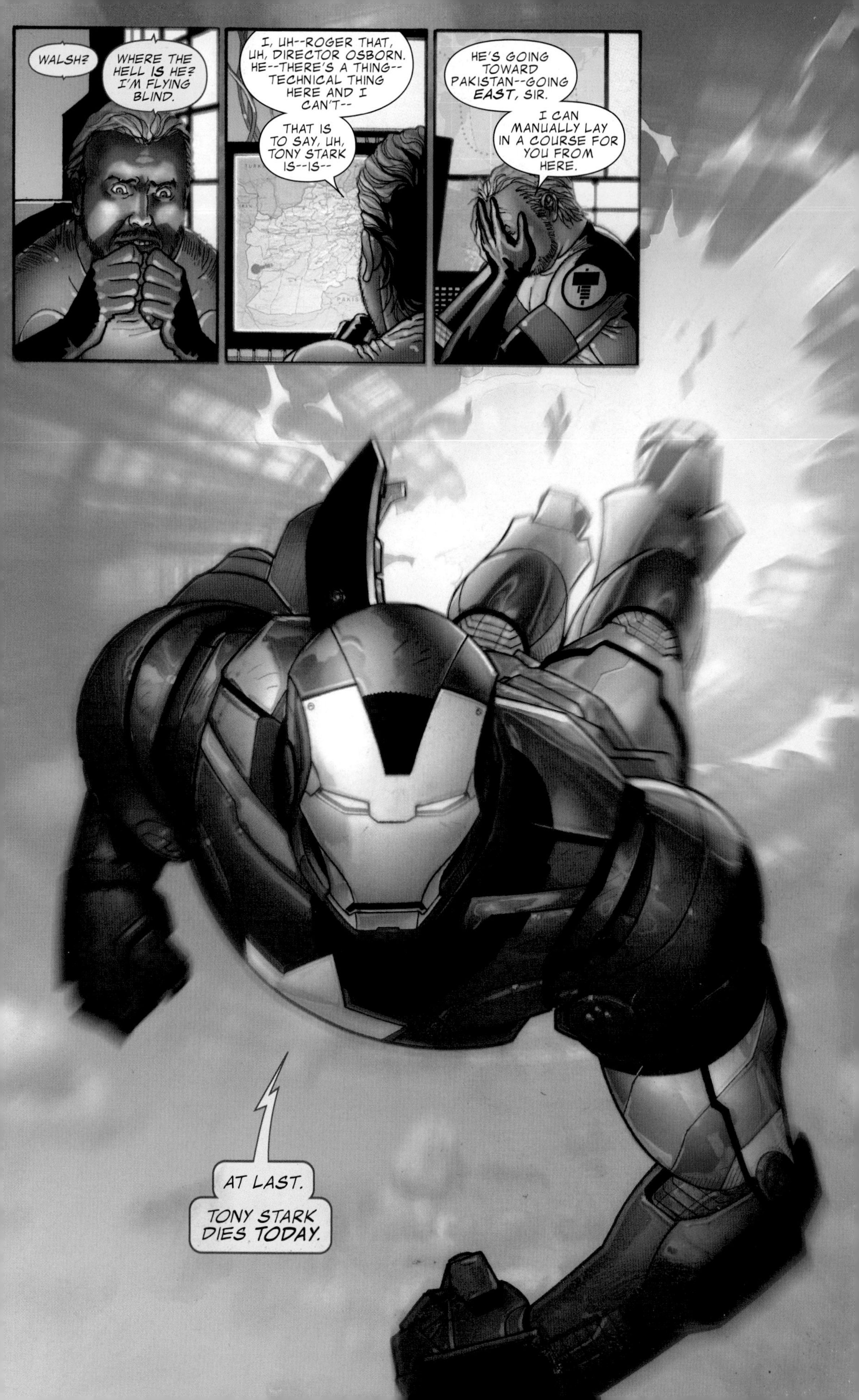
WALSH?
WHERE THE HELL IS HE? I'M FLYING BLIND.
I, UH--ROGER THAT, UH, DIRECTOR OSBORN. HE--THERE'S A THING--TECHNICAL THING HERE AND I CAN'T--
THAT IS TO SAY, UH, TONY STARK IS--IS--
HE'S GOING TOWARD PAKISTAN--GOING EAST, SIR.
I CAN MANUALLY LAY IN A COURSE FOR YOU FROM HERE.
AT LAST.
TONY STARK DIES TODAY.

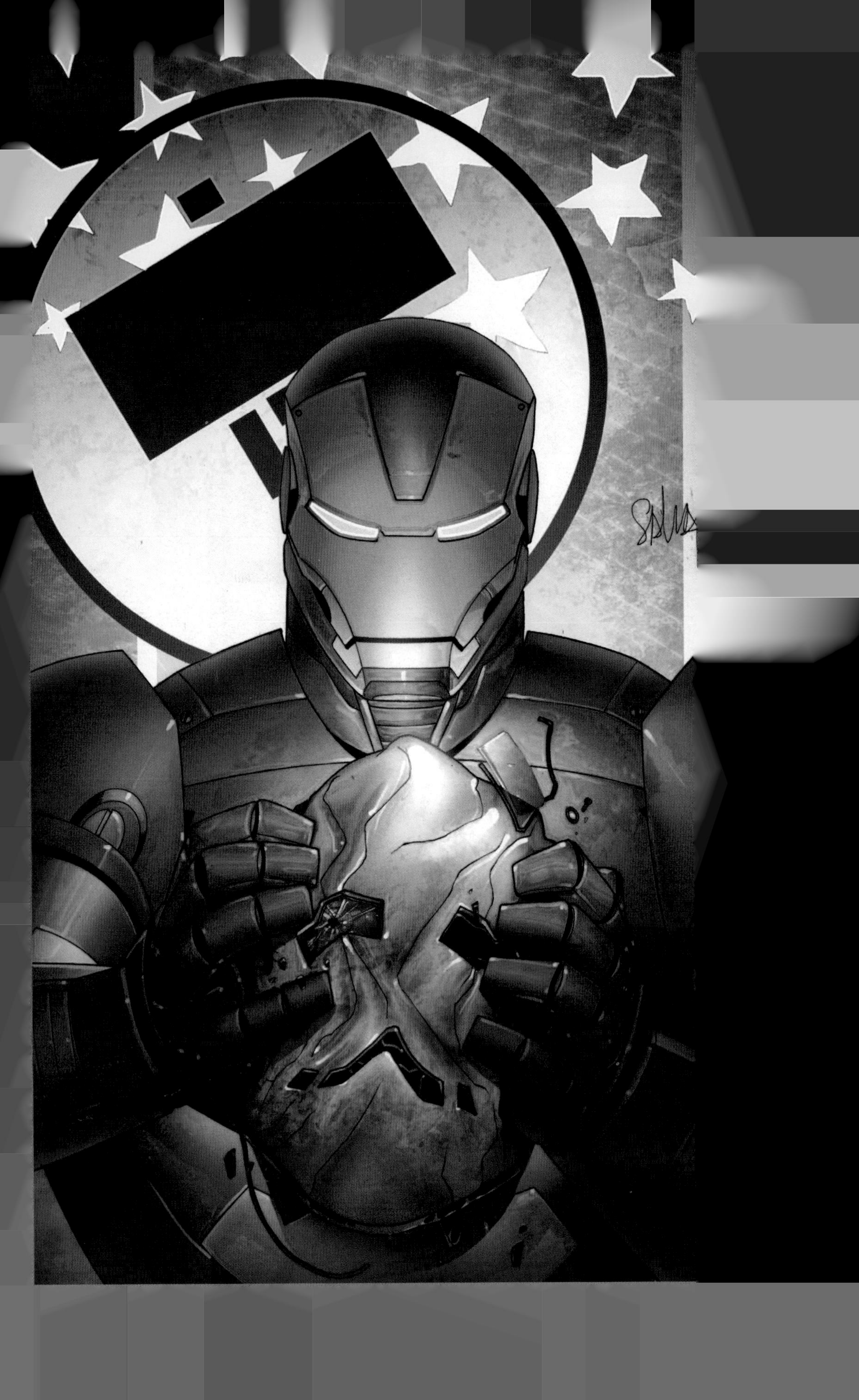

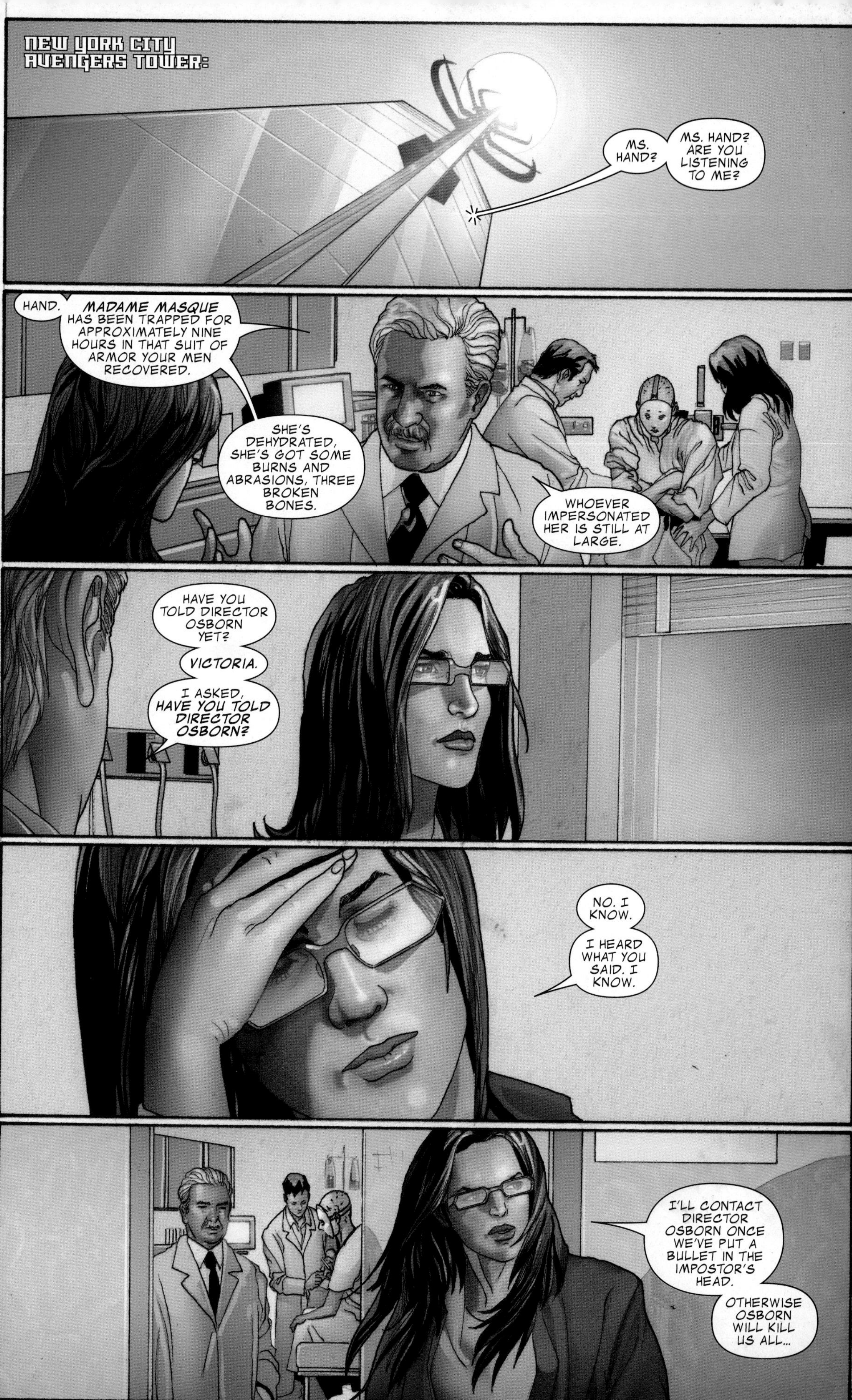

NEW YORK CITY
AVENGERS TOWER:
MS. HAND?
MS. HAND? ARE YOU LISTENING TO ME?
HAND.
MADAME MASQUE HAS BEEN TRAPPED FOR APPROXIMATELY NINE HOURS IN THAT SUIT OF ARMOR YOUR MEN RECOVERED.
SHE'S DEHYDRATED, SHE'S GOT SOME BURNS AND ABRASIONS, THREE BROKEN BONES.
WHOEVER IMPERSONATED HER IS STILL AT LARGE.
HAVE YOU TOLD DIRECTOR OSBORN YET?
VICTORIA.
I ASKED, HAVE YOU TOLD DIRECTOR OSBORN?
NO. I KNOW.
I HEARD WHAT YOU SAID. I KNOW.
I'LL CONTACT DIRECTOR OSBORN ONCE WE'VE PUT A BULLET IN THE IMPOSTOR'S HEAD.
OTHERWISE OSBORN WILL KILL US ALL...

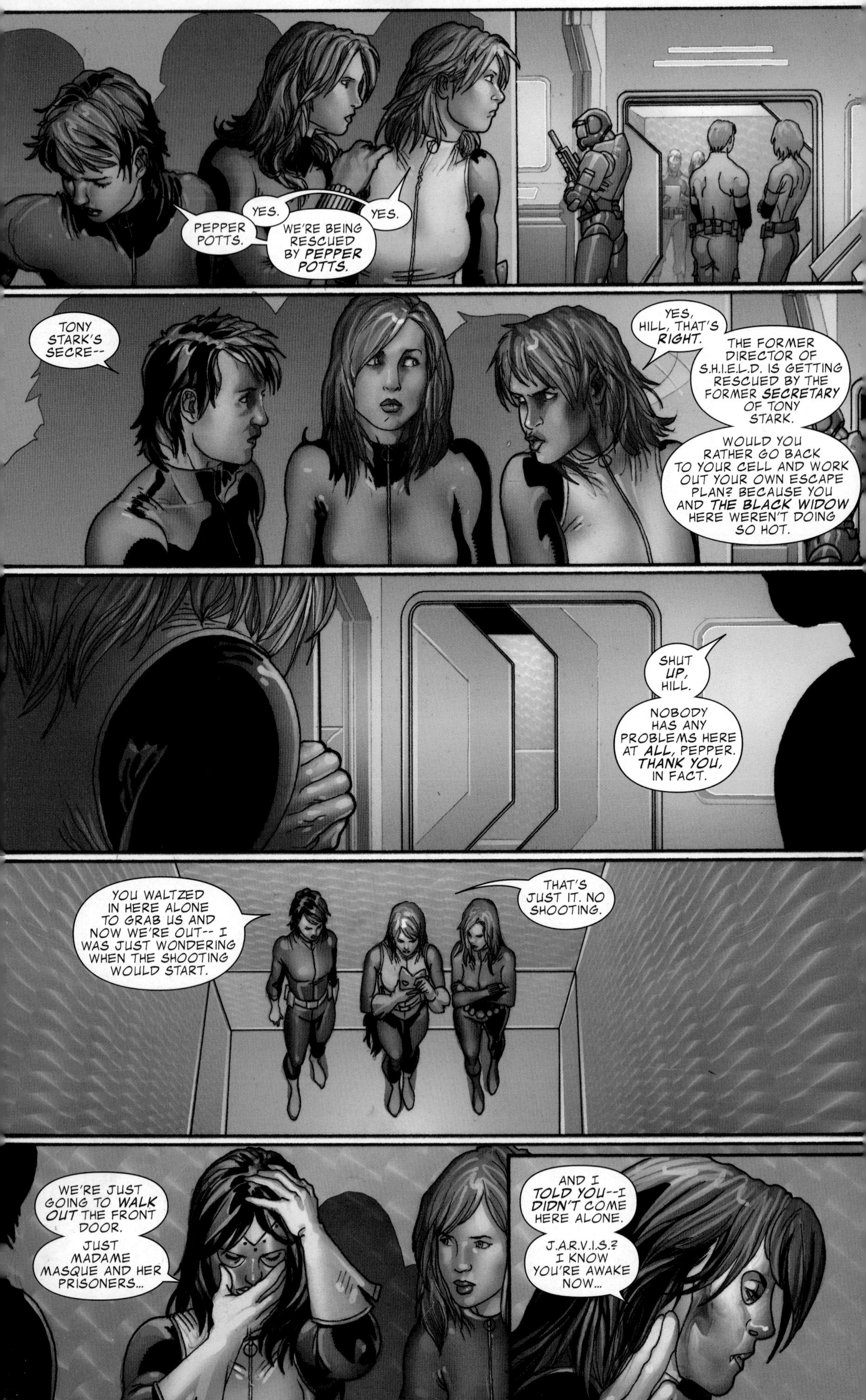

PEPPER POTTS.
YES.
YES.
WE'RE BEING RESCUED BY PEPPER POTTS.
TONY STARK'S SECRE--
YES, HILL, THAT'S RIGHT.
THE FORMER DIRECTOR OF S.H.I.E.L.D. IS GETTING RESCUED BY THE FORMER SECRETARY OF TONY STARK.
WOULD YOU RATHER GO BACK TO YOUR CELL AND WORK OUT YOUR OWN ESCAPE PLAN? BECAUSE YOU AND THE BLACK WIDOW HERE WEREN'T DOING SO HOT.
SHUT UP, HILL.
NOBODY HAS ANY PROBLEMS HERE AT ALL, PEPPER. THANK YOU, IN FACT.
YOU WALTZED IN HERE ALONE TO GRAB US AND NOW WE'RE OUT-- I WAS JUST WONDERING WHEN THE SHOOTING WOULD START.
THAT'S JUST IT. NO SHOOTING.
WE'RE JUST GOING TO WALK OUT THE FRONT DOOR.
JUST MADAME MASQUE AND HER PRISONERS...
AND I TOLD YOU--I DIDN'T COME HERE ALONE.
J.A.R.V.I.S.? I KNOW YOU'RE AWAKE NOW...

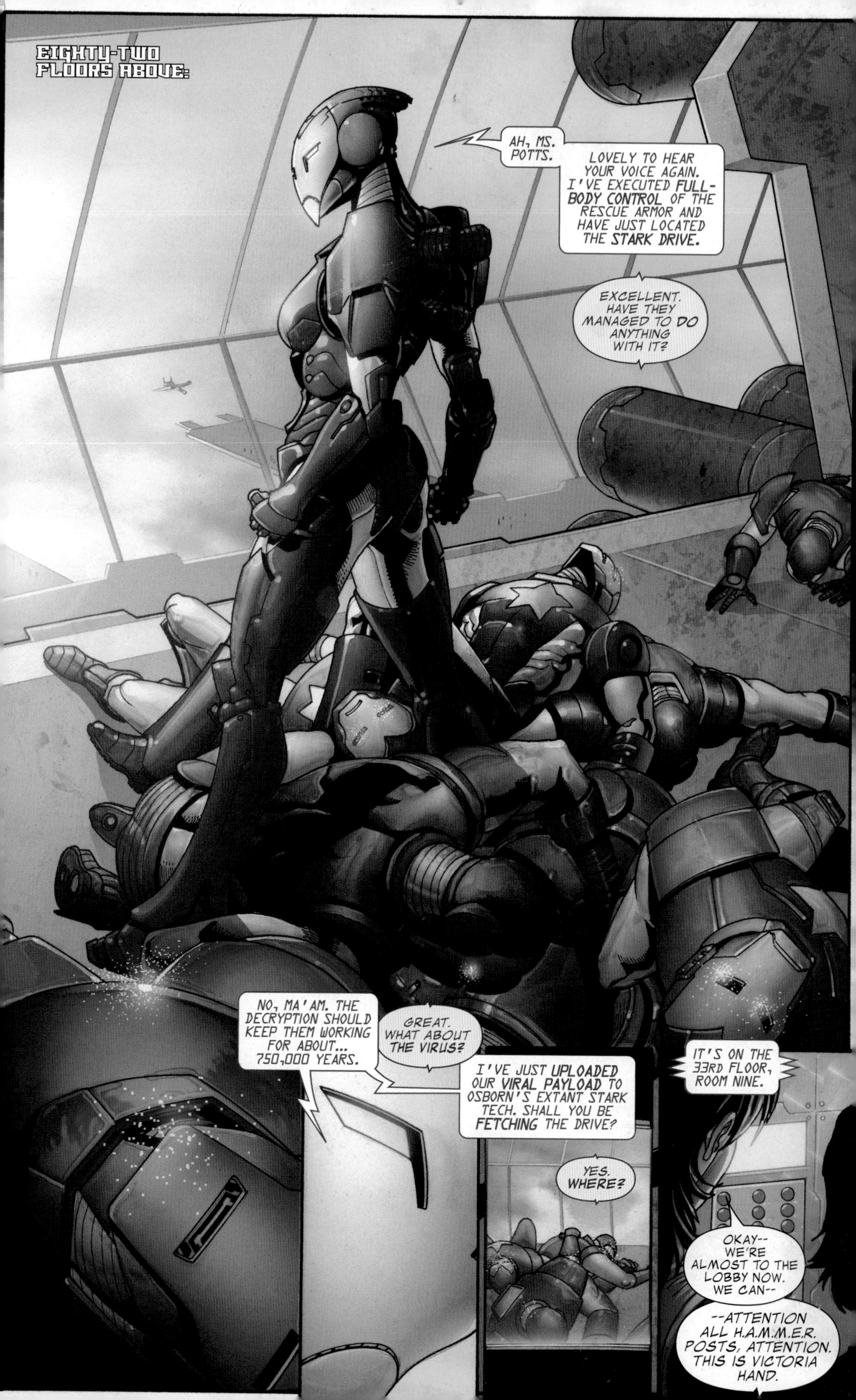
EIGHTY-TWO FLOORS ABOVE:
AH, MS. POTTS.
LOVELY TO HEAR YOUR VOICE AGAIN. I'VE EXECUTED FULL-BODY CONTROL OF THE RESCUE ARMOR AND HAVE JUST LOCATED THE STARK DRIVE.
EXCELLENT. HAVE THEY MANAGED TO DO ANYTHING WITH IT?
NO, MA'AM. THE DECRYPTION SHOULD KEEP THEM WORKING FOR ABOUT... 750,000 YEARS.
GREAT. WHAT ABOUT THE VIRUS?
I'VE JUST UPLOADED OUR VIRAL PAYLOAD TO OSBORN'S EXTANT STARK TECH. SHALL YOU BE FETCHING THE DRIVE?
YES. WHERE?
IT'S ON THE 33RD FLOOR, ROOM NINE.
OKAY-- WE'RE ALMOST TO THE LOBBY NOW. WE CAN--
--ATTENTION ALL H.A.M.M.E.R. POSTS, ATTENTION. THIS IS VICTORIA HAND.

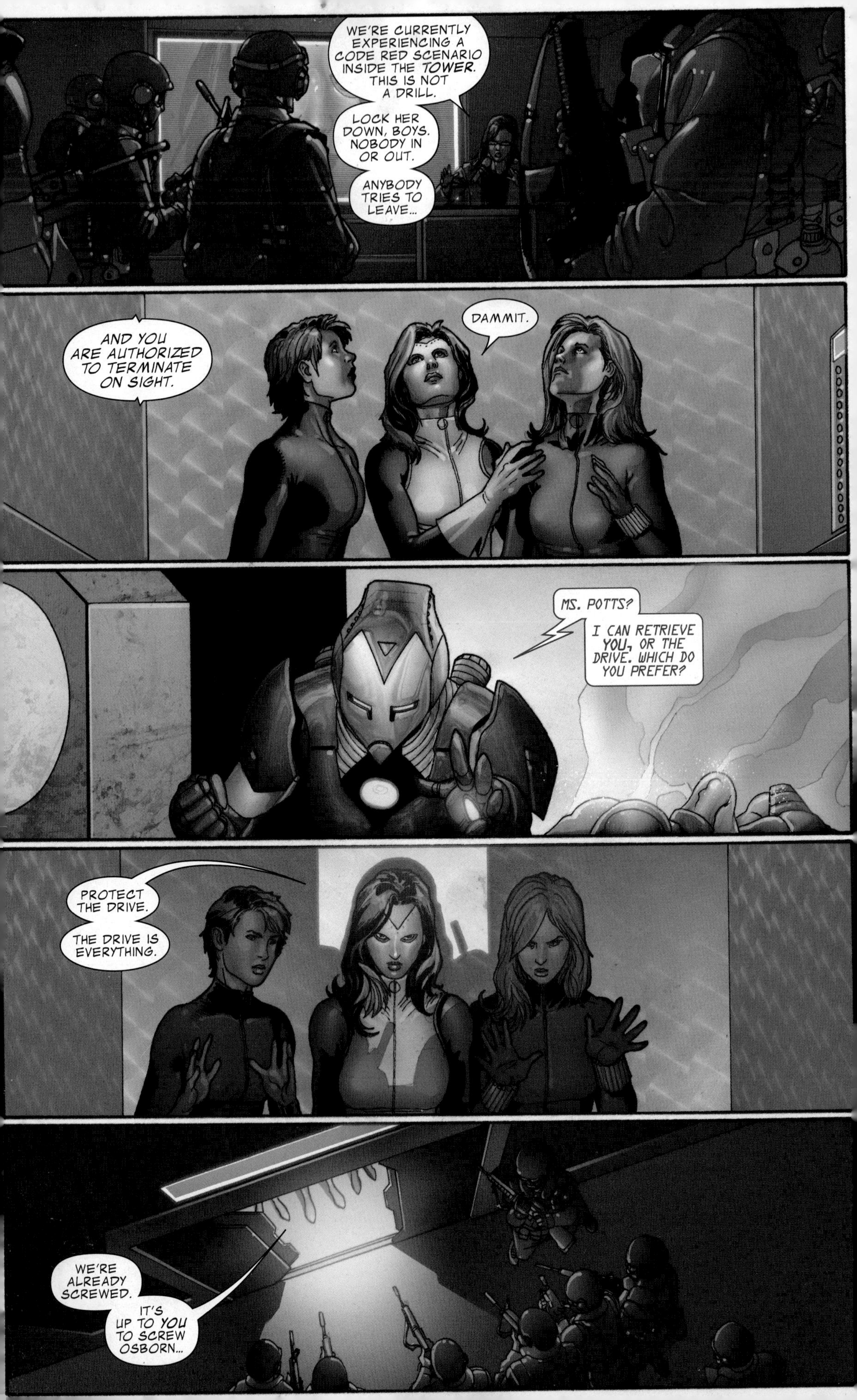
WE'RE CURRENTLY EXPERIENCING A CODE RED SCENARIO INSIDE THE TOWER. THIS IS NOT A DRILL.
LOCK HER DOWN, BOYS. NOBODY IN OR OUT.
ANYBODY TRIES TO LEAVE...
AND YOU ARE AUTHORIZED TO TERMINATE ON SIGHT.
DAMMIT.
MS. POTTS?
I CAN RETRIEVE YOU, OR THE DRIVE. WHICH DO YOU PREFER?
PROTECT THE DRIVE.
THE DRIVE IS EVERYTHING.
WE'RE ALREADY SCREWED.
IT'S UP TO YOU TO SCREW OSBORN...

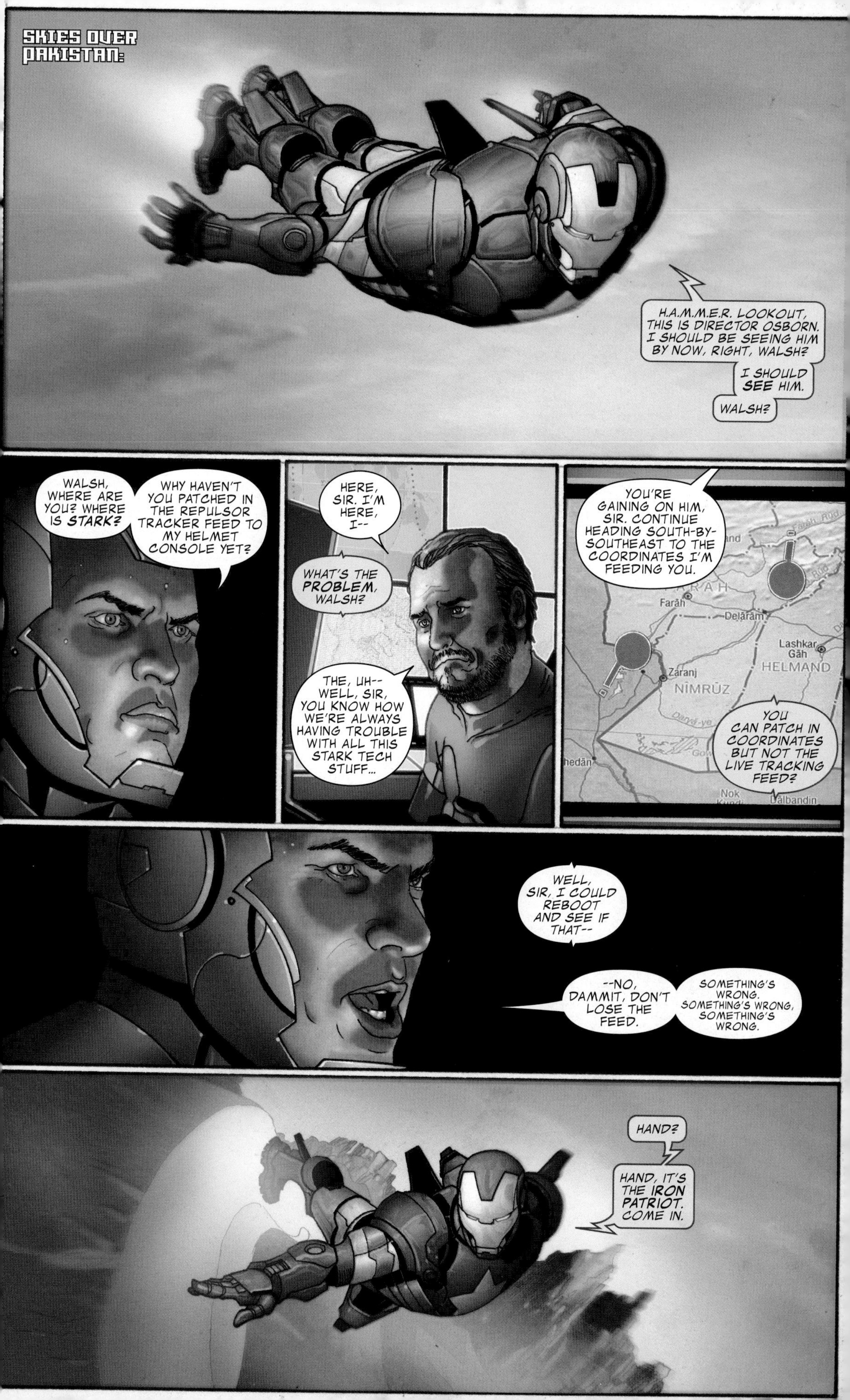
SKIES OVER PAKISTAN:
H.A.M.M.E.R. LOOKOUT, THIS IS DIRECTOR OSBORN. I SHOULD BE SEEING HIM BY NOW, RIGHT, WALSH?
I SHOULD **SEE** HIM.
WALSH?
WALSH, WHERE ARE YOU? WHERE IS ***STARK?***
WHY HAVEN'T YOU PATCHED IN THE REPULSOR TRACKER FEED TO MY HELMET CONSOLE YET?
HERE, SIR. I'M HERE, I--
WHAT'S THE ***PROBLEM,*** WALSH?
THE, UH-- WELL, SIR, YOU KNOW HOW WE'RE ALWAYS HAVING TROUBLE WITH ALL THIS STARK TECH STUFF...
YOU'RE GAINING ON HIM, SIR. CONTINUE HEADING SOUTH-BY-SOUTHEAST TO THE COORDINATES I'M FEEDING YOU.
Farāh
Delārām
Lashkar Gāh
HELMAND
Zaranj
NĪMRŪZ
Dalbandin
YOU CAN PATCH IN COORDINATES BUT NOT THE LIVE TRACKING FEED?
WELL, SIR, I COULD REBOOT AND SEE IF THAT--
--NO, DAMMIT, DON'T LOSE THE FEED.
SOMETHING'S WRONG. SOMETHING'S WRONG, SOMETHING'S WRONG.
HAND?
HAND, IT'S THE ***IRON PATRIOT.*** COME IN.

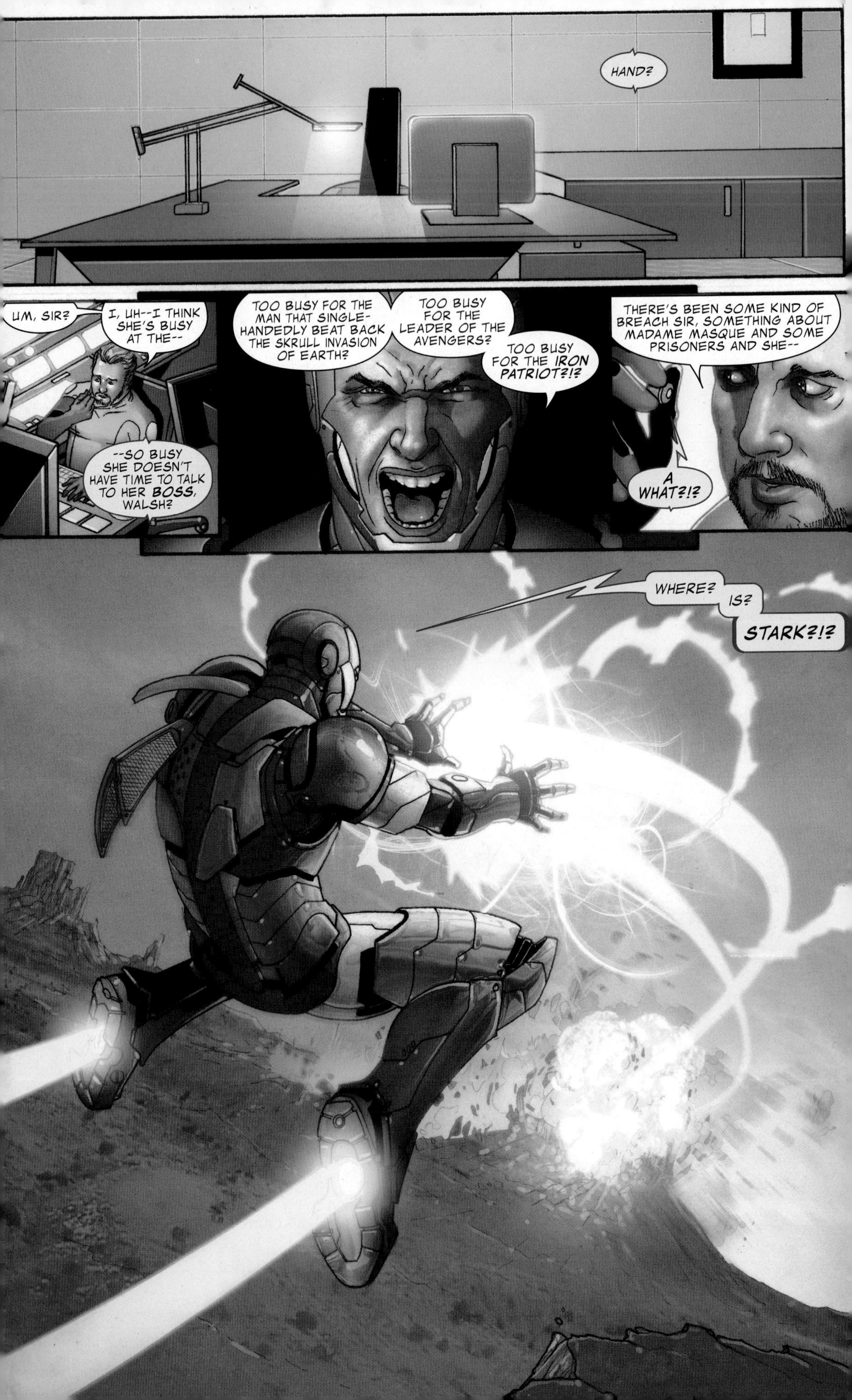
HAND?
UM, SIR?
I, UH--I THINK SHE'S BUSY AT THE--
--SO BUSY SHE DOESN'T HAVE TIME TO TALK TO HER BOSS, WALSH?
TOO BUSY FOR THE MAN THAT SINGLE-HANDEDLY BEAT BACK THE SKRULL INVASION OF EARTH?
TOO BUSY FOR THE LEADER OF THE AVENGERS?
TOO BUSY FOR THE IRON PATRIOT?!?
THERE'S BEEN SOME KIND OF BREACH SIR, SOMETHING ABOUT MADAME MASQUE AND SOME PRISONERS AND SHE--
A WHAT?!?
WHERE?
IS?
STARK?!?

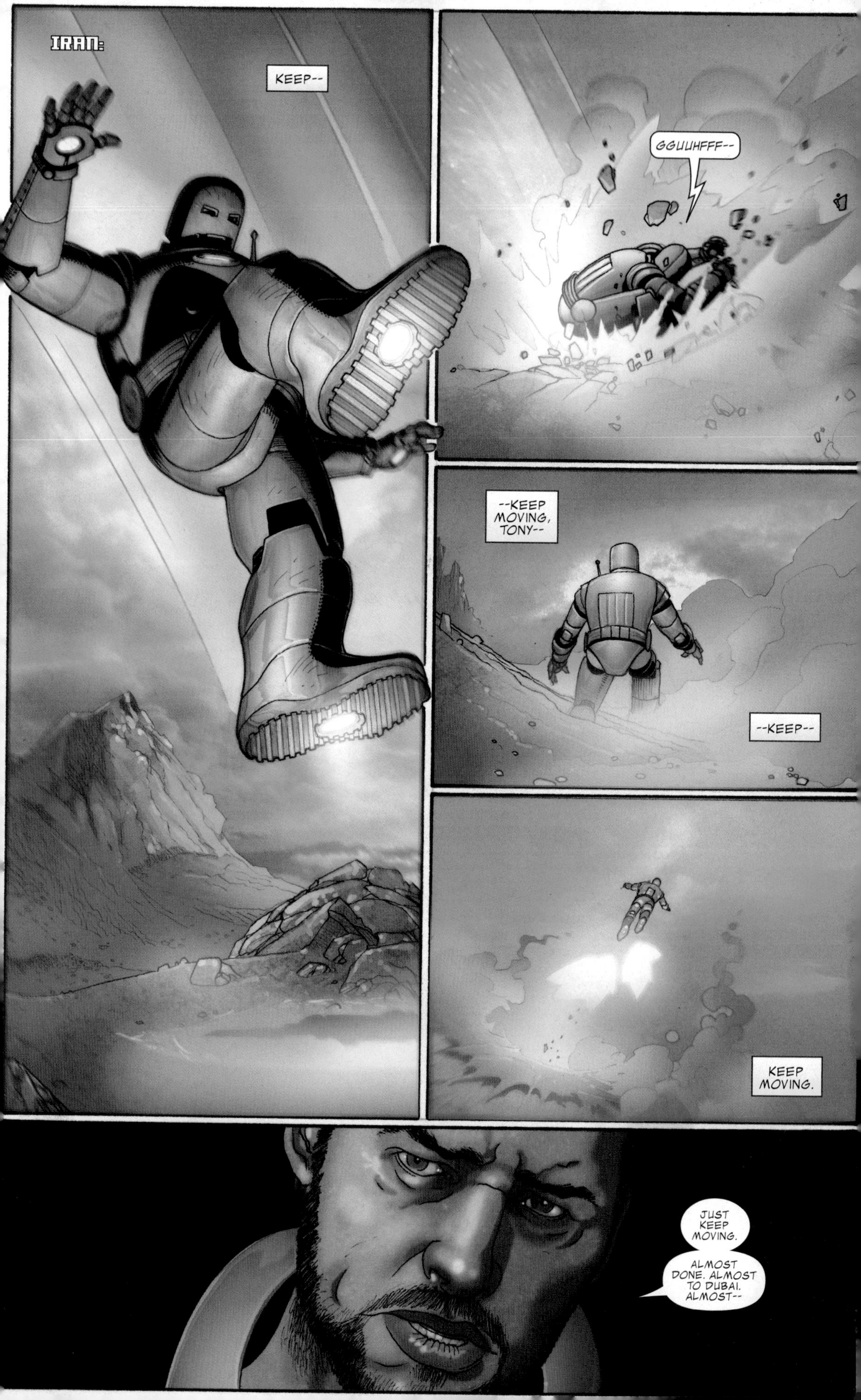
IRAN:
KEEP--
GGUUHFFF--
--KEEP MOVING, TONY--
--KEEP--
KEEP MOVING.
JUST KEEP MOVING.
ALMOST DONE. ALMOST TO DUBAI. ALMOST--

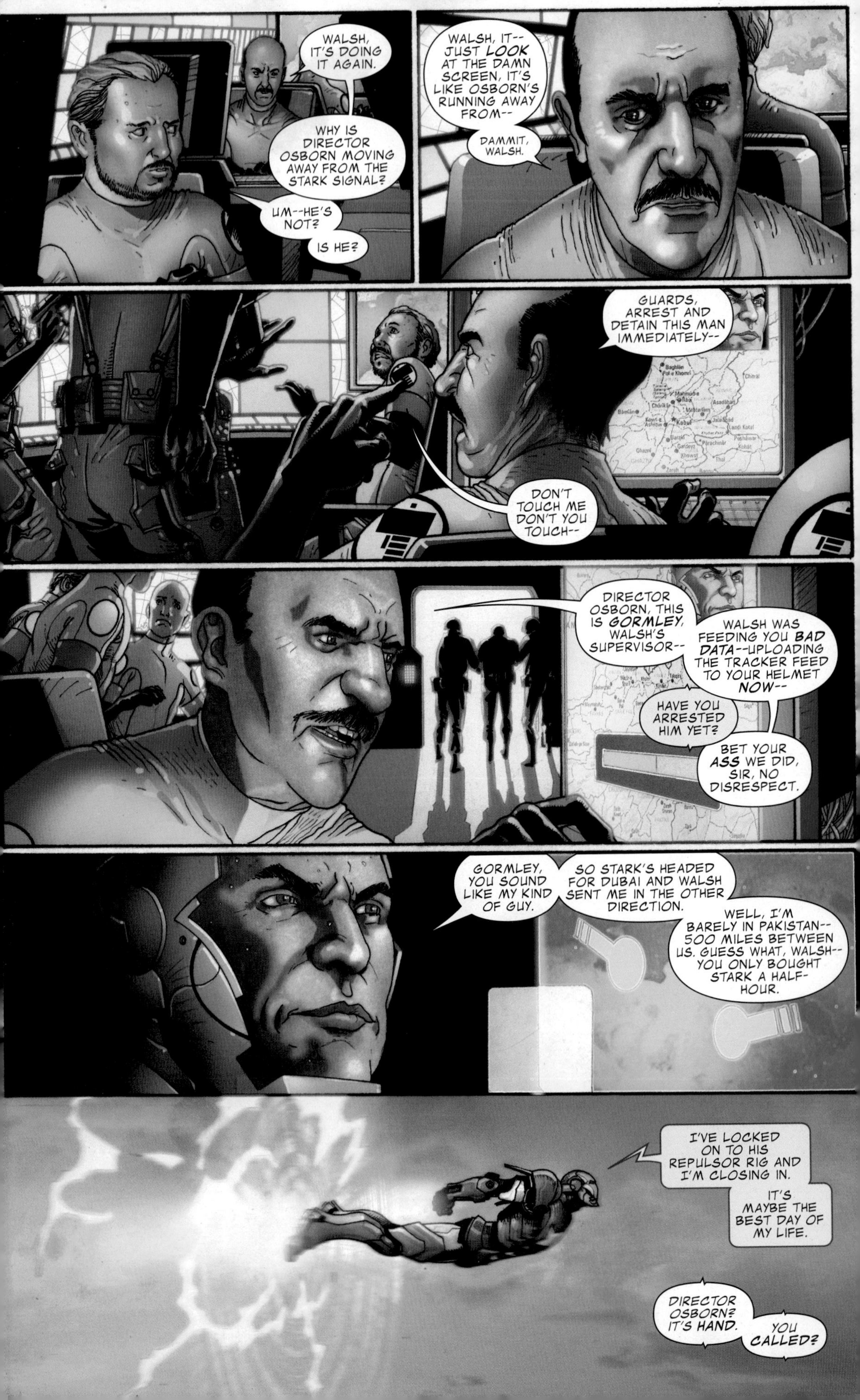
WALSH, IT'S DOING IT AGAIN.
WHY IS DIRECTOR OSBORN MOVING AWAY FROM THE STARK SIGNAL?
UM--HE'S NOT?
IS HE?
WALSH, IT-- JUST LOOK AT THE DAMN SCREEN, IT'S LIKE OSBORN'S RUNNING AWAY FROM--
DAMMIT, WALSH.
GUARDS, ARREST AND DETAIN THIS MAN IMMEDIATELY--
DON'T TOUCH ME DON'T YOU TOUCH--
DIRECTOR OSBORN, THIS IS GORMLEY, WALSH'S SUPERVISOR--
WALSH WAS FEEDING YOU BAD DATA--UPLOADING THE TRACKER FEED TO YOUR HELMET NOW--
HAVE YOU ARRESTED HIM YET?
BET YOUR ASS WE DID, SIR, NO DISRESPECT.
GORMLEY, YOU SOUND LIKE MY KIND OF GUY.
SO STARK'S HEADED FOR DUBAI AND WALSH SENT ME IN THE OTHER DIRECTION.
WELL, I'M BARELY IN PAKISTAN-- 500 MILES BETWEEN US. GUESS WHAT, WALSH-- YOU ONLY BOUGHT STARK A HALF-HOUR.
I'VE LOCKED ON TO HIS REPULSOR RIG AND I'M CLOSING IN.
IT'S MAYBE THE BEST DAY OF MY LIFE.
DIRECTOR OSBORN? IT'S HAND.
YOU CALLED?

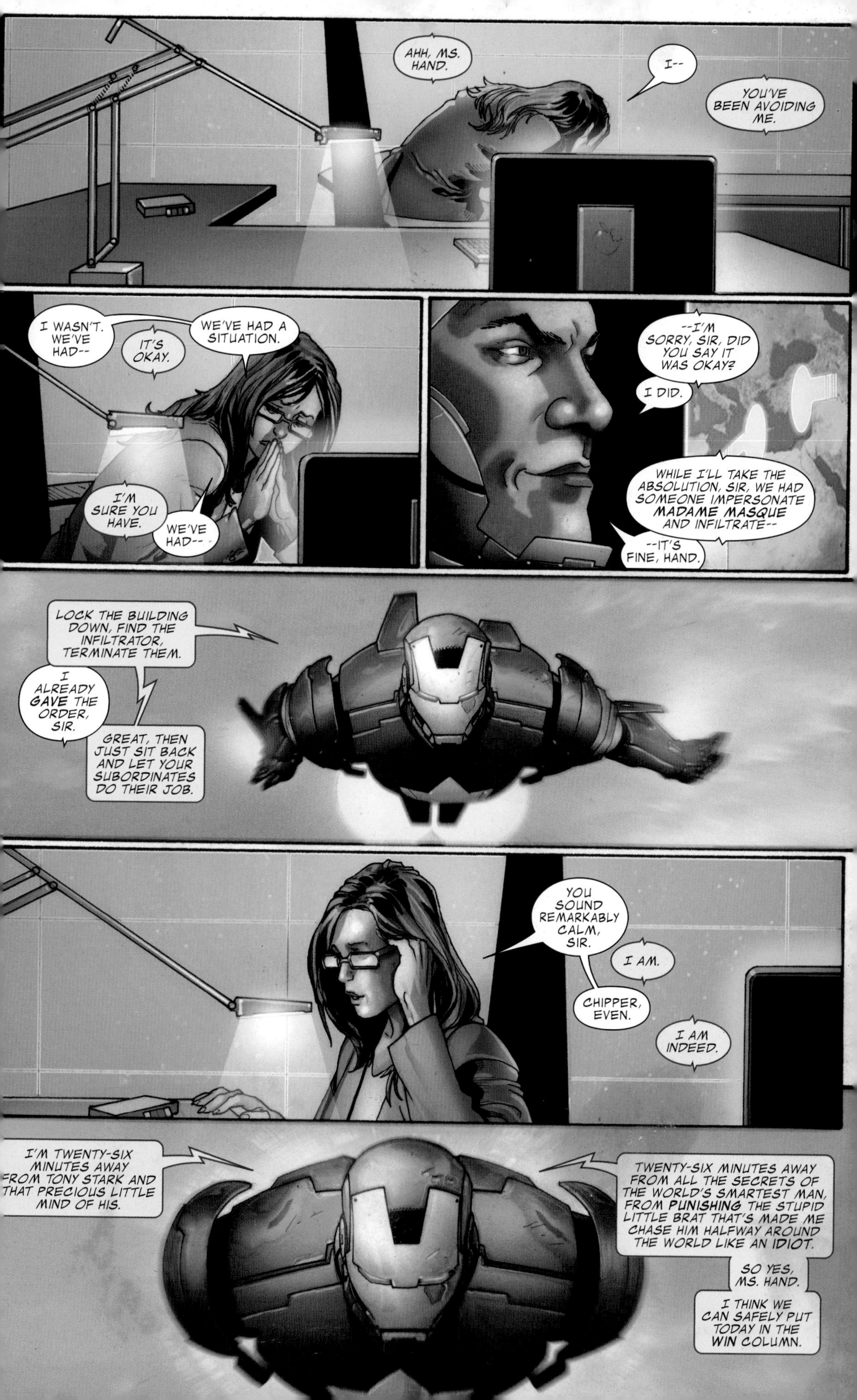
AHH, MS. HAND.
I--
YOU'VE BEEN AVOIDING ME.
I WASN'T. WE'VE HAD--
IT'S OKAY.
WE'VE HAD A SITUATION.
I'M SURE YOU HAVE.
WE'VE HAD--
--I'M SORRY, SIR, DID YOU SAY IT WAS OKAY?
I DID.
WHILE I'LL TAKE THE ABSOLUTION, SIR, WE HAD SOMEONE IMPERSONATE MADAME MASQUE AND INFILTRATE--
--IT'S FINE, HAND.
LOCK THE BUILDING DOWN, FIND THE INFILTRATOR, TERMINATE THEM.
I ALREADY GAVE THE ORDER, SIR.
GREAT, THEN JUST SIT BACK AND LET YOUR SUBORDINATES DO THEIR JOB.
YOU SOUND REMARKABLY CALM, SIR.
I AM.
CHIPPER, EVEN.
I AM INDEED.
I'M TWENTY-SIX MINUTES AWAY FROM TONY STARK AND THAT PRECIOUS LITTLE MIND OF HIS.
TWENTY-SIX MINUTES AWAY FROM ALL THE SECRETS OF THE WORLD'S SMARTEST MAN, FROM PUNISHING THE STUPID LITTLE BRAT THAT'S MADE ME CHASE HIM HALFWAY AROUND THE WORLD LIKE AN IDIOT.
SO YES, MS. HAND.
I THINK WE CAN SAFELY PUT TODAY IN THE WIN COLUMN.

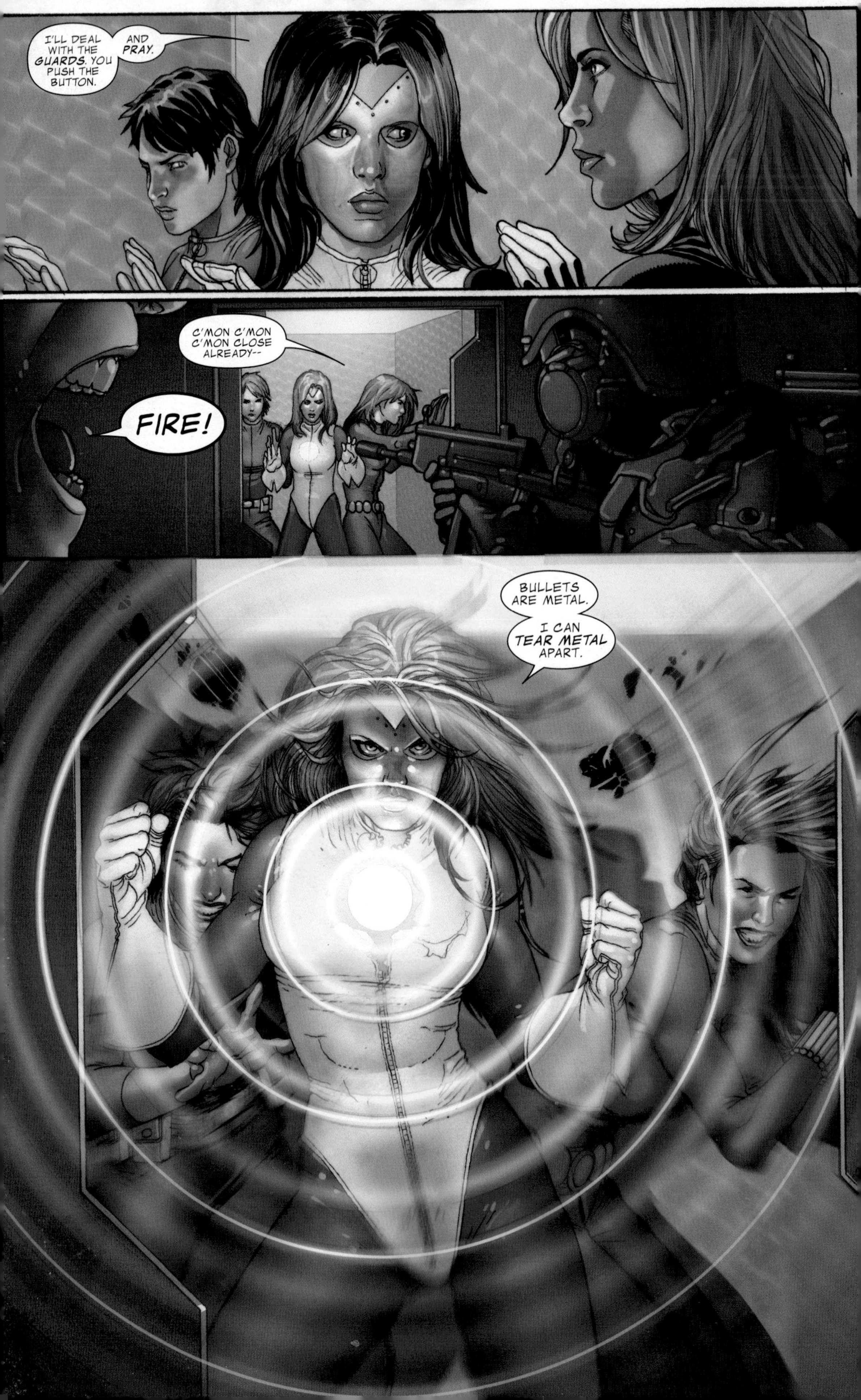
I'LL DEAL WITH THE GUARDS. YOU PUSH THE BUTTON.
AND PRAY.
C'MON C'MON C'MON CLOSE ALREADY--
FIRE!
BULLETS ARE METAL.
I CAN TEAR METAL APART.

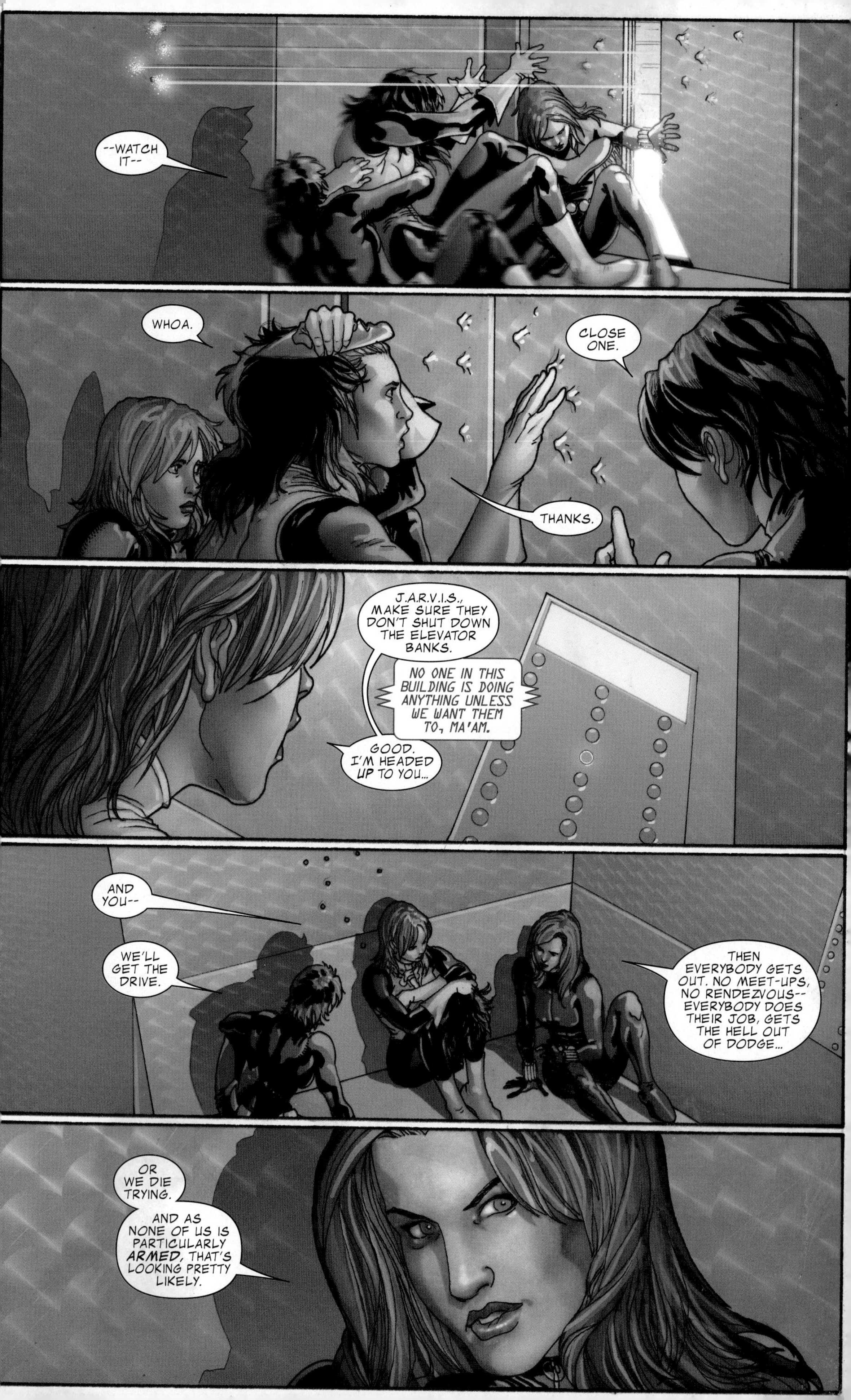
--WATCH IT--
WHOA.
CLOSE ONE.
THANKS.
J.A.R.V.I.S., MAKE SURE THEY DON'T SHUT DOWN THE ELEVATOR BANKS.
NO ONE IN THIS BUILDING IS DOING ANYTHING UNLESS WE WANT THEM TO, MA'AM.
GOOD. I'M HEADED UP TO YOU...
AND YOU--
WE'LL GET THE DRIVE.
THEN EVERYBODY GETS OUT. NO MEET-UPS, NO RENDEZVOUS--EVERYBODY DOES THEIR JOB, GETS THE HELL OUT OF DODGE...
OR WE DIE TRYING.
AND AS NONE OF US IS PARTICULARLY ARMED, THAT'S LOOKING PRETTY LIKELY.

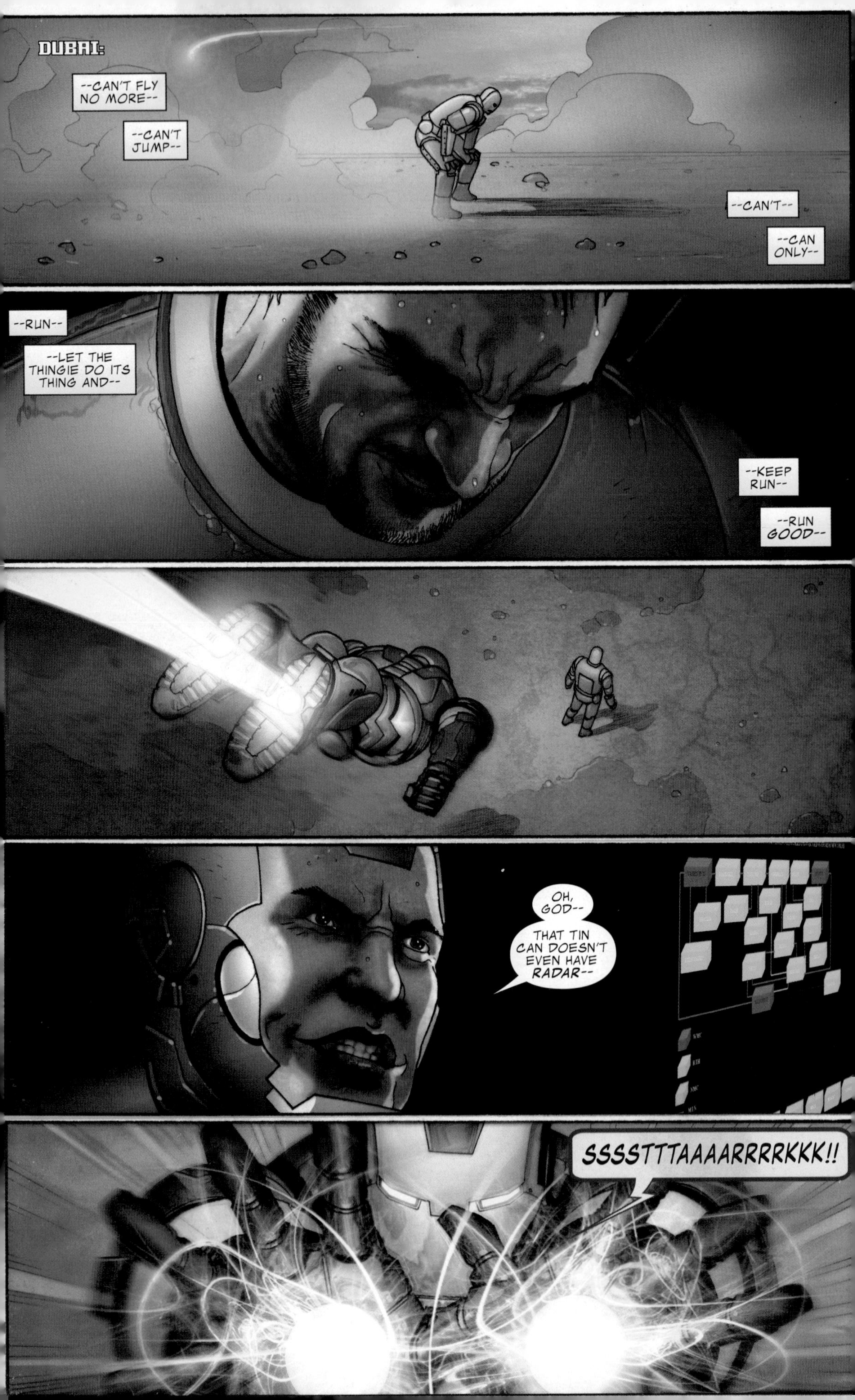
DUBAI:
--CAN'T FLY NO MORE--
--CAN'T JUMP--
--CAN'T--
--CAN ONLY--
--RUN--
--LET THE THINGIE DO ITS THING AND--
--KEEP RUN--
--RUN GOOD--
OH, GOD--
THAT TIN CAN DOESN'T EVEN HAVE RADAR--
SSSSTTTAAAARRRRKKK!!

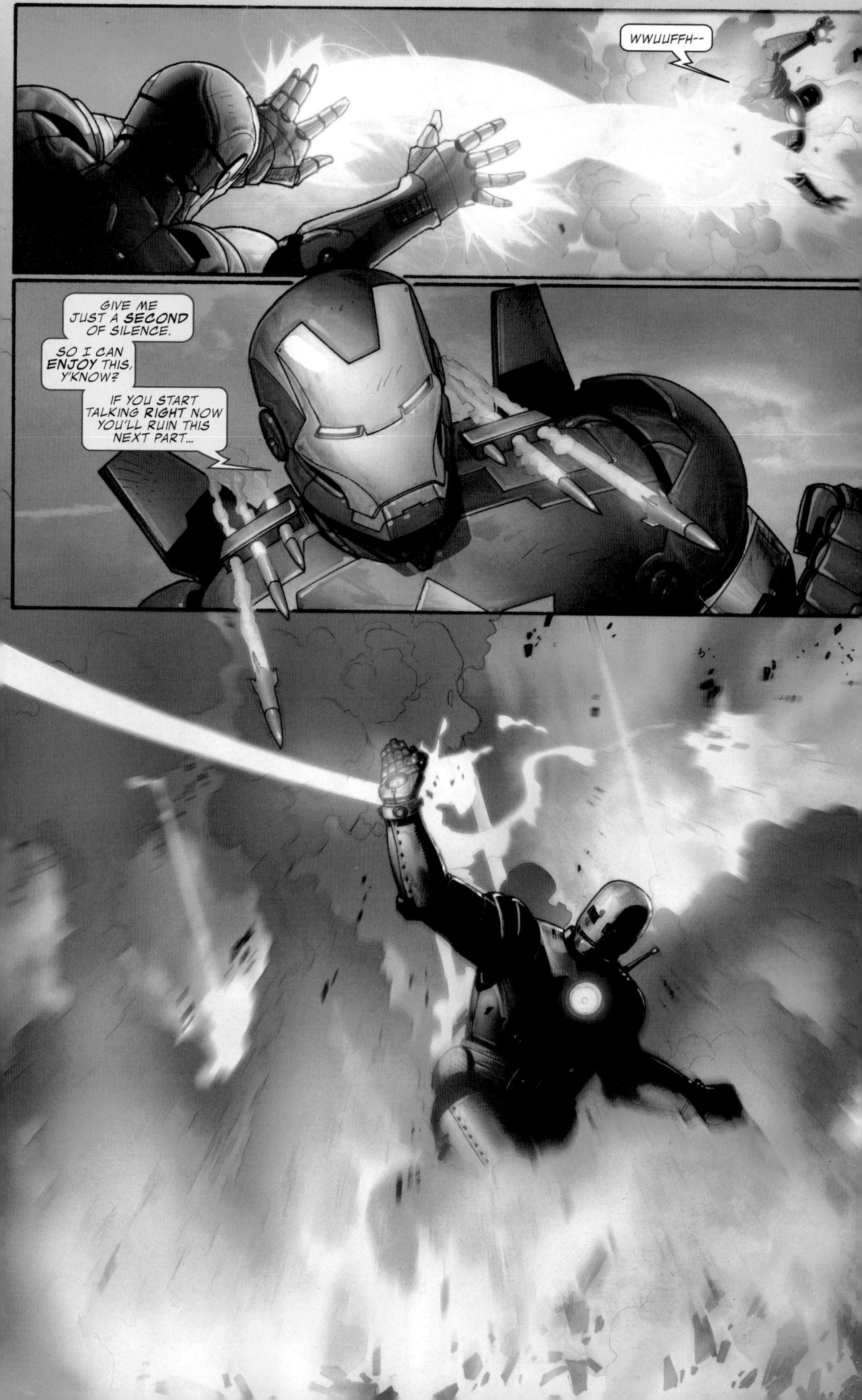

WWUUFFH--
GIVE ME JUST A SECOND OF SILENCE.
SO I CAN ENJOY THIS, Y'KNOW?
IF YOU START TALKING RIGHT NOW YOU'LL RUIN THIS NEXT PART...

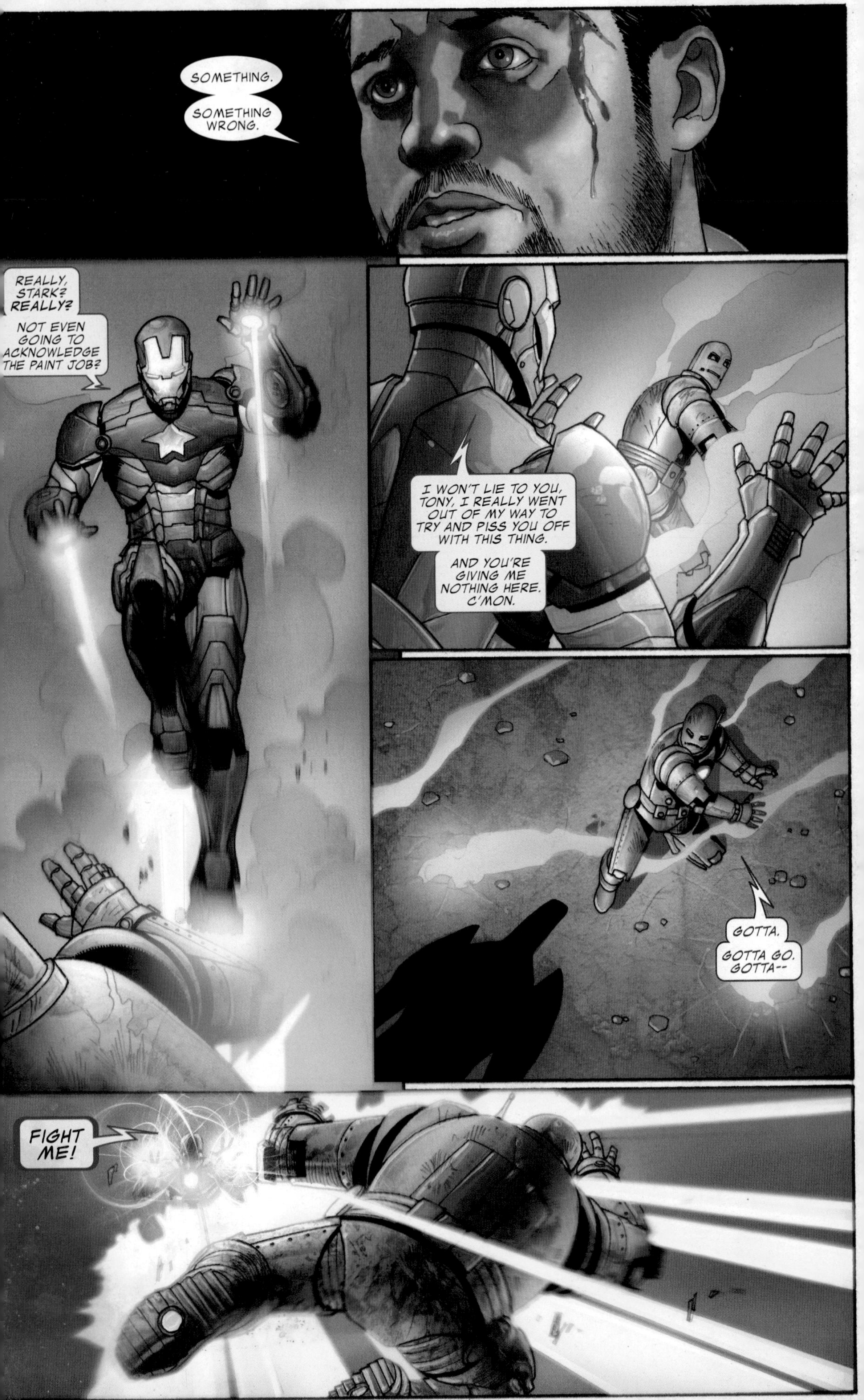
SOMETHING.
SOMETHING WRONG.
REALLY, STARK? REALLY?
NOT EVEN GOING TO ACKNOWLEDGE THE PAINT JOB?
I WON'T LIE TO YOU, TONY, I REALLY WENT OUT OF MY WAY TO TRY AND PISS YOU OFF WITH THIS THING.
AND YOU'RE GIVING ME NOTHING HERE. C'MON.
GOTTA.
GOTTA GO. GOTTA--
FIGHT ME!

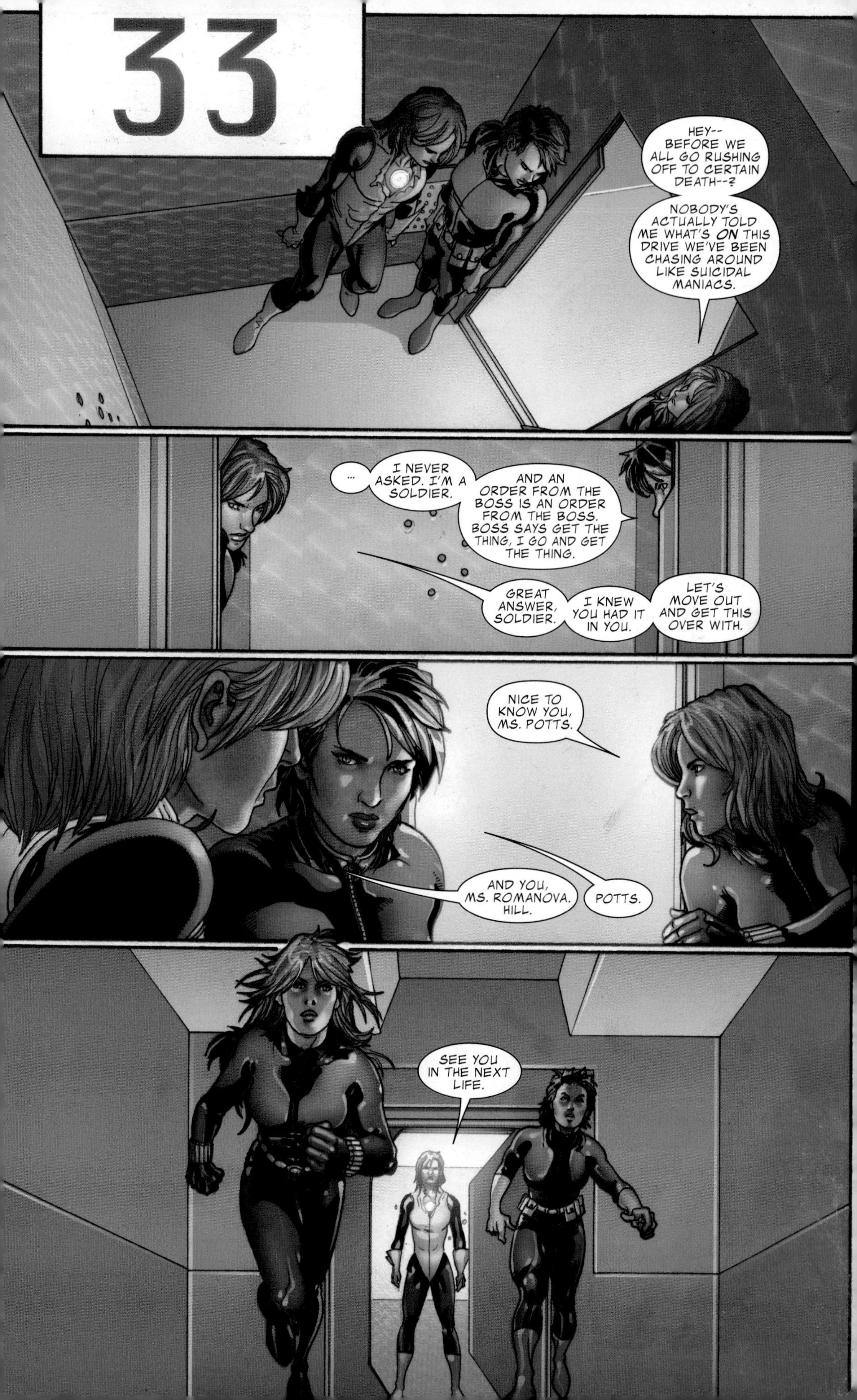
33
HEY-- BEFORE WE ALL GO RUSHING OFF TO CERTAIN DEATH--?
NOBODY'S ACTUALLY TOLD ME WHAT'S ON THIS DRIVE WE'VE BEEN CHASING AROUND LIKE SUICIDAL MANIACS.
...
I NEVER ASKED. I'M A SOLDIER.
AND AN ORDER FROM THE BOSS IS AN ORDER FROM THE BOSS. BOSS SAYS GET THE THING, I GO AND GET THE THING.
GREAT ANSWER, SOLDIER.
I KNEW YOU HAD IT IN YOU.
LET'S MOVE OUT AND GET THIS OVER WITH.
NICE TO KNOW YOU, MS. POTTS.
AND YOU, MS. ROMANOVA. HILL.
POTTS.
SEE YOU IN THE NEXT LIFE.

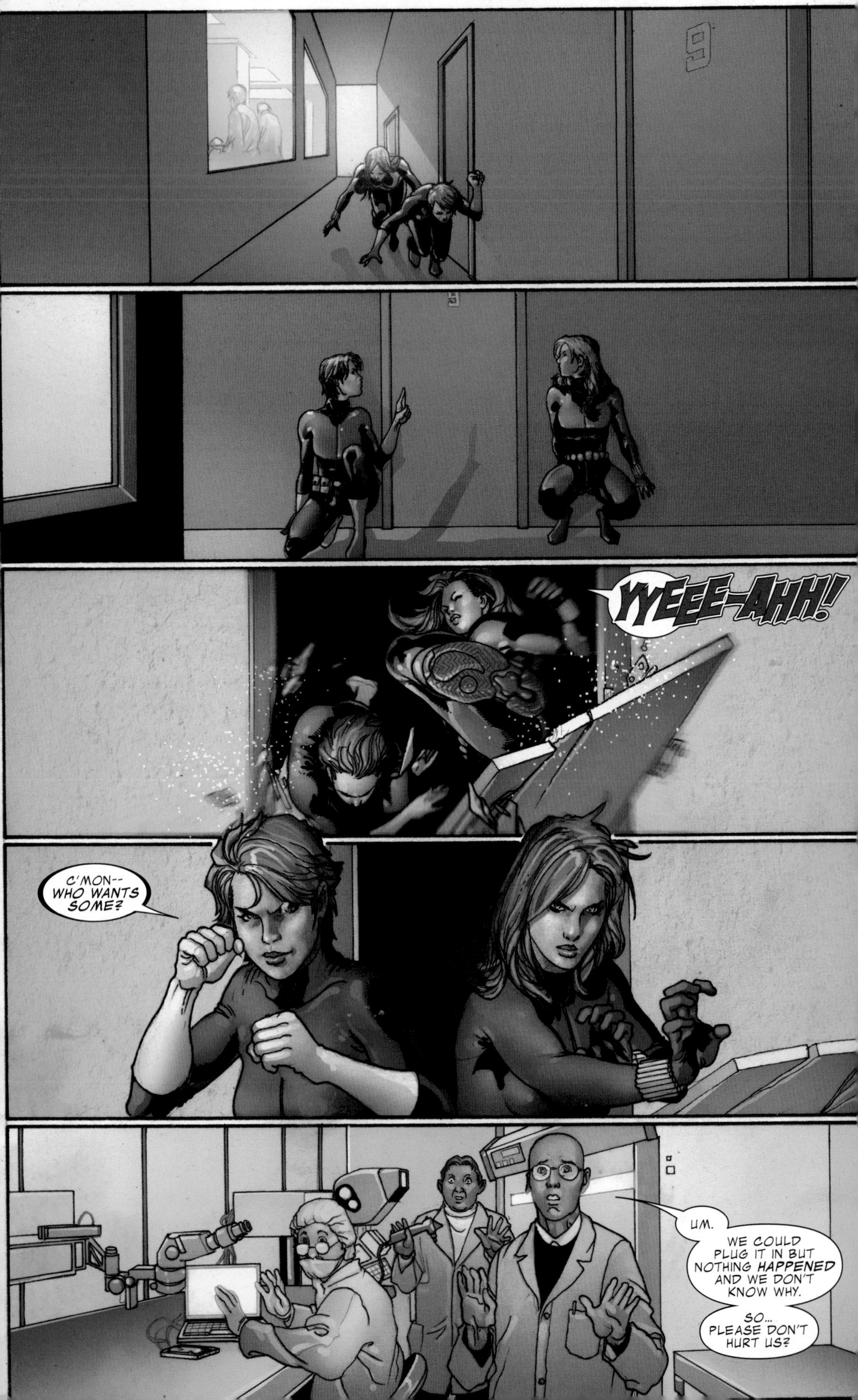
YYEEE-AHH!
C'MON-- WHO WANTS SOME?
UM.
WE COULD PLUG IT IN BUT NOTHING HAPPENED AND WE DON'T KNOW WHY.
SO... PLEASE DON'T HURT US?

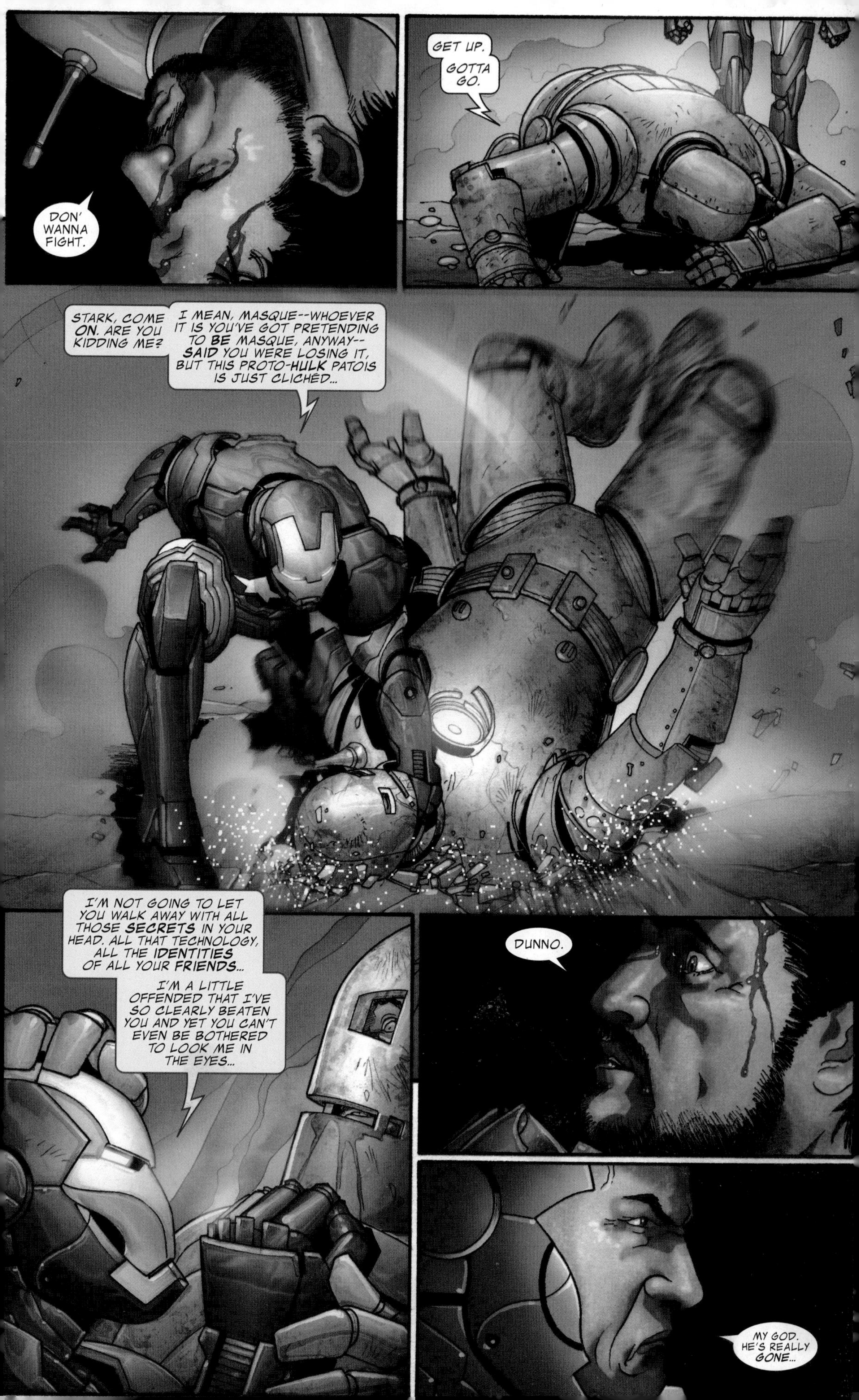
DON' WANNA FIGHT.
GET UP. GOTTA GO.
STARK, COME ON. ARE YOU KIDDING ME?
I MEAN, MASQUE--WHOEVER IT IS YOU'VE GOT PRETENDING TO BE MASQUE, ANYWAY--SAID YOU WERE LOSING IT, BUT THIS PROTO-HULK PATOIS IS JUST CLICHÉD...
I'M NOT GOING TO LET YOU WALK AWAY WITH ALL THOSE SECRETS IN YOUR HEAD. ALL THAT TECHNOLOGY, ALL THE IDENTITIES OF ALL YOUR FRIENDS...
I'M A LITTLE OFFENDED THAT I'VE SO CLEARLY BEATEN YOU AND YET YOU CAN'T EVEN BE BOTHERED TO LOOK ME IN THE EYES...
DUNNO.
MY GOD. HE'S REALLY GONE...

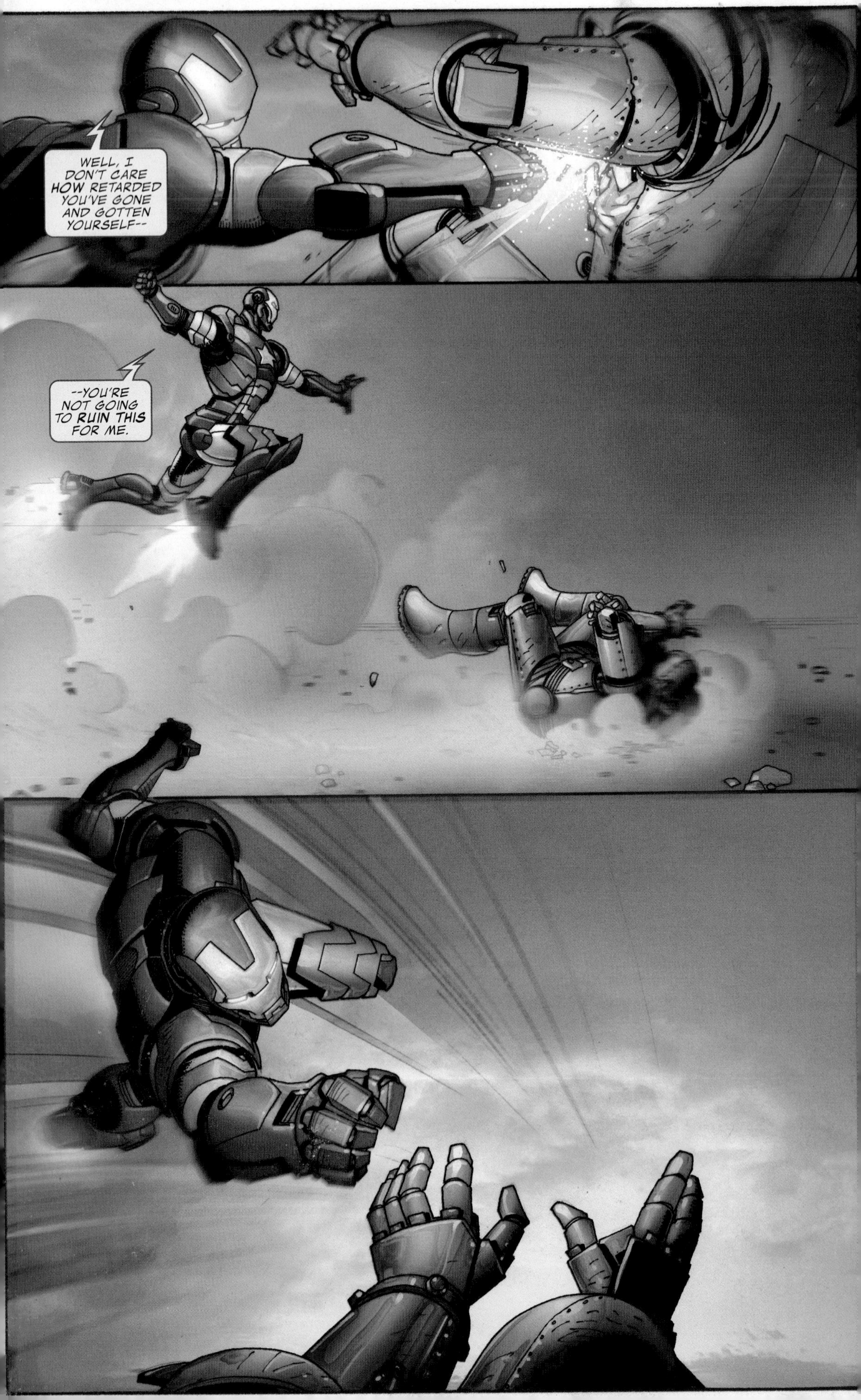
WELL, I DON'T CARE HOW RETARDED YOU'VE GONE AND GOTTEN YOURSELF--
--YOU'RE NOT GOING TO RUIN THIS FOR ME.

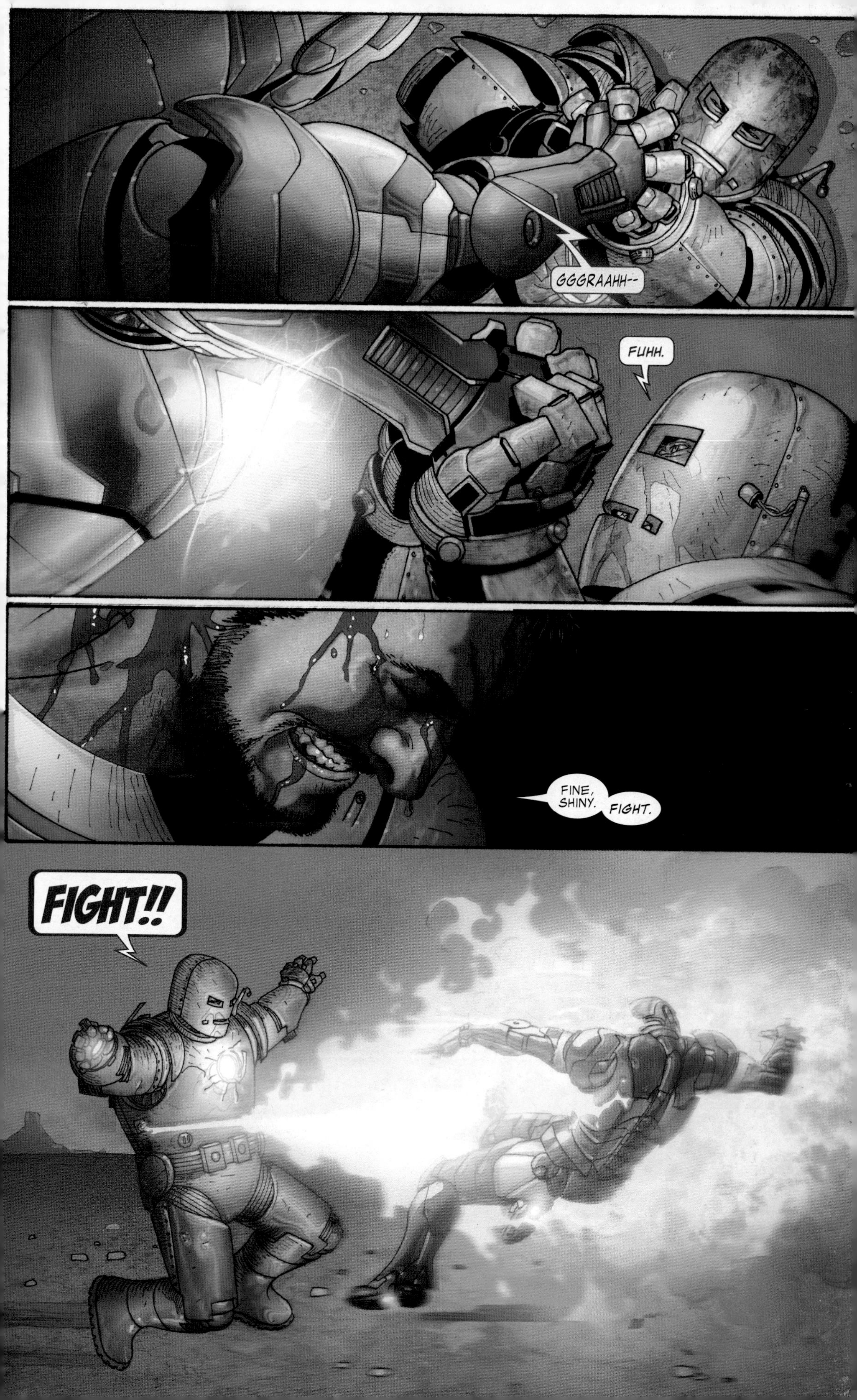
GGGRAAHH--
FUHH.
FINE, SHINY.
FIGHT.
FIGHT!!

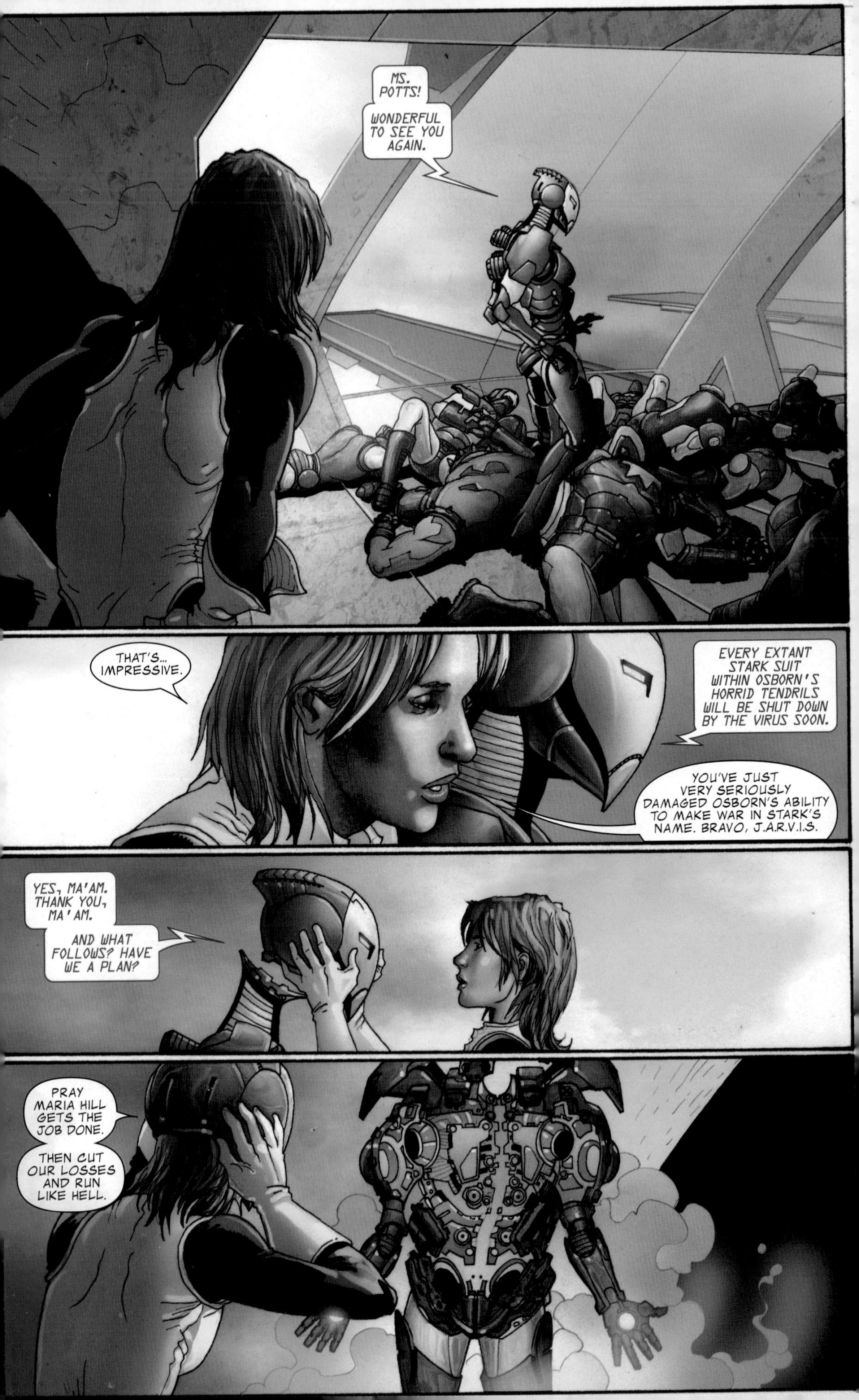
MS. POTTS!
WONDERFUL TO SEE YOU AGAIN.
THAT'S... IMPRESSIVE.
EVERY EXTANT STARK SUIT WITHIN OSBORN'S HORRID TENDRILS WILL BE SHUT DOWN BY THE VIRUS SOON.
YOU'VE JUST VERY SERIOUSLY DAMAGED OSBORN'S ABILITY TO MAKE WAR IN STARK'S NAME. BRAVO, J.A.R.V.I.S.
YES, MA'AM. THANK YOU, MA'AM.
AND WHAT FOLLOWS? HAVE WE A PLAN?
PRAY MARIA HILL GETS THE JOB DONE.
THEN CUT OUR LOSSES AND RUN LIKE HELL.

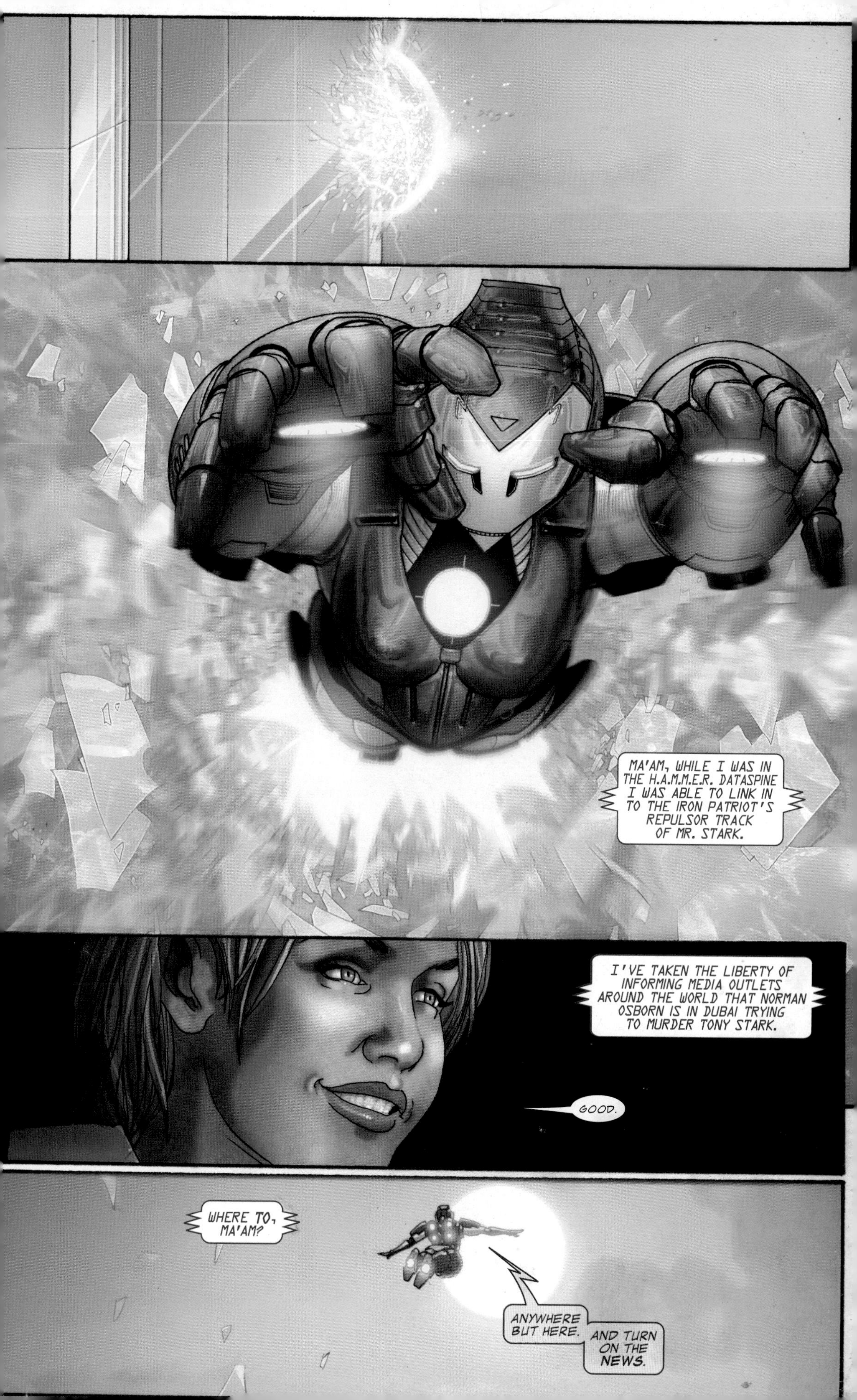
MA'AM, WHILE I WAS IN THE H.A.M.M.E.R. DATASPINE I WAS ABLE TO LINK IN TO THE IRON PATRIOT'S REPULSOR TRACK OF MR. STARK.
I'VE TAKEN THE LIBERTY OF INFORMING MEDIA OUTLETS AROUND THE WORLD THAT NORMAN OSBORN IS IN DUBAI TRYING TO MURDER TONY STARK.
GOOD.
WHERE TO, MA'AM?
ANYWHERE BUT HERE.
AND TURN ON THE NEWS.

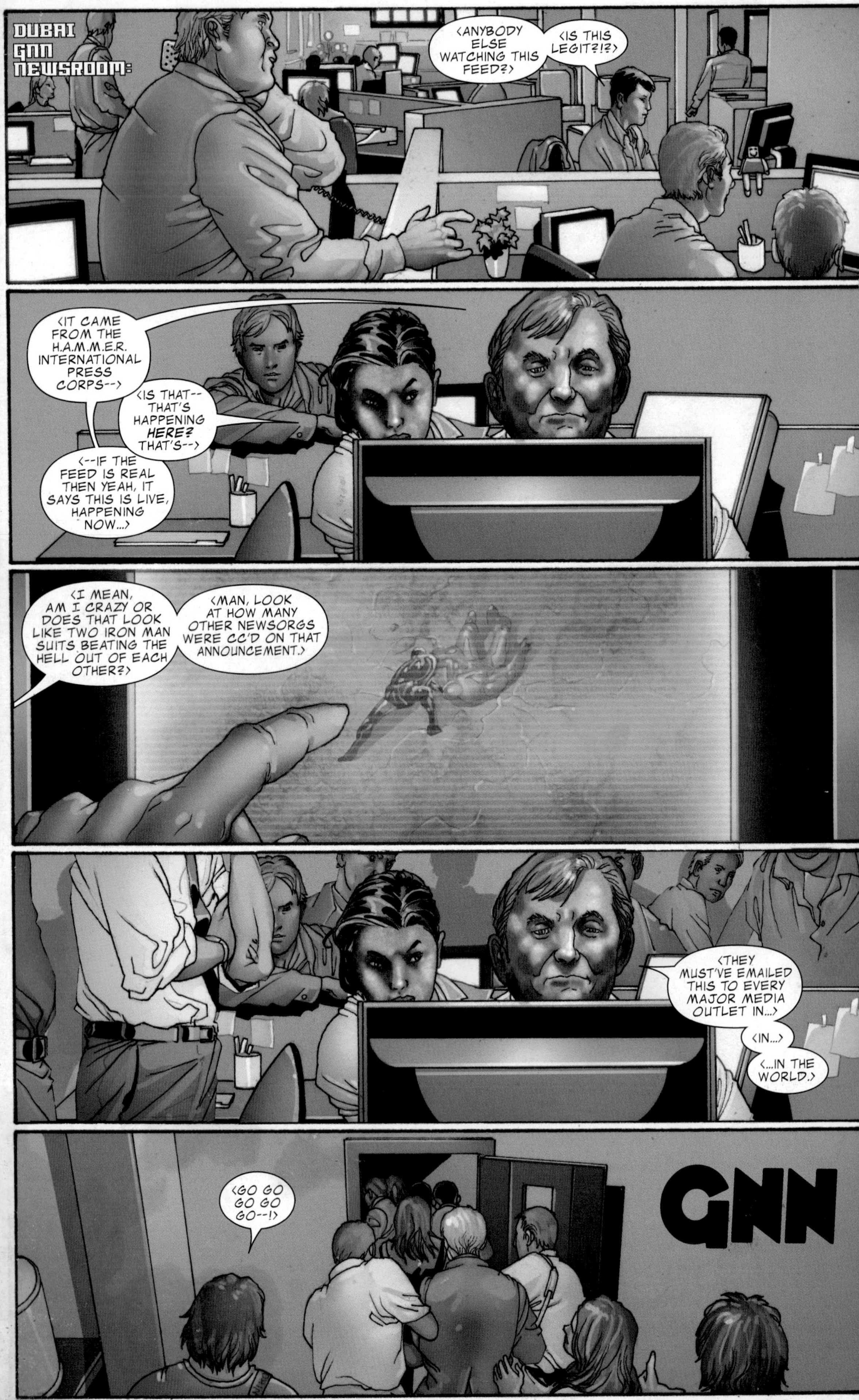
DUBAI GNN NEWSROOM:
<ANYBODY ELSE WATCHING THIS FEED?>
<IS THIS LEGIT?!?>
<IT CAME FROM THE H.A.M.M.E.R. INTERNATIONAL PRESS CORPS-->
<IS THAT--THAT'S HAPPENING HERE? THAT'S-->
<--IF THE FEED IS REAL THEN YEAH, IT SAYS THIS IS LIVE, HAPPENING NOW...>
<I MEAN, AM I CRAZY OR DOES THAT LOOK LIKE TWO IRON MAN SUITS BEATING THE HELL OUT OF EACH OTHER?>
<MAN, LOOK AT HOW MANY OTHER NEWSORGS WERE CC'D ON THAT ANNOUNCEMENT.>
<THEY MUST'VE EMAILED THIS TO EVERY MAJOR MEDIA OUTLET IN...>
<IN...>
<...IN THE WORLD.>
<GO GO GO GO GO--!>
GNN

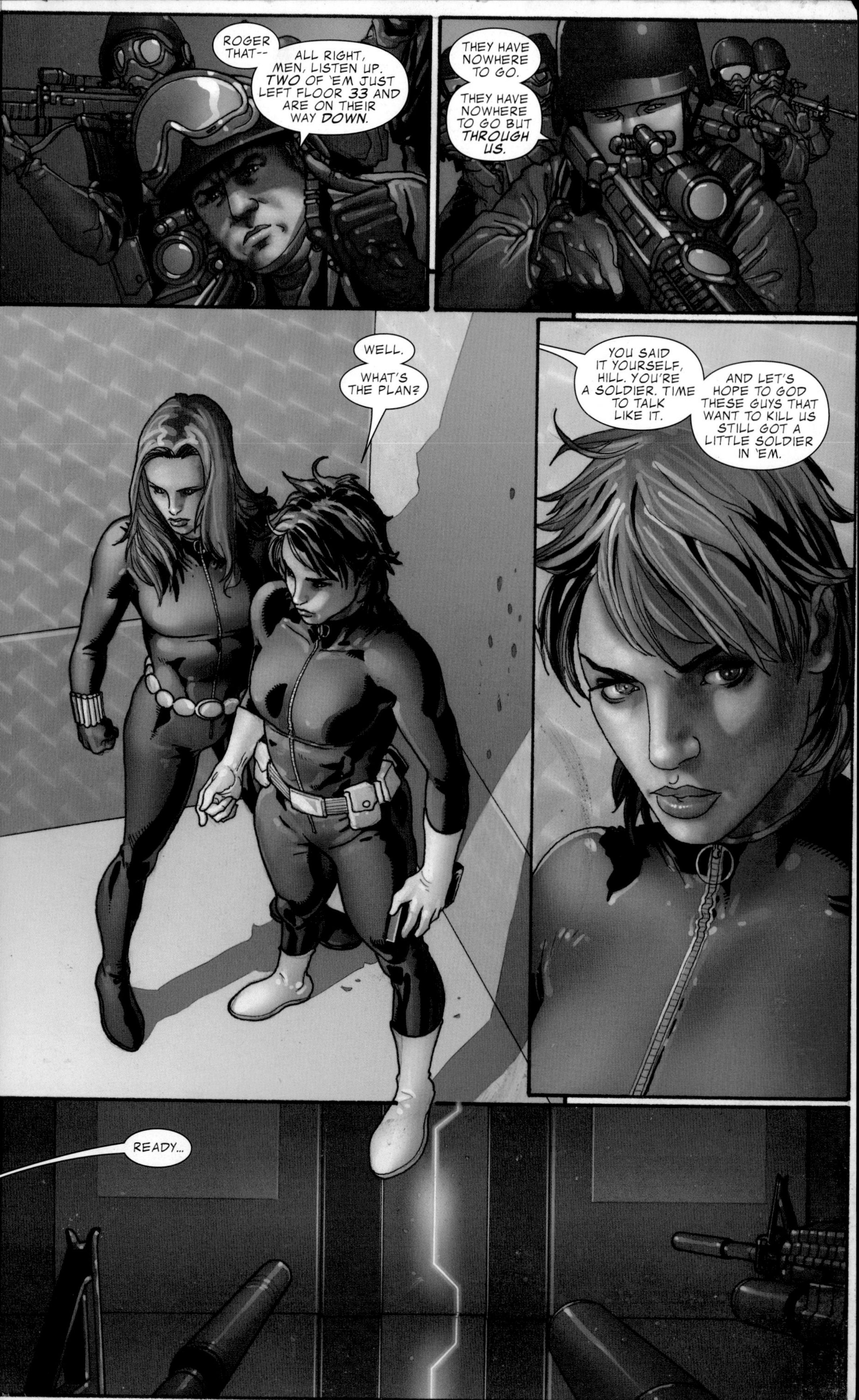
ROGER THAT--
ALL RIGHT, MEN, LISTEN UP. TWO OF 'EM JUST LEFT FLOOR 33 AND ARE ON THEIR WAY DOWN.
THEY HAVE NOWHERE TO GO.
THEY HAVE NOWHERE TO GO BUT THROUGH US.
WELL.
WHAT'S THE PLAN?
YOU SAID IT YOURSELF, HILL. YOU'RE A SOLDIER. TIME TO TALK LIKE IT.
AND LET'S HOPE TO GOD THESE GUYS THAT WANT TO KILL US STILL GOT A LITTLE SOLDIER IN 'EM.
READY...

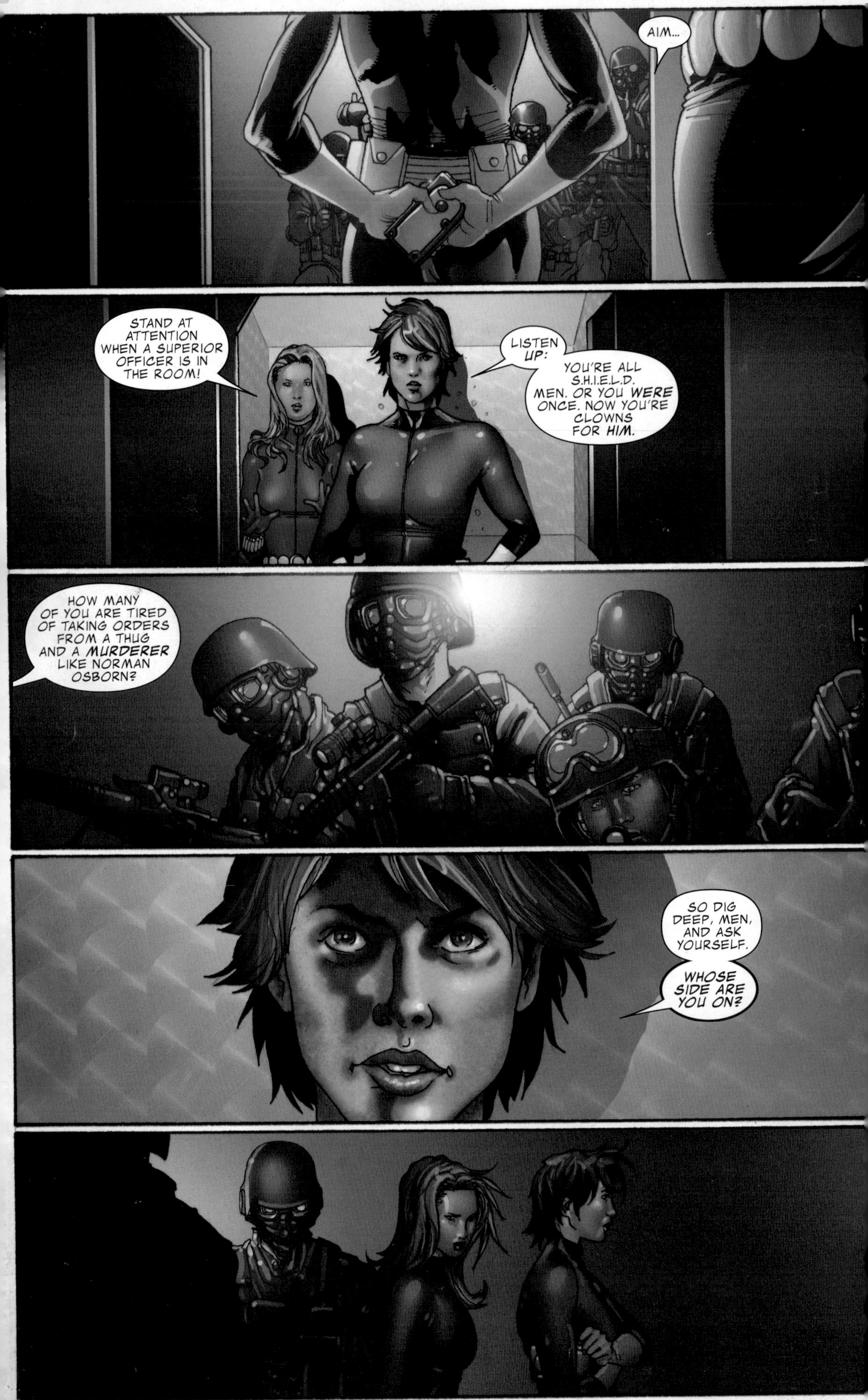
AIM...
STAND AT ATTENTION WHEN A SUPERIOR OFFICER IS IN THE ROOM!
LISTEN UP:
YOU'RE ALL S.H.I.E.L.D. MEN. OR YOU WERE ONCE. NOW YOU'RE CLOWNS FOR HIM.
HOW MANY OF YOU ARE TIRED OF TAKING ORDERS FROM A THUG AND A MURDERER LIKE NORMAN OSBORN?
SO DIG DEEP, MEN, AND ASK YOURSELF.
WHOSE SIDE ARE YOU ON?

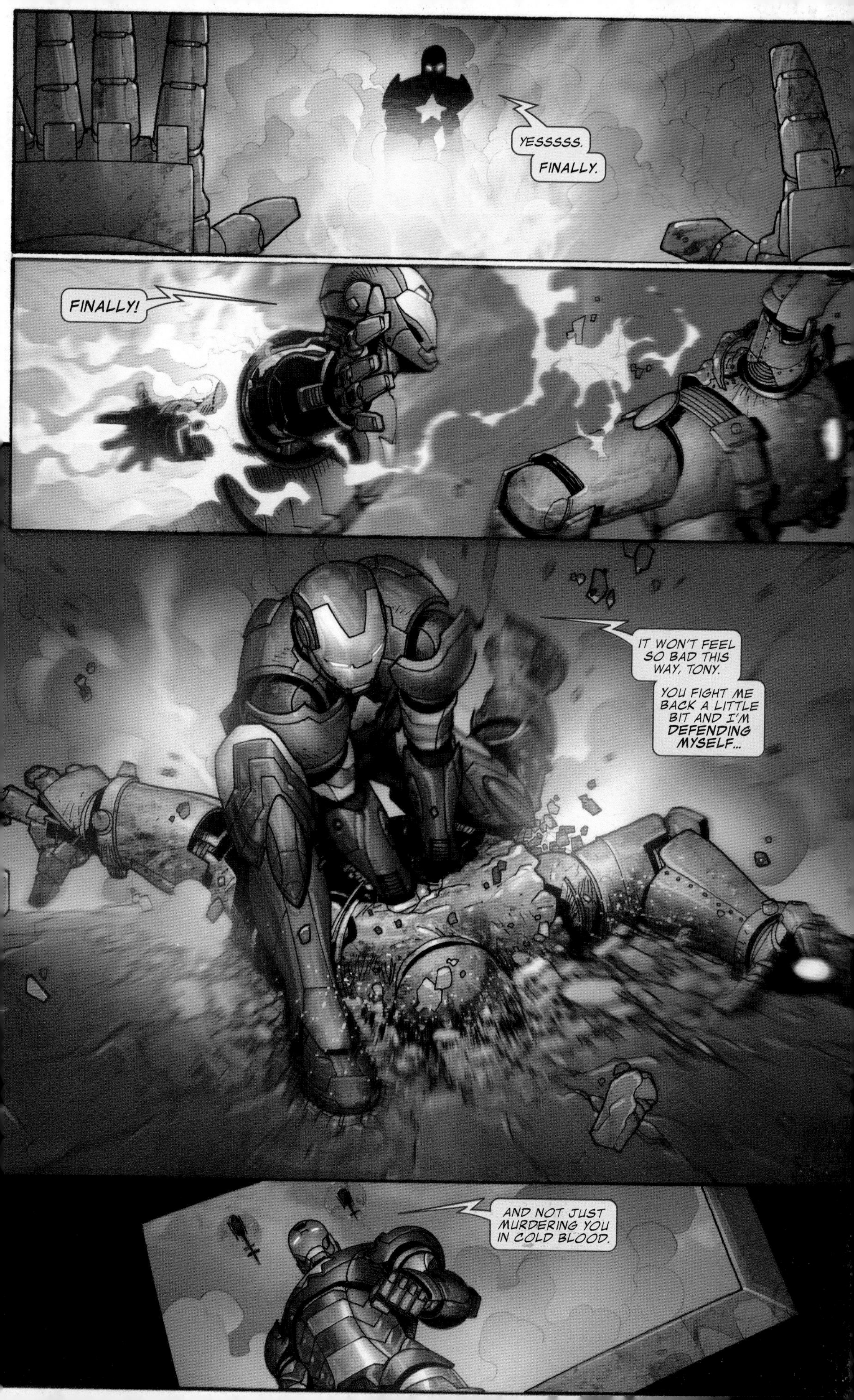
YESSSSS.
FINALLY.
FINALLY!
IT WON'T FEEL SO BAD THIS WAY, TONY.
YOU FIGHT ME BACK A LITTLE BIT AND I'M DEFENDING MYSELF...
AND NOT JUST MURDERING YOU IN COLD BLOOD.

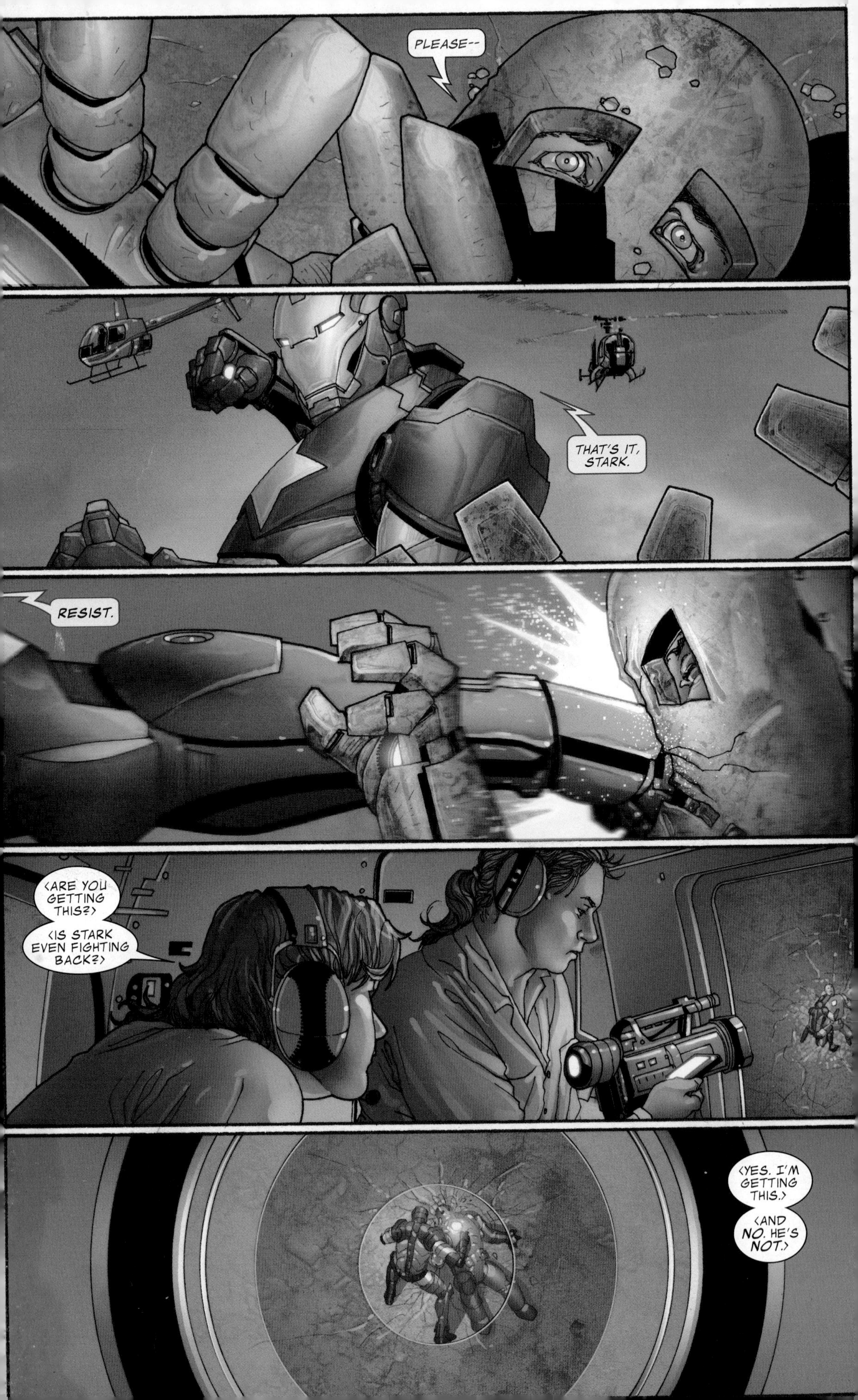
PLEASE--
THAT'S IT, STARK.
RESIST.
<ARE YOU GETTING THIS?>
<IS STARK EVEN FIGHTING BACK?>
<YES. I'M GETTING THIS.>
<AND NO. HE'S NOT.>

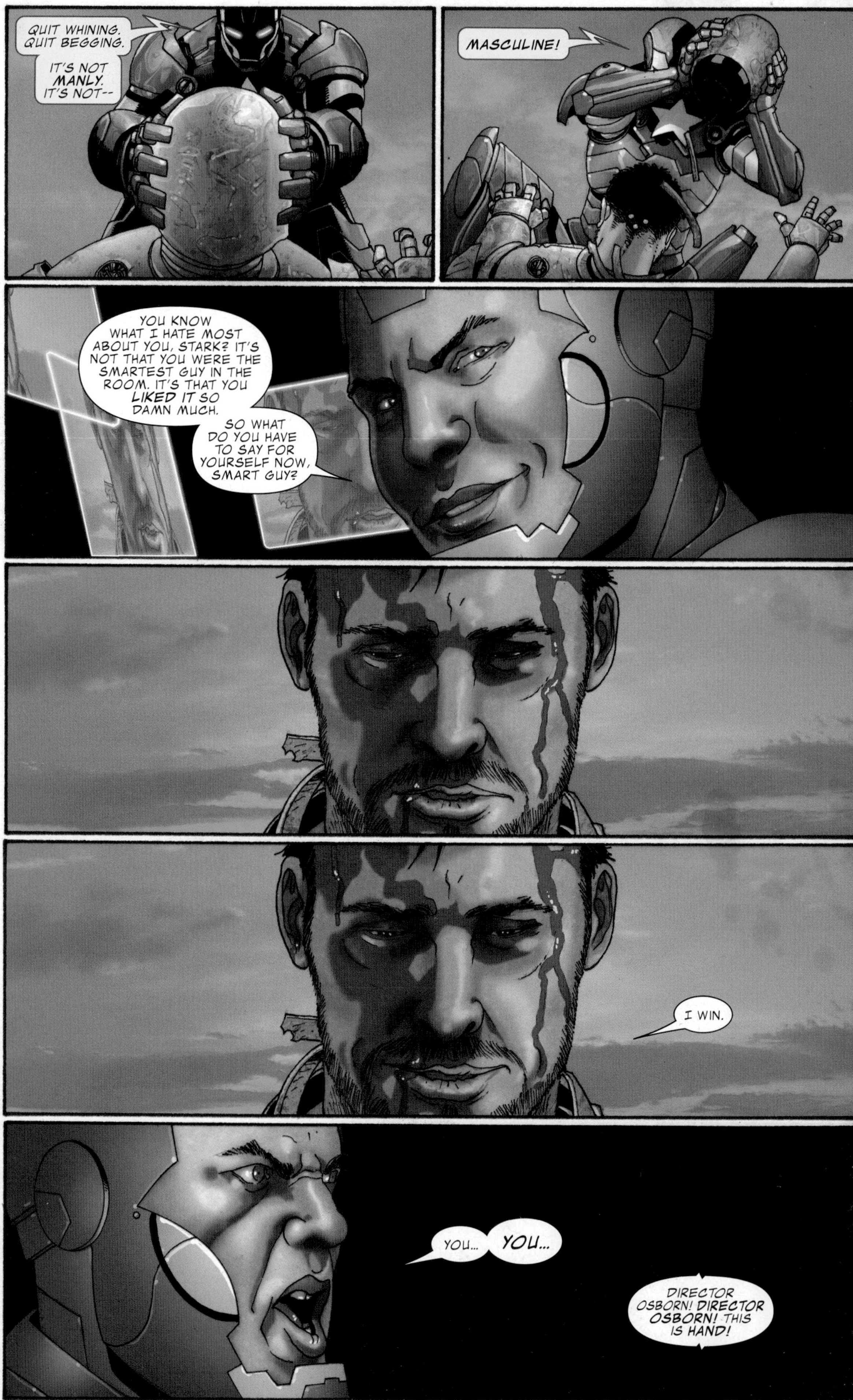
QUIT WHINING. QUIT BEGGING.
IT'S NOT MANLY. IT'S NOT--
MASCULINE!
YOU KNOW WHAT I HATE MOST ABOUT YOU, STARK? IT'S NOT THAT YOU WERE THE SMARTEST GUY IN THE ROOM. IT'S THAT YOU LIKED IT SO DAMN MUCH.
SO WHAT DO YOU HAVE TO SAY FOR YOURSELF NOW, SMART GUY?
I WIN.
YOU...
YOU...
DIRECTOR OSBORN! DIRECTOR OSBORN! THIS IS HAND!

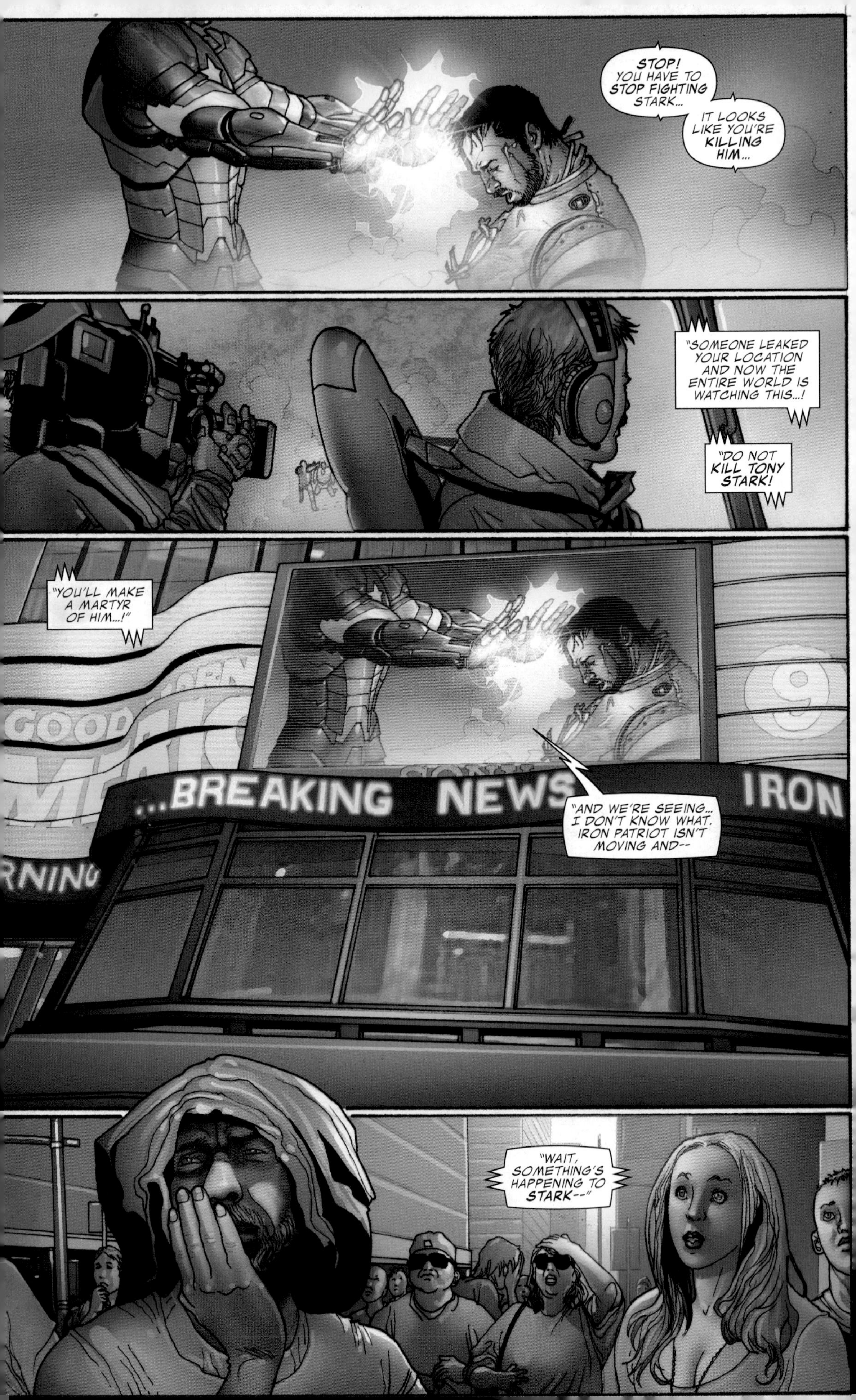

STOP! YOU HAVE TO STOP FIGHTING STARK...
IT LOOKS LIKE YOU'RE KILLING HIM...
"SOMEONE LEAKED YOUR LOCATION AND NOW THE ENTIRE WORLD IS WATCHING THIS...!
"DO NOT KILL TONY STARK!
"YOU'LL MAKE A MARTYR OF HIM...!"
GOOD
...BREAKING NEWS
IRON
RNING
"AND WE'RE SEEING... I DON'T KNOW WHAT. IRON PATRIOT ISN'T MOVING AND--
"WAIT, SOMETHING'S HAPPENING TO STARK--"

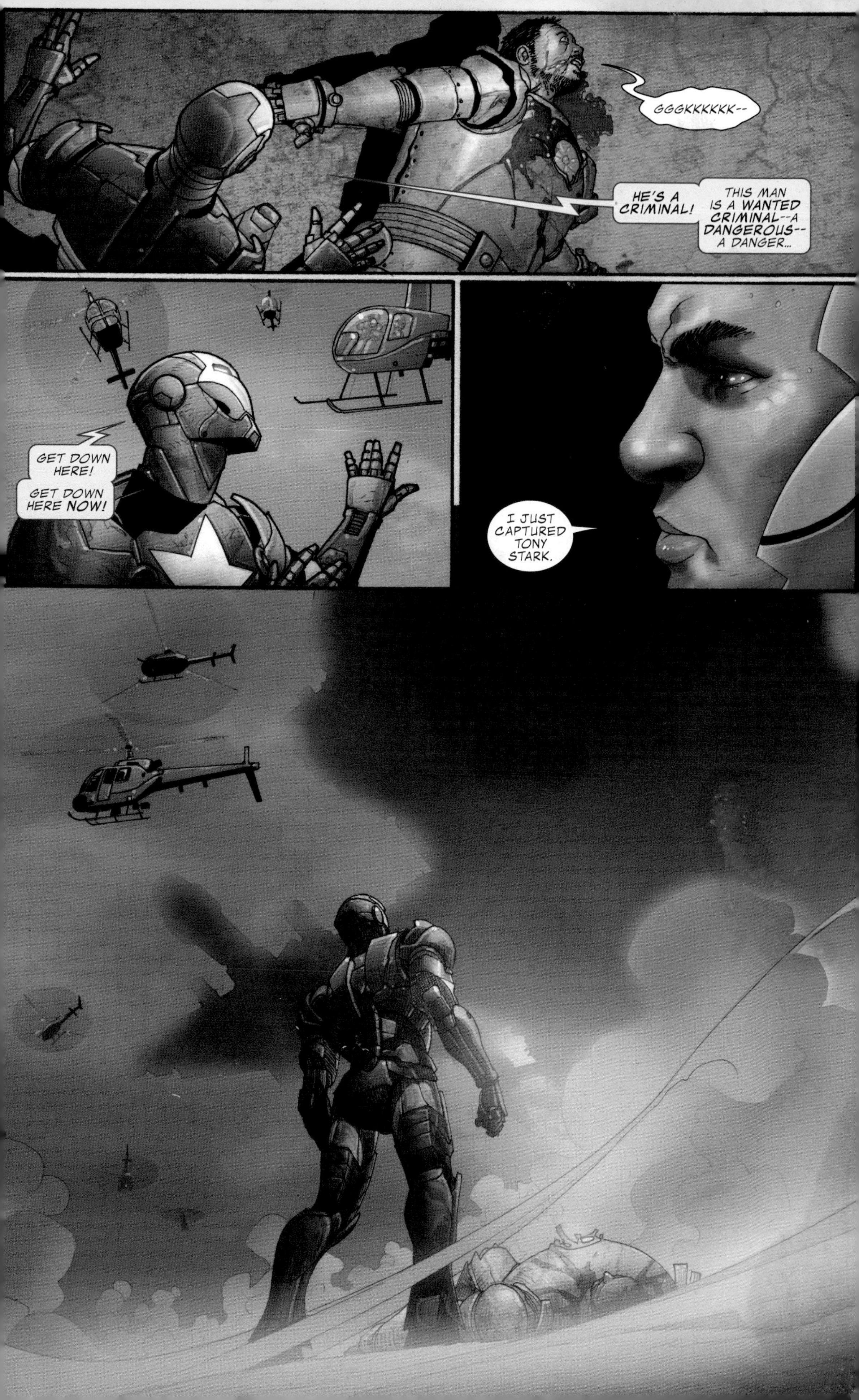
GGGKKKKKK--
HE'S A CRIMINAL!
THIS MAN IS A WANTED CRIMINAL--A DANGEROUS--A DANGER...
GET DOWN HERE!
GET DOWN HERE NOW!
I JUST CAPTURED TONY STARK.

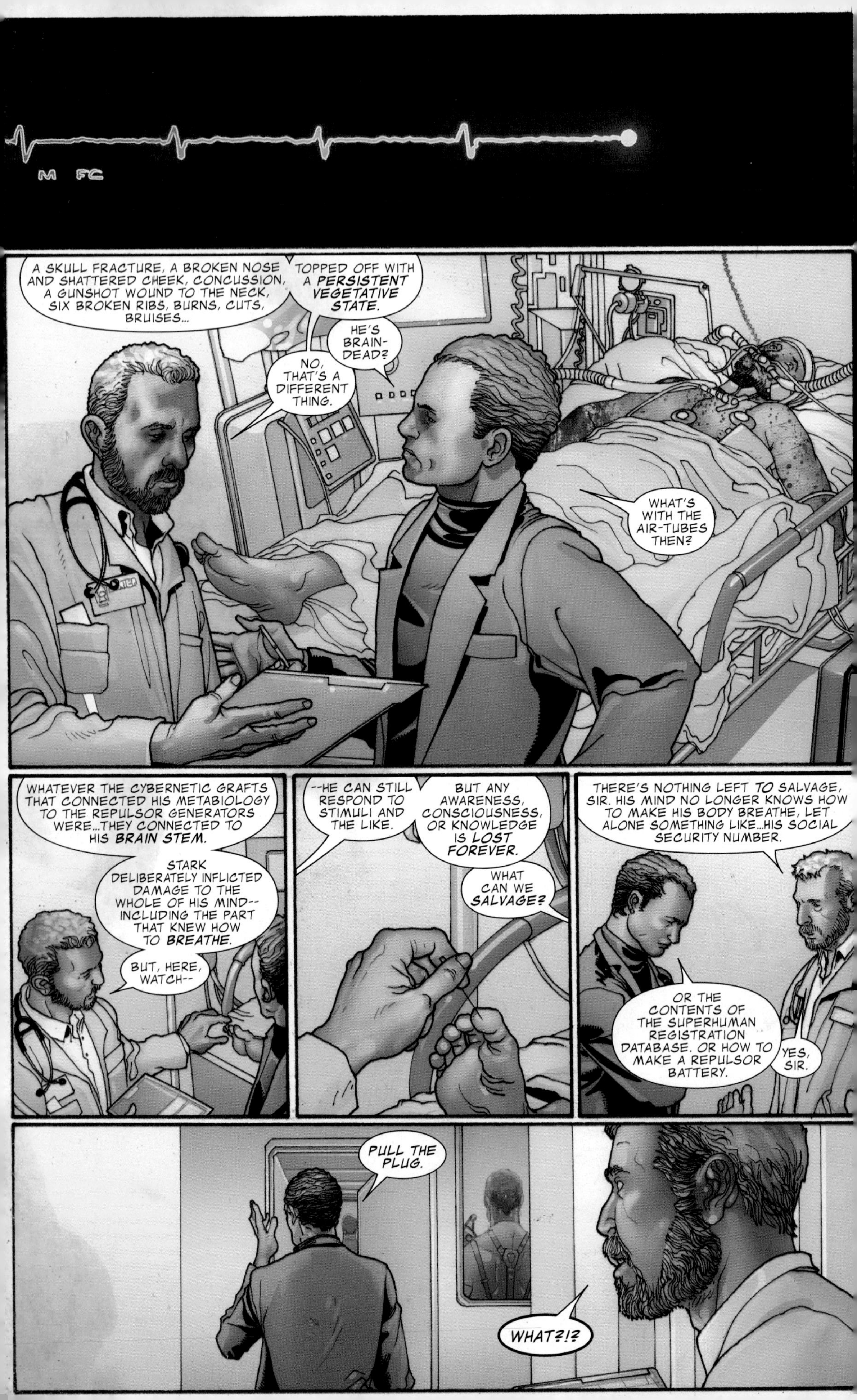
M FC
A SKULL FRACTURE, A BROKEN NOSE AND SHATTERED CHEEK, CONCUSSION, A GUNSHOT WOUND TO THE NECK, SIX BROKEN RIBS, BURNS, CUTS, BRUISES...
TOPPED OFF WITH A PERSISTENT VEGETATIVE STATE.
HE'S BRAIN-DEAD?
NO, THAT'S A DIFFERENT THING.
WHAT'S WITH THE AIR-TUBES THEN?
WHATEVER THE CYBERNETIC GRAFTS THAT CONNECTED HIS METABIOLOGY TO THE REPULSOR GENERATORS WERE...THEY CONNECTED TO HIS BRAIN STEM.
STARK DELIBERATELY INFLICTED DAMAGE TO THE WHOLE OF HIS MIND--INCLUDING THE PART THAT KNEW HOW TO BREATHE.
BUT, HERE, WATCH--
--HE CAN STILL RESPOND TO STIMULI AND THE LIKE.
BUT ANY AWARENESS, CONSCIOUSNESS, OR KNOWLEDGE IS LOST FOREVER.
WHAT CAN WE SALVAGE?
THERE'S NOTHING LEFT TO SALVAGE, SIR. HIS MIND NO LONGER KNOWS HOW TO MAKE HIS BODY BREATHE, LET ALONE SOMETHING LIKE...HIS SOCIAL SECURITY NUMBER.
OR THE CONTENTS OF THE SUPERHUMAN REGISTRATION DATABASE. OR HOW TO MAKE A REPULSOR BATTERY.
YES, SIR.
PULL THE PLUG.
WHAT?!?

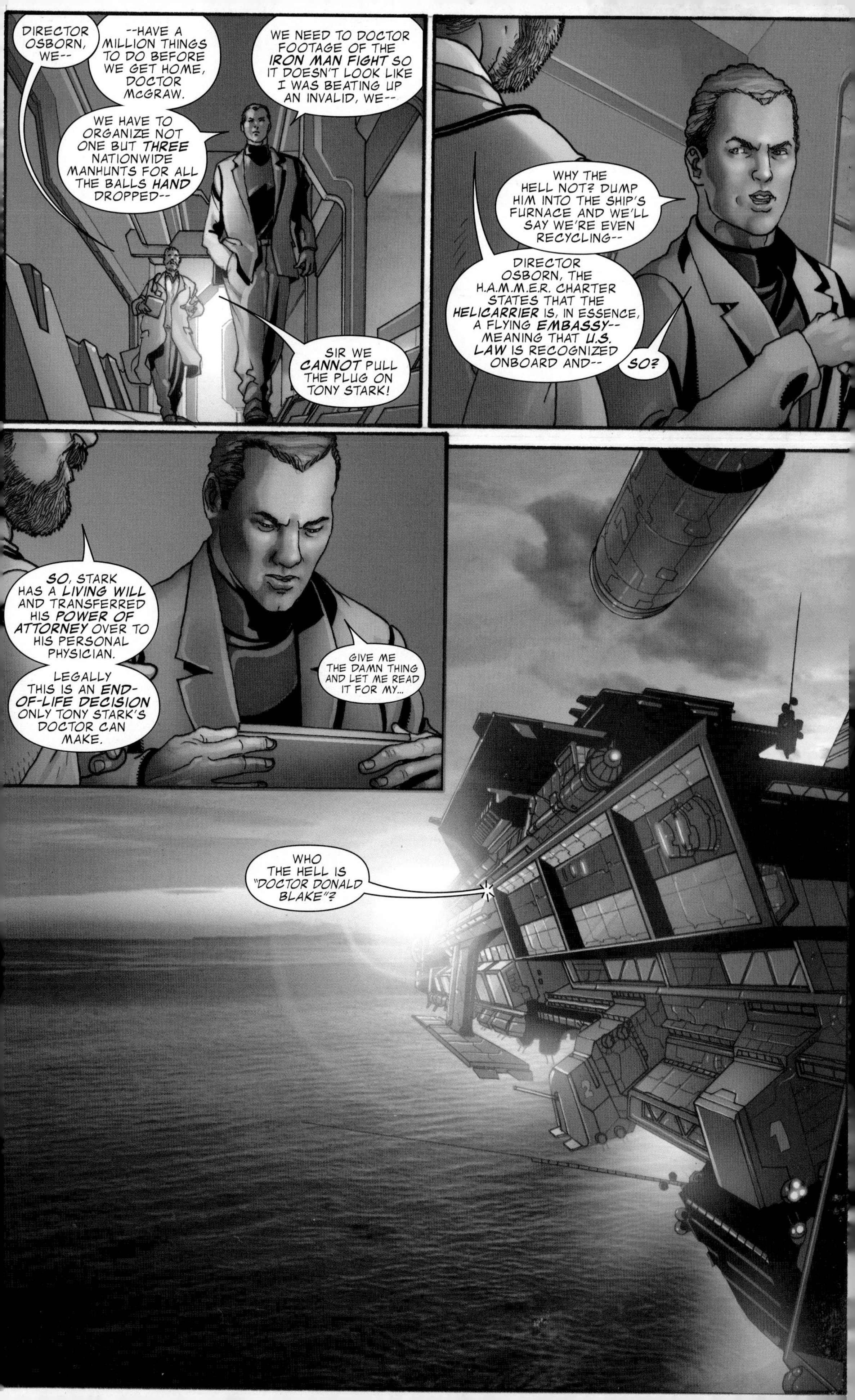
DIRECTOR OSBORN, WE--
--HAVE A MILLION THINGS TO DO BEFORE WE GET HOME, DOCTOR McGRAW.
WE HAVE TO ORGANIZE NOT ONE BUT THREE NATIONWIDE MANHUNTS FOR ALL THE BALLS HAND DROPPED--
WE NEED TO DOCTOR FOOTAGE OF THE IRON MAN FIGHT SO IT DOESN'T LOOK LIKE I WAS BEATING UP AN INVALID, WE--
SIR WE CANNOT PULL THE PLUG ON TONY STARK!
WHY THE HELL NOT? DUMP HIM INTO THE SHIP'S FURNACE AND WE'LL SAY WE'RE EVEN RECYCLING--
DIRECTOR OSBORN, THE H.A.M.M.E.R. CHARTER STATES THAT THE HELICARRIER IS, IN ESSENCE, A FLYING EMBASSY-- MEANING THAT U.S. LAW IS RECOGNIZED ONBOARD AND--
SO?
SO, STARK HAS A LIVING WILL AND TRANSFERRED HIS POWER OF ATTORNEY OVER TO HIS PERSONAL PHYSICIAN.
LEGALLY THIS IS AN END-OF-LIFE DECISION ONLY TONY STARK'S DOCTOR CAN MAKE.
GIVE ME THE DAMN THING AND LET ME READ IT FOR MY...
WHO THE HELL IS "DOCTOR DONALD BLAKE"?

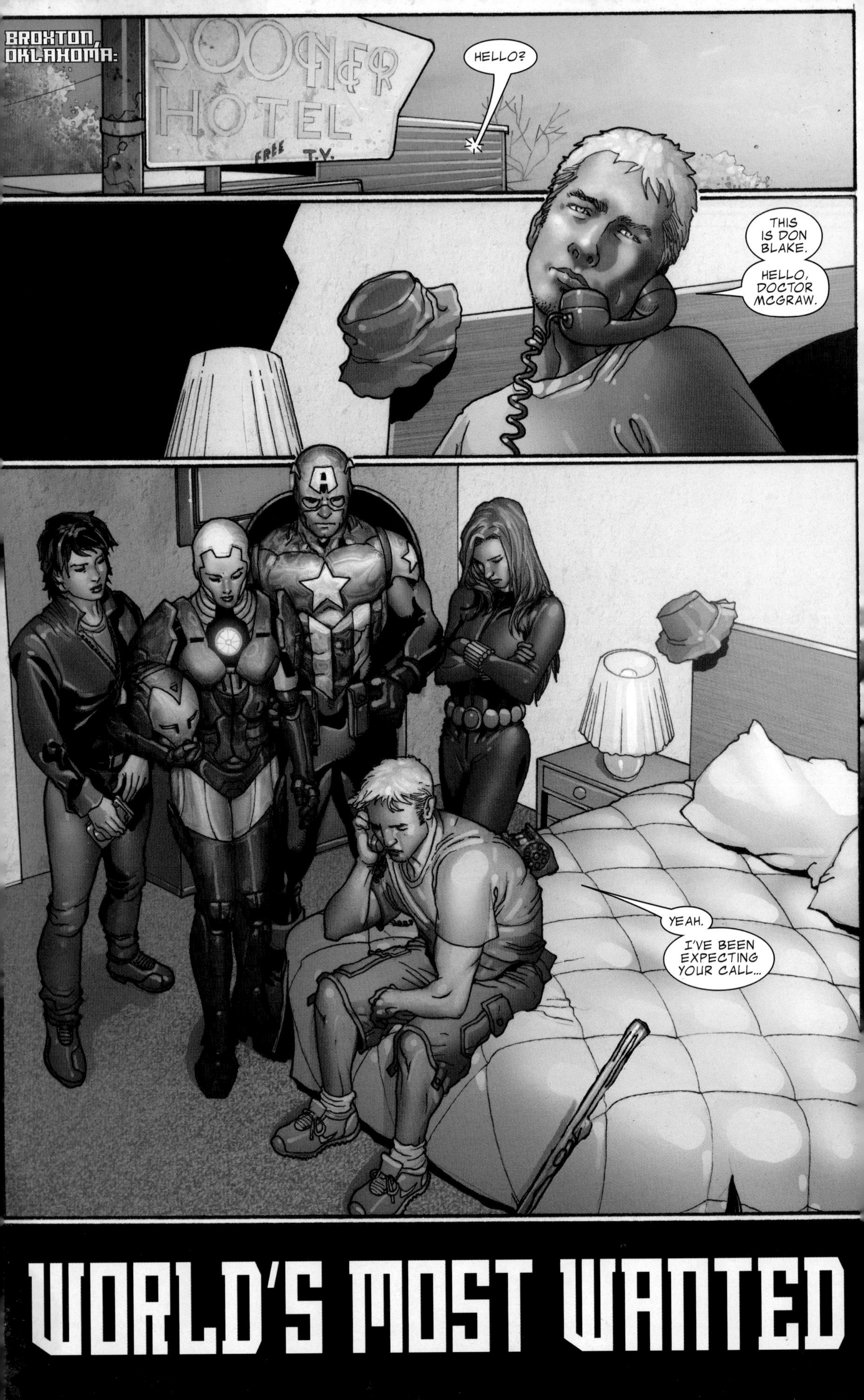
BROXTON, OKLAHOMA:
SOONER HOTEL
FREE T.V.
HELLO?
THIS IS DON BLAKE.
HELLO, DOCTOR MCGRAW.
YEAH.
I'VE BEEN EXPECTING YOUR CALL...
WORLD'S MOST WANTED

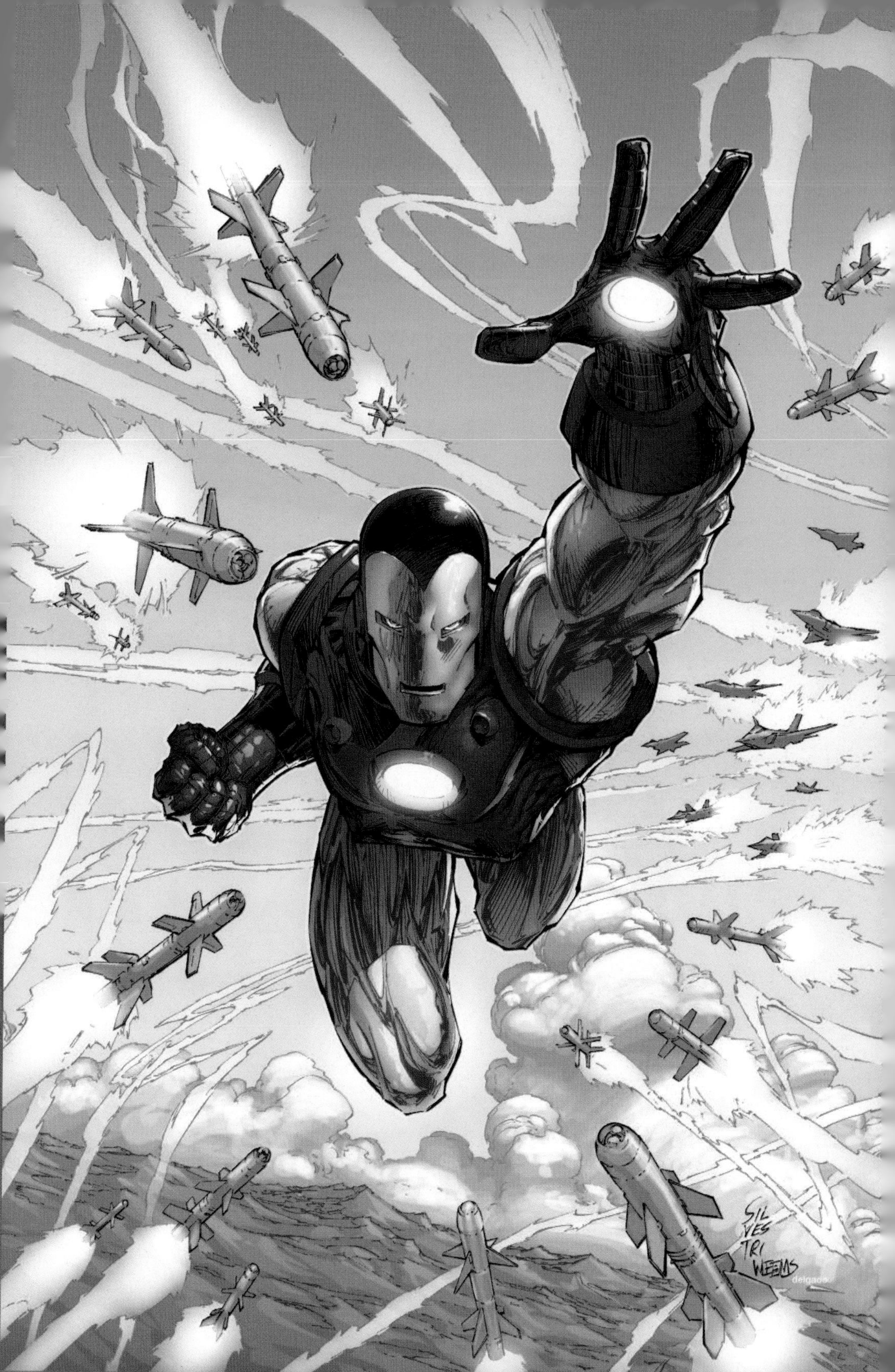
SIL
VES
TRI
WEEMS
delgado

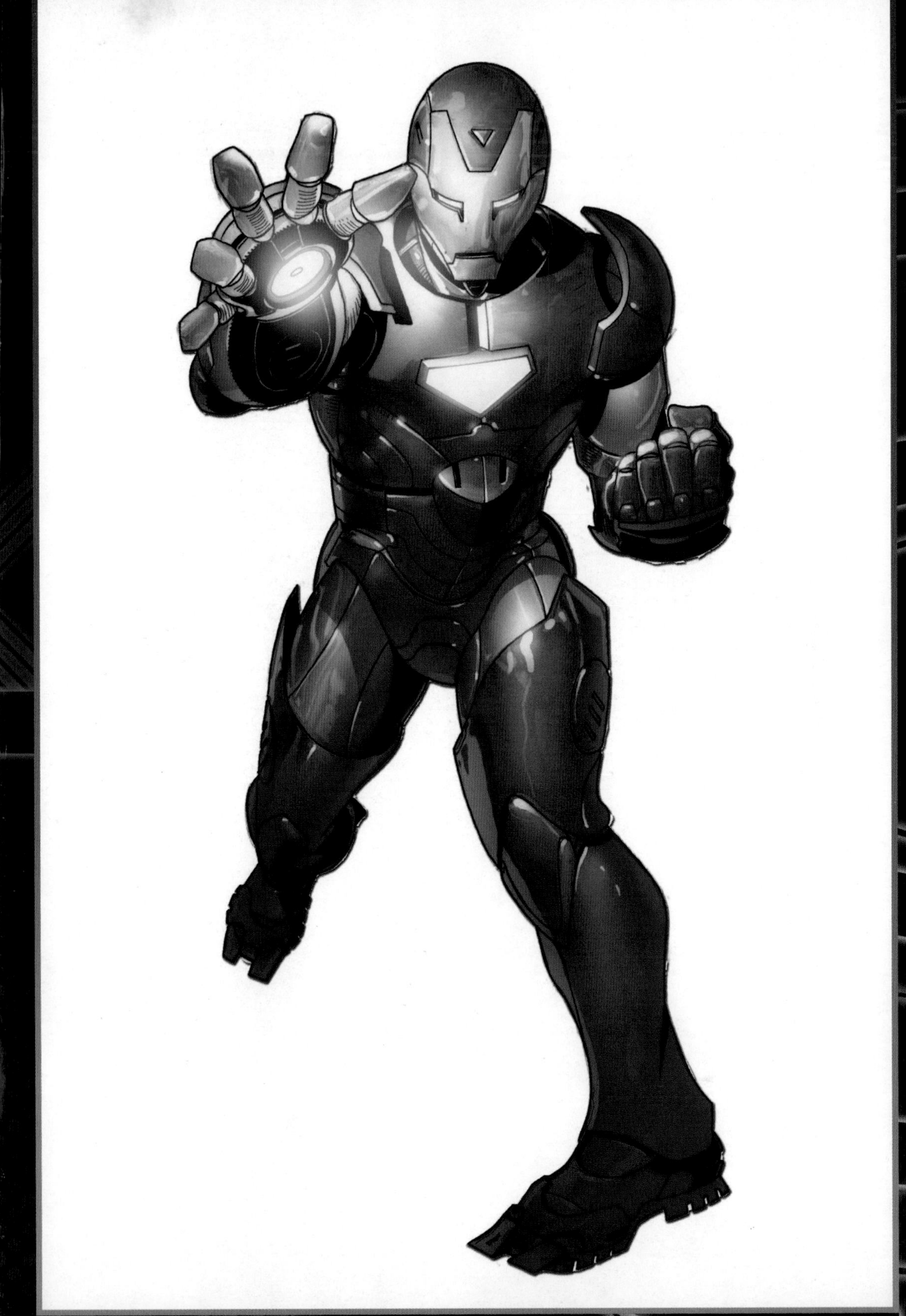

#16 70TH ANNIVERSARY FRAME VARIANT
BY SALVADOR LARROCA

THE INVINCIBLE IRON MAN

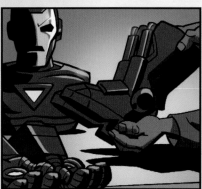

#19 SUPER HERO SQUAD VARIANT

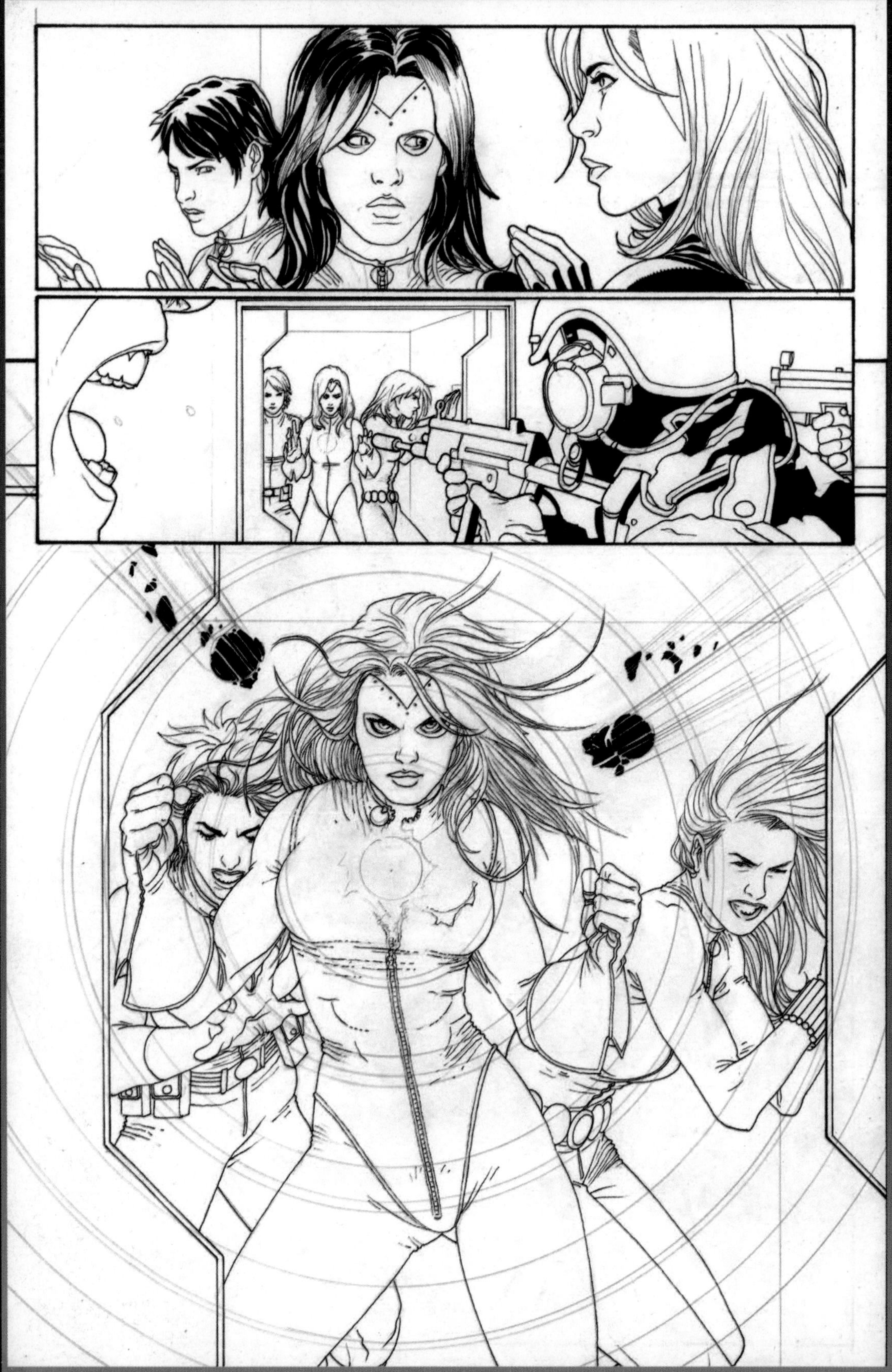

#19 PAGE 10 PENCILS
BY SALVADOR LARROCA

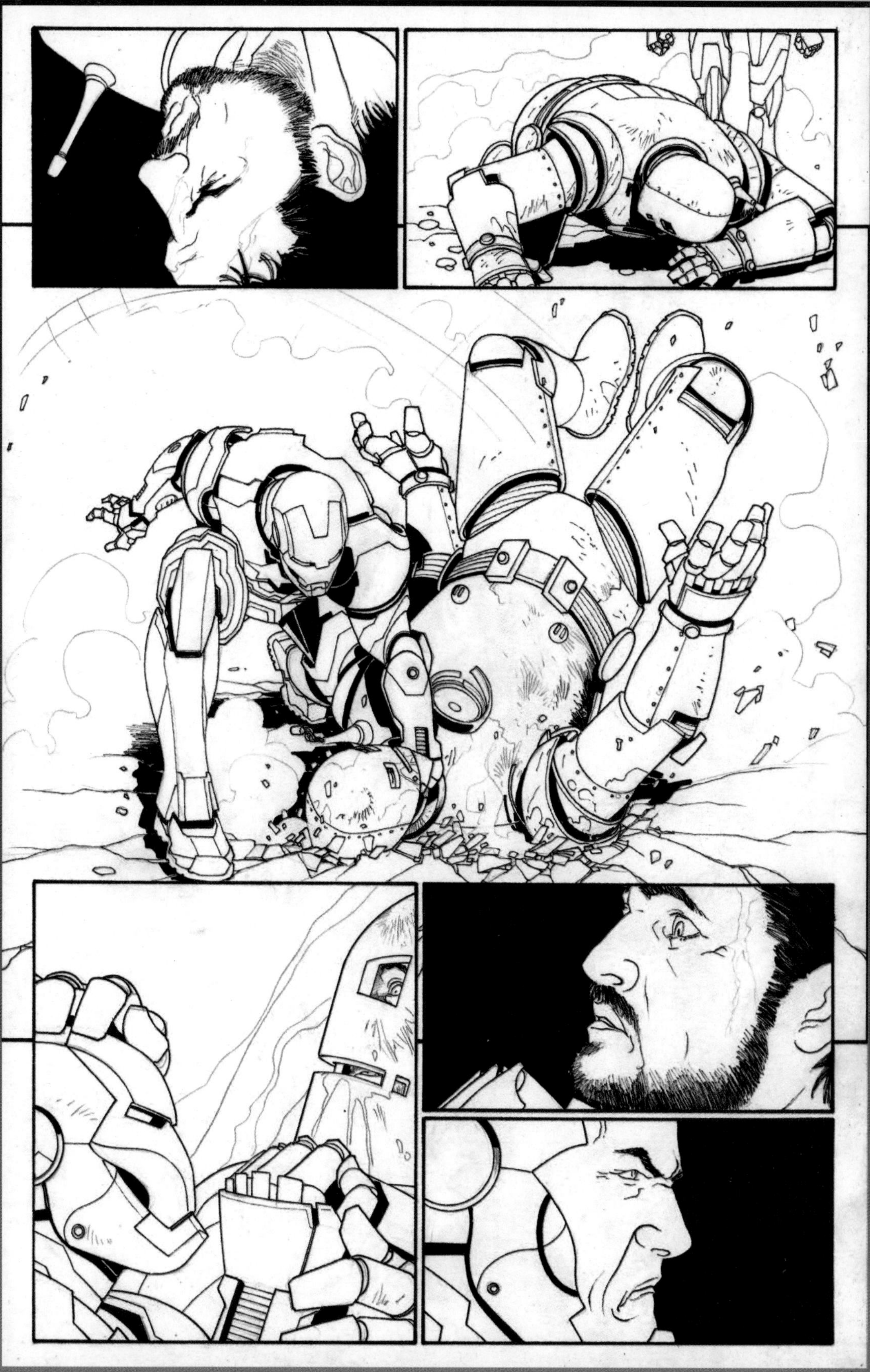

#19 PAGE 17 PENCILS
BY SALVADOR LARROCA

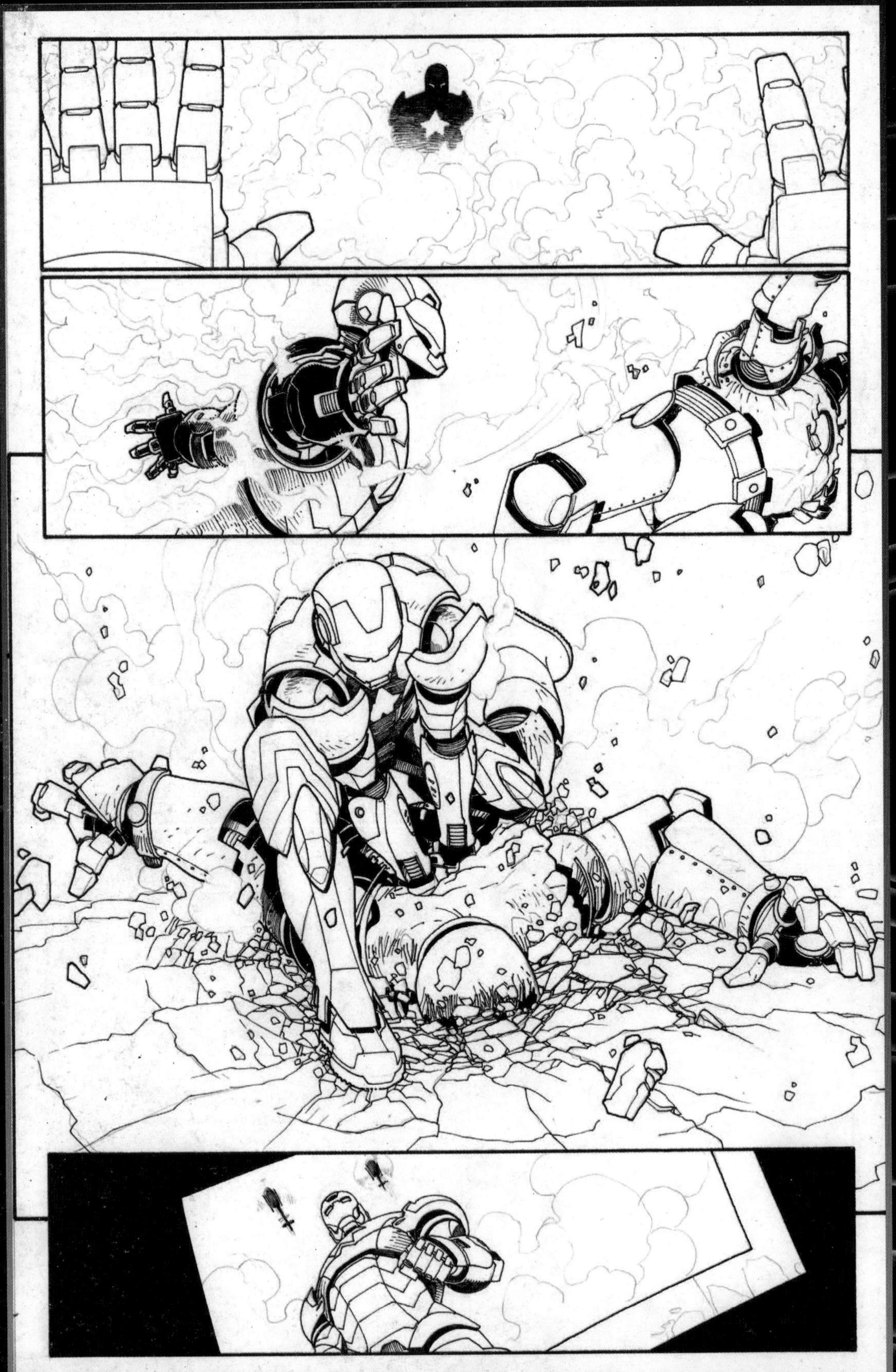

#19 PAGE 25 PENCILS

BY SALVADOR LARROCA